T0316267

Language Planning in the Asia Pacific

This volume covers the language situation in Hong Kong, Timor-Leste and Sri Lanka explaining the linguistic diversity, the historical and political contexts and the current language situation, including language-in-education planning, the role of the media, the role of religion and the roles of non-indigenous languages. Two of the authors are indigenous to the situations described while the other has undertaken extensive field work and consulting there. The three sections contained in this volume draw together the literature on each of the polities to present an overview of the research available about each of them, while providing new research-based information. The purpose of the volume is to provide an up-to-date overview of the language situation in each polity based on a series of key questions in the hope that this might facilitate the development of a richer theory to guide language policy and planning in other polities where similar issues may arise.

The sections in this book were published as special issues of *Current Issues in Language Planning*.

Robert B. Kaplan, Emeritus Professor of Applied Linguistics, University of Southern California, has published numerous books and refereed articles, was founding Editor-in-Chief of the *Annual Review of Applied Linguistics*, member of the editorial board of the *Oxford International Encyclopedia of Linguistics* (2002) and is editor of the first and second editions of the *Oxford Handbook of Applied Linguistics*.

Richard B. Baldauf Jr., Professor of TESOL, School of Education, University of Queensland, has published numerous articles in refereed journals and books, is co-author of *Language Planning from Practice to Theory* (1997), *Language and Language-in-Education Planning in the Pacific Basin* (2003), and *Planning Chinese Characters: Evolution, Revolution or Reaction* (2007).

Language Planning in the Asia Pacific
Hong Kong, Timor-Leste and Sri Lanka

Edited by
Robert B. Kaplan and Richard B. Baldauf Jr.

LONDON AND NEW YORK

First published 2011
by Routledge
2 Park Square, Milton Park, Abingdon, Oxon, OX14 4RN

Simultaneously published in the USA and Canada
by Routledge
711 Third Avenue, New York, NY 10017

Routledge is an imprint of the Taylor & Francis Group, an informa business

This book is a reproduction of two special issues of *Current Issues in Language Planning*: vol.10, issue 1 and vol.11, issue 1. The Publisher requests to those authors who may be citing this book to state, also, the bibliographical details of the special issue on which the book was based.

Typeset in Times New Roman by Taylor & Francis Books

British Library Cataloguing in Publication Data
A catalogue record for this book is available from the British Library

ISBN13: 978-0-415-61851-9

Disclaimer
The publisher would like to make readers aware that the chapters in this book are referred to as articles as they had been in the special issue. The publisher accepts responsibility for any inconsistencies that may have arisen in the course of preparing this volume for print.

Contents

Notes on contributors

Robert B. Kaplan, Emeritus Professor of Applied Linguistics, University of Southern California, USA has published numerous books and refereed articles, was founding Editor-in-Chief of the *Annual Review of Applied Linguistics,* member of the editorial board of the *Oxford International Encyclopedia of Linguistics* (2002) and is editor of the first and second editions of the *Oxford Handbook of Applied Linguistics* (2002; 2010).

Richard B. Baldauf Jr., Professor of TESOL, School of Education, University of Queensland, Australia has published numerous articles in refereed journals and books, is co-author of *Language Planning from Practice to Theory* (1997), *Language and Language-in-Education Planning in the Pacific Basin* (2003), and *Planning Chinese Characters: Evolution, Revolution or Reaction* (2007).

Sandagomi Coperahewa BA (Colombo) MA (Lancaster) MPhil (Peradeniya) PhD (Cambridge) is a Senior Lecturer in Sinhala at the University of Colombo, Sri Lanka. His research areas are modern Sinhala, sociology of Sinhala language, and language policy planning. He has worked as a consultant to the Department of Official Languages, Sri Lanka on various language planning projects.

Anita Y.K. Poon is an Associate Professor in the Department of Education Studies at Hong Kong Baptist University. She obtained her PhD from Queensland University of Technology in Australia. She has published seven books, some book chapters and refereed journal articles in language policy and planning, English language education, and education policies in journals like: *Current Issues in Language Planning, International Journal of Bilingual Education and Bilingualism*, and *International Review of Education*.

Kerry Taylor-Leech is a lecturer and researcher in Applied Linguistics at the University of Southern Queensland, Australia. Her research focuses on multilingualism, in particular the intersections between language policy, development, identity, education and literacy. She also researches the relationship between language and settlement for adult immigrants. In addition she has an ongoing interest in the teaching and learning of languages. Kerry's connections with Timor-Leste date from 2001.

Introduction: Language planning in the Asia Pacific: Hong Kong, Timor-Leste and Sri Lanka – Some common issues

Robert B. Kaplan
Professor Emeritus, Applied Linguistics, University of Southern California

Richard B. Baldauf Jr.
Professor, TESOL, School of Education, University of Queensland, Brisbane

Introduction

This volume brings together polity studies of language policy and planning related to three Asia Pacific regional polities[1], while the addendum at the end of this chapter provides an opportunity for each of the study's authors briefly to update their work. (See Appendix A: 'Polity Studies Overview' for a more general discussion of the rationale for these studies, Appendix B for the 22 questions each study sets out to address, and Kaplan *et al.* (2000) for a discussion of the underlying concepts for the studies themselves.) This introduction provides a brief summary of the three monographs that follow and draws out some of the more general issues raised by these studies.

All three polities have been plagued by extensive colonial periods, the interaction of indigenous languages and colonial languages and in more recent history issues of what languages to use for what purposes, especially in education. These conditions define both their achievements and the problems with which they have had to wrestle.

Hong Kong

Hong Kong, occupying a small peninsula and 235 islands hanging off of the Chinese mainland, has a history as a British settlement dating from 1841, starting as a tiny fishing port and ending in 1997 with its return to China. Hong Kong, a capitalist city of 1,104.3 square kilometers and one of the most densely populated areas in the world, having practiced a free economy for 155 years, was handed back to a socialist regime in China and now functions as a Special Administrative Region of the People's Republic of China (PRC) under the "One Country Two Systems" policy. The population of Hong Kong consists of ethnic Chinese – 95 per cent – most of whom are migrants from China's Guangdong province. The remaining 5 per cent who are not ethnic Chinese originate from South Asia (i.e. India, Pakistan and Nepal), and South East Asia (i.e. Vietnam, The Philippines, Indonesia and Thailand), while others are British, continental Europeans, North Americans, Australians, Japanese or Koreans, who are largely employed in the local commercial, financial and educational sectors.

The Chinese language, as understood in the context of Hong Kong, employs written Modern Standard Chinese and spoken Cantonese, while the spoken form of Modern Standard Chinese is *Putonghua* (or Mandarin), the national language of China (PRC) and Taiwan. Written Cantonese is a variant of Modern Standard Chinese, the writing system accepted in Chinese communities world-wide. Since Modern Standard Chinese is based on Mandarin and other northern Chinese dialects while Cantonese is a southern dialect, Modern Standard Chinese and Cantonese are considerably different in lexis, syntax, pronunciation and phonology, to such an extent that from a Western-based linguistic perspective Cantonese and Mandarin (i.e. Modern Standard Chinese) constitute different languages, a view rejected by Chinese-based linguists where language is more often defined in historical and political terms.

Cantonese is an umbrella term for a group of similar dialects spoken in two southern provinces in China – the western half of Guangdong province and the southern half of Guangxi province. *Standard Cantonese* refers to the variant of Cantonese spoken in Guangzhou, the capital of Guangdong. The other variants of Cantonese are classified as sub-dialects of Cantonese – i.e. *Donggun* spoken in Tung Kwun, *Baoan* spoken in Po On, *Taishan* spoken in Toi Shan, and *Zhongshan* spoken in Chung Shan. Before British colonization, the inhabitants of Hong Kong spoke the Cantonese sub-dialects *Donggun* and *Baoan*, as well as several other Chinese dialects; i.e. *Hakka, Chiu Chow* and *Tanka* which are unintelligible to Cantonese speakers. After British settlement began in 1842, a large number of workers and merchants migrated to Hong Kong from Guangzhou; consequently, standard Cantonese became the majority language used among the Chinese in Hong Kong. The Cantonese spoken in Hong Kong before 1949, the year in which the Hong Kong government closed the border with the PRC in order to arrest the influx of mainlanders, was not much different from the Cantonese spoken in Guangzhou. However, the Cantonese spoken in Hong Kong has gradually deviated from the standard Cantonese used in Guangzhou and has developed into a new variant now known as *Hong Kong Cantonese*. This has occurred primarily for four reasons:

(1) Because of the influence of the English language, borrowing has taken place and many loanwords have passed into Hong Kong Cantonese; e.g. */pa:si:/* (bus), */tIksi:/* (taxi), */tsi:si:/* (cheese).

(2) As a result of increasing English literacy rate in the general population, the use of mixed code (i.e. use of English words or phrases in Cantonese structures) has become popular, e.g. *right-click mouse highlight mon* (you can right-click the mouse to highlight the monitor).

(3) As dialects have been stigmatized in Mainland China, Cantonese has been downgraded to the status of a home and community language; as a consequence, the development of Cantonese has been constrained, and some colloquial Cantonese expressions and vocabulary have been replaced by written Chinese, which is closer to Mandarin than is Cantonese but it fails to represent the vitality and subtlety of Cantonese.

(4) By contrast, Cantonese continues to be used in all domains in Hong Kong society. Many neologisms and a number of jargon terms related to Hong Kong life have been created, especially in the entertainment sector; e.g. in television soap-operas and "Canto- pops" (i.e. Cantonese pop songs).

Although there is only one recognized written Chinese (i.e. Modern Standard Chinese), two sets of characters are currently in general use to represent written Chinese; i.e. one system using traditional Chinese characters as used in Mainland China prior to 1949 and in Taiwan, and another system using simplified Chinese characters which were created in the PRC after 1949 (see Zhou, 2008). Hong Kong always has adopted the traditional writing system.

Historically, Hong Kong was composed of two monolingual communities – the Chinese-speaking community, consisting of large numbers of local people, and a small English-speaking community, consisting of colonialists from Britain. The two communities had little contact with each other in their daily lives, and their communication, if any, was accomplished through linguistic middlemen – i.e. Chinese translators able to speak English reasonably well. This mode of communication persisted until Hong Kong started to expand its educational system after World War II. As a result of the educational expansion, more locals have gradually become cognizant of the English language. However, as inter-ethnic communication is formal and always related to study, work or official encounters (Johnson, 1994), English is typically used by the English-speaking Chinese in a rather limited way, only in the domains of education, administration, the judiciary, business and the media, and seldom in daily social interaction among the Chinese. Strictly speaking, English does not function as a second language in the usual sense as it is used in such places as Singapore; rather it is used as an "auxiliary language." Consequently, there is a cline of English use by Chinese speakers in Hong Kong (except for a small group of ethnic Chinese who are native or near-native English speakers), ranging from English used as a foreign language to its use somewhere between a second language and a foreign language, to its use as a second language.

Sri-Lanka

Sri-Lanka, a tropical island in the Indian Ocean with an area of 65,610 sq. km. (25,332 sq. miles), became a free, sovereign and independent republic within the British Commonwealth on 22 May 1972. Sri-Lanka has a recorded history extending over some 2,000 years. The most important socio-historical event of the early period was the introduction of Buddhism to the island from India by Mahinda, the emissary of the great Buddhist emperor, Asoka, during the 3rd century BCE. At the same time, writing was also introduced to the island. Sinhala has its own script, the origins of which go back to the ancient Indian script known as 'Brāhmi' – a unique cursive script of South Indian type. Theravada Buddhism expected its adherents to be literate, and from very early times the Buddhist monks developed the custom of recording events connected with the institution to which they were attached and with the sacred objects that they honored and worshipped. The most significant feature of this tradition was the development of the literary genre known as *vamsa;* as a result, the Sinhalese claim a special place in the region as the earliest people to keep such historical records. The two chronicles, the *Mahāvamsa* (possibly compiled about the 6th century CE) and its continuation the *Culavamsa* (compiled in the 13th century CE) provide a remarkably full account of the island's ancient and medieval history.

Sri Lankan culture and the language have been exposed to various European influences over the past 500 years. The arrival of the Portuguese on the island in 1505 introduced a European language for the first time. Some parts of the island were under Portuguese domination for a century and a half. The Dutch replaced the Portuguese (1656-1796); in turn, the British displaced the Dutch (1815-1948). In the 19th century, as a result of British colonial rule, English was introduced as a medium of instruction. English was the official language of Sri Lanka from 1815 to 1956 – even after independence in 1948, it was used in all official domains until 1956. It still exerts a tremendous influence on both the vocabulary and the structure of Sinhala. In 1956, the Sinhala language entered a new phase in its history, ushering in changes not only in its 'status' as the official language, but also changes in its structure. As the official language, Sinhala was now required to cope with a variety of new roles, in effect, as the medium of official communication in the Parliament, in state departments, and in the courts of law. With the expansion of modern Sinhala literature in the mid-20th century, the Sinhala language became a popular vehicle for its new reading public. The new status accorded to Sinhala in 1956 broadened its usage as a medium in education, in government activity, and in the mass media; in other words, the shift to Sinhala from English inevitably increased the functional load on the Sinhala language.

The official status of English underwent a dramatic change with the introduction of the *Official Language Act of 1956*, more commonly known as the *Sinhala-Only Act*. In 1987, as a result of the 13th amendment to the Sri Lankan Constitution, Tamil was raised to the status of an official language, and English was declared a "link language," although no further definition or clarification of its use and status was provided. The provisions of the 13th amendment were clarified and indeed consolidated by the 16th amendment. Shortly after the enactment of the 16th Amendment, the Commissioner of Official Languages and the International Centre for Ethnic studies (ICES), Colombo, together organized a conference to examine the implications of bilingualism and the effective implementation of the language policy. This conference adopted twenty proposals, in three stages – *'immediate'*, *'transitional'*, and *'long term'* – for the successful implementation of the new official language policy in administration. Sinhala, an Indo-Aryan language, the language of the majority (70%) of the Sri Lankan population, has its roots in classical Indian languages (e.g. Hindi, Bengali, Gujarati, Marathi, Punjabi and Kashmiri) but is spoken nowhere else in the region. Moreover, Maldivian, or *Divehi*, an offshoot of Sinhala, separated from the latter around the 10th century CE. Sinhala and Divehi are the only two Indo-Aryan languages that are geographically and linguistically separated from the main Indo-Aryan linguistic area. Sinhala is a diglossic language; that is, two different varieties are in use – one for spoken/colloquial (*bhāshana*) and one for writing (*lēkhana*). Tamil, a Dravidian language, is also spoken in South India and comes from the same linguistic source of such modern South Indian languages as Malayalam, Telugu, and Kannada. Tamil is the language of Sri Lanka's close neighbor – South India. From about the 3rd century BCE, there appear to have been trade relations between Sri Lanka and South India. As a result, the Tamils came to Sri Lanka as traders and subsequently as invaders. Tamil has had a long history in Sri Lanka. It played a key role in trade and business along the Indian coasts as well as along the Sri Lanka coasts, as it was the main language used for commercial communication.

In Sri Lanka, there are only a few minority languages and dialects. Most of these lesser known languages and creoles – generally considered to be endangered – are spoken by small groups or tiny communities in remote areas. There is no government policy or program for the comprehensive documentation of these languages; however, a few researchers located outside Sri Lanka have launched projects to document them.

A Creole based on an original Vedda language with Sinhala as the second contributor currently spoken by the Veddas – thought to be either the so-called aboriginal people descended from a tribe living on the island prior to the advent of the Aryans or a group that moved to the island from the Indian mainland in prehistoric times – is used in addition to Sinhala. A second Creole – Sri Lanka Portuguese Creole – flourished as a *lingua franca* in some parts of the island from the 16th to mid-19th century. Since the Portuguese settlements initially lay along the coast, the Creole originated and has persisted in those areas, having developed from a Portuguese base with Sinhala as the second contributor. Sri Lanka Malay speakers – only about three-tenths of a per cent of the population – use the variety, but it is no longer a home language for the younger generation; indeed, it is at present only a spoken dialect. It is considered to consist of Malay lexicon with a syntactic surface structure of Sri Lanka Tamil, best defined as a mixed language resulting from typological convergence. There is evidence of a Malay presence in Sri Lanka as early as the 13th century, but large numbers of Malays migrated to the island during Dutch period, in the 18th and 19th centuries, when they came as constituents of the work force and as soldiers. The Creole of the 'Rodi' community – a low-caste group, initially socially ostracized but eventually progressively assimilated into the general population – is used by that population in addition to Sinhala. Sri Lankan-Telugu or *Ahikuntika* – i.e. "those who play with serpents and make them dance" – is spoken in a group of isolated communities in which the males are snake charmers, the women soothsayers. The variety – used only within the communities – is considered a dialect of Telugu – a major Dravidian language spoken in Andra Pradeh. In addition, both Sinhala and Tamil each exhibit some regional variations. Sri Lanka Tamil can be considered to be a major hyper-system consisting of a number of subordinate varieties – e.g. 1) North variety centered on Jaffna; 2) Northeastern variety centered on Trincomalee; 3) Northwestern variety centered on Chilaw; 4) Southeastern variety centered on Batticaloa; 5) Muslim variety; and 6) Plantation variety.

There are four classical/religious languages spoken in Sri Lanka that are used respectively in Buddhist, Hindu, Islamic and Christian religious communities; i.e. Buddhist schools use *Pali*, universities use Sanskrit, Muslim schools use Arabic, old public schools and Christian schools use Latin. *Pali* is the classical language used in Buddhist religious activities. It is an Indo-Aryan language, descending from the ancient Indian language *Magadhi*, spoken in the state of Magadha where the Buddha spent the greater part of his life. *Pali* has no script of its own; consequently, it is written using different orthographies in different parts of the Buddhist world. In Sri Lanka, it is written mainly in Sinhala, but the Roman script is also used occasionally. Much of the *Tripitaka* (The Three Baskets), the Theravada Buddhist scriptures, is written in *Pali*, and *Pali* was the medium of communication in the ancient Buddhist world. Sri Lanka is famous as a stronghold of *Pali* learning. The Colleges known as *Pirivenas* attach much importance to the teaching of *Pali* in the traditional manner. Moreover, the

Sunday Dhamma Schools (*Daham Pāsala*) conduct lessons on the *Pali* language for school children, and *Pali* is also offered as a subject in schools. Sanskrit – one of the official languages of modern India – is the classical language of Hinduism, having its own script that is shared with Hindi. Arabic is the classical language of Islam, used to recite the *Koran,* the most sacred religious text. Latin is the classical language of the Christian Church. It is still used in the chanting of certain hymns although there is a trend to replace Latin with national languages.

At independence, the successor states of the British Empire in South Asia confronted the critical issue of deciding which language – or languages – should replace English as the official language/s. In the first decade after independence, all three nations, India, Pakistan and Sri Lanka, faced language problems that arose in the formulation of language policies especially with reference to the question of official/national language. In Sri Lanka (as in most South Asian states) the language issue has historically been an "arena for struggle," where the majority of the country's population has sought to exercise power over minority ethnic groups. The attempt to ensure the primacy of the majority language by legal enactment disturbed the civil peace of the country for five decades. Language has often been used as a weapon in the power struggle. Therefore, the selection of an official language(s) has proven to constitute a policy decision of great controversy and emotion.

Language lies at the root of the present ethnic struggle in Sri Lanka between the Sinhalese[2] majority and the Sri Lankan Tamils – a conflict that originated in the mid -1950s over the selection of an official language after the country became independent of the British Empire. Fifty years (1956-2006) have passed since Sinhala was made the official language, and eighteen years (1988-2006) have elapsed since the Tamil language was declared as the other official language of Sri Lanka by the 13th amendment to the Constitution. National language policy and planning exercises in Sri Lanka have experienced a series of twists and turns as politicians grappled with the consequences of the policy changes they had introduced. Much of status planning has been bound up with the 'one language, one nation,' myth, an idea that emerged as the primary argument during the period of nation building after independence. Both government and individual language planning activities aimed at the *cultivation* of Sinhala as an official language.

Language planning in general gained momentum in the second half of the 20th century in response to new needs resulting from the changing status of Sinhala. A comprehensive language-planning program was carried out under the auspices of the government during the policy implementation transition period. Corpus planning activities carried out by the Department of Official Languages during the period between 1955 and 1965 enabled Sinhala to cope with its extended role and new function as an 'official language'. The terminological modernization of Sinhala generated extensive discussion in the area of corpus planning. As an official language, Sinhala has been increasingly used in various domains and in the educational and administrative system; Sinhala as a modern language must serve the communicative needs of the modern epoch. In order to survive, Sinhala needs modern terminology for all specialized fields. As a result of lexical expansion, Sinhala has become a more efficient medium for instruction and communication. However, due to the lack of government sponsored language planning in the past few years, no language planning agency or academy was set up to look into the language related problems of the society. The Official Languages Department and the Cultural Affairs Department are the only government bodies actually charged to act in the area of language and cultural problems. Non-governmental organizations are also not active in the area of language policy and planning. As a result, various language issues have arisen in Sinhala society related to Sinhala orthography – the acceptability of a standard, the development of specific registers and modernization.

Since the end of the internal fighting between government forces and the Tamil separatists, one of the ways the Government has sought to bring about national reconciliation is through the implementation of the official bilingual language policy. However, implementation of this key activity still lags far behind expected levels according to the most recent Language Resources Needs Assessment Survey conducted by the Official Languages Commission (OLC) and the government realizes more needs to be done to make the public service bilingual to meet the needs of all Sri Lankans.

Timor-Leste

Timor-Leste is situated on the easternmost tip of the Archipelago of the Lesser Sunda Islands, comprising the eastern half of the island of Timor; the Oecussi (Ambeno) exclave on the northwest portion of the island of Timor; and the islands of Ataúro to the north, and Jaco to the east, encompassing approximately 14,900 square kilometers in area, sharing a border with Indonesia and being a close neighbor of Australia. The population is 1,154,625 according to the World Fact Book (2010), but is increasing rapidly. The people of Timor-Leste have endured a long history of colonialism, underdevelopment, conflict, human rights abuse, civil unrest and dramatic political change. Although independence was originally declared in 1975, it was formally celebrated on 20th May 2002 when the United Nations handed over administration to the independent state after over four centuries of Portuguese colonialism and 24 years of occupation by Indonesia. The composition of the present population, the language profile of the country, language choice and patterns of language use, maintenance and spread can only be fully understood in the light of these experiences.

The National Constitution of the new nation declared the endogenous lingua franca (*Tetum*) and the former colonial language (Portuguese) to be co-official. The remaining local languages were given the status of national languages, while Indonesian and English have been designated working languages "for as long as is deemed necessary." The socio-political agendas and linguistic ideologies of Australia, Indonesia and Portugal have shaped the course of the modern history of Timor-Leste. As a consequence, literacy rates are extremely low; 54.2 per cent (at least 400, 000 people over the age of six) cannot read or write in any of the official languages. Some 45 per cent of the population aged 15 and older survives on subsistence labor while at least 42 per cent lives below the poverty line. The situation is further complicated by the fact that Timor-Leste is beset with significant linguistic variety. The Papuan languages with the greatest numbers of speakers are *Makasai* and *Bunak*. The three largest Austronesian languages are *Baikenu* (spoken in the East Timorese exclave of Oecussi and in West Timor), *Mambae* (spoken in eastern Timor) and *Tetum* (spoken in the east and the west of Timor island) – *Tetum* is not simply the lingua franca of Timor-Leste; it is also the most commonly spoken language on both sides of the island. At least 16 other language varieties are spoken in Timor-Leste compared to only seven in West Timor. *Baikenu, Tetum, Kemak* and *Bunak* are spoken on both sides of the border with West

Timor. The *Wetarese* and *Galoli* languages (and their dialectal varieties) are spoken on both sides of the border between Timor-Leste and Maluku. With one exception – only *Lóvaia,* also known as *Makuva*, is seriously endangered – the endogenous languages are considered to have high linguistic vitality. If high language diversity can be defined as a situation in which less than 50 per cent of the population speaks the same language, no language variety is spoken as a first language in Timor-Leste by more than 18 per cent of the population and most languages are spoken by far smaller numbers of speakers. Such concepts as *majority* and *minority* languages are irrelevant in Timor-Leste. In Timor-Leste, even *Tetum* is a minority language in certain regions; the number of speakers of *Tetum* as a first language is as low as 1.4 per cent in some districts and in some other districts less than 20 per cent of the population can speak, read or write it. Given the difficulty of arriving at accurate counts of speakers of a given language, all figures are necessarily estimates. Consequently, definitions of what constitutes a language must be operationally stated, and such statements may differ from what speakers themselves consider a language.

There is also the difficult problem of what constitutes the difference between dialects and languages; many languages are known by more than one name. There are also differences of opinion about how to measure both proficiency and literacy. Some of these difficulties are manifested in any estimation of language actively spoken in Timor-Leste. Colonial legacies continue to pose significant problems in the curriculum. Although Portuguese was introduced as a subject in the junior secondary grades from 2005, at the time of writing the curriculum in junior high schools and senior high schools still uses the Indonesian model. Indonesian, the most recent colonial language, is the most common language of instruction in the universities and high schools. Moreover, textbooks are still largely in Indonesian. At the National University of Timor-Leste, the degree structure, syllabi and methods of assessment still remain predominantly in Indonesian. By 2003, Indonesian was no longer taught as a subject in schools or in the national university. However, students in junior secondary school and secondary school have continued to use Indonesian books whilst learning Portuguese. In this educational context, a *language as problem* orientation is inevitable. A key goal of the Education Policy framework has been to reintroduce Portuguese and to develop *Tetum* as languages of instruction.

Problems faced by the several polities

As these brief summaries show, all three of the polities are faced with the problem created by the presence of colonial languages – English in Hong Kong, Dutch, English and Portuguese in Sri Lanka, and Portuguese, Indonesian and English – through globalization – in Timor-Leste. The colonial languages are in competition with the indigenous languages – Cantonese and Standard Written Chinese in Hong Kong, Sinhala and Tamil in Sri-Lanka, and *Tetum* in Timor-Leste. With the cessation of European colonial rule, their governments were faced with an immediate and urgent problem – the need to have a vehicle for communication with the populace. Looking at the history of the western states, the "one language/one nation" myth, inherited from Europe and the colonial powers in their histories, seemed a viable solution. Regrettably, the choice of a single language to serve that objective proved to be far more complicated than was initially imagined. That difficulty has been amply demonstrated by any number of states – both small and large, developed and developing, relatively rich or relatively poor – in Africa, Asia and Latin America.[3]

The chaos resulting from various attempts to identify a single language for unification was in several cases exacerbated by the adoption of a colonial language for that purpose. Since the colonial language had rarely been spoken by the populace at large, that solution was not successful. Another tactic was to adopt a "global" language – which in most cases turned out to be English. As a result, English has been subjected to a great deal of criticism – sometimes because it was perceived as a "killer" language (i.e. one responsible for the extinction of smaller indigenous languages), sometimes because it was perceived as benefiting from its global use. These criticisms of the language are somewhat unreasonable, since languages are not, in any sense, actors (Zhao, 2011); rather, only speakers of languages can be accused of having intentions, benevolent or evil. "Language contact exists only between speakers and language communities, not between languages" (Nelde, 2010: 378).

In addition, the universal learning of English in the school population has turned out to be rather impractical – an activity involving huge cost for relatively small success (See Hamid & Baldauf, 2008 for Bangladesh). In any case, the solution to the problem has been devolved to the education sector. In all three polities, a significant language-in-education legislation has been enacted, at times resulting in contradictory trends. In all three cases, language policy has turned out to be a political activity, entrusted into the hands of politicians rather than the hands of educators or those of linguists. As a result, language planning has drawn a large number of criticisms that, like criticisms directed at the English language, have been unjust and undeserved; it has not been language planning which has been at fault; rather it has been language planners who have been guilty of unsuccessful planning, or using language planning for political purposes. Planning often has been unsuccessful either because the assumptions about language learning, the time necessary for successful learning, the training of qualified teachers, the types of assessment employed to determine success, the nature of success, the time required to permit a reasonable trial period and other matters, or because the implementation of a language plan has been inadequately funded, inadequately extended, and inadequately disseminated across the educational system. Indeed, it seems amazing that, in the face of all the evidence to the contrary, education administrators around the world are (as they are in these three polities) still happy to promulgate instructional programs in which the rate of forgetting is quite likely to exceed the rate of learning, in which time on task is so brief as essentially to insure fractured acquisition, and in which teacher-training, materials development as well as achievement and project assessment are conducted in blissful ignorance of the accumulated wealth of knowledge about language policy and planning, language learning, language teaching and language testing. These problems arise in part because the key decision-makers in charge of the process normally remain largely unaware of the extant research, unfamiliar with researchers who are experts in the field, and unlikely or unwilling to seek the advice even of the teachers at the chalk face.

Studies such as those presented here are intended to help inform not only education administrators but also language planners, the authors of language policy and the political figures responsible for language legislation at every level, from the local school to the multinational regulatory body. It is increasingly urgent that all those who control the power of governments and of government ministries relating to language regulation, language education and language rights both with respect to the largest, most influential majority languages and minority languages exerting the least influence over their own survival increase their ability to understand what language is, what language does and what language needs to assure the survival of as many languages as possible with the least conflict.

Notes

1 The studies in this volume were previously published as follows: Taylor-Leech, K. (2010) The language situation in Timor-Leste. *Current Issues in Language Planning* 10 (1), 1-68; Coperahewa, S. (2010) The language-planning situation in Sri Lanka. *Current Issues in Language Planning* 10 (1), 69-150; Poon, A. Y. K. (2011) Language use, and language and planning in Hong Kong. *Current Issues in Language Planning* 11 (1), 1-66.

2 To clarify some terminological difficulties, some writers have suggested using *Sinhala* for the language, and *Sinhalese* for the people who speak it, or alternatively using *Sinhala* as the adjective (as in 'Sinhala Culture') and *Sinhalese* as the noun, (as in 'we are *Sinhalese*'). The origin of the name lies in the myth of origin, as recorded in the *Dipavamsa* and *Mahāvamsa*. According to this myth, the Sinhalese are said to be descendants of an Indian prince, named *Vijaya*, the grandson of a *Sinha*, i.e., a literary lion.

3 The language planning literature is too large to permit selecting a small sample set to represent the scholarly activity over the past half-century, although the polity studies referenced in Appendix A provide a starting point. Based on a corpus review of published Language Policy and Planning (LPP) literature found in *Linguistic and Language Behavior Abstracts* (LLBA) from 1973 to 2008 and as available on WebSPIRS (up to 1988) and CSA Illumina (1989-2008), there are 10,999 articles related either to 'language policy' or to 'language planning' out of a total of 285,540 items related to 'language' generally (26%) in the LLBA database. This literature is scattered across a wide range of publications related to many different disciplines and is published more frequently in languages other than English than the LLBA literature in general. The references per 1,000 articles shows how, in the 1970s, the LPP literature grew as a field relative to the language literature – from only 6 articles per 1,000 in 1973 to 41.1 articles per 1,000 in 1979. The 10-year period from 1979 to 1988 saw 1,840 or 49 articles per 1,000 published, while the period from 1989 to 1998 saw 4,192 or 39.4 articles per 1,000 published and 1999 to 2008 saw 4,114 or 39.4 articles per 1,000 published, indicating the emerging strength of the field in the 1980s and reflecting a gradual leveling off of interest in relative terms since (see Baldauf, 2010).

References

Baldauf, R. B., Jr. (2010). Methodologies for policy and planning. In R. B. Kaplan (Ed.) *Oxford handbook of applied linguistics* (pp. 427-451). New York: Oxford University Press.

Coperahewa, S. (2010). The language planning situation in Sri Lanka. *Current Issues in Language Planning*, 10 (1), 69-150.

Hamid, M. O. & Baldauf, R. B., Jr. (2008). Will CLT bail out bogged down ELT in Bangladesh? *English Today*, 24(3), 19-27.

Johnson, R. K. (1994). Language policy and planning in Hong Kong. *Annual Review of Applied Linguistics*, 14 (1), 177-199.

Kaplan, R. B., Baldauf, R. B., Jr., Liddicoat, A, J., Bryant, M.-T. & Pütz, M. (2000). Current issues in language planning. *Current Issues in Language Planning*, 1 (2), 135-144.

Nelde, P. H. (2010). Language contact. In R. B. Kaplan (Ed.) *Oxford handbook of applied linguistics* (pp. 373-381). New York: Oxford University Press.

Poon, A. Y. K. (2011). Language use, and language and planning in Hong Kong. *Current Issues in Language Planning*, 11 (1), 1-66.

Taylor-Leech, K. (2010). The language situation in Timor-Leste. *Current Issues in Language Planning*, 10 (1), 1-68.

Zhao, S. H. (2008). Chinese character modernization in the digital era: A historical perspective. In R. B. Kaplan & R. B. Baldauf, Jr. (Eds) *Language planning and policy in Asia, vol.1: Japan, Nepal, Taiwan and Chinese characters* (pp. 38-101). Bristol: Multilingual Matters.

Zhao, S. H. (2011). Actors in language planning. In E. Hinkel (Ed.) *Handbook of research in second language teaching and learning* (2nd Edn), pp. 905-923. London: Routledge.

Appendix A: Polity Studies Overview

Polity studies addressing the language situation in particular polities have been published fairly regularly over the past dozen years – initially in 1998 and 1999 in the *Journal of Multilingual and Multicultural Development* and subsequently in *Current Issues in Language Planning (CILP)* which began publication in 2000. Over that time span, 30* polity studies (and one study of Chinese character modernization) have been published. These studies have all addressed, to a greater or lesser extent, 22 common questions or issues (Appendix B), thus giving them some degree of consistency. As we have been keenly aware, these polity studies have been published in *CILP* in the order in which we have received manuscripts – an order entirely appropriate to journal publication. However, it has seemed to us that bringing out the polity studies in geographic volumes might be of greater use to area specialists and might make the studies more accessible to the general public. As the number of available polity studies has increased, we have undertaken to make them available in areal volumes, updating them where necessary, to present the studies in a more logical configuration.

The first such volume appeared in 2004 and was concerned with Africa due to a significant number of studies becoming available, because Africa constituted an area that is significantly under-represented in the language planning literature, and because African language policy is marked by extremely interesting policy developments and planning issues. The polity studies available at the time that were included in the volume were on Botswana, Malawi, Mozambique and South Africa.

The response from readers has led us to believe that this process is indeed useful. In 2008, a perturbation in the publishing industry required a change in the preparation of these volumes. All of the initial volumes were made available as a boxed set.** Subsequently, there has been a two year hiatus in the production of the areal volumes; the current volume presents studies of Hong Kong, Timor-Leste and Sri Lanka, grouped into an areal volume from the Asia Pacific region. We hope to continue publishing additional areal volumes as sufficient studies are submitted for initial publication in *CILP*.

In the mean time, we plan to continue to publish *CILP*, adding not only additional polity studies but also continuing to assemble thematic issues concerned with language policy and planning issues.

Assumptions concerning polity studies

A number of assumptions concerning the nature of language policy, the actors involved in policy production, and the issues that appear to concern policy makers underlie the polity studies that already have appeared. It has seemed to us as we have worked with the polity studies that no broad, coherent paradigm for addressing the complex questions of language policy/planning development yet exists. At the same time, we are convinced that the need for a coherent paradigm depends on the collection of a large body of more or less comparable data and the careful analysis of that data. Consequently, in our efforts to solicit polity studies from potential authors, we have asked those potential contributors to address some two-dozen questions (to the extent that such questions were pertinent to each particular polity) in order to enlarge the probability of comparable data. The questions were designed to serve as suggestions for organizing the topics addressed in the polity studies (See Appendix B). Contributors have responded to these suggestions in various ways, some using the questions literally as an outline for their efforts; others have been more independent in approaching the task. Obviously, in framing the questions, we were – consciously and unconsciously – moving from a perhaps inchoate understanding of what might be an underlying theory. The inchoate quality of our questions has been demonstrated in each of the polity studies produced.

In addition, we have tried to approach potential authors who had had a direct experience in working with the language planning and policy decisions made in the polity about which they were writing; i.e. we explicitly sought insider knowledge and perspectives about the polities and the evolving policies and plans. As insiders were, in fact, part of the developmental process, they sometimes found it difficult to assume the role of the 'other' – that is to be critical of the process in which they were involved. However, it has seemed to us that it is neither necessary nor appropriate that they should be. As Pennycook (1998: 126) argues:

> One of the lessons we need to draw from this account of colonial language policy [i.e. Hong Kong] is that, in order to make sense of language policies we need to understand both their location historically and their location contextually. What I mean by this is that we cannot assume that the promotion of local languages instead of a dominant language, or the promotion of a dominant language at the expense of a local language, are in themselves good or bad. Too often we view these things through the lenses of liberalism, pluralism or anti-imperialism, without understanding the actual location of such policies.

Many of the studies we receive are basically descriptive, illustrating the activities of language planning in the polity with which they are concerned, even though some authors are able to write critically or to employ a theoretical approach. All of the reports are useful in the sense that they describe actual events and views. Thus, all reports constitute valuable contributions to an evolving theoretical paradigm even though the descriptions may employ existing paradigms – e.g. language management, language rights, linguistic imperialism – or offer information based on somewhat general frameworks (e.g. Hornberger, 2006; Nekvapil, 2009; Spolsky, 2004, 2009). The reality is that the contemporary condition of knowledge about language policy and planning remains partial. Indeed, we admit that we ourselves have not been innocent of relying on general frameworks – e.g. Kaplan & Baldauf, 2003, Chapter 12. Thus, the emergence of a sufficient body of work to permit the generation of an adequate paradigm remains an essential prerequisite.

We acknowledge that the foundation on which much contemporary language planning is normally undertaken is quite inadequate to the task. The development of a successful language plan involves much more information than is conventionally assumed. First of all, it is essential to recognize that language planning is a highly political activity – see Hogan-Brun, *et al.*, 2007. Clearly, traditional linguistic research is necessary but not sufficient; indeed, the publication of scholarly articles constitutes only the first step in a complex process. Such articles may need to be re-oriented to consider not only linguistic matters but also sociological concerns surrounding language use and even further the ecological conditions surrounding language, its spread, and its functions in areas like education, health, the economy and governance and development (see Djité, 2008, 2011). The research evidence essential to the general understanding of a language plan needs to be presented in a form understandable to the lay public; unfortunately, the ideal transmission of such information rarely falls to traditional academic authors (Kaplan & Baldauf, 2007). We believe that this series of polity studies may contribute not only to a clearer understanding of the formation of language policy but also to a more acceptable means of communicating the advantages and disadvantages of a policy to the speakers of a language under discussion.

An Invitation to Contribute

Contributions of additional polity studies are welcome. The editorial views on various issues are available in Kaplan and Baldauf (1997); examples of publishable polity monographs are available in the extant issues *Current Issues in Language Planning* [*CILP*] and in the earlier publication in this series. (See the listing of prior volumes that follows.) Any potential authors should contact the editors, present a proposal for a monograph, and provide a sample list of references. A brief biographical note (especially one citing any relevant research/publication in language policy and planning) would also be useful. All contributions should, of course, be original, unpublished works. We expect to work closely with contributors during the preparation of monographs. All monographs will, of course, be reviewed for quality, completeness, accuracy, and style. Experience suggests that co-authored contributions may be very successful, but we want to stress that we are seeking a unified monograph concerning the polity, not an edited compilation of various authors' efforts. Questions may be addressed to either of us:

Robert B. Kaplan
rkaplan@olypen.com

Richard B. Baldauf, Jr.
richard.baldauf@bigpond.com

INTRODUCTION

Notes

* Polities in print include:
1. Algeria
2. The Baltics
3. Botswana
4. Cameroon
5. Côte d'Ivoire
6. Czech Republic
7. Ecuador
8. European Union
9. Fiji
10. Finland
11. Hong Kong
12. Hungary
13. Ireland
14. Italy
15. Malawi
16. Mexico
17. Mozambique
18. Nepal
19. Nigeria
20. Northern Ireland
21. Paraguay
22. The Philippines
23. South Africa
24. Sri Lanka
25. Sweden
26. Taiwan
27. Timor-Leste
28. Tunisia
29. Vanuatu
30. Zimbabwe

A 31st monograph on Chinese Character Modernization is also available.

** Areal volumes currently in print include:

Language Planning and Policy in Europe, Vol. 1: Hungary, Finland and Sweden (2005)

Language Planning and Policy in Europe, Vol. 2: The Czech Republic, The European Union and Northern Ireland (2006)

Language Planning and Policy in the Pacific, Vol. 1: Fiji, the Philippines and Vanuatu (2006)

Language Planning and Policy in Africa, Vol. 2: Algeria, Côte d'Ivoire, Nigeria and Tunisia (2007)

Language Planning and Policy in Latin America, Vol. 1: Ecuador, Mexico and Paraguay (2007)

Language Planning and Policy in Europe, Vol. 3: The Baltics, Ireland and Italy (2007)

Language Planning and Policy in Asia, Vol. 1: Japan, Nepal, Taiwan and Chinese Characters (2008)

References

Djité, P. G. (2008). *The sociolinguistics of development in Africa*. Clevedon: Multilingual Matters.

Djité, P. G. (2011). *The language difference: Language and development in the greater Mekong sub-region*. Bristol: Multilingual Matters.

Hogan-Brun, G., Ozolins, U., Ramonien, M. & Rannut, M. (2007). Language politics and practices in the Baltic States. *Current Issues in Language Planning*, 8(4), 469–631.

Hornberger, N. H. (2006). Frameworks and models in language policy and planning. In T. Ricento (Ed.) *An introduction to language policy: Theory and method* (pp. 24 – 41). Oxford: Blackwell.

Kaplan, R. B. & Baldauf, R. B., Jr. (2007). Language policy spread: Learning from health and social policy models. *Language Problems & Language Planning*, 31 (2), 107–129.

Kaplan, R. B. & Baldauf, R. B., Jr. (2003). Language planning in perspective. In *Language and language-in-education planning in the Pacific Basin* (pp. 201 – 226). Dordrecht: Kluwer.

Kaplan, R. B. & Baldauf, R. B., Jr. (1997). *Language planning from practice to theory*. Clevedon, Avon: Multilingual Matters.

Nekvapil, J. (2009). The integrative potential of language management theory. In J. Nekvapil & T. Sherman (Eds.) *Language management in contact situations: Perspectives from three continents* (pp. 1 – 11). Frankfurt am Main: Peter Lang.

Pennycook, A. (1998). *English and the discourses of colonialism*. London and New York: Routledge.

Spolsky, B. (2004). *Language policy*. Cambridge: Cambridge University Press.

Spolsky, B. (2009). *Language management*. Cambridge: Cambridge University Press.

Appendix B

Part I The Language Profile of...

1. Name and briefly describe the national/official language(s) (*de jure* or *de facto*).
2. Name and describe the major minority language(s).
3. Name and describe the lesser minority language(s) (include "dialects", pidgins, creoles and other important aspects of language variation); the definition of minority language/dialect/pidgin will need to be discussed in terms of the sociolinguistic context.
4. Name and describe the major religious language(s); in some polities religious languages and/or missionary policies have had a major impact on the language situation and provide *de facto* language planning. In some contexts religion has been a vehicle for introducing exogenous languages while in other cases it has served to promote indigenous languages.
5. Name and describe the major language(s) of literacy, assuming that it is/they are not one of those described above.
6. Provide a table indicating the number of speakers of each of the above languages, what percentage of the population they constitute and whether those speakers are largely urban or rural.
7. Where appropriate, provide a map(s) showing the distribution of speakers, key cities and other features referenced in the text.

Part II Language Spread

8. Specify which languages are taught through the educational system, to whom they are taught, when they are taught and for how long they are taught.
9. Discuss the objectives of language education and the methods of assessment to determine whether the objectives are met.
10. To the extent possible, trace the historical development of the policies/practices identified in items 8 and 9 (may be integrated with 8/9).
11. Name and discuss the major media language(s) and the distribution of media by socio-economic class, ethnic group, and urban/rural distinction (including the historical context where possible). For minority language, note the extent that any literature is (has been) available in the language.
12. How has immigration effected language distribution and what measures are in place to cater for learning the national language(s) and/or to support the use of immigrant languages?

Part III Language Policy and Planning

13. Describe any language planning legislation, policy or implementation that is currently in place.

14. Describe any literacy planning legislation, policy or implementation that is currently in place.
15. To the extent possible, trace the historical development of the policies/practices identified in items 13 and 14 (may be integrated with these items).
16. Describe and discuss any language planning agencies/organisations operating in the polity (both formal and informal).
17. Describe and discuss any regional/international influences affecting language planning and policy in the polity (include any external language promotion efforts).
18. To the extent possible, trace the historical development of the policies/practices identified in items 16 and 17 (may be integrated with these items).

Part IV Language Maintenance and Prospects

19. Describe and discuss intergenerational transmission of the major language(s), and whether this is changing over time.
20. Describe and discuss the probabilities of language death among any of the languages/language varieties in the polity, any language revival efforts as well as any emerging pidgins or creoles.
21. Add anything you wish to clarify about the language situation and its probable direction of change over the next generation or two.
22. Add pertinent references/bibliography and any necessary appendices (e.g. a general plan of the educational system to clarify the answers to questions 8, 9 and 14).

Addendum

Since the three studies presented here were published some time ago, the authors have provided some brief updating, together with some more recent references, attached here as an addendum.

Latest development in Hong Kong's language policy scene

Anita Y. K. Poon

• *Recent 'Safeguard Cantonese Movement' in Guangzhou and Hong Kong.*

A member of Chinese People's Political Consultative Conference (CPPCC) of Guangzhou put forward a motion on 5 July 2010 suggesting changing the language of the major Guangzhou TV channel from Cantonese to Putonghua. His reasons were two-fold:

1. To facilitate visitors from other provinces during the period of the Asian Games, which will be held in Guangzhou in December 2010.
2. To help Guangzhou to become an international city.

The news agitated Guangzhou people. Thousands of them took to the street on 25 July and on 1 August 2010; the participants were mostly young people born in the 1980s and 1990s. Some young people in Hong Kong responded to the call, crossed the border and participated in the second rally held in Guangzhou on 1 August 2010 while several hundred youngsters organised a similar rally in Hong Kong on the same day. It was the second time in history that people in Guangzhou and Hong Kong had participated in demonstrations over the same issue (the first demonstration had been against the 4 June 1989 massacre.) The cause for such a strong reaction to the CPPCC member's proposal is deep-rooted. On the one hand, it reveals the dissatisfaction of Guangzhou people about the communist regime's attempt over the past five decades to eradicate traditional Cantonese language and culture; on the other hand it illustrates the emergence of civil society in Mainland China. (See Ng, August 8, August 15, 2010; Poon, August 5, 2010; Tse, August 15, 2010; Yung, 2010).

INTRODUCTION

• *Implication of 'Safeguard Cantonese Movement' for Hong Kong.*

The PRC's "Promote Putonghua and abolish Cantonese" policy has been continuously implemented since 1958 (Yung, 2010). This language policy has far-reaching impact on the future development of Cantonese, the first language of 95% of Hong Kong inhabitants. Cantonese – as well as other dialects – has been replaced by Putonghua as the medium of instruction in primary and secondary schools on the Mainland since 1958. Subsequently, Cantonese has been relegated to the status of a home and community language; it has been forbidden in such other public domains as the government, the judiciary, and other official domains. The Guangdong authorities also issued a paper in 1960 entitled "Cantonese pronunciation scheme" intended to standardise the phonetic symbols of Cantonese based on Putonghua symbols, as a consequence forcing some sounds unique to Cantonese to be modified in order to align pronunciation with Putonghua (Yung, 2010). As a result of such linguistic hegemony, the use of Cantonese has been decreasing in southern China. Similarly, the same outcome has occurred with respect to other dialects in other parts of China; e.g. a recent survey indicates that the younger generation in Shanghai is not able to speak Shanghainese well. (See Poon, August 11, 2010).

In Hong Kong, the teaching in Putonghua of the Chinese language subject at school has been placed on the agenda of the Curriculum Reform document as a long-term goal (Curriculum Development Council, 2000). Given the poor experience in implementing compulsory Chinese-medium instruction policy in junior secondary schools over the past 12 years, the Hong Kong government is being rather more cautious this time. Instead of pushing the policy forward, the Education Bureau has adopted a soft approach. HK$200 million (equivalent to US$25.64 million) was invested in a pilot scheme to allow 120 primary and secondary schools to try out using Putonghua as the medium of instruction for the Chinese language subject during 2008–2011. Parents and schools welcomed the move since they believe that Putonghua offers better job opportunities for their children, and students' standard Chinese (i.e. written Chinese) will be enhanced because, once students become fluent speakers of Putonghua through the constant use of the language as the medium of instruction, they will be able to write what they think and say. Poon (2001, December 8; 2010, August 11) argues that there is a misconception concerning any improvement in standard Chinese through using Putonghua to teach the Chinese language subject. The assumption underlying the notion of being better able to write what one thinks and says is based on the use of the language as one's first language. In the case of Hong Kong, if one really wrote what one thought and said, it would be in the written form of Cantonese, which is very different from Modern Standard Chinese, the written form of Putonghua. Being able to speak Putonghua well will not necessarily lead to improvement in standard Chinese; there is no supporting research evidence (SCOLAR, 2003). It is likely that the teaching of the Chinese language subject through the medium of Putonghua will enhance proficiency in Putonghua as a result of increased exposure to the language, but Hong Kong society would have to pay a high price for this enhanced proficiency (Poon, 2010, August 5). Should Putonghua be adopted as the teaching medium of the Chinese language subject, other subjects presently taught in Chinese will sooner or later shift to the Putonghua-medium. It can be anticipated that the use of Cantonese in Hong Kong will gradually decline, as is likely to happen in Guangzhou and in other parts of southern China, if Putonghua is adopted as the medium of instruction.

INTRODUCTION

A Guangzhou youth born in the 1980s was asked by a Hong Kong magazine to comment on the "Safeguard Cantonese Movement." The interviewee said:

> If you don't rebel, the government will suppress everything. First, the issue of Putonghua, then freedom of expression. We Guangzhou people are frightened because we are aware of the danger. If Hong Kong people aren't aware and aren't frightened, I'll be heart-broken because Hong Kong is the last fortress for our ethnic Cantonese community and culture. If Hong Kong can't remain autonomous, our situation will be even more difficult. I hope Hong Kong people will not be so naïve; they should have heightened awareness....Hong Kong people should not value only money (Chan, 2010, p. 43).

• *Trendy language included in Oxford Dictionary.*

The *Oxford Chinese Dictionary* containing English-Chinese and Chinese-English translation was released on 9 September 2010. It is the largest single-volume dictionary, containing about 670,000 words and phrases, 1,098 of which are newly added. These new words are the so-called "trendy language" [...] used in Chinese newspapers and magazines published in Beijing, Hong Kong, Macau, Shanghai, Singapore and Taipei over the past ten years. Although the trendy words are taken mainly from Mainland China, there are approximately 5% from Hong Kong Cantonese.

References

Chan, C. (2010). Cantonese: Life or death. *Ming Pao Weekly*, August 21 (In Chinese).
Curriculum Development Council (2000). *Learning to learn: Key learning area Chinese language education (Consultation document)*. Hong Kong: Government Printer.
Ng, W. (2010). Thousands of people took to the street to safeguard Cantonese in Guangzhou. *Asia Weekly*, August 8 (In Chinese).
Ng, W. (2010). Another demonstration to safeguard Cantonese in Guangzhou. *Asia Weekly*, August 15 (In Chinese).
Poon, A.Y.K. (2010, August 5). Linguistic hegemony. *Ming Pao*. p. A29.
Poon, A.Y.K. (2010, August 11). Should Hong Kong people also safeguard Cantonese? *Ming Pao*. p. B14.
Poon, A.Y.K. (2001, December 8). Using Putonghua as the medium of instruction is not the key to learning Chinese well. *Ming Pao*.
SCOLAR (2003). *Action plan to raise language standards in Hong Kong*. Hong Kong: SCOLAR, Education and Manpower Bureau.
Tse, H.Y. (2010). The understatement of Hong Kong people's action to safeguard Cantonese. *Asia Weekly*, August 15 (In Chinese).
Yung, Y. (2010). Historical reasons for 'Safeguard Cantonese movement' and people's awakening. *Ming Pao Monthly*, September 2010 (In Chinese).

Recent developments in language policy planning in Sri Lanka

Sandagomi Coperahewa

In the post war scenario, as Government seeks to bring about national reconciliation, the implementation of the official language policy which is expected to play a key role in the success of the effort still lags far behind expected levels according to the most recent Language Resources Needs Assessment Survey conducted by the Official Languages Commission (OLC). A striking factor of the survey, covering 50 state institutions, was the fact that the proportion of officers proficient in Tamil serving in the public administration sector was very low. The report revealed that, in areas outside the North and East, the percentage of officers proficient in Tamil was 9.5 per cent, compared with 18.1 per cent of officers proficient in Sinhala in the north and east. Sinhala is the language of administration in areas outside the north and east while Tamil is the language of administration in these two areas.

For a Tamil speaking population of around 1.1 million in areas outside the two provinces, there was a total of only 6,626 officers proficient in Tamil at executive, subordinate and minor employee level or around 9.5 per cent, while in the northern and eastern provinces for around 365,000 Sinhalese speaking persons, there were 540 officers proficient in Sinhalese at different levels or around 18.1 per cent. The institutions where language was found to be an obstacle to around 50 per cent of members of the public questioned were base-hospitals, police stations, local authorities, head offices and Divisional and District Secretariats.

Many of those surveyed faced hindrances in matters like filling of forms and communication with state institutions. Even though in around 60 per cent of state institutional forms were printed in all three languages as the law stipulates, there were many institutions where this rule was not enforced. There was also a low level of compliance with regard to the display of name and signboards, direction boards and information displays in the two official languages. The survey also found that the degree of awareness of the language policy among all categories of public servants/corporation employees was either poor or very poor, the same being true of members of the general public who were unaware of their language rights. The non-availability of physical resources such as typewriters and computers to produce documents in both official languages was another drawback (*Sunday Times* 2010/02/14).

In November 2009, Constitutional Affairs and National Integration Minister D.E.W. Gunasekera noted that the achievements realised through the implementation of language policy for the promotion of peace, unity and cohesion was incredible. The support provided for the resolution of the ethnic problem through the implementation of the Official Language Policy was enormous, he said. The Minister further remarked that, according to the Official Languages policy, classes and examinations for public officers were being conducted by the Department of Official Languages to facilitate the bilingualisation of the Public Service.

He said that, since the Cabinet had decided in 2005 on the bilingualisation of the Public Service, incentives for public officers who were in service for achieving proficiency in the second official language was impressive. Newly recruited public officers should have proficiency in the second language within a prescribed period. Minister Gunasekera said 2,635 officers were successful at the written examination held in March 2008, and 2,962 were successful at the level of the oral examination. A great number – 5,875 public officers – sat for the examination on September 27, 2008. The Minister pointed out that the proposal on the vigorous implementation of official languages policy in the Mahinda Chintana program provided added strength and support to the implementation of official language policy (*Daily News* 2009/11/23).

To position the National Language Policy on a pragmatic footing, Government servants with fluency in Tamil and Sinhala will, in due course, get special salary increments based on the merits of their being bilingual represents a strategy contemplated by the National Languages and Social Integration Ministry. The Official Language Policy requires that state institutions and departments should be bilingual. A time span of three years had been established for Government servants to become proficient in Tamil, in the event that they are native Sinhala speakers. The native Tamil speakers are also required to learn the Sinhala language to become entitled to receive the salary increments that are to be introduced in due course by the Ministry to promote bilingual education. (*Daily News*, 2010/07/14).

References

Daily News, http://www.dailynews.lk/2010/07/14/news21.asp.
Daily News, http://www.dailynews.lk/2009/11/23/news40.asp.
Sunday Times, http://www.sundaytimes.lk/100214/News/nws_21.html.

Recent developments in language policy planning in Timor-Leste

Kerry Taylor-Leech

Since this monograph was written there have been some encouraging developments on the language front in Timor-Leste. These developments highlight the unpredictable, organic ways in which policy can be reshaped. Since the country emerged from the crisis of 2006-07, relative stability has returned, although the country's pressing economic and social problems are still far from resolution. The present government has achieved the important milestone of establishing nine years free, basic compulsory schooling for all East Timorese children. The Education System Framework Law 14/ 2008 reaffirms that the languages of the education system are Tetum and Portuguese and guarantees that by the end of primary school each student shall have mastery (sic) of these languages along with the learning of an (unspecified) first foreign language. However, while the policy guidelines directing teachers to use Portuguese as the language of instruction with Tetum as a pedagogic aid remain the same, initiatives from outside government are combining to bring about change. The aid industry shows increasing sensitivity to Tetum and the national languages; indeed UN and non-government organisations have taken a leading role in campaigning for their use as languages of instruction in schools. In April, 2008 Care International, UNICEF, and UNESCO sponsored an international conference entitled *"Helping children learn"* in the capital city of Dili with the Ministry of Education. In a bold initiative, the new Minister of Education placed multilingual education and educational quality squarely on the agenda by posing three key questions to the conference:

1. What should be considered the mother tongue in any given district given the linguistic diversity of Timor-Leste?
2. Should teachers decide the language of instruction in each classroom?
3. Is the current language-in-education policy giving stress to children by expecting too much from them?

Given the sensitivities surrounding language in Timor-Leste, the debate was intense but the emergent recommendations have opened the way for change. Following from the conference, the National Education Commission established a working group to elaborate a language-in-education policy by the end of 2010. This working group was mandated to work in close collaboration with international language policy experts and conduct consultations with education stakeholders, including teachers, students and Ministry of Education officials. In November, 2009 and April, 2010 two international missions were invited to advise the working group on operationalising the constitutional provisions for language in the school system.

The First Meeting on the National Languages of Timor-Leste, attended by 100 delegates representing almost every East Timorese language variety, was held by the Ministry of Culture, UNESCO and the Nippon Cultural Centre in August, 2010 with the theme of *Dalen oi-oin, povo ida deit (Many languages, just one people)*. The meeting called on the government to honour its commitment to developing the national languages by establishing councils for the promotion of each national language and boosting its funding support for the *Instituto Nacional de Linguística/Instituto Nasionál Linguística Nian (National Institute of Linguistics)* as the body entrusted with safeguarding and developing the languages of Timor-Leste, including the development of a standard orthography to be used for all national languages. Finally, the meeting urged the government to give serious consideration to a role for the national languages in the education system. In a high profile gesture, the meeting launched the first-ever national languages writing competition, *Ha'u nia lian, ha'u nia rai (My language, my country)* in the presence of the President and advertised on national television.

Another encouraging development can be seen in the considerable expansion of adult and non-formal education. With the return of stability since 2007, the government has made a major investment in promoting adult literacy through its National Literacy Program. The National Directorate of Non-formal Education and the Ministry of Education in collaboration with the organisations and teachers involved in literacy education outside the formal education system have developed core curriculum guidelines for organisations and personnel conducting adult literacy training. The *Sim eu posso/Los Ha'u bele (Yes I can)* literacy campaign has resumed with Cuban aid and the alphanumeric method used in the three-month courses mentioned in the monograph has targeted 250,000 adults to achieve basic literacy by 2014 (retrieved 26 September, 2010 from http://www.smh.com.au/world/cubans-bring-democracy-one-letter-at-a-time-20090904-fbh5.html). Despite criticisms of its methods (see Fernandes, 2010), the campaign has reached a great number of adults who can now sign their names and read basic functional texts.

As far as the schooling system is concerned, nothing has translated into formal policy to date; however, these developments have generated new discourses concerning language and identity in Timor-Leste and give good reason to be optimistic about more inclusive language policy directions.

References

Fernandes, Z., (2010). The significance of using the Cuban method in literacy learning. In M. Leach, N. Mendes, A. Da Silva, A. Ximenes, & B. Boughton (Eds). *Understanding Timor-Leste. Refereed proceedings of the understanding Timor-Leste conference*, Universidade Nasional Timor Lorosa'e, Dili, Timor-Leste, 2-3 July 2009. pp. 278-83.

Language use, and language policy and planning in Hong Kong

Anita Y.K. Poon

Department of Education Studies, Hong Kong Baptist University, Hong Kong

This monograph provides an overview of the language situation in Hong Kong from a historical perspective. Hong Kong has evolved in the past 167 years from a small fishing port to an international financial centre which forms part of a financial network hailed by *Time Magazine* as Ny.Lon.Kong (i.e. New York-London-Hong Kong). Hong Kong has gone through changes of sovereignty twice, once in 1842 as a Chinese territory ceded to Britain after the first Opium War, and a second time in 1997 as a British colony returned to China. It is a micro polity with no natural resources except its deep harbour. Economically, Hong Kong has gradually developed from a fishing port when British settlement began in 1841, to an entrepôt during 1945–1950s, to a manufacturing hub during 1960–1970s, to an international financial centre since the 1980s. The historical, political and economic development has had a great impact on the language situation in Hong Kong. Its language community started with two separate monolingual groups: one consisting of local Chinese speaking Cantonese and other Chinese dialects, and the other composed of British colonists speaking English. Because of language spread and language shift as a result of political, economic and social changes, the monolingual group of Chinese speakers has become trilingual, speaking Cantonese, English and *Putonghua*, whereas the monolingual group of English speakers has expanded to include native speakers of such other English varieties as American English, Australian English, Canadian English, Indian English and Singaporean English. In addition, there is a large group of minorities composed of bilingual speakers of English and a south Asian language. Although the development of language use is a natural process, it can be influenced by the government's language policy and planning. In 1997 there was a major political change, and Hong Kong, a capitalist city that practised a free economy for 155 years, was handed back to a socialist regime in China and now functions as a Special Administrative Region of the People's Republic of China (PRC) under the 'One Country Two Systems' policy. Hong Kong's prospects for a changing language situation depend on its political and economic development as well as PRC's policy.

Introduction

Outline of the monograph

This monograph consists of four parts:

Part I presents the language profile of Hong Kong: the official languages, the national language, major minority languages, foreign languages and major religious languages. The statuses of the majority languages and the phenomena of actual language use are depicted: diglossia and triglossia, code mixing and code switching, and bilingualism and biliteracy.

Part II describes the ways in which Chinese and English are spread through the education system, the changing society, pop culture and the media.

Part III focuses on language policy and planning in Hong Kong. The following language-in-education policies are discussed: language enhancement policy and medium-of-instruction policy. In addition, there are some society-wide language policies that are the outcomes of political, economic, regional and international influences: the biliterate tri-lingual policy, Workplace English Campaign and policies to promote *Putonghua*.

Part IV discusses the intergenerational transmission of the major languages and language shift as well as the language attitudes of the younger generation towards English, Cantonese and *Putonghua*. This part also suggests a probable direction for change in the language situation over the next generation.

The following introduction provides a backdrop to this monograph. Some general background information pertaining to Hong Kong involves commenting on the location of Hong Kong, on the population and the work force, and on the impact of historical, political and economic development on the language situation in Hong Kong.

Location of Hong Kong

Hong Kong, a Special Administrative Region (SAR) of the PRC, is a city of 1104.3 km^2 located on the south coast of China, bordering the mainland city of Shenzhen in Guangdong province to its north, and surrounded by the South China Sea on its east, south and west. Macau, the other Chinese SAR, is 60 km west of Hong Kong on the opposite side of the Pearl River Delta. Geographically Hong Kong is situated in the mid-point of Asia along the Pacific Ocean, with Japan and Korea to the north and Indonesia to the south. Hong Kong is also described as the meeting point of the east and the west, a point at which both Chinese culture and western culture co-exist (Figure 1).

Hong Kong city is composed of a main island known as Hong Kong Island (the second largest and the most populated island), the Kowloon Peninsula, the New Territories (new towns on the outskirts of the Kowloon Peninsula), Lantau Island (the largest island), and 233 small islands.

Population and work force

Hong Kong is one of the most densely populated areas in the world. Its population reached 7 million in 2008 (Census and Statistics Department, 2009a). Approximately 95% of the population are ethnic Chinese, most of whom are migrants from China's Quangdong province. The remaining 5% are not ethnic Chinese, some of whom are permanent residents originating from India, Pakistan and Nepal, as well as refugees from Vietnam. Some are foreign domestic helpers from the Philippines, Indonesia and Thailand (a total of 252,178 as at July 2008), while others are British, continental Europeans, North Americans, Australians, Japanese or Koreans, largely employed in the commercial, financial and educational sectors.

As of 2008, the work force of Hong Kong was estimated at 3.66 million. Approximately half of the work force is involved in major industries such as finance, insurance, real estate, air and sea logistics services, wholesale/retail, import/export trades, restaurants, hotels, tourism and manufacturing. The GDP in 2007 was US$ 207.2 billion; the per capita GDP was US$29,900. The GDP real growth rate in 2007 was 6.4%. Because of the

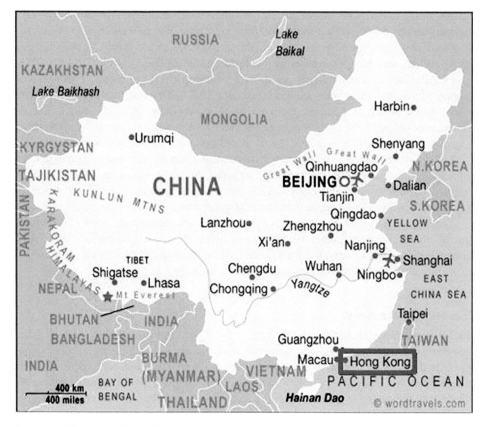

Figure 1. The map of Hong Kong.
Source: Retrieved June 24, 2009, from http://www.wordtravels.com/Travelguide/Countries/China/Map

global financial tsunami, the GDP real growth rate in 2008 dropped to 2.4% (Census and Statistics Department, May 15, 2009b).

Impact of historical, political and economic development on the language situation in Hong Kong

Historical and political development

The Chinese name of Hong Kong (香港) means 'fragrant harbour' or 'incense harbour'. Hong Kong was incorporated into the territory of Imperial China during the Qin Dynasty (221–206 BCE), and served as a trading post and naval base during the Tang Dynasty (CE 618–907) and the Song Dynasty (CE 960–1279). During the Qing Dynasty (CE 1644–1911) trade restrictions were imposed, and international trade was allowed in Canton (Quangzhou) only through imperially sanctioned monopolies.

Sino-British trade became imbalanced by the early 19th century in the sense that more goods (largely tea and silk) were exported from China to Britain while Britain mainly exported silver to China. In order to curb the flow of silver out of the country and strike a balance in trade, Britain increased the importation of opium to China from India, which was then under British rule. Consequently, millions of Chinese became drug addicts. In 1839, the Qing Emperor appointed Lin Zexu as special commissioner of

Canton to stamp out the opium trade. Lin ordered that all opium stocks be surrendered and burnt. The First Opium War broke out between China and Britain in 1840 and ended in 1842, the year in which the Treaty of Nanking was signed and Hong Kong Island was ceded to Britain. China was defeated again in the Second Opium War (1856–1858), and Kowloon Peninsula south of Boundary Street was ceded to Britain under the Convention of Peking signed in 1860. In 1898 Britain obtained a 99-year lease of the New Territories, which comprised the area north of the Kowloon Peninsula up to the Shum Chun (Shenzhen) River and including 235 islands. Hong Kong was declared a free port and served as an entrepôt of the British Empire.

On 8 December 1941, during World War II, Japan invaded Hong Kong. Britain surrendered Hong Kong to Japan on 25 December 1941. During the Japanese occupation, Hong Kong lost more than half of its population, from 1.6 million in 1939 to about 600,000 in 1945 (Hong Kong Government, 2008). Japan surrendered in August 1945, and the United Kingdom (UK) resumed its rule of the colony. The population of Hong Kong recovered quickly to an estimated 1.8 million in 1947 because of the post-war baby boom as well as immigration from Mainland China resulting from the civil war between the Kuomintang (KMT; i.e. the Chinese Nationalist Party) and the Chinese Communist Party (CCP). The KMT fled to Taiwan, and the People's Republic of China (PRC) was subsequently founded on 1 October 1949. As a result, more migrants fled to Hong Kong for fear of persecution by the CCP, and 'Hong Kong received an influx unparalleled in its history' with the population reaching 4 million in 1971 (Hong Kong Government, 2008, p. 420). Many corporations in Shanghai and Guangzhou also shifted their business to Hong Kong. International trade with Mainland China was interrupted during the Korean War (1950–1952) as the United Nations ordered a trade embargo against the Chinese communist government. Hong Kong became the sole contact point between Mainland China and the Western world.

As the 99-year lease of the New Territories was due to expire in 1997, the United Kingdom and the People's Republic of China held many rounds of discussions in the early 1980s over the future of Hong Kong. A Sino-British Joint Declaration was signed on 19 December 1984, stipulating that Hong Kong would be returned to China on 1 July 1997. Under Deng Xiao-ping, the then Chinese communist leader, it was mutually agreed (i) that the principle of 'One Country Two Systems' would be honored, (ii) that 'the socialist system and policies shall not be practised in the Hong Kong Special Administrative Region (HKSAR) [of the PRC] and (iii) that Hong Kong's previous capitalist system and life-style shall remain unchanged for 50 years' (later encapsulated in The Basic Law of the HKSAR, 1990). The Basic Law of the HKSAR was adopted on 4 April 1990 by the Seventh National People's Congress of the PRC, and came into effect on 1 July 1997. Despite the reassurances of the Chinese government, many thousands of Hong Kong people made every effort to obtain a passport and the necessary foreign visa, and the number of emigrants to Western countries during 1984–1997 was 604,000 (Census and Statistics Department, 2004; Figure 2).

However, a large number of these emigrants returned to Hong Kong prior to or after the handover. The estimated number of individuals returning to Hong Kong in 2000 was 118,400, but this figure included not only the returning emigrants, but also those who had studied abroad (Census and Statistics Department, May 30, 2000).

Economic development

Hong Kong is a micro-polity with no natural resources except its deep harbour. One might wonder how it could have developed over the past 160 years from a fishing

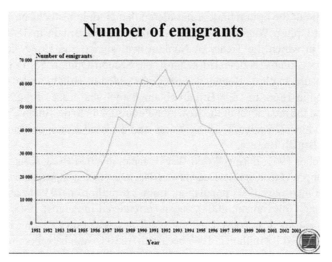

Figure 2. Number of emigrants to western countries.
Source: Census and Statistics Department, 2004.

port when British settlement began in 1841, to an entrepôt from 1945 through the 1950s, to a manufacturing hub during 1960s and 1970s, to an international financial centre since the 1980s. The changing economy has been due largely to the political changes in China and the world at large. The Korean War (as mentioned previously) and the cold war – between the capitalist states led by the USA and the UK, and the communist states dominated by the former USSR and the PRC – provided Hong Kong with an opportunity to act as an entrepôt conducting export/import trade between Mainland China and Western countries during the embargo in the 1950s, and continuing until China implemented its open-door policy in 1978. In addition, trade as well as communications between Taiwan and Mainland China had been made possible via Hong Kong until agreements were signed by representatives of the two respective governments on 4 November 2008.

The massive influx of migrants from Mainland China during the years between 1945 and the mid-1960s resulting from political instability, as mentioned previously, brought capital, know-how in the textile and garment industry, and labour to Hong Kong. Thus Hong Kong became an important manufacturing hub in Southeast Asia during the 1960s and 1970s, exporting things like garments, toys, plastic flowers, and radios to North America and Europe. This blooming of the economy in the 1970s was the basis for Hong Kong's gradual evolution as an international financial centre in the 1980s. Meanwhile, the economy of Asia was also flourishing; Hong Kong had been designated one of the 'four little dragons' in Asia in the 1970s (the other three were Taiwan, Singapore and South Korea), and the Asian economic miracle persisted until the Asian financial crisis in late 1997, a disaster that did not hit Hong Kong until one year later. The stock market and the real estate market collapsed overnight in late 1998. The economy of Hong Kong gradually revived in 2000, but it dipped again in 2001 because of the 9/11 terrorist attack in the USA. It then went through another uphill battle until the deadly SARS pandemic in March 2003.

The economic development of Hong Kong went through another cycle after the handover to the PRC, viz. economic amalgamation with Mainland China, especially with the Pearl River Delta of Quangdong, adjacent to Hong Kong and sharing the same Southern Chinese language (i.e. Cantonese) and culture. Hong Kong was not enthusiastic about the amalgamation during the first few years after the handover until its economic downturn caused by SARS in 2003. To help Hong Kong to recover economically, Mainland China allowed the mainlanders to visit Hong Kong as individual travellers starting from July 2003.[1] In addition, a free trade agreement entitled 'The Mainland and Hong Kong Closer Economic Partnership Arrangement' (CEPA) was signed in June 2003. 'CEPA is a win–win agreement, bringing new business opportunities to the Mainland, Hong Kong and all foreign investors' (Trade and Industry Department, 2008). Consequently, Hong Kong's economy gradually improved, flourished and underwent another transformation. Hong Kong was seen to be economically on par with New York and London for the very first time in history as Ny.Lon.Kong – 'three cities linked by a shared economic culture … have … created a financial network that has been able to lubricate the global economy, and critically, ease the entry into the modern world of China' (Elliott, 2008, January 28, p. 32). Yet Hong Kong is currently facing challenges from other metropolises in the world as well as in the region – e.g. Singapore, and especially Shanghai, which has recently obtained Beijing's blessing to become 'a global financial and shipping centre by 2020' (Ren, Zhou, Wong, & So, 2009, March 26).

How historical, political and economic development impacts on the language situation

Owing to its colonial history and its changing economy, Hong Kong is far from being a linguistically homogeneous city like other cities in China, although 95% of the Hong Kong population are of Chinese descent (Hong Kong Government, 2008). Unlike some other post-colonial polities in Asia such as Malaysia, Indonesia, Vietnam and Taiwan, which forsook their respective former colonial language after independence, Hong Kong retained English as a co-official language alongside Chinese after the change of sovereignty in June 1997. The reasons for keeping the colonial language are related to the changing status of English as well as the changing economy in Hong Kong. English remained a colonial language in Hong Kong until the end of the 1970s. People's attitude towards English then was negative; bilingualism had been imposed on Hong Kong society. Because of the economic boom and the subsequent change of Hong Kong's status from a manufacturing hub to an international centre of finance and trade, coupled with the decolonisation policy during the late 1970s and the 1980s, the status of English in Hong Kong also underwent a metamorphosis from a colonial language to an international language. Thus, people's attitude towards English changed fundamentally, and the demand for bilingualism began to surge. This change is further elaborated in what follows.

Part I: the language profile of Hong Kong

The majority languages

Cantonese, English and *Putonghua* are the majority languages spoken in Hong Kong both as the usual languages of interpersonal communication and as additional languages/dialects. According to the statistics from the mid-decade bi-census conducted in 2006 (see Table 1), the proportion of the population aged 5 and over able to speak Cantonese is 90.8%, English is 41.9% and *Putonghua* is 40.2%, respectively.

Table 1.   Proportion of the population able to speak Cantonese, English and *Putonghua*, 1996, 2001 and 2006.

| | Proportion of Population(1) Aged 5 and Over (%) | | | | | | | | |
| | As the Usual Language | | | As Another Language/Dialect | | | Total | | |
Language/Dialect	1996	2001	2006	1996	2001	2006	1996	2001	2006
Cantonese	88.7	89.2	90.8	6.6	6.8	5.7	95.2	96.1	96.5
English	3.1	3.2	2.8	34.9	39.8	41.9	38.1	43.0	44.7
Putonghua	1.1	0.9	0.9	24.2	33.3	39.2	25.3	34.1	40.2
Hakka	1.2	1.3	1.1	3.6	3.8	3.6	4.9	5.1	4.7
Chiu Chau	1.1	1.0	0.8	3.9	3.8	3.2	5.0	4.8	3.9
Fukien (including Taiwanese)	1.9	1.7	1.2	2.0	2.3	2.1	3.9	3.9	3.4
Indonesian (Bahasa Indonesia)	0.2	0.2	0.1	0.7	1.2	1.5	0.9	1.3	1.7
Filipino (Tagalog)	0.2	0.2	0.1	1.6	1.7	1.3	1.8	1.9	1.4
Japanese	0.3	0.2	0.2	1.0	1.2	1.1	1.2	1.4	1.2
Shanghainese	0.5	0.4	0.3	1.1	1.1	0.9	1.6	1.5	1.2

Source: Census and Statistics Department (2006a).
Note: The figures exclude mute persons.

Chinese

'Chinese' itself has never been defined in the three official legal documents in Hong Kong, i.e.:

- the Official Languages Ordinance enacted in 1974 makes Chinese a co-official language alongside English;
- the Official Languages Ordinance amended in 1987 requires all new legislation to be enacted bilingually in both English and Chinese; and
- the Basic Law, a mini-constitution enacted by the PRC on 4 April 1990 for the Hong Kong SAR, stipulates the co-official language status of English alongside Chinese after the handover in 1997.

Though ill-defined, Chinese as understood in the context of Hong Kong means written Modern Standard Chinese and spoken Cantonese. The spoken form of Modern Standard Chinese is *Putonghua* (or Mandarin), which is the national language in Mainland China and Taiwan. The written form of Cantonese is not accepted as standard written Chinese used in formal writing because Modern Standard Chinese is unanimously accepted as the only written form used in Mainland China, Taiwan, Hong Kong and overseas Chinese communities. Modern Standard Chinese is based on Mandarin and other northern Chinese dialects whereas Cantonese is a southern dialect. Modern Standard Chinese and Cantonese are, therefore, considerably different in lexis, syntax, pronunciation and phonology, to the extent that 'Western-based linguists tend to view Cantonese and Mandarin [i.e. Modern Standard Chinese] as different languages (Bauer, 1984, p. 294), a view rejected by China-based linguists (Zhou, 1981, pp. 3–6)' (So, 1989, p. 38).

Cantonese is an umbrella term for a group of similar dialects spoken in two southern provinces in China – the western half of Quangdong province and the southern half of Quangxi province (Chao, 1947). Standard Cantonese refers to the variant of Cantonese spoken in Quangzhou, the capital of Quangdong. The other variants of Cantonese are classified as sub-dialects of Cantonese, e.g. those spoken in Tung Kwun (Donggun), Po On (Baoan), Toi Shan (Taishan), and Chung Shan (Zhongshan). Before British colonisation, the inhabitants of Hong Kong spoke the sub-dialects of Cantonese – Tung Kwun (Donggun) and Po On (Baoan) – as well as other Chinese dialects – Hakka, Chiu Chow and Tanka – unintelligible to Cantonese speakers. After British settlement in 1842, a large number of workers and merchants migrated to Hong Kong from Quangzhou, so standard Cantonese became the majority language used among the Chinese in Hong Kong. The Cantonese spoken in Hong Kong before 1949, the year in which the Hong Kong government closed the border in order to stop the influx of mainlanders from PRC, was not much different from the Cantonese spoken in Quangzhou. However, the Cantonese spoken in Hong Kong has gradually deviated from the standard Cantonese used in Quangzhou since then and has developed into a new variant identified as Hong Kong Cantonese for four reasons:

(1) Because of the influence of English, borrowing has taken place and many loan-words have passed into Hong Kong Cantonese: e.g. 巴士 (/pa:si:/) (i.e. bus), 的士 (/tIksi:/) (i.e. taxi), 芝士 (/tsi:si:/) (i.e. cheese), 朱古力 (i.e. /tsy:ku:llk/).

(2) As a result of the increasing English literacy rate among the general public, the use of mixed code (i.e. mixing English words or phrases in Cantonese sentences) has become popular: e.g. 佢地好 friend (meaning 'they are good friends'), 你可以 right-click 個 mouse 嚟 highlight 個 mon (meaning 'you can right-click the mouse to highlight the monitor').

(3) As dialects are undermined in Mainland China, Cantonese has been relegated to the status of a home and community language. Hence the development of Cantonese is constrained and some colloquial Cantonese expressions and vocabulary are replaced by written Chinese which is closer to Mandarin than Cantonese and fails to represent the vitality and subtlety of Cantonese.

(4) By contrast, Cantonese continues to be used in all domains in Hong Kong society. Many new expressions and jargon related to Hong Kong life have been created especially in the entertainment sector, e.g. in TV soap operas and Canto pops (i.e. Cantonese pop songs). This matter will be discussed subsequently.

Although there is only one recognised written Chinese (i.e. Modern Standard Chinese), two writing systems (scripts) are currently used to represent written Chinese – viz. one system using the traditional Chinese characters as they are used in Taiwan now and were used in Mainland China prior to 1949, and another system using simplified Chinese characters, created by PRC after 1949 (Zhao, 2008). Hong Kong continued to use the traditional writing system even after the handover in 1997.

English

Hong Kong was essentially composed of two monolingual communities (Luke & Richards, 1982; Poon, 2000; So, 1989) – the Chinese-speaking community, consisting of large numbers of local people, and the English-speaking community, a small percentage of the population consisting of colonists from Britain. The two communities had little contact with each other in daily living, and their communication, if any, was accomplished through the linguistic middlemen (Luke & Richards, 1982) – Chinese who were able to speak both languages. This mode of communication persisted until Hong Kong started to expand its educational system after World War II. As a result of the educational expansion, more locals have gradually become cognizant of the English language. However, as inter-ethnic communication is formal and largely related to study, work or official encounters (Johnson, 1994), English is typically used by the English-speaking Chinese in a rather restricted manner, only in the domains of education, administration, the judiciary, business and the media, and seldom in daily social interaction among the Chinese (Fu, 1987; Lord, 1987; Luke & Richards, 1982; Poon, 2000; So, 1989). Strictly speaking, English does not function as a second language in the sense that it is used in other places like Singapore, but rather as an 'auxiliary language' (Luke & Richards, 1982, p. 55). Therefore, there is a cline of English use by Chinese speakers in Hong Kong starting with a small group of ethnic Chinese who are native or near-native English speakers, to those who speak English as a second language, to those who speak English as a foreign language, to those who speak some variety of Chinglish, a mixture of English and Chinese (Qiang & Wolff, 2003).

In addition, Hong Kong as an international financial and trade centre has attracted a large number of people from various parts of the world. These non-Chinese residents use English as a lingua franca. The proportion of the population using English as a lingua franca has increased from 29.4% in 1991 to 41.9% in 2006 (Census and Statistics Department, 2006a).

British English was the dominant variety of English used in Hong Kong prior to the 1980s. The number of varieties of English has gradually broadened as people have flocked from all over the world to this international financial centre and Pearl of the Orient since the 1980s. Thus, such different varieties as Australian English, Indian English, North American English and Singaporean English are spoken in the territory. There is a tendency to mix British vocabulary, spelling and pronunciation with North American varieties, for instance, 'garbage bin' instead of 'rubbish bin' (British) or 'garbage can' (American), and North American terms such as 'highway' and 'eggplant' are used in texts spoken/written in British English.

'Hong Kong English' is a term used to describe a variant (not a variety) of English spoken by Hong Kong people. This term carries a connotation associated with erroneous and improper use of English with respect to pronunciation, grammar and idiomatic expressions. Because of the influence of their first language, Hong Kong people tend to replace some English phonemes which do not exist in Cantonese with other phonemes, e.g. /v/ replaced by /w/ or /f/, /z/ replaced by /s/, /r/ replaced by /w/. Hong Kong speakers of English tend to pronounce the phonemes /w/ and /h/ in words like 'Greenwich', 'Birmingham' and 'Beckham' as the sounds are reflected in the translation of these words into Chinese (e.g. 'Beckham' is translated as 碧咸 /bik-ham/). As for grammar, verb tenses and articles are the most problematic areas because they do not have direct equivalents in Chinese; consequently, errors in the uses of tenses and omission/redundancy in the use of articles are not uncommon. Hong Kong people also have difficulty in the structure of English sentences. A common error caused by first language influence is the use of 'although ... but', which is directly translated from the Chinese structure '雖然 ... 但是'. Some Cantonese expressions are directly translated into English and have become very popular among Hong Kong people, e.g. 'People mountain people sea' directly translated from '人山人海' meaning 'a very crowded place', 'Open the door, see the mountain' directly translated from '開門見山' meaning 'go straight to the point' in a conversation. Additional characteristics of Hong Kong English are code-mixing and code-switching. It is common to hear Hong Kong people mix some English words or phrases into the Chinese sentences; e.g. '下個 weekend 究竟去 Ocean Park 抑或去 barbecue 啫?我好耐冇去 Ocean Park, 聽 D friend 講多咗好多 ride 同埋 show' (meaning: 'where shall we go next weekend – Ocean Park or having a barbecue? I haven't been to Ocean Park for ages. I've heard some friends say there are more rides and shows there'). The use of code-mixing and code-switching is elaborated subsequently.

The official languages

English was the sole official language – in administration, the law, education, and other formal registers – from the early colonial days until 1974, the year in which the Official Languages Ordinance was enacted (Hong Kong Government, 1974). Chinese was made a co-official language as a result of Britain's decolonisation policy in Hong Kong after the riots in 1967 and the colonial government's response to the popular demands of the masses as pledged in the 'Chinese as Official Language Movement'[2] during the late 1960s and the early 1970s (Poon & Wong, 2004, p. 142). Both English and Chinese remained as the official languages of Hong Kong even after the changeover of sovereignty under the Basic Law. According to the most recent version of the Official Languages Ordinance (1997, June 30):

> The official languages possess equal status and, subject to the provisions of this Ordinance, enjoy equality of use for the purposes of communication between the Government or any public officer and members of the public and for court proceedings. (Chapter 5, Section 3)

The national language

The concept of 'national language' was vague to Hong Kong people during the colonial period for two reasons: the first was the obvious reason that national identity was not advocated during the colonial era; the second was the linguistic difference between Cantonese, the language spoken by the majority of Hong Kong people, and *Putonghua* (or Mandarin), the national language spoken in Mainland China and Taiwan, as previously noted. After the handover of sovereignty in 1997, the Hong Kong SAR government has put strenuous efforts into nurturing the national identity of Hong Kong citizens through the school curriculum and also through co-curricular activities, the media, community activities, territory-wide events and exhibitions, etc. In addition, the national language, *Putonghua*, is promoted through a new language policy – i.e. the biliterate trilingual policy announced in 1997, which gradually has gained momentum and spread within the society (Poon, 2004a). The biliterate trilingual policy and the spread of *Putonghua* in Hong Kong is discussed subsequently.

The minority languages

Five per cent of the residents in Hong Kong are not ethnic Chinese. There are permanent Hong Kong residents and transient Hong Kong residents. The former form approximately 0.6% of the entire population; the group includes Indians, Pakistanis, and Nepalese, who have been resident in Hong Kong for two or three generations. The Indians in Hong Kong mostly speak Hindi as well as such other Indian varieties as Punjabi, Tamil, Bengali, and Gujrati. The Pakistanis in Hong Kong mostly speak Urdu and such other varieties as Punjabi, Arabic, and Pashto.

The Nepalese in Hong Kong speak Nepali. The transient residents are composed of Filipinos, Indonesians and Thais (who form the largest group of ethnic minorities, many serving as domestic helpers in Hong Kong), the British, North Americans (including Canadians), Japanese and other temporary residents. The Filipinos in Hong Kong largely speak

Table 2.   Population by Nationality, 1996, 2001 and 2006.

	1996		2001		2006	
Nationality	Number	%	Number	%	Number	%
Chinese						
Place of domicile – Hong Kong	5,623,467	90.4	6,261,864	93.3	6,374,211	92.9
Place of domicile – other than Hong Kong	64,717	1.0	76,898	1.1	86,062	1.3
Filipino	120,730	1.9	143,662	2.1	115,349	1.7
Indonesian	22,057	0.4	54,629	0.8	110,576	1.6
British	175,395	2.8	25,418	0.4	24,990	0.4
Indian	20,955	0.3	16,481	0.2	17,782	0.3
Pakistani, Bangladeshi and Sri-Lankan			12,161	0.2	12,181	0.2
Thai	15,993	0.3	14,791	0.2	16,151	0.2
Nepalese	N.A.	N.A.	12,379	0.2	15,845	0.2
Japanese	19,010	0.3	14,715	0.2	13,887	0.2
United States of America	28,946	0.5	14,379	0.2	13,608	0.2
Canadian	32,515	0.5	11,862	0.2	11,976	0.2
Others	93,771	1.5	49,150	0.7	51,728	0.8
Total	6,217,556	100	6,708,389	100	6,864,346	100

Source: Census and Statistics Department (2006b).

Tagalog, as well as such other Philippine varieties as Cebuano. The Indonesians in Hong Kong mostly speak Bahasa Indonesia while the Thais in Hong Kong mainly speak Thai, although some speak Chiu Chow, a Chinese dialect. Table 2 shows the distribution of Hong Kong's population by nationality.

According to a survey of Hong Kong's ethnic minorities commissioned by the Home Affairs Bureau (2000) and the Census and Statistics Department (2000), an average 49.9% of the ethnic minorities claimed to be able to speak Cantonese, the majority language; the average ranged from 21% of the Nepalese to 100% of the Thais. At the same time, an average of 87.9% of the ethnic minorities were able to speak English, another majority language; the average ranged from 38.2% of the Pakistanis to 97.5% of the Indians and the Nepalese. Table 3 below shows the distribution.

Foreign languages

The foreign languages taught at universities, international schools and private language institutes in Hong Kong are mostly European languages, among which French, Spanish, German and Italian are the preferred choices. People learn these European languages because they aspire to the high culture of Europe. Japanese is traditionally a popular foreign language for youngsters, many of whom are attracted to the Japanese comics, gadgets, computer games, pop songs, films and fashion. Korean, another Asian language, caught the attention of young people several years ago because of some popular Korean TV soap operas and films, but this interest has diminished recently.

Bilingualism and biliteracy in Hong Kong

Diglossia and triglossia

The diglossic situation in Hong Kong refers to the different statuses and allocated functions not only of English, Cantonese and *Putonghua*, but also of other varieties of Chinese, as

Table 3. Persons belonging to ethnic minorities arranged by: whether they can speak Cantonese/English, fluency in Cantonese/English and ethnic group.

Whether could speak Cantonese/English, fluency in Cantonese/English	No. of persons ('000)/Percentage							
	Ethnic group							
	Filipinos	Indonesians	Indians	Nepalese	Thais	Pakistanis	Others	Overall
Could speak Cantonese	75.1 (47.5%)	32.4 (80.8%)	5.2 (43.0%)	1.7 (21.0%)	10.1 (100.0%)	3.1 (56.4%)	12.0 (26.4%)	139.5 (49.5%)
Fluency in Cantonese								
Fluent	9.1 (5.8%)	7.7 (19.1%)	3.8 (31.6%)	–	4.6 (45.1%)	0.6 (10.3%)	5.6 (12.4%)	31.3 (11.2%)
Conversational	27.1 (17.1%)	19.4 (48.4%)	0.6 (4.6%)	0.4 (4.8%)	5.0 (49.7%)	2.5 (46.1%)	2.1 (4.6%)	57.0 (20.4%)
Simple words only	38.9 (24.6%)	5.3 (13.3%)	0.8 (6.8%)	1.3 (16.2%)	0.5 (5.2%)	–	4.3 (9.5%)	51.1 (18.3%)
Could not speak Cantonese	83.0 (52.5%)	7.7 (19.2%)	6.9 (57.0%)	6.4 (79.0%)	–	2.4 (43.6%)	33.4 (73.6%)	140.1 (50.1%)
Overall	158.1 (100.0%)	40.1 (100.0%)	12.1 (100.0%)	8.1 (100.0%)	10.1 (100.0%)	5.5 (100.0%)	45.4 (100.0%)	279.6 (100.0%)
Could speak English	151.7 (96.0%)	24.0 (59.9%)	11.8 (97.5%)	7.9 (97.5%)	4.5 (44.6%)	2.1 (38.2%)	43.8 (96.5%)	245.8 (87.9%)
Fluency in English								
Fluent	108.7 (68.7%)	6.5 (16.4%)	10.4 (85.4%)	3.3 (40.9%)	2.7 (26.6%)	0.8 (15.1%)	36.4 (80.2%)	168.8 (60.4%)
Conversational	43.1 (27.3%)	14.6 (36.5%)	1.5 (12.1%)	4.6 (56.6%)	1.3 (12.8%)	1.2 (23.1%)	5.8 (12.7%)	72.1 (25.8%)
Simple words only	–	2.8 (7.0%)	–	–	0.5 (5.2%)	–	1.6 (3.6%)	5.0 (1.8%)
Could not speak English	6.4 (4.0%)	16.1 (40.1%)	0.3 (2.5%)	0.2 (2.5%)	5.6 (55.4%)	3.4 (61.8%)	1.6 (3.5%)	33.8 (12.1%)
Overall	158.1 (100.0%)	40.1 (100.0%)	12.1 (100.0%)	8.1 (100.0%)	10.1 (100.0%)	5.5 (100.0%)	45.4 (100.0%)	279.6 (100.0%)

Notes: 'Zero' in value.
Others included British, Japanese, European (excluding British), United States of American, Canadian, Australian, New Zealander, South African, Korea, Bengali, Sri Lankan.
Source: Home Affairs Bureau (2000). *Sample survey of the characteristics of the ethnic minorities in Hong Kong: main findings.* Paper No. CB(2)590/00-01(01), Annex B, Table 6.

described in Ferguson (1959) and Fishman (1971). I will first examine the diglossic situation pertaining to English and Chinese. As in any colony, English as a colonial language enjoyed supreme status in Hong Kong despite the small population of speakers before the handover – i.e. according to the 1991 population census only 2.2% of the population used English as the language of normal communication (Census and Statistics Department, 1991, p. 43). English functioned as a 'high' language in the domains of government administration, the legislature and the judiciary, whereas Chinese was the 'low' language, used at home and in daily social contact by the majority of the population (Fu, 1987; Lord, 1987; Luke & Richards, 1982; Poon, 2000; So, 1989). The diglossic situation ameliorated after the enactment of the Chinese as co-official language ordinance in 1974. Consequently, the use of Chinese in government administration was legalised, and bilingual versions of ordinances, government reports and announcements have appeared regularly since then. However, the *de facto* status of English was considerably higher than that of Chinese, while the *de jure* status was consistently even higher, as was evident in the exclusive use of English in all levels of the Courts as well as in the Legislative Council and in the Executive Council (the highest policymaking body of the government).

The English version of the ordinances and of all government reports and announcements was (and still is) deemed the only correct version whenever questions of interpretation arose. After the handover in 1997, the *de facto* status of Chinese improved. Chinese has replaced English as the common language in government administration, the Legislative Council and the Executive Council. Even the judiciary has permitted the use of Chinese in the District Court (the lowest level Court), but not in the Court of Appeal or in the Final Court of Appeal. Although diglossia has greatly diminished in the public sector, it still exists in the minds of Hong Kong people as reflected in their practices. The controversy surrounding language policy to be discussed subsequently in Part III demonstrates that people in Hong Kong attach a higher value to English than to Chinese.

An additional form of diglossia occurs through the use of the two varieties of spoken Cantonese in Hong Kong. The 'high' variety of Cantonese is used on such formal occasions as giving public speeches and lectures, while the 'low' variety of Cantonese is spoken at home and in conversations with friends. The two forms of diglossia (i.e. English versus Chinese, 'high' Cantonese versus 'low' Cantonese), the mismatch between Modern Standard written Chinese and spoken Cantonese – as mentioned previously – together with the lack of standardization and purification in Chinese contribute to the confusing language situation in Hong Kong.

Diglossia has gradually given way to triglossia as Hong Kong entered the later stage of transition in the early 1990s. The proportion of the population of Hong Kong speaking *Putonghua*, the national language of China, as their first language is very small according to census statistics – ranging from 1.1% in 1996 to 0.9% in both 2001 and 2006 (Census and Statistics Department, 2006a). However, the status of *Putonghua* has grown in Hong Kong since 1997, although *Putonghua* has not yet been accorded any official status. The spread of *Putonghua* is discussed subsequently in Part II.

Bilingualism and trilingualism

Is Hong Kong a bilingual city in which people are able to speak two different languages? Bilingualism is normally seen as consisting of two types – societal bilingualism and individual bilingualism (Baker, 2006). Arguably the former is apparent in Hong Kong whereas the latter is more difficult to define. Because of the colonial history of Hong Kong, the provision of social facilities has been bilingual for many years, e.g. English-medium schools beside Chinese-medium schools, English-speaking churches beside Chinese-speaking churches, English radio/TV channels beside Chinese radio/TV channels, or English news-papers/magazines beside Chinese newspapers/magazines. On the other hand, individual bilingualism did not become widespread until after the expansion of education following the end of World War II. Even at the present time, the proportion of the population who claim to be able to speak English as a second/foreign language is not as high as might be expected. The following statistics are revealing.

These figures reveal that there was a 12.5% increase in the proportion of the population able to speak English as a second/foreign language between 1991 and 2006. A careful look at the figures reveals that two minority groups – the Filipinos and the Indonesians, serving mostly as domestic helpers in Hong Kong – have increased dramatically from 1.3% of the population in 1991 (1.2% for Filipinos and 0.1% for Indonesians) to 3.3% in 2006 (1.7% for Filipinos and 1.6% for Indonesians) (Census and Statistics Department, 2006b). English serves as the main lingua franca that these groups employ at work as well as in the local community. It might be more appropriate to assume that approximately 37% of the ethnic Chinese population were able to speak English in addition to Chinese in 2006 (i.e. 41.9% minus 5% of not ethnic Chinese, 3.3% of whom were Filipinos and Indonesians and 1% were English speakers; i.e. British, Australians and North Americans, as well as Indians and Pakistanis residing in Hong Kong – see Table 4).

As *Putonghua* has increased in importance in Hong Kong since the early 1990s (the causes of the increase will be discussed subsequently), more people have come to recognise the need to learn *Putonghua*. The figures in Table 5 show the dramatic increase in the popu-lation who claim to be able to speak *Putonghua* as an additional language.

The situation concerning *Putonghua* in Hong Kong differs from that of English. The people who claim to be able to speak *Putonghua* in Hong Kong are ethnic Chinese. Very few members of non-Chinese minorities in Hong Kong speak *Putonghua*, and those who claim to be able to speak Chinese only speak Cantonese. It is probable that, as the trend to use *Putonghua* persists, more and more people in Hong Kong will become trilingual.

Table 4.   Proportion of the population able to speak English as another language.

1991	29.4%
1996	34.9%
2001	39.8%
2006	41.9%

Source: Census and Statistics Department (1991, 2006a).

Table 5.   Proportion of the population able to speak *Putonghua* as another language.

1991	16.9%
1996	24.2%
2001	33.3%
2006	39.2%

Sources: Census and Statistics Department (1991, 2006a).

Biliteracy

Hong Kong children enter kindergarten at approximately three years of age, and the minimum age for attending school is 5 years and 9 months. With the provision of 12 years' free and compulsory education,[4] all children studying at local government-aided schools learn both Chinese and English from Primary 1 for 12 years through the end of senior secondary education. Hence they are biliterate. The *adult literacy rate* in Hong Kong is 94.6 percent, ranking 67th among 177 countries listed, according to UNESCO's 'Human development report 2007/2008' (UNESCO, 2009). The term *adult literacy rate* means adult ability in reading and writing in their first language. The adult literacy rate of Hong Kong cannot reach 100% despite free, compulsory education, for two reasons. First, a quota of 150 persons per day is granted to Chinese mainlanders for family reunion purpose, and the majority of these new migrants are not well educated. Second, 5% of the population are not ethnic Chinese, and the education level of some minorities is relatively low.

The Programme for International Student Assessment (PISA) initiated by the Organization for Economic Co-operation and Development (OECD) assesses the ability of 15-year-old students in acquiring the knowledge and skills essential for participation in society. To date, three cycles of assessment have been completed: PISA 2000 & 2002, PISA 2003 and PISA 2006. In each cycle a country or region invites about 5000 students from at least 150 schools to participate. The reading literacy, mathematical literacy and scientific literacy of the students is assessed. Hong Kong has participated in all of these cycles of assessment, and achieved outstanding performance, particularly in mathematics and science, ranking among the top three countries each time. In reading, Hong Kong placed in 6th position in 2000, 10th position in 2003 and in 3rd position in 2006, respectively, as shown in Table 6.

Code-mixing and code-switching

There is no consensus about the terms used to describe switches between languages in conversation (Baker, 2006; Myers-Scotton, 1997). Appel and Muysken (1987) distinguish between switches at the lexical level within a sentence (code-mixing) and switches over phrases or sentences across sentences (code-switching). Lin (2008) uses 'code-switching' as a general term to describe all types of switches, whereas Muysken (2000) prefers 'code-mixing' as a general term. I adopt Appel and Muysken's (1987) definitions of code-mixing and code-switching, as they describe this aspect of language use in Hong Kong over time more precisely.

As mentioned previously, the use of code-mixing and code-switching is a characteristic of Hong Kong English. Prior to the introduction of 9-year free, compulsory education in 1978, access to education was limited, particularly at the tertiary level, and English was not widely spoken in the society. As Meissel (2004, p. 93) points out, 'bilinguals have available additional communicative means which monolingual speakers lack', so they tend to switch between languages. Code-mixing and code-switching were popular among professionals such as lawyers and medical doctors, persons who were likely to be highly proficient in both English and Chinese. Being able to speak English well was a symbol of high social status. This trend was extended to those who aspired to be 'westernized' and 'well educated', especially during the 1970s and 1980s. The group involved included students studying at universities and Anglo-Chinese schools (i.e. the old name for English-medium secondary schools), and white-collar workers. Unlike professionals,

Table 6. Reading performance of Hong Kong students in PISA (2000, 2003, 2006).

	2000			2003			2006		
	Country	Mean	S.E.	Country	Mean	S.E.	Country	Mean	S.E.
1	Finland	546	(2.60)	Finland	543	(1.60)	Korea	556	(3.80)
2	Canada	534	(1.60)	Korea	534	(3.10)	Finland	547	(2.10)
3	New Zealand	529	(2.80)	Canada	528	(1.70)	Hong Kong, China	536	(2.40)
4	Australia	528	(3.50)	Australia	525	(2.10)	Canada	527	(2.40)
5	Ireland	527	(3.20)	Liechtenstein	525	(3.60)	New Zealand	521	(3.00)
6	Hong Kong, China	525	(2.90)	New Zealand	522	(2.50)	Ireland	517	(3.50)
7	Korea	525	(2.40)	Ireland	515	(2.60)	Australia	513	(2.10)
8	United Kingdom	523	(2.60)	Sweden	514	(2.40)	Liechtenstein	510	(3.90)
9	Japan	522	(5.20)	Netherlands	513	(2.90)	Poland	508	(2.80)
10	Sweden	516	(2.20)	Hong Kong, China	510	(3.70)	Sweden	507	(3.40)

Source: HKPISA, 2000, 2003 and 2006, reports [Note that only the top 10 countries are given for each year.].

the latter groups were not necessarily very proficient in English; therefore, they used more code-mixing than code-switching in their conversation. With the continuing spread of English in Hong Kong society since the 1990s, more people have acquired the ability to code-mix (but not to code-switch, which seems to require a much higher level of proficiency in English).

On the other hand, because of the general decline in English standards after 1997 among students – especially those students attending Chinese-medium schools (Poon, 2009; Stone, 1994; Wong, 2008), those students generate a smaller quantity of English mixed with Cantonese. Even those who continue to generate code-mixing do not demonstrate a high level of English proficiency. Another form of code-mixing (i.e. using Cantonese with English words mixed in) – a characteristic of Hong Kong Cantonese, has become more popular. Pennington, Balla, Detaramani, Poon, and Tam (1992) suggest the language used in Hong Kong is 'a move away from both the pure Cantonese and especially the pure English extremes and towards a blend of the two languages in a unique form of Cantonese with English-based lexis' increased over a period of 15 years (Pennington et al., 1992, p. 64). Low and Lu (2006) also found that this type of code-mixing and code-switching has been extended into the domain of home and leisure activities, causing this blended variety to become a reality in Hong Kong society.

In addition to social communication, code-mixing and code-switching is used in the classroom. Traditionally, English-medium schools have been required to teach all subjects except Chinese and Chinese History in English; likewise, Chinese-medium schools are required to teach all subjects except English in Chinese. The distinction had been clear before the early 1980s, but gradually it became 'blurred with the expansion of universal junior secondary education, and both languages are, in fact, being used in varying degrees in different types of schools' (Education Commission, 1984, p. 40). Over the past two decades, the phenomenon has gradually spread from junior secondary to senior secondary classes, and then to university tutorials and lectures. The main reason for using code-mixing and code-switching in some English-medium schools is that the English standards of students have not reached the threshold level[5]. As English-medium schools are generally perceived to be higher status schools, they are more popular among parents, and therefore most schools opt for English-medium identification in order to attract more students.

The major religious languages

Protestantism, Catholicism, Buddhism and Taoism are the four largest religions practised in Hong Kong. Both the Protestant and the Catholic churches run separate sessions for their Chinese-speaking and English-speaking congregations, whereas Chinese is used exclusively in Buddhist and Taoist worships. Islam, Sikhism and Hinduism are mainly practised by the respective minorities using their own languages, i.e.:

- Indonesians in the practice of Islamism essentially use the Arabic of the *Koran* and/or Bahasa Indonesia,
- Pakistanis in the practice of Islamism use the Arabic of the *Koran* and/or Urdu, while
- People from various parts of India probably use their respective local languages in pursuing Sikhism and/or Hinduism (e.g. Hindi, Bengali, Gujarati, Kannada, Kashmiri, Malayam, Marathi, Punjabi, Tamil, Telugu, Urdu, depending on their point of origin).

Table 7. Proportion of population aged 5 and over able to speak English and *Putonghua* (Census and Statistics Department, 2006a).

	1996	2001	2006
English	38.1%	43%	44.7%
Putonghua	25.3%	34.1%	40.2%

Part II: language spread

The spread of languages

The majority languages

Hong Kong has witnessed the spread of various languages used in the polity in its 167 years of history. The numbers of users of both the majority written languages (i.e. Chinese and English) and the majority spoken languages (i.e. Cantonese, English and *Putonghua*) have increased manifold times as Hong Kong has developed from a fishing village with a population of about 5000–7,500 in 1842 to an international financial centre with a popu-lation of 7 million in 2009. As mentioned previously, the Cantonese spoken in Hong Kong has gradually deviated from the standard Cantonese used in Quangzhou as a result of colo-nization and localization. Hence a Hong Kong Cantonese variety has emerged since the 1970s, containing a large number of words from English, along with a variety of jargon from Canto pops, local films and TV soap operas. Hong Kong Cantonese has spread to the Quangdong and Quangxi provinces in Mainland China, to the Chinese communities in such Southeast Asian countries as Singapore and Malaysia, and to Chinese communities in such Western countries as the USA and Canada and to Australia as well. The causes for this language spread are elaborated subsequently.

The percentage of people who claimed to be able to speak English and *Putonghua* either as their common language or as another language has been on the rise (see Table 7).

The minority languages

Some minority languages – Tagalog and Bahasa Indonesian – have also spread in Hong Kong because of the increase in the number of Filipino and Indonesian domestic workers from about 25,000 in 1982 to 252,178 in 2008. Tagalog or Bahasa Indonesian can be heard in the streets much more often at present than was the case in the past, especially since domestic workers are, by law, permitted to enjoy their free time on Sundays and statutory holidays.[6] The use of those minority languages is, nonetheless, con-fined to their respective communities; there has been no evidence that either Tagalog or Bahasa Indonesia has spread to other language communities.

The languages spoken by two permanent resident minority groups in Hong Kong – Indians and Pakistanis – are also confined to their respective communities. Unlike the numbers of Filipinos and Indonesians, the number of Indians and Pakistanis has remained stable over the years, constituting only 0.3% of the population (Census and Statistics Department, 2006b).

Reasons for language spread

The causes of the spread of the two majority written languages (Chinese and English) and three majority spoken languages (Cantonese, English and *Putonghua*) lie in: (i) the education system, (ii) the changing society, (iii) pop culture and the media, and (iv) language policy.

The Current Academic Structure of Hong Kong

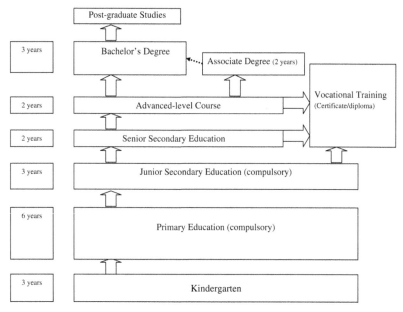

Figure 3. The current 6–5–2–3 academic structure of Hong Kong.

Spread through the education system

The education system in Hong Kong traditionally follows the British system, adopting the 6–5–2–3 structure; i.e. six years of primary education, five years of secondary education, two years of matriculation (i.e. preparation for entering the university), and three years of university. The system is illustrated in Figure 3.

A new 6–3–3–4 academic structure was proposed when Hong Kong SAR launched an education reform 'of unprecedented depth and magnitude ... covering the entire education system – academic structure, admissions system, curriculum, assessment methods, medium of instruction, and teacher certification and training' in 2000 (Poon & Wong, 2008, p. 35). The new academic structure abolished the earlier British system and adopted the American model which is more in line with the system practised in Mainland China; i.e. six years of primary school, three years of junior secondary school, three years of senior secondary school and four years of university. The new system is now being put in place.[7] Hong Kong will see the first cohort of Senior Secondary 1 students in September 2009. The current 6–5–2–3 academic structure is going to be phased out when the first cohort of Senior Secondary graduates begin their 4-year university studies in September 2012. Figure 4 illustrates the new academic system.

The school curriculum traditionally focuses on Chinese, English and Mathematics. There are only four academic subjects in primary school – i.e. Chinese, English, Mathematics and General Studies. Secondary students must pass the three core subjects (i.e. Chinese, English and Mathematics) plus two other subjects in the Hong Kong Certificate of Education Examination (HKCEE), equivalent to Britain's GCSE (O-Level), to be taken at the end of secondary education in order to graduate. A pass grade in Chinese and English is also obligatory in the Hong Kong Advanced Level Examination (HKAL), a

The New Academic Structure of Hong Kong

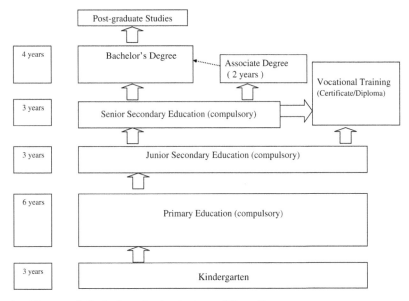

Figure 4.   The new 6−3−3−4 academic structure of Hong Kong.

university-entrance examination. University students are required to take general English proficiency courses as well as English for Academic Purposes courses. They are also encouraged to take the Exit Test of English, which is compulsory upon graduation for such programmes as Business. Among the three main subjects in the curriculum – Chinese, English and Mathematics – English is the most heavily emphasized, increasingly so as students progress through the system. In addition to being the most important subject in the curriculum, English has been adopted as the medium of instruction in one-fourth of secondary schools (in more than 80% of secondary schools prior to 1998), and in all universities. English-medium instruction has certainly contributed to the spread of English in the education sector, if not in Hong Kong society at large.

Putonghua did not receive any attention at school until after the handover. It was made a compulsory subject in the school curriculum in 1998, and was added to the HKCEE as an elective subject in 2000. *Putonghua* has also become a very popular elective course offered by the Language Centres of all universities in Hong Kong since 1997.

Although a focus on Chinese, English and *Putonghua* in the curriculum does not necessarily lead to the spread of these languages in the society, it does provide a solid foundation for language spread.

Spread through changes in society

As mentioned previously, Hong Kong society has undergone drastic changes in all respects throughout its short history. Its historical, economic, political and social developments do have impact on the spread of standard written Chinese, English, Cantonese and *Putonghua*.

Firstly, colonial history accounts for the initial spread of English in Hong Kong as it did 'in all parts of the periphery-English world where the British flag once flew' (Phillipson, 1992, p. 110). The influence of the English language did not diminish when the British Empire began to disintegrate after World War II; instead, it gathered momentum when the USA arose as a world super power. In the 1980s, English gradually changed its status from a colonial language to an international language in the global arena as well as in Hong Kong. This change paved the way for the further spread of English in Hong Kong which was increasingly becoming an international city.

Secondly, the economic development of Hong Kong discussed in Part I raised the status of Hong Kong as an international financial centre, subsequently boosting the demand for English in the polity. The force of globalisation over the past two decades has further augmented the demand for English and thus supported the increasing spread of English in Hong Kong. Likewise, because of the economic boom and globalisation, the status of Hong Kong has been greatly enhanced not only in the world, but also in the Chinese Diaspora. As a result, Hong Kong Cantonese has spread to the southern part of Mainland China as well as to overseas Chinese communities. On the other hand, *Putonghua*, the national language of China, which had been ignored during the colonial era in Hong Kong, also spread in Hong Kong, initially because of economy. China's open door policy, announced in 1978, attracted many thousands of Hong Kong manufacturers to transfer their business across the border. Hence 'China trade' became very popular in the 1980s and 1990s, and *Putonghua* started to spread in Hong Kong. After 20 years of rapid economic development in China, the mainlanders were economically better off, and organised package tours began to flood into Hong Kong in the mid-1990s; the number of mainland tourists has continued to increase since then. In addition, the Beijing government relaxed the restriction on mainlanders' visits to Hong Kong by launching the so-called 'Visit Hong Kong as an Individual Traveller' Scheme implemented during the SARS period in July 2003. Figure 5 shows the dramatic increase in the number of tourists coming to Hong Kong after 2003 – from 15 million in 2003 to almost 30 million in 2008. As the number of tourists coming mostly from the mainland increased, more and more working people in Hong Kong – especially those in the tourism and related industries – have felt the need to improve their *Putonghua*.

Thirdly, the political change – i.e. the changeover of sovereignty on 30 June 1997 – has been an additional factor contributing to the spread of *Putonghua* in Hong Kong. According to the Basic Law of the Hong Kong SAR, both Chinese and English are stipulated as the official languages. As mentioned previously, the meaning of 'Chinese' is blurred, and *Putonghua* is not stipulated as an official language. Despite this, *Putonghua* as the national language of the PRC, is gradually gaining recognition in the Hong Kong community as Hong Kong is being amalgamated into Mainland China. For the very first time, Hong

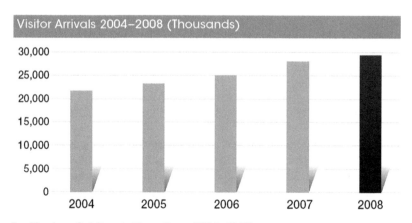

Figure 5.   Number of visitors to Hong Kong (2004–2008).
Source: Hong Kong Tourism Board, 2009.

Kong has been included in the PRC's long-term blueprint for the development of Pan-Pearl River Delta, announced on 9 January 2009 (Huang, 2009, January 9). A closer tie with the Mainland mediates the further spread of *Putonghua* in Hong Kong. On the other hand, the change of sovereignty might have had some impact on the use of English – the language of the former colonist – as has happened in other former colonies in Asia; e.g. Malaysia, Indonesia and Korea abandoned the use of their former colonial languages (respectively, English, Dutch and Japanese) as official languages soon after they achieved independence. In contrast, due to the changing status of English in Hong Kong, as mentioned previously, the language remains valued and continues to spread in the territory, except in secondary schools where the use of English as medium of instruction is restricted as a result of the Hong Kong government's language policy following the handover. This matter is discussed subsequently in Part III.

Fourthly and finally, social development has also played a part in language spread. Chinese was not granted any official status and was considered a low language in Hong Kong during most of the colonial period. Hence, Chinese was precluded from being used in government administration and the judiciary. It was partly due to the social movement of the 'Chinese as Official Language Movement' that Chinese was finally enacted as a co-official language in 1974. Consequently, Chinese has been included in the domains of government administration and the judiciary, as well as in other formal registers. Meanwhile, Cantonese has evolved into a new Hong Kong variant of Cantonese, embodying the Hong Kong identity and spreading both within and beyond Hong Kong. The spread of Cantonese is subsequently discussed.

Spread through pop culture and the media

Pop culture and the media have played a significant role in the spread of Hong Kong Cantonese both within and beyond Hong Kong. Hong Kong Cantonese is marked by the use of local jargon derived from TV soap operas or 'the talk of the town', with large numbers of English loanwords, and also with a mixture of some English words or part of the English words into Cantonese sentences; e.g. '嗰個 secure 好似係阿燦嚟' (English translation: 'That security guard looks like Ah Charn'). 'Ah Charn', the name of a character in a popular TV soap opera produced in the 1980s, was a new migrant from the Mainland portrayed as a country bumpkin. This term carries a pejorative connotation.

To trace the development of Hong Kong Cantonese, it is necessary to look into the changing psyche of Hong Kong people over the past 50 years. As the majority of Hong Kong residents (or their parents) were originally from the Mainland, they shared one common characteristic of migrants – i.e. the inability to take root in the new place of residence. Colonialism further aggravated the situation. Local Chinese felt that they were second-class citizens and that their first language (i.e. Cantonese or such other sub-dialects as Hakka, Chiu Chow, etc.) was only a low language in the colony. Therefore, few people were able to cultivate a sense of belonging to Hong Kong – a city generally perceived as a 'Borrowed place, Borrowed time' (Hughes, 1976).

The 1970s marked a turning point in Hong Kong's history. The second generation of migrants, the majority of whom were post-war baby-boomers, came of age and joined the labour force. Unlike their parents, they had a stronger tie to Hong Kong. That tie explains why the social movements, which started during the late 1960s, were led by a group of awakened elites flourishing during the 1970s. The economic boom, which started during the decade of the 1970s, engendered in the hearts of people a sense of pride and thus a sense of belonging to the place where they were born or had lived for most of their lives. A Hong Kong spirit, characterized as tough and able to overcome hardships in order to create miracles, was nurtured. The Hong Kong identity was further strengthened by then Governor Lord Maclehose's wide range of infrastructural and social policies implemented during the 1970s with a view to building a better home for Hong Kong people; e.g. the construction of the mass transit railway, 9-year free, compulsory education, the expansion of senior secondary education and tertiary education, the public housing scheme, the establishment of the Independent Commission Against Corruption, the enactment of Chinese language as a co-official language ordinance, and the like.

The 1970s also marked the beginning of Canto-pops (Cantonese pop songs). Prior to the 1970s, Western English pop songs (e.g. hit songs by The Beatles, The Rolling Stones, etc.) and Mandarin pop songs from Taiwan catering to different audiences dominated the scene. Sam Hui, a baby-boomer and graduate of The University of Hong Kong, is the first singer and composer of Canto-pops. He popularised Canto-pops by incorporating the then unknown idiosyncrasies of Western popular music into the Canto-pop genre. What permitted him to earn the title 'God of Songs' (a direct translation from Cantonese, better translated as 'King of Canto-pops'), were the lyrics he wrote himself. All his songs reflect different facets of life in Hong Kong, especially life at the grass roots. His passion for Hong Kong deeply touched the hearts of people from all walks of life in Hong Kong. He is not only a singer, composer and lyric writer, but also a film star whose films further popularise his Canto-pops. Canto-pops, which embody the Hong Kong spirit, have continued to flourish since then because of the efforts of other superstars and because the genre spread to Taiwan, to Quangdong province, to Shanghai, to Beijing and even to the hinterland of China where Cantonese is not spoken (e.g. to Tibet). Canto-pops have also spread to the Chinese communities in Malaysia, Singapore, Thailand, Vietnam, the Philippines, Indonesia, the USA, Canada, the UK, Australia, etc.

Apart from Canto-pops, Hong Kong films (e.g. Kung Fu films and films about the triads) as well as TV soap operas (usually with theme songs) reflecting the lifestyle of Hong Kong are equally popular and have also reached the widespread Chinese communities. Consequently, Hong Kong Cantonese has been spread beyond the territory.

Recently, a new development has occurred with respect to using the written form of Hong Kong Cantonese – a form not accepted as standard written Chinese in the media (i.e. newspapers, magazines, advertisements, etc.). On the contrary, the written form of Hong Kong Cantonese with English inclusions now regularly occurs in blogs and on Facebook, MSN, and other online fora.

Through language policy spread

Compared with the three reasons listed for language spread – the education system, a changing society, and pop culture and the media – language policy is a more direct cause of language spread because 'Language policy is either a macro- or microsociological activity involving deliberate and organized efforts to solve language problems' (Poon, 2000, p. 117). Hong Kong government's language policy is dealt with in detail subsequently in Part III.

Effects of language spread

The spread of the majority languages (i.e. Cantonese, English and *Putonghua*) over the past 35 years has not only changed the self-esteem and identity of the Chinese people living in Hong Kong, but it has also changed their attitudes towards English and *Putonghua*. The decolonization policy initiated by the British government after the riot in 1967 brought

Table 8.   Social identity of Hong Kong young people in 1996 and 2006.

	1996	2006
Hong Kong people	33.9%	28.7%
Hong Kong people, and next option is Chinese	40.0%	39.4%
Chinese people, and next option is Hong Kong people	15.8%	22.3%
Chinese people	10.4%	9.6%

Sources: Lam et al. 2007, Executive Summary.

about the enactment of the Chinese Ordinance in 1974, establishing the official status of the Chinese language and permitting the use of Chinese in government administration. The local Chinese people, who were considered second class citizens prior to the 1970s, gradually achieved a higher degree of self-esteem. The localization process coincided with the economic development through the 1970s to the mid-1990s. All these developments provide the backdrop for the spread of Hong Kong Cantonese, since Canto-pops became popular in the 1970s as previously noted. Hong Kong Cantonese distinguishes the Cantonese spoken in Hong Kong from that used in its place of origin – Quangdong (Bolton & Kwok, 1990). Hong Kong Cantonese embodies the spirit of Hong Kong – a spirit that Hong Kong people are proud of. As a result, Hong Kong identity has been created coincident with the spread of the language. As Lai's study (2009, p. 82) indicated, 'students expressed their strong affection for Cantonese because it is a distinct characteristic of Hong Kong and the local culture'. Some surveys have been conducted to find out how young people look at their identity. For instance, Lam, Lau, Chiu, and Hong (2007) report that young people's sense of Hong Kong identity remained quite high between 1996 and 2006 although there also was a tendency to add Chinese identity because of the changing political (1999) and economic situation in Hong Kong (see Table 8). The respondents were also proud of being Hong Kongers (mean score: 5.1; 7 = very proud, 1 = not very proud).

Hong Kong people's attitudes towards English have undergone changes over historical time. Prior to the 1950s, very few local Chinese were able to speak English. They regarded English as the colonist's language, something absolutely foreign to them. Not knowing English did not matter to the locals as their businesses had a local focus, except for a small group of people who wanted to work in the civil service. With the expansion of school education during the 1960–1970s, English spread so that it was no longer alien to the locals. Students began to recognise the instrumental value of English because English was a compulsory subject in the university entrance examination. Despite the fact that knowing English was instrumentally important to students, some negative attitudes towards the use of English were reported in the research conducted during the 1970s. Fu (1975) reported that 66% of her respondents (secondary school students) felt uneasy when a Chinese used English with them outside the classroom, and that 51% felt uneasy if their classmates conversed with them in English. In Pierson, Fu, and Lee's study (1980), more than 60% of the students agreed with the following statements:

When using English, I do not feel that I am Chinese any more;

At times I fear that by using English I will become like a foreigner;

If I use English, it means that I am not patriotic.

Speaking English seemed to betray one's national identity. This conflict between instrumental purposes and English as a colonial identity diminished as the status of English

Table 9. Proportion of population aged 5 and over able to speak *Putonghua* as the usual language.

	1991	1996	2001	2006
Putonghua as the usual language	1.1%	1.1%	0.9%	0.9%

Sources: Census and Statistics Department (2001, 2006a).

changed from a colonial language to an international language during the 1980s. People's attitude towards English and English language learning has become much more positive since then (Hyland, 1997; Lin & Detaramani, 1998; Lu, Li, & Huang, 2004; Yang & Lau, 2003). The ability to speak English even gives Hong Kong people a higher feeling of self-esteem because they feel they are able to speak the global language – English – better than their counterparts on the mainland and in Taiwan.

Hong Kong people's attitude towards *Putonghua*/Mandarin has also changed. The number of Hong Kong residents using *Putonghua*/Mandarin as their usual language (or their first language) has always been low because the majority of ethnic Chinese in Hong Kong are native speakers of Cantonese. According to the 1961 Population Census, only 0.99% of the population spoke Kuo Yu (i.e. *Putonghua*/Mandarin) (Census and Statistics Department, 1961). The number has remained quite stable in the past 15 years as indicated in Table 9.

Prior to the late 1980s, Cantonese speakers in Hong Kong adopted a neutral position towards *Putonghua*/Mandarin; i.e. they were not eager to learn the national language of the mainland and Taiwan partly because *Putonghua*/Mandarin was not included in the curriculum, but mostly because they did not see the need to learn this language. On the other hand, they did not reject it. As a matter of fact, Mandarin films and pop songs imported from Taiwan dominated the film and entertainment industry in Hong Kong during the 1960s and 1970s. *Putonghua*/Mandarin in a sense has been familiar to Hong Kong ears. The demand for *Putonghua* began to increase when 'China trade' was in full swing and mainland tourists started to come to Hong Kong in ever increasing numbers during the late 1980s and early 1990s. Hong Kong people then realized the importance of *Putonghua*, and the proportion of the population able to speak *Putonghua* as another language more than doubled from 16.9% in 1991 to 39.2% in 2006 (for details, see Table 5).

However, *Putonghua* was welcomed for its instrumental value rather than for its integrative value, even after the handover. *Putonghua* as the national language of the PRC has not yet instilled nationalism or patriotism – not to mention the sense of national identity – in the hearts of Hong Kong people. A recent study of Hong Kong students' language attitudes found that:

> . . . it was surprising to find students expressing stronger integrative orientation towards English, the colonial language, than *Putonghua*, the national language of China. As in the instrumental domain . . . English was the most highly valued as a gatekeeper for upward and outward social mobility. Cantonese ranked second . . . *Putonghua* ranked last. (Lai, 2009, p. 81)

Part III: language policy and planning

Language legislation

The Joint Declaration signed between the Chinese and British governments on 19 December 1984 set out the basic policies of the PRC concerning Hong Kong: i.e. the 'One Country, Two Systems' principle:

> The socialist system and policies shall not be practised in the Hong Kong Special Administrative Region, and the previous capitalist system and way of life shall remain unchanged for 50 years. (The Basic Law of the HKSAR, 1997, July 1, Chapter 1, Article 5)

Therefore, the official languages of Hong Kong remain unchanged as spelled out in the latest version of the Official Languages Ordinance (1997, June 30):

> The English and Chinese languages are declared to be the official languages of Hong Kong for the purposes of communication between the Government or any public officer and members of the public and for court proceedings. (Chapter 5, Section 3)

The Official Languages Ordinance, enacted in 1974 and revised since then, is the only ordinance governing languages used in Hong Kong. Both Chinese and English are granted the status of official languages in Hong Kong. However, the variant(s) of spoken and written Chinese are not defined, nor is a variety of English mentioned. These language-planning-related issues are not specifically stipulated in the colonial legislation, or in post-1997 Hong Kong SAR legislation for reasons that are discussed subsequently.

Language policy and planning agencies

The term 'language policy' is at times interchangeably used with other terms such as 'language planning' and 'language-in-education policy' (Baldauf, 1990, 1994; Cooper, 1989; Kaplan, 1990; Rubin, 1984). Poon (2000, pp. 119–124) made an attempt to clarify the murky conceptual terrain of the language planning field by proposing a Model of Hierarchical Order of Language Planning and Language Policy as shown in Figure 6.

'Language planning' and 'language policy' are 'two different yet related concepts', which 'share some common characteristics' (Poon, 2000, p. 119). They are both top down, 'involving deliberate and organized efforts to solve language problems, which very often have a social, political and/or economic orientation' (Poon, 2000, p. 116). The major difference between these two constructs is that language planning is 'a macrosociological activity ... at a governmental and national level' *only* whereas language policy can be 'either a macro- or microsociological activity ... at a governmental and national level or at an institutional level' (Poon, 2000, pp. 116–117). That means language planning must be government-led, and language policy is not necessarily so. Language planning deals with status planning and corpus planning[8] while language policy deals with corpus planning and acquisition planning.[9] Within the framework of Hierarchical Order of Language Planning and Language Policy, language planning, which undertakes the same processes of identification of problems, analysis, policy setting and predicting outcomes as language policy, assumes a higher order than language policy in the policy area of language. Specific language policies derive out of language planning. Nevertheless, language policy may operate at either a governmental or an institutional level in the absence of language planning. Therefore, language policy covers a wider range of situations than language planning, which is government-directed and deals with status planning and corpus planning only.

After carefully examining the government documents and the language policy scene prior to the handover, Poon concluded that 'Hong Kong has no language planning, but it does have language policy' (Poon, 2000, p. 116). Hong Kong adopts a cultivation approach to language problems as opposed to the policy approach adopted by developing countries (for the notions of cultivation approach and policy approach, see Neustupný, 1974[1970]).

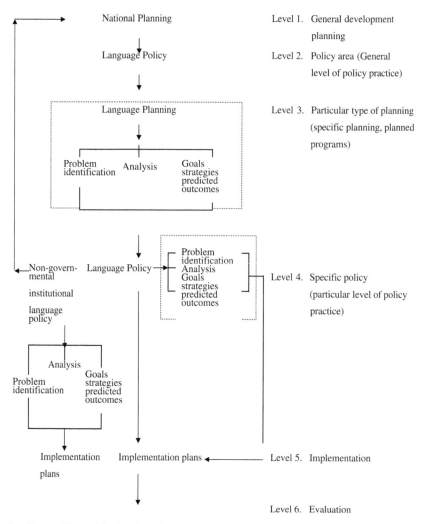

Figure 6. Poon's Hierarchical Order of Language Planning and Language Policy.
Source: Poon, 2000, p. 123.

So throughout the 155 years of colonial rule no attempt was ever made by the Hong Kong government to plan the status of Chinese and English, or to standardize the usage of Chinese. Prior to 1974, status planning was not important because Chinese could by no means compete with the colonial language – English – as an official language. Chinese was made the second official language only in 1974 (Hong Kong Government, 1974) under tremendous pressure from the public, not as an outcome of language planning. Based on the principle of 'One Country Two Systems', the post-handover Hong Kong SAR government follows the practice of the former government by *not* setting up a particular bureau taking care of language planning matters, like the one in Mainland China.

Poon postulates that there are four types of language policy as shown in Figure 7:

(1) the normal type of government-led language policy that emerges out of language planning and that deals with corpus planning;

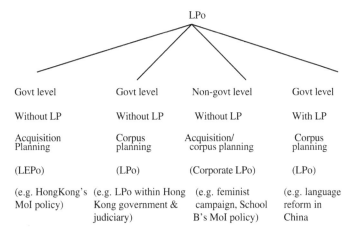

Figure 7. Poon's Four Types of Language Policy.
Source: Poon, 2000, p. 125.

(2) the government-led language policy that deals with acquisition planning in the absence of language planning;

(3) the government-led language policy that deals with corpus planning in the absence of language planning; and

(4) the non-government-led language policy that deals with acquisition planning or corpus planning in the absence of language planning (Poon, 2000, p. 125).

Hong Kong's language policy belongs to the second type. To be more precise, Hong Kong's language policy both prior to and after the handover is basically language-in-education policy (a type of language policy in the realm of education), among which the most prominent sub-types are medium-of-instruction policy (with a focus on content-based learning) and language enhancement policy (with a focus on Chinese and English).

Since language-in-education policy is within the policy area of education, Hong Kong's language policy is an outcome of education planning rather than language planning. The policymaking and planning of language is taken up by the Education Bureau. Before the handover, it was the Education Commission, an advisory body directly appointed by the Hong Kong Governor with a group of experts and educationists serving voluntarily on the committee, that was responsible for the policymaking of education policies (including language-in-education policies) pertaining to the school sector. After thorough research and consultations, the Education Commission then made recommendations to the Education and Manpower Bureau (the former name of the Education Bureau), the *de jure* education policymaker for endorsement and implementation. However, after the handover the Hong Kong SAR government gradually abolished the British advisory system and re-centralized its governance in different respects including educational governance (Poon & Wong, 2004). The educational advisory body, Education Commission, lost its role in education policymaking. SCOLAR (Standing Committee on Language Education and Research) – a sub-committee under Education Commission designed to advise the government specifically on language education policies and issues – was relocated and put under the Education Bureau. The Education Bureau thus became the sole agent of educational policymaking and implementation, including language-in-education policies.

Language policy before the handover

Language problems

According to Neustupný's (1968, 1983) Theory of Language Problems, Model of Language Correction and Language Management Theory (e.g. Neustupný & Nekvapil, 2006 for a detailed example from the Czech Republic), there are some language problems of which society is conscious. The declining language standards of English during the 1980s and early 1990s[10], issues around the medium of instruction, and the subsequent use of mixed code in teaching were the major language problems of which Hong Kong society was conscious before the handover. As mentioned in Part I, the mismatch between written Chinese (Modern Standard Chinese) and spoken Chinese (Cantonese), while not a problem unique to Hong Kong, also poses a serious problem for students (Llewellyn et al., 1982; Poon, 1999; So, 1989), who cannot write what they say. They think in Cantonese, their first language, and its written form is not recognised as standard written Chinese. They have to learn to write in Modern Standard Chinese, the spoken form of which (*Putonghua*) they do not use. Consequently, mastering Chinese presupposes much effort in the context of Hong Kong. On the other hand, bilingualism was imposed on Hong Kong society through the process of colonialism prior to the 1980s. Because of 'superposed bilingualism' (So, 1989), students had to (even at present still have to) struggle between the languages of Cantonese (spoken), Modern Standard Chinese (written) and English (both written and spoken) starting from Primary 1 (in actual practice, from kindergarten – i.e. at the age of three).

Given the complications of the language situation, language learning has presupposed more effort on the parts of both students and teachers than might otherwise be the case. Prior to the implementation of the curriculum reform of 2001 (Curriculum Development Council, 2001), the teaching methods adopted by both Chinese and English language teachers were very traditional. Rote learning was the dominant mode of learning in the Chinese Language class, which was typically conducted as follows: The teacher read out a text written in classical Chinese (if the text was written in Modern Standard Chinese, the teacher would ask students to read once on their own), and then explained to students the meaning of words, phrases, sentences, paragraphs and the whole text, followed by asking students to do some exercises. As Chinese is an ideographic language rather than a phonetic language, there is no way to pronounce Chinese characters by merely looking at the script. Nor is there any systematic way to guide learners how individual Chinese characters are written. The only way to learn to write and pronounce Chinese characters is through rote learning; therefore, dictation of Chinese words and phrases is a compulsory component in Chinese language learning. English language teaching, on the other hand, is presumably more varied as there is a body of teaching methods underpinned by the communicative approach that has been developed over the past four decades in the West.

However, English language lessons in Hong Kong remained very traditional because they were based on audiolingualism where repeated drilling of sentence patterns and vocabulary was the dominant English language teaching methodology, adopted although communicative language teaching had been advocated for more than two and a half decades by the English curriculum (Curriculum Development Council, 1983, 1999, 2002). What made this situation even more problematic was that teaching did not take into account differences between first language acquisition and second language acquisition in terms of language structure, language environment and stages of development. Local English teachers taught English modeled upon the way Chinese was taught and dictation was made an important part in English language teaching especially in primary schools (Poon, 2001,

Table 10. Survey of students' motivation in Chinese Language, English Language and *Putonghua* (conducted in March 2002) (SCOLAR, 2003, p. 29).

	Percentage of students with 'strong' or 'very strong' motivation to learn languages		
	Students' self-perception	Parents' perception	Teachers' perception
Chinese language	47%	35%	11%
English language	44%	26%	8%
Putonghua	25%	20%	N/A*

Note: *Only Chinese and English Language teachers were surveyed.

June 15; Poon, 2004b). Students are merely asked to spell the words without being taught how to pronounce them and relate the letters to the corresponding sounds. Research on primary school students' strategies used in English oral reading (e.g. sounding out, phonic substitution) indicates that the students over-relied on memory for word recognition rather than on applied phonic rules (Tinker Sachs & Mahon, 1997). Such traditional language teaching methods doubtlessly demotivated students as shown in the perception surveys conducted by SCOLAR in March 2002 (see Table 10).

The low motivation in English together with other factors (e.g. a large number of untrained English teachers, traditional teaching methods, lack of an English environment, an examination-oriented educational system and large class size) all contributed to the declining English standards.

The problems of language learning in primary education just described lingered, and the effects of these problems were felt in secondary schooling (Cheng, Shek, Tse, & Wong, 1979 [1973]; Education Commission, 1990, 1996; Llewellyn, Hancock, Kirst, & Roeloffs, 1982). The problems were magnified because, traditionally, after using Chinese as the medium of learning content-based subjects (e.g. Mathematics, General Studies, etc.) for six years in primary schools, students would need to make a shift to English-medium of learning when they entered Secondary 1[11] because of 'superposed bilingualism' (So, 1989) where the majority of students were forced to learn through the medium of English. The sudden shift in the medium of instruction from Chinese to English in secondary education generated language confusion in school. Prior to 1978, there was a clear distinction between two types of secondary schools: namely, Anglo-Chinese schools using English as the medium of instruction, and middle schools using Chinese as the medium of instruction. The problem with using English as a medium of instruction in secondary schools was not so serious then, in that the education system was basically elitist, and those who were offered government subsidized places in secondary schools could overcome the hurdle of language in one way or another (Poon, 1999). However, with the introduction of 9 years of free, compulsory education in 1978, Hong Kong's education entered the mass-education era. More secondary schools were established, and most of them claimed to be Anglo-Chinese schools (i.e. English-medium schools) to cater for the demand of the public. This made the problem of medium of instruction more acute, reaching alarming proportions by the 1980s because of the move from elite to universal education. The distinction between Anglo-Chinese schools and Chinese middle schools was blurred. Using English only or Chinese only as the medium of instruction became rare. The majority of teachers in effect resorted to the use of mixed code, i.e. mixing both English and Chinese in their discourse. The extent of the use of the two languages varied, ranging from using English most of the time mixed with some Chinese explanation, to using Chinese most of the time mixed with some English terminology. In a study on the modes of teacher-talk in Anglo-Chinese schools, Johnson (1983) found that the teachers used 43% English, 48% Cantonese and 9% mixed-code (Cantonese mixed with English terms). The percentage of English used in a class varied from 100% to 2%, depending on the English proficiency of teachers and students. Likewise, Chinese middle schools did not use Chinese exclusively for lessons other than English language. Shek, Johnson, and Law (1991) found that only 4% of the 193 Chinese-medium schools studied used Chinese textbooks for all subjects other than English, whereas the remaining 96% of the schools – claiming to use Chinese as the medium of instruction – used English textbooks for one or more subjects.

The language issue pertaining to the problems of declining language standards and the use of mixed code in medium-of-instruction programs previously described emerged as an important issue in education before the handover, as reflected in most of the education reports published during the 1980s and the 1990s (Education Commission, 1984, 1986, 1990, 1994, 1995, 1996; Education Department, 1989; Hong Kong Government, 1981; Llewellyn, Hancock, Kirst, & Roeloffs, 1982). The significance of the language issue to the Hong Kong educational sector as well as to Hong Kong society as a whole was evident. The language-in-education policies, subsequently described, were the Hong Kong government's responses to the language problems during the time immediately preceding the handover.

Medium-of-instruction policy: from laissez-faire policy to streaming policy

Laissez-faire policy. Medium of instruction has been among the thorniest and trickiest issues facing Hong Kong education. Traditionally, the Hong Kong government under British rule adopted a *laissez-faire* attitude towards the question of medium of instruction (Poon, 2000). For the very first time in its history, the Hong Kong government formally proposed using Chinese as the medium of instruction in junior secondary schools and documented the proposal in a 1973 Green Paper (i.e. a consultation paper) (Board of Education, 1973). Because of public pressure, the proposal was toned down in the White Paper (i.e. a policy paper) (Board of Education, 1974), and schools were granted the autonomy to select their own instructional medium. There was, in fact, no implementation plan included in the 1974 medium-of-instruction policy paper, thus rendering the paper a policy *on paper* only. The *laissez-faire* policy persisted until the 1980s.

Perceiving the increasing detrimental effects on students' educational development of using English as the medium of instruction and the subsequent alternative of using mixed code, the Hong Kong government invited an international panel headed by Sir John Llewellyn to review Hong Kong's education system in 1981. Consequently, an insightful report entitled *A Perspective on Education in Hong Kong* (often referred to as the *Llewellyn Report*) was produced in 1982. The panel considered the language situation of Hong Kong as:

> a classic public policy dilemma: whether to jeopardise the educational progress of the majority (and perhaps endanger the culture itself) in order to guarantee a sufficient number of competent English speakers; or to value the whole group (and in so doing conserve the culture) but accept the loss in capacity to deal with the international environment and hence a possible decline in the economic prosperity. (Llewellyn, Hancock, Kirst, & Roeloffs, 1982, p. 30)

Based on the assumption 'the mother tongue is, all other things being equal, the best medium of teaching and learning' (Llewellyn, Hancock, Kirst, & Roeloffs, 1982, p. 28), and practically constrained by the linguistic dilemma in Hong Kong, they put forward the following compromise solution:

> This [the proposal] would involve, in the long term, a shift towards complete mother tongue education in the early compulsory years ... Such a solution would support a wholehearted push towards genuine bilingualism after P6 [Primary 6], including the tertiary level. From FI [Secondary 1] there should be a progressive shift to genuinely bilingual programmes so that by the end of F III [Secondary 3] students are receiving approximately half of their instruction in each language. (Llewellyn, Hancock, Kirst, & Roeloffs, 1982, p. 30)

The panel chose not to define the term 'bilingualism', nor did the panel specify the type of bilingual education Hong Kong would need. No concrete measures were proposed. Despite these shortcomings:

> the Llewellyn Report adopted a broad perspective, and expressed the view that it is necessary to move to areas beyond education, for example, public policy, in order to find a solution to the language problem. (Poon, 2000, p. 158)

Improving language teaching alone would not lend itself to the solution of the medium-of-instruction problem in Hong Kong, because medium of instruction is more than a linguistic problem; rather the problem has cultural and economic ramifications as well (Llewellyn, Hancock, Kirst, & Roeloffs, 1982, pp. 25–26).

A permanent advisory body – the Education Commission – was created in 1984 to formulate education policy and to co-ordinate the planning and development of education at all levels (Education Commission, 1984, p. 1). The Commission issued six Reports (ECR1 to ECR6), four of which provided a wide range of suggestions on ways to deal with the language problems. ECR1 encouraged schools to adopt Chinese as the medium of instruction through the 'positive discrimination' policy (i.e. intended to provide support and resources) favouring schools that would adopt Chinese as the teaching medium. In other words, schools were free to select their own medium of instruction although they were encouraged to adopt Chinese as the medium of instruction. However, Poon argues:

> The scope of these reports (except ECR6) is narrow, just within the domain of language, and most of the suggestions are *ad hoc*: they are *not* guided by clear goals and long-term planning. (Poon, 2000, p. 158)

Streaming policy. Streaming policy refers to the medium-of-instruction policy proposed in ECR4 (1990) with a view to resolving the problem of using mixed code in English-medium secondary schools and subsequently aimed at raising the English standards. Instead of having only English-medium and Chinese-medium schools, schools were re-labeled and required to adopt the appropriate medium of instruction rather than to use mixed code. In order to place them in suitable schools, students were streamed into different categories based on their language ability. Details of the streaming policy are discussed subsequently.

The language situation worsened throughout the decade of the 1980s. Approximately 88% of secondary students were placed in the so-called English-medium schools, i.e. schools that in effect adopted mixed-code teaching because of students' limited English ability. Research indicated 'only around 30% of students may be able to learn effectively through English' (Education Commission, 1990, p. 102). However, many parents believed (and presently still believe) that English-medium instruction would provide better tertiary education and employment opportunities for their children. As a result of parental attitudes, schools dared not abandon the label of English-medium teaching, fearing that should they switch to Chinese-medium, they would receive lower band students (Education Commission, 1990, pp. 104–105)[12]. To resolve the dilemma arising from language of instruction issues, the Education Commission (1990) put forward a framework for language-in-education reform in its ECR4, claiming to offer a coherent and comprehensive framework catering for the demands of different stake-holders. Under the streaming policy, students were grouped into the following categories based on the results of an objective assessment – the Medium-of-Instruction Grouping Assessment (MIGA):

C [i.e. Chinese] – Students who would learn best through the Chinese medium;

B [i.e. bilingual] – Students who would probably learn better through the Chinese medium but who are possibly able also to learn in English; and

E [i.e. English] – Students who are able to learn effectively in English many of whom could learn in Chinese equally well, should they so wish. (Education Commission, 1990, p. 107)

Schools were grouped into three types: Chinese-medium, English-medium and two-medium schools. The results of MIGA were issued to both parents and schools. Parents were free to choose any of the three types of school for their children:

… but armed with objective information on their children's achievement, they would be in a position to select schools best suited for their children's educational development. (Education Commission, 1990, p. 108)

On the other hand, the overriding belief of the Education Commission (1990) was that school authorities should be given free and responsible choice to make decisions for their own schools:

With the results of the assessments to hand, secondary schools would be in a better position to choose an appropriate medium of instruction to meet the needs of their student intake. (Education Commission, 1990, p. 108)

A detailed implementation time-table of the streaming policy was set out. The plan was implemented as of September 1994 following a three-year period of preparation. Poon (2000) did an extensive study of the streaming policy *per se* as well as of its implementation in schools. Poon found a number of factors signifying that the streaming policy was not likely to be implemented to any great extent territorially. There were such macro factors as policymaking, social values, political force, economic development and cultural factors, as well as such micro factors as the attitudes of the schools, the values and beliefs of the teachers, the English proficiency of the students and the ways government officials handled things. Poon also found that the use of mixed code was predominant in the majority of the so-called English-medium schools at the time of her study. On the other hand, some studies investigated the stake-holders' attitudes towards the streaming policy. Evans, Jones, Rusmin, and Cheung (1998) and Tung, Lam, and Tsang (1997) employed surveys to explore the attitudes of students, parents and/or teachers as well as business people towards the streaming policy. The finding in Evans et al. (1998) showed that most respondents disagreed with the streaming policy because it deprived them of a free choice of medium of instruction; the respondents appeared to prefer multi-medium education (i.e. using English, Chinese and *Putonghua* as the medium of instruction). Tung et al. (1997, p. 441) found that 'students and their parents consistently value English over

Chinese ... although they agree ... that instruction in Chinese is educationally more effective'.

The streaming policy was scheduled to be fully operational in the academic year 1997–1998. However, the streaming policy suddenly came to a halt and was replaced by the compulsory Chinese-medium-instruction policy in September 1998. This matter will be further explored subsequently.

Debates over medium-of-instruction policy

Poon (2009) postulates that the debate on medium of instruction in Hong Kong has undergone three stages amid political, economic and social changes during the past three decades. The intensity of the debate in each of the three stages has remained great albeit with a different focus and content each time. The first stage of debate took place from the late 1960s to the late 1970s, the second stage from the 1980s to 1997, and the third stage has occurred since 1997. This section describes the two stages prior to the handover.

The first round of debate was political-oriented (Poon, 2009). It started in 1967 in the aftermath of a riot organized by pro-Beijing workers and students against the colonial rule of the then Hong Kong government in 1967 as mentioned in Part I. Anti-colonial feeling was high. As mentioned previously, because of the impact of the progressive movement in the West, social movements initiated by the young baby boomer elite began to take root in Hong Kong, and the 'Chinese as Official Language Movement' was the one that had a bearing on the debate concerning medium of instruction. The principal argument of the activists at this stage was that English-medium instruction was imposed on students through colonialism, and that learning through a foreign language was detrimental to children's intellectual and educational development, as well as their creativity and sensitivity (Cheng, 1979; Cheng, Shek, Tse, & Wong, 1979 [1973]; S.K. Poon, 1979). Consequently, the medium of instruction should be rectified, moving away from the imposed English-medium instruction towards Chinese-medium instruction. On the other hand, the supporters of English-medium instruction argued that English-medium instruction should be maintained because English provided students with opportunities for well-paid jobs and for higher education.

The second round of debate was much less politically oriented because anti-colonial feeling had diminished (Poon, 2009). This movement took place during the 1980s through until 1997, a period in which Hong Kong established itself as an international financial centre as a result of the major economic boom mentioned previously in Part I. The changing economic environment together with the accelerating decolonization process completely changed the status of English in Hong Kong from a colonial language to an international language (Johnson, 1994; Lord, 1987; Pennington & Yue, 1994; Poon, 2000). English became even more highly valued in society than before. English medium instruction which was originally imposed on students during the previous period, then turned out to be the preferred choice of students and their parents (Poon, 1999, 2000, 2004a, 2009). However, many students in the so-called English-medium schools during this period were not able to learn through the English medium. Therefore, the focus of the medium-of-instruction debate shifted to declining standards in English among students and the subsequent reliance on mixed code resulting from the expansion of education during the mass education era (Education Commission, 1984, 1986, 1990, 1996; Lin, 1991; Pennington, 1995). The advocates of Chinese-medium instruction reiterated their position that the first language was the best medium for learning and argued that the use of mixed code impinged on students' language development. Alternatively, supporters of English-medium instruction emphasized the practical value of English as an international language and the urgent need for fluent English in Hong Kong as an international city.

The Hong Kong government's *laissez-faire* attitude towards medium of instruction prior to 1997 favoured the English medium supporters, thus deepening the differences between the two camps. The debate continued, but it took a major turn after the handover. This development is elaborated subsequently.

Language enhancement policy: English and Chinese subjects

As mentioned previously, one undesirable effect of nine-year compulsory education, in effect as of 1978 was the declining language standards – and especially English standards – among students. On the one hand, the Hong Kong government was not willing to admit the fact of declining English standards and argued that 'the gap between demand and supply has led to a perception that language standards are falling' (Education Commission, 1994, p. 15, 1995, 1996). On the other hand, the government has made strenuous efforts since the early 1980s to combat the declining language standards; e.g. following are some measures taken by the Hong Kong government prior to 1997 to enhance the language standards of students in the school sector as well as in the university sector.

School sector. Both the Education Department and the Education Commission set up working groups to investigate the language issue in 1988 and again in 1993, respectively, and four comprehensive reports exclusively concerning the language issue were published prior to 1997 (Education Commission, 1994, 1995, 1996; Education Department, 1989) in addition to the Education Commission Reports nos. 1, 2 and 4 that had previously offered some sections concerning the means to enhance the language standards of students (Education Commission, 1984, 1986, 1990). Following are some examples of measures aimed at language enhancement implemented prior to the handover:

- revising the Chinese and English syllabuses in primary and secondary schools,
- introducing task-oriented curriculum to the English curriculum,
- providing additional resources for remedial English classes adopting split-class teaching (i.e. splitting a regular class into two smaller classes to be taught by two different teachers),
- increasing library funds for schools to implement their reading programmes,
- offering English bridging courses for Secondary 1 students in English-medium schools,
- providing additional Chinese and English language teachers in secondary schools,
- trying out the Expatriate English Teachers scheme in secondary schools,
- recruiting local native speakers of English for secondary schools, and
- recruiting expatriate lecturers of English for school teacher training courses in Colleges of Education (Education Commission, 1984, 1986, 1990, 1994, 1995, 1996).

University sector. University education underwent a substantial expansion following the Policy Address of the then Governor Lord David Wilson delivered at the re-opening of the Legislative Council session on 11 October 1989. The number of universities funded by the University Grants Committee, (i.e. the UGC commissioned by the Hong Kong government to oversee the financial affairs and development of universities) increased from two in the 1980s to seven in the 1990s. The provision of additional first-year, first-degree places intended to increase the enrolment from 2.4% of the relevant age group in 1982 to 18% by 1995. In view of this significant expansion, it was anticipated that 'the overall educational standards of Hong Kong's tertiary students [would be] worse than before', including English standards (Education Commission, 1988, p. 23). Accordingly, a series of language enhancement measures were undertaken: e.g.:

- providing language enhancement funds for universities to develop self-access language learning centres,
- offering extensive Chinese and English enhancement programmes with effect from the early 1990s,
- strictly enforcing the minimum entrance requirements regarding English language proficiency, and
- offering bridging courses for Secondary 6 and 7 students to make the transition from Chinese-medium secondary education to English-medium tertiary education.

Effect of language enhancement policy

The language enhancement policy seemed to bear little fruit as the debate pertaining to a decline in English standards among Hong Kong students started in the 1980s and has persisted until the present time. Some studies conducted prior to the handover reported that the English proficiency of both secondary school students and university students was not up to the standard required; e.g. the survey reported in Evans et al. (1998) included interviews with students, teachers, parents and business people who rated their own abilities in English as being slightly below average. These four groups of participants blamed each other for the declining English standards. Two additional studies examined the actual medium of instruction used at presumably English-medium universities. The findings revealed that the English language proficiency of students was inadequate because instruction was in reality basically in Chinese (Flowerdew, Li, & Miller, 1998; Walters & Balla, 1998). More specifically, Stone (1994) found that university students in Hong Kong had insufficient lexical and semantic knowledge. He concluded 'the results of this study are consistent with general anecdotal and research evidence suggesting that the English proficiency of Hong Kong undergraduates is low' (Stone, 1994, p. 97).

The use of code-mixing and code-switching appears to be a consequence of declining English standards as well as a further indicator of the ineffectiveness of the language enhancement policy implemented prior to 1997. Teaching using code switching spread from junior secondary to senior secondary classes, and then to university tutorials and lectures over the past 25 years. The main reason for using code-mixing in some English-medium schools derives from the fact that the English proficiency of students did not reach the threshold level. A finding common among some studies (Johnson & Lee, 1987; Lin, 1991) demonstrated that code-mixing and code-switching often were included in the medium of instruction in the classroom, not only in content subjects, but also in English lessons.

Although the Hong Kong government had expended billions of dollars on schools and universities, the language enhancement policy in place before the handover proved to be ineffective, because the policy failed to address the crux of the problem. According to second language acquisition theories (Gardner & Lambert, 1959; Gardner, 2001; Giles & Byrne, 1982; Schumann, 1978), motivation is a key factor influencing learners' level of language attainment. Research on Hong Kong students indicates that both tertiary and school students found English important to them and they were very positive about English language learning (Axler, Yang, & Stevens, 1998; Lai, 1999; Lin & Detaramani, 1998). Hong Kong students' positive attitudes towards English language learning should have permitted the achievement of high standards in English. However, in reality Hong Kong teachers continued (and still continue) to complain about the low motivation of their students and about the perception that the English standards of students were (and still are) declining.

The problem lies with the type of motivation for English language learning that Hong Kong students have. As Gardner (2001, p. 5) argues, 'Integrativeness reflects a genuine interest in learning the second language in order to come closer to the other language community.' 'Integrativeness' together with 'attitudes toward the learning situation' and toward 'other support' contribute to motivation. Despite their positive attitudes supported by the above cited research findings, Hong Kong students' orientation to English language learning is instrumental rather than integrative (Hyland, 1997; W. Poon, 1988). According to Gardner's (2001) Socio-Educational Model of Second Language Acquisition, motivation is only one factor, albeit an important one, contributing to students' language achievement. There are also other factors such as language aptitude, as well as school-based (e.g. the teacher factor, the teaching materials, the teaching methods, the curriculum) and background factors (e.g. policy decisions, family background, or the environment). The factors of family background and the environment are beyond the control of the government, but the other factors are within the scope of policymaking. In terms of policy, Hong Kong follows quite closely the English language teaching methodology developed in the West. In the 1983 English syllabus (Curriculum Development Council, 1983) the previously used Oral-Structural Approach was replaced by the Communicative Approach. In the 1999 English syllabus (Curriculum Development Council, 1999) task-based language learning was introduced alongside the Communicative Approach. However, in reality many English teachers continue to practise the traditional grammar and structural approaches. English skills are not taught integratively. Emphasis continues to be placed on grammar and English usage exercises, and practice in listening and speaking is minimal – just the reverse of the natural approach to language acquisition advocated by Krashen and Terrell (1983) and Krashen (1982).

The teaching medium is an additional problem. At secondary level, but not necessarily at primary level, English is taught mostly through the target language. Consequently, primary students are not provided with sufficient English input. The issues of student motivation, English language teaching approach, methods and medium of instruction are, in fact, related to a bigger issue of teacher qualifications and training. Because of a high demand on the supply of English teachers, quite a large number of them were not subject-trained before the handover and some even demonstrated problems with their own English proficiency. According to the 2001 Teacher Survey conducted by the former Education Department, the percentage of primary and secondary English teachers who possessed a first degree in English plus a diploma in education specializing in English was only 6.3% and 22.7%, respectively (SCOLAR, 2003). The actual percentage at the point of handover must have been even lower.

Language policy after the handover

Language problems

The language problems pertaining to declining language standards and medium of instruction persist to the present time, 12 years after the handover. According to the results of 2008

Territory-wide System Assessment – a public assessment of approximately 200,000 Primary 3, Primary 6 and Secondary 3 students on English, Chinese and Mathematics – the scores on the English subject were the lowest among the three subjects, and more than 30% of Secondary 3 students failed to achieve basic competency in English. Even worse, 7.8% of Secondary 3 students reached the basic competency level when they studied in Primary 6 in 2005, but their English had deteriorated after three years (Ming Pao, 2008, November 1). In addition, the number of Secondary 5 students taking Syllabus A, an easier syllabus than Syllabus B, of the English Language paper[13] in another public examination – HKCEE – increased by approximately four times from 7567 candidates in 1997 to 29,322 candidates in 2006. The statistics in Table 11 clearly indicate a gradually increasing decline in English standards after the handover.

The Statistics from public examinations in Table 11 corroborate the teachers' views. In Poon (2009), the English teachers in 10 secondary schools who had taught in those schools for at least eight years have witnessed the falling English standards of the students in their own schools. In addition, prominent public figures in business, politics and the judiciary have, from time to time, strongly criticized the English proficiency of Hong Kong students. A recent example appears in the criticism provided by Stephen Bradley, the former British consul general, prior to his departing Hong Kong in March 2008: 'It [English] has significantly declined as a language in general use' (Wong, 2008, March 14). A further decline in English standards aggravated the situation in Hong Kong after the handover, not only in the education sector, but also in the economy. Globalisation has triggered a demand for English throughout the world in the past 15 years. Becoming increasingly globalised as an international financial centre, Hong Kong is in serious need of competent English users, increasingly so after 1997. Unfortunately the rapidly increasing demand for English is not likely to be alleviated unless the problem of declining English standards is promptly and properly addressed.

Medium of instruction always carries a political implication. The change of sovereignty in 1997 had a great effect on Hong Kong society as a whole and specifically on education. For some people the issue of using the colonial language – English as the medium of instruction – had to be rectified after the PRC regained sovereignty over Hong Kong. For others, Hong Kong is not just a city in China; rather it is an international financial centre, and the 'One Country Two Systems' principle must be upheld. As a result, English medium instruction should continue. The continuing medium-of-instruction problem carried over from the pre-1997 era is considered subsequently.

Table 11. Number of candidates taking Syllabus A and Syllabus B of the English Language subject (1997–2006).

科目 Subject		考試年份 Examination Year											
		1997	1998	1999	2000	2001	2002	2003	2004	2005	2006	2007	2008
英國語文(課程甲) English Language (Syllabus A)	出席人數 No. sat	7 567	8 564	9 616	11 776	13 279	14 255	16 528	20 236	25 901	29 322	–	–
	A%	0.8	0.5	0.6	0.6	0.5	0.5	1.1	0.9	1.1	0.7	–	–
	C⁺%	11.6	9.9	10.3	9.7	9.0	9.6	10.9	10.8	13.4	17.9	–	–
	E⁺%	45.8	39.9	43.1	41.2	41.8	41.6	44.3	44.6	49.1	55.9	–	–
英國語文(課程乙) English Language (Syllabus B)	出席人數 No. sat	55 415	57 265	56 864	55 311	52 432	50 342	46 609	43 686	43 121	39 176	–	–
	A%	2.4	2.4	2.5	2.7	2.8	2.5	2.7	2.6	2.8	3.2	–	–
	C⁺%	9.6	10.0	10.2	10.9	11.3	11.3	11.8	12.9	13.6	15.1	–	–
	E⁺%	57.9	59.0	60.4	63.3	66.0	66.4	64.5	69.6	75.2	78.6	–	–

Source: Hong Kong Examination and Assessment Authority, 2009, HKCEE statistics of entries and results over the years.

In addition to the two older problems previously cited, a new language problem for the Hong Kong SAR government has emerged because of political change – i.e. how to instill a sense of national identity in the populace through education and language. As education involves many other matters, the present focus is exclusively on language. *Putonghua* (Mandarin) was not promoted by the colonial government prior to 1997. As a consequence, setting a policy to promote *Putonghua* became a high priority of the Hong Kong SAR government in the aftermath of the handover.

Medium-of-instruction policy: from compulsory Chinese medium instruction policy to fine-tuning policy
Compulsory Chinese medium instruction policy. As mentioned previously, the streaming policy – presumably a long-term policy with a framework to resolve the decades-old lingering problem of medium of instruction – started in September 1994; it was scheduled to complete one full cycle by September 1997. Surprisingly, on the brink of the changeover of sovereignty when implementation of the streaming policy was in full swing, the Hong Kong SAR government suddenly issued a consultation document ('the Firm Guidance') in April 1997, proposing a *compulsory* Chinese medium-of-instruction policy (Education Department, 1997a). That meant *all* secondary schools would need to change to Chinese medium whether or not they liked it. Due to strong opposition from schools, students and parents (Ming Pao Daily, May 3, 1997; Sing Tao Daily, May 3, 1997; May 13, 1997; *South China Morning Post*, September 19, 1997), the 'Firm Guidance' was subsequently revised to 'Guidance' in September 1997, allowing for some schools to be exempted from the compulsory Chinese medium instruction policy (Education Department, 1997b). Under the *compulsory* Chinese medium instruction policy 114 schools were granted exemptions, and approximately 70% of schools were designated Chinese medium. The number of Chinese-medium schools increased from 12% during the *laissez-faire* period to 38% during the period of the streaming policy, and further to 70% in 1998 when the compulsory Chinese medium instruction policy was strictly enforced.

How was the compulsory Chinese medium instruction policy received at the point of introduction? The Chinese medium instruction policy was welcomed by some educational bodies for different reasons, e.g. on educational grounds by the Professional Teachers' Union of Hong Kong and Hong Kong Government Secondary Schools Principals Association, and on patriotic grounds by the Hong Kong Federation of Education Workers (Ming Pao Daily, May 30, 1997; *Wen Wei Po Daily*, March 25, 1997). Nonetheless, the policy was poorly received territorially by students, parents and schools. In a survey conducted by the Hong Kong Federation of Youth Groups during July and August 1997, 55% of the respondents – students and parents – admitted Chinese medium instruction was more effective, but 73% believed English standards would be lowered and 50% thought the change would hurt the students' chances of finding a job and getting a place in university (*South China Morning Post*, September 19, 1997). Some schools and some Parent–Teacher Associations even advertised in the newspapers reiterating their firm support for English medium education (Sing Tao Daily, May 3, 1997).

The 'Firm Guidance' and the 'Guidance' were originally meant to help implement fully the streaming policy according to the framework stipulated in Education Commission Report No. 4 in 1990 (Education Commission, 1990). In effect, the policies abolished the streaming policy and proposed a new direction for Hong Kong's medium-of-instruction policy – the compulsory Chinese medium-of-instruction policy. Poon argues:

it was a political move – a gesture to appease China. Hong Kong was on the brink of returning to China: it seemed legitimate to enforce the use of Chinese as the medium of instruction especially when a myriad of problems have arisen during implementation of the streaming policy. (Poon, 1999, p. 139)

The compulsory Chinese medium instruction policy has been in place for more than 11 years, and the impact had been deeply felt. The most worrying consequence lies in the declining English standards as mentioned previously. A further impact resulted in a divided education sector as a result of the third stage of debate on medium of instruction triggered by the compulsory Chinese medium instruction policy. This division is sub-sequently discussed. The greatest concern for educators as well as parents is the teaching and learning effectiveness of Chinese-medium instruction. Tsang's (2002, 2004, 2008) three longitudinal studies investigated the effects of different medium-of-instruction arrangements on students' learning at three different stages – i.e. junior secondary (S1–S3), senior secondary (S4–S5) and matriculation (S6–S7). It was found that junior secondary students studying at Chinese-medium schools outperformed their counterparts at English-medium schools in science and social studies subjects by 30%, but their performance in English subject dropped by 20%. When the same cohort of stu-dents reached senior secondary, the value-added advantages in science and social studies subjects that Chinese-medium schools students had achieved over English-medium schools students had declined as shown in the Hong Kong Certificate of Education Exam-ination, whereas their English results continued to deteriorate. By the time the same cohort of students reached matriculation level, Chinese-medium school students' value-added advantages in science and social studies subjects had completely disappeared. Their English results were very poor because their motivation for English learning and their self-esteem resulting from English competence were much lower than were those of their counterparts in English-medium schools. What was worse, the chances of Chinese-medium school students to enter university were only half that of English-medium school students. The findings of Poon's study (2009) corroborated some of Tsang's – e.g. teachers (especially English teachers) were not satisfied with students' motivation in learning; teachers were not sure whether the present students learning through Chinese-medium were more motivated than had been their past students learning through English-medium. Teachers regardless of school bandings shared the same view that the present students did not necessarily achieve better results than had been achieved by past students before the shift in the medium of instruction from English to Chinese in 1998. Additionally, Poon found that students:

> ...were generally quite positive about studying in CMI [Chinese-medium] schools in the sense that learning is faster, better and more interactive through the Chinese medium (Findings 6, 8). However, surprisingly, though, quite a large number of students chose to study in English-medium schools if they were given an offer irrespective of their bandings (Findings 9, 10). (Poon, 2009, p. 219)

The apparent discrepancy in the findings reveals that the schools and students' choices of medium of instruction 'are to quite a large extent determined by the dominant social values, which are framed by various forces in their social milieu' (Poon, 2009, p. 219). The high value traditionally accorded to English in Hong Kong society has thus been intensified by the compulsory Chinese-medium instruction policy as the number of English-medium schools has been dramatically reduced, thus creating keen competition among students and between schools. Chinese-medium schools, which should presumably have benefited from the compulsory Chinese medium instruction policy, were ironically classified as lower-level schools.

A formal evaluation of the Chinese medium instruction policy was scheduled to be conducted by a Review Committee comprising members of the former Board of Education and SCOLAR (Standing Committee on Language Education and Research) after a 3-year cycle – i.e. in the school year 2001–2002. Based on the Review Committee's recommendation, the Hong Kong government would decide whether to maintain this language-in-education policy. As medium of instruction is more than an educational issue in Hong Kong involving the interests of different parties, immense pressure has been put on the government either to continue with or to discontinue the policy. As in the past, the Hong Kong government's stand towards the medium of instruction has been shifting. By the end of 2002, the views of the Review Committee were still so divided that the Hong Kong government decided to put off the formal review for two additional years on the grounds that a long-term medium-of-instruction policy should be considered in conjunction with the review of the Secondary School Places Allocation System in the school year 2003–2004. In the final review report on language education, entitled 'Action plan to raise language standards in Hong Kong' (SCOLAR, 2003), released in June 2003, the support for Chinese medium-of-instruction policy was reiterated, but SCOLAR's position towards the use of English medium was less rigid than it had previously been. It averred: 'If schools wish to use a second language as the MOI (medium of instruction), they should ensure that the preconditions mentioned in paragraph 3.2.3 above are fulfilled' (SCOLAR, 2003, p. 34). Whether the compulsory Chinese medium-of-instruction policy would become a long term policy was yet to be determined at that point.

The formal review of medium of instruction was finally completed, and a report was issued in December 2005. A so-called 'Changing Train' policy was proposed. According to this policy, the first language would continue to be upheld as the principal medium of instruction, and those schools that had been granted an exemption to use English medium would be subject to a review every six years for quality assurance. A new mechanism to allow the change of teaching medium from Chinese to English was proposed based on three criteria:

(1) Student ability – schools adopting English medium must have at least 85% of its Secondary 1 intake being able to learn through English according to the Medium-of-Instruction Grouping Assessment (MIGA) issued by the Education Bureau;
(2) Teacher capability – non-language subject teachers teaching through English should possess a grade C or above in English Language of the Hong Kong Certificate of Education Examination or other recognized qualifications; and
(3) Support measure – schools must provide a language environment conducive to learning in English medium (Education Commission, 2005).

Chinese-medium schools could apply to change to English-medium if they fulfilled the prescribed criteria. Likewise, English-medium schools would risk being forced to change to Chinese-medium if they failed to fulfil the prescribed criteria. The 'Changing Train' policy was scheduled to be implemented in September 2010. However, it was poorly received since it was meant to further tighten the compulsory Chinese-medium-of-instruction policy with a view to limiting the existing number of English-medium schools.

Fine-tuning policy. The 'Changing Train' policy would have been implemented had the decision-makers of the Education Bureau – Arthur Lee (former Secretary for Education and Manpower) and Fanny Law (former Permanent Secretary for Education and Manpower) – not stepped down in June 2007 because of a scandal pertaining to infringement of academic freedom. The new Bureau chief, Michael Suen, instituted a drastic policy change after taking into consideration the stakeholders' concerns (Education Bureau, 2009a). The major criticism of the previously proposed 'Changing train policy' was fourfold:

(1) 'Students learning in their mother tongue have limited exposure to English' – a limitation which may affect their transition to senior secondary and post-secondary levels;
(2) 'The bifurcation of schools into CMI schools and EMI schools may not fully meet the needs of individual students';
(3) The labelling effect will create pressure on teachers and students of Chinese-medium schools; and
(4) The review mechanism under which schools will change their medium of instruction 'will cause consequential destabilizing effect on the development of schools' (Education Bureau, 2009b, pp. 2–3).

Consequently, a 'fine-tuning policy' was put forward for consultation in June 2008. It was announced in May 2009 that the new medium-of-instruction policy would be put in place in September 2010.

In the new fine-tuned medium-of-instruction framework, schools would no longer be bifurcated into Chinese-medium and English-medium schools. More flexibility will be given to schools, and 'there will be a spectrum of MOI arrangements across schools, ranging from total CMI at one end, CMI or EMI in different subjects between the extremes, and EMI in full immersion at the other end' (Education Bureau, 2009b, p. 5). However, schools would be expected to follow closely the three prescribed criteria recommended in the review report (Education Commission, 2005) in selecting an appropriate medium of instruction for their students. Schools would be required to develop a coherent school-based medium-of-instruction strategy as part of their whole-school language policy.

Although the fine-tuning policy paper purports that the 'aim is not to overturn the MOI policy [i.e. to continue with the compulsory Chinese medium instruction policy] recommended by the EC (Education Commission)' (Education Commission, 2005, p. 3); in effect, it deviates drastically from the compulsory Chinese medium instruction policy that has been in place since September 1998. It basically follows the bilingual education model proposed by Poon (2000, 2004a).

Debates on medium-of-instruction policy

As mentioned previously, the debate on medium of instruction started in the late 1960s and passed through two stages during the colonial period. The third stage of the debate erupted immediately after the handover. The issue of medium of instruction has once again become politicized, mainly because of the Hong Kong SAR government's tightening its grip on governance in education (Poon & Wong, 2004) and its subsequent new language policy put forward in September 1997 (Education Department, 1997b). For the patriots, nationalism should come first, and the return of Hong Kong's sovereignty to Mainland China is a golden opportunity for enforcing first language (i.e. Chinese) rather than a foreign language (i.e. English) as the medium of instruction in all secondary schools. The new policymaker is inclined towards the patriotic view, especially when the education scene is taken into consideration – i.e. the English standards of local students continue to decline, the problems of using English as a medium of instruction linger, and the use of mixed code in the classroom has become widespread. The education groups that had been fighting for Chinese medium of instruction for decades join hands with the government. Nonetheless, enormous pressure keeps coming from the business sector, and the demand for better English proficiency has increased as a result of: (a) globalisation, (b) Hong Kong's repositioning in the world economy, and (c) China's strategic planning. Meanwhile, parents and the majority of schools have pledged more English-medium schools, because the number of English-medium schools had shrunken from about 340 to 114 since the compulsory Chinese medium-of-instruction policy was put in place in September 1998. Obviously, since English is an international language, it provides better opportunities for a career trajectory and thus for a brighter future. The reversing of the compulsory Chinese medium-of-instruction policy through the introduction of the 'fine-tuning policy' triggers the opportunity for further political debates.

Language enhancement policy: biliterate/trilingual policy

The language enhancement policy implemented after 1997 is called the biliterate/trilingual policy. The term 'biliterate/trilingual' in the context of Hong Kong means two written languages (i.e. Modern Standard Chinese and English) and three spoken languages (i.e. Cantonese, English and *Putonghua*). The biliterate/trilingual policy was first proposed in the Education Commission Report No. 6 (Education Commission, 1996). No framework and no implementation plan was put forward, not even following the official announcement of the policy in the first Policy Address delivered by Tung Chi Hwa, the first Chief Executive of Hong Kong SAR in October 1997. Initially the biliterate/trilingual policy was proposed as a language-in-education policy to enhance students' language ability and train them to be biliterate and trilingual. The measures taken since 1997 are *ad hoc*. The policy has gradually evolved, having been extended from the education sector into the wider community since 2000. The measures taken by the Hong Kong government to enhance biliteracy and trilingualism in various sectors can be summarised as follows.

Education sector. Billions of dollars have been injected into schools and universities to promote English, Chinese and *Putonghua* since the biliterate/trilingual policy was announced in 1997. For the school sector, four main steps were taken to improve Chinese and English:

(1) an additional HK\$4.2 million (equivalent to US\$0.54 million) library fund was allocated to each school for the purchase of Chinese and English books, teaching materials and teaching aids;
(2) Chinese and English Extensive Reading Schemes were launched to nurture reading culture in the schools;
(3) Multi-Media Language Centres were set up in schools to facilitate language teaching and learning; and
(4) a Language Teaching Support Unit was established in the Education Bureau in 2003 to support language teachers at school in such areas as curriculum development, teaching methods and strategies, reflective teaching, collaborative teaching, and assessment.

Additional measures have been taken to enhance English including:

(1) HK$1.1 billion (equivalent to US$0.14 billion) was added to the Language Fund in 2006 to support English language teaching in secondary schools. A Chinese-medium secondary school was entitled to a total of an additional HK$3 million (equivalent to US$0.39 million) spread over six years whereas an English-medium secondary school received a one-off additional sum of HK$0.5 million (equivalent to US$64,432);

(2) HK$0.6 billion (equivalent to US$0.08 billion) was used to launch a NET (Native English Teachers) scheme in 1998 to enable each secondary school to employ one NET; the scheme was extended to primary schools in 2002;

(3) To ensure the quality of language teachers[14], Benchmark requirements for teachers' language competence in English and *Putonghua* were established in 2000, and the Benchmark Test has been required since 2001. All new English and *Putonghua* teachers are required to meet the respective language benchmark before joining the profession since September 2004, and all serving language teachers must also meet the benchmark since September 2006;

(4) An overseas English immersion programme was made a mandatory component in the full-time Diploma in Education programme for training English teachers in 2004–2005. HK$0.3 billion (equivalent to US$38.65 million) was put aside to subsidize the English major student-teachers' participation in the immersion programme; and

(5) HK$0.3 billion (equivalent to US$38.65 million) was drawn from the Language Fund to establish the Professional Development Incentive Grant Scheme for Language Teachers. Each applicant is to be reimbursed 50% of the tuition fee of an entire programme of study, up to a maximum of HK$30,000 (equivalent to US$3846.15).

For *Putonghua*, HK$30 million (equivalent to US$3.87 million) was initially allocated to schools to train *Putonghua* teachers immediately after the handover in 1997. The school curriculum was revised in 1998 to make *Putonghua* a compulsory subject in primary and secondary schools, and in 2000 *Putonghua* was made an elective subject in the public examination of the HKCEE. Starting from 2001, *Putonghua* teachers are required to take the Benchmark Test; they are also subsidized to enter the *Putonghua* immersion programme. SCOLAR published an 'Action Plan' in 2003 to promote biliteracy and trilingualism, with a special emphasis on the use of *Putonghua* to teach the Chinese language subject in the schools (SCOLAR, 2003). Subsequently, HK$0.2 billion (equivalent to US$25.8 million) was drawn from the Language Fund to do research comparing the use of Cantonese and *Putonghua* as medium of instruction and to investigate the conditions under which schools could implement *Putonghua* as the medium of instruction in the Chinese language subject. The research was completed in 2007. Forty schools in each of the past two school years (30 primary and 10 secondary in 2008–2009, and 34 primary and six secondary in 2009–2010) participated in a longitudinal study trying out the use of *Putonghua* to teach the Chinese language subject. The results of the research testing the effectiveness of the two approaches are yet to be announced.

As for universities, a mandatory pass in both Chinese and English subjects in the HKCEE has become a basic entry requirement. The requirement for English is even higher – i.e. students must obtain a pass in the Use of English paper in the Hong Kong Advanced Level Examination (HKALE) in addition to a pass in the HKCEE. In his first Policy Address in 1997, the former Chief Executive encouraged universities to develop an English Exit Test for their graduates to provide a reference for employers as well as to set standards for universities for the design of their English courses. In response to this policy directive, the University Grants Committee announced in July 2002 that IELTS (International English Language Testing System) would be adopted as the English Exit Test for all universities in Hong Kong starting from the 2002–2003 academic year on a voluntary basis. In addition, all universities will continue to offer Chinese, *Putonghua* and mandatory English language courses to enhance the language proficiency of their students.

Workplace sector. Although the biliterate/trilingual policy was initially confined to the education sector, it has subsequently been adopted in the workplace and in the wider society. The business sector initiated the change because there was great concern about the declining English standards of students in Hong Kong. In 1999, in response to the education reform, a 'Coalition on Education in the Business Sector' was formed by the Federation of Hong Kong Industry and 10 Chambers of Commerce to examine Hong Kong's education system and to propose ways of improving it from the perspective of the business world (Ming Pao Daily, 1999, September 3). The areas of concern were: (a) co-operation between the business sector and the schools, (b) the English standards of those joining the business sector, (c) vocational training and (d) continuing education. The Hong Kong government fully supported the Coalition's initiative, creating a historic government-business sector effort to reform Hong Kong's education system. After incorporating the initiatives of the Coalition, the Hong Kong government officially launched a one-year 'Workplace English Campaign' on 28 February 2000, with the aim of enhancing the English proficiency of employees to meet the increasing demands of Hong Kong as an international centre of commerce, finance and tourism (*South China Morning Post*, 2000, February 29).

The one-year campaign covered three areas of work: (a) the English training subsidy scheme, (b) the business and schools partnership program, and (c) benchmarking. One-off funding of HK$62 million (equivalent to US$7.99 million) was put into the campaign. HK$50 million (equivalent to US$6.44 million) was allocated to the first item – the English training subsidy scheme. Out of the HK$50 million (equivalent to US$6.44 million), HK$40 million (equivalent to US$5.15 million) was used to subsidize employees to take English courses and to sit for the relevant English tests (i.e. half of the fees were to be covered by this scheme and the remainder being the responsibility of the employer). This scheme targeted four types of lower level working people who need English at work – secretaries, clerks, frontline service personnel and receptionists/telephone operators. These four job types were chosen because they account for about one-third of Hong Kong's workforce. The scheme was quite successful, gaining the support of many companies (*South China Morning Post*, 2000, 29 February). The second area supported consisted of a program to promote co-operation between the business sector and the schools, the two areas having seldom had any contact with each other. Some visits by the company directors to the schools were organised so that they could have a deeper understanding of the schools and could at the same time share their business experience with students. Secondary school students also were given an opportunity to visit companies or to receive some training in the companies.

The third area of work of the Workplace English Campaign was to set 'the standards of English in writing and speaking that employees of different industries in Hong Kong should strive to attain' (Workplace English Campaign, 2009, October 30). The language benchmarks were developed based on the performance of about 2000 employees from various industries (e.g. banking, financial services, tourism, retailing, manufacturing, shipping, trading, real estates, IT, communications and medical services) in the pilot tests conducted by four independent bodies:

- the London Chamber of Commerce and Industry Examining Board;
- Pitman Qualifications;
- Test of English for International Communications; and
- the University of Cambridge Local Examination Syndicate.

The benchmarks reflect the level of proficiency in English deemed desirable by employers in six different job types, i.e.:

- low proficiency jobs;
- frontline service personnel jobs;
- receptionist/telephone operator jobs;
- clerical jobs;
- secretarial jobs; and
- executive/administrative/associate professional jobs.

The benchmarks provide four levels of achievement ranging from Level 1 to Level 4, and serve as a reference for employers in recruitment and staff development. SCOLAR continues to steer workplace English benchmarks.

As there has been an increasing concern about the declining English standards of employees and an escalating demand for English proficiency from the workforce, the English requirement to enter some professions has been tightened; for example, the teaching profession, the civil service (Ming Pao Daily, 2001, 16 November; SCOLAR, 2003), the legal profession (Wan, 2001, August 11). While this requirement implies that employees will need to enhance their English proficiency in order to secure a job in the current stringent job market, it does not mean that, as a result of this language policy, English use as a genuine second language in people's daily lives is likely to become widespread in the territory.

Society. With the launching of the Workplace English Campaign in 2000, the biliterate/ trilingual policy has gradually gained momentum and has expanded more widely in society in such domains as the media, public transport services and the community. A *Putonghua* radio channel has been set up on the government service, Radio Hong Kong. SCOLAR also has launched a project entitled 'English in the air' involving commercial TV stations during 2003–2004 and has produced some English TV programmes using English subtitles and related learning materials designed for teenagers; the programmes have successfully attracted some 100,000 viewers. Apart from *Putonghua* and English, SCOLAR has supported both the government and commercial radio and TV stations to produce programmes on the problem of 'lazy articulation' of Cantonese with a view to helping parents correct children's pronunciation of Cantonese. In the public transport service domain, *Putonghua* has been added as the third language in the announcements on the trains and mass transit railway stations. Territory- and community-wide, SCOLAR has sponsored different organisations to provide various activities to promote English and *Putonghua*: e.g. an English Drama Fest, an English Public Speaking Contest, *Putonghua* Month, or a Vocational *Putonghua* Public Speaking Contest.

Effect of biliterate/trilingual policy

While billions of dollars have been invested to promote biliteracy and trilingualism since the handover in 1997, ironically, language standards of students in Hong Kong – particularly those of students of English – have declined still further (Poon, 2009). Employers in the business sector continue to be dissatisfied with the English standards of their employees. For example, in the Business Prospect Survey conducted by the Hong Kong General Chamber of Commerce (2007) the percentage of employers who 'reflected dissatisfaction with language skills' was 65.9% for English and 45.8% for *Putonghua*. The Business Outlook Survey conducted by the American Chamber of Commerce in Hong Kong in 2008 also showed the level of English proficiency was one of the factors 'low on performance ... but high in importance' (see Table 12).

As previously mentioned in the section on *Language policy after the handover*, prominent individuals (e.g. former British Consulate General in Hong Kong Stephen Bradley, see Wong, 2008, March 14) and the 2008 Territory-wide system assessment ('Thirty percent', 2008) also noted the decline in English performance. After the handover, Evans and Green (2007) investigated the actual language use at universities which were presumably English-medium. Their findings revealed that the students' English skills in actual practice were inadequate, and the instruction was basically in Chinese or mixed code rather than in English. These indicators of the continuing decline in English standards show the ineffectiveness of the biliterate/trilingual policy.

Under the biliterate/trilingual policy, significant resources have been allocated to improve the training and qualifications of English teachers, and the percentage of primary and secondary English teachers who possess a first degree in English (6.3%) or a degree plus a diploma in education specialising in English (22.7%) has increased from 2001 (SCOLAR, 2003) to 54.0% and 70.4%, respectively, in September 2008 (statistics provided by Education Bureau in May 2009). These improvements presumably mean that the English proficiency of English teachers has been raised; however, on average only between 40% and 50% of candidates attained the benchmark in the two productive skills in English (i.e. speaking and writing) as shown in Table 13.

Part IV: prospects for a changing language situation

Intergenerational transmission of the majority languages and language shift

The metamorphosis of Hong Kong basically started after the Second World War. The population increased from around 600,000 just after the war to nearly 7 million in 2008, of whom the majority consists of ethnic Chinese who migrated from the southern part of Mainland China and who speak Cantonese, some sub-dialects of Cantonese and other southern Chinese dialects as their first languages. The past six and a half decades have witnessed changes in language transmission and language shift as a consequence of the changing language situation in Hong Kong. In the sections that follow, intergenerational transmission of the three majority languages – Cantonese, English and *Putonghua* – as well as language shift in the younger generations is discussed.

Cantonese

The percentage of Cantonese speakers is increasing, if the 1961 (the earliest record that can be found, see Table 14) and 2006 census figures are compared.

Table 12.   Business Outlook Survey of the American Chamber of Commerce in Hong Kong (2008).

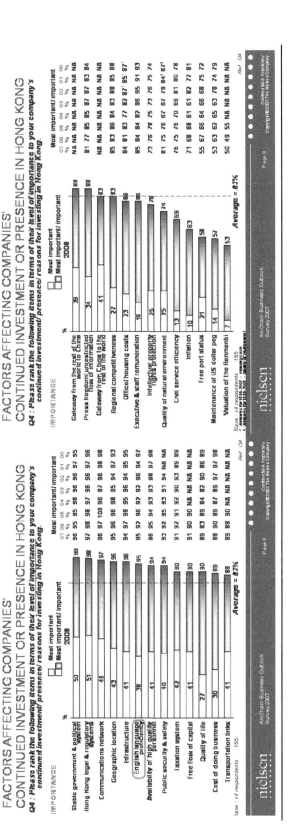

Table 13. Attainment rates on the English Benchmark Test.

Paper	2001	2002	2003 (March)	2003 (Sept)	2004 (March)	2004 (Sept)	2005 (March)	2005 (Sept)	2006	2007	2008	2009
						Attainment rates on the English Benchmark test						
Listening	68.35%	39%	72%	63%	49%	71%	62%	64%	74.3%	80.4%	71.8%	69.5%
Speaking	50.71%	58%	45%	46%	47%	43%	45%	39%	37%	47.7%	62%	50.6%
Reading	85.68%	55%	63%	68%	71%	66%	71%	59%	85.5%	78.8%	81.8%	80.3%
Writing	33.33%	29%	41%	32%	40%	28%	41%	30%	45.9%	39.6%	42%	46.2%
Classroom Language	89.25%	91%	89%	85%	88%	90%	89%	92.5%	92.7%	92.7%	94.6%	97.2%

Note: Taken from Education Bureau, ELPAT results 2001–2009, retrieved Nov 9, 2009 http://www.edb.gov.hk/index.aspx?langno=2&nodeid=1365.

In 1961, the percentage of Cantonese speakers in the total population was 79.02% whereas in 2006 people using Cantonese as their usual language was 90.8%. By comparison, the percentage of speakers of other Cantonese sub-dialects such as Sze Yap (4.36% in 1961/0 in 2006) and Hakka (6.26% in 1961/1.1% in 2006) as well as speakers of such other Chinese dialects as Chiu Chow/Hoklo (6.26% in 1961/ 0.8% in 2006) and Shanghainese (2.65% in 1961/ 0.3% in 2006) has decreased. The substantial decrease in the number of these dialect or sub-dialect users indicates that a language shift has taken place from Cantonese sub-dialects and other Chinese dialects to Cantonese. The old migrants who took root in Hong Kong about 60 years ago can still speak their first languages, while the second generation may understand the dialects/sub-dialects without being able to speak them well, while the third generation finds these dialects/sub-dialects unintelligible. Furthermore, the influx of migrants from Mainland China has continued especially from the period of the famine and the Cultural Revolution in the 1960s to the instigation of the Open Door policy in the 1980s. After 1997, the Mainland authorities issued 150 one-way permits a day to facilitate Mainland residents to re-unite with their families in Hong Kong. These new migrants are mostly from Quangdong province while some come from Fujian (Fukien) province. As Hong Kong culture has become very popular on the Mainland in the past three decades, the new migrants have been ready to assimilate; they learn Hong Kong Cantonese very quickly. Intergenerational transmission of their first languages (i.e. Cantonese sub-dialects or other Chinese dialects) is less likely to occur than it was six decades ago.

Therefore, the ethnic Chinese in Hong Kong as a whole have undergone two language shifts since the end of the Second World War. The first language shift was from Cantonese sub-dialects and other Chinese dialects to Cantonese, as demonstrated in the Census statistics. Although the second language shift from standard Cantonese to Hong Kong Cantonese is not reflected in the Census statistics, it has been occurring since the 1980s as Hong Kong people speak Cantonese using expressions from local popular culture mixed with English borrowings.

Table 14. 1961 Census figures compared with the proportion of the population able to speak Cantonese, English and *Putonghua* as their usual language 1996, 2001 and 2006 (Census and Statistics Department, 1961, 2006a).

Language/dialect	As their usual language				
	1961 No. speakers	1961	1996	2001	2006
Cantonese	2,076,210	79.02	88.7	89.2	90.8
English	31,824	1.21	3.1	3.2	2.8
Putonghua	–	–	1.1	0.9	0.9
Hakka	128,432	4.89	1.2	1.3	1.1
Hoklo	184,537	6.26	–	–	–
Chiu Chau	–	–	1.1	1.0	0.8
Sze Yap	114,484	4.36	–	–	–
Kuo Yu	26,021	0.99	–	–	–
Fukien (including Taiwanese)	–	–	1.9	1.7	1.2
Shanghainese	69,523	6.65	0.5	0.4	0.3
Indonesian (Bahasa Indonesia)	–	–	0.2	0.2	0.1
Filipino (Tagalog)	–	–	0.2	0.2	0.1
Japanese	–	–	0.3	0.2	0.2
Other East Asian languages	877	0.05	–	–	–
Any other language	7225	0.28	–	–	–

English

Table 15 indicates that English used as a primary language has increased from 1.21% in 1961 to 2.8% in 2006; the change in the use of English as an additional language has been even greater, from not being recorded in 1961 to 29.4% in 1991, and then to 41.9% in 2006. Apart from the conventional domains of education, government administration, the judiciary, business and the media, English now is more frequently used in the home than it has been earlier as a result of English spread in Hong Kong. People below the age of 40 brought up in Hong Kong should all be able to speak English with some degree of proficiency. Middle class families (or those having higher socioeconomic status) tend to push their children to learn more English through measures like employing native English speakers as private tutors at home or sending infants (some just a few months old) to playgroups conducted by native English speakers (Sing Tao Daily, 2007, January 4; *'Pre-School' Magazine*, 2006). Older children may be sent to English classes taught by native speakers of English, children may be enrolled in short overseas English immersion programmes during the summer holiday, parents may communicate with their own children in English rather than in Chinese at home, or the Filipino domestic helpers may be required to talk to the children in English. This kind of intergenerational transmission of a second language is more effective, and consequently those children who get such strong family support have a much higher level of English proficiency than others who learn English only at school.

An emerging trend in Hong Kong pertaining to English use at home relates to Chinese residents who emigrated to overseas countries (e.g. to Canada, the USA or Australia) for a number of years and who returned to Hong Kong after 1997. The children of these returnees were born overseas and do not speak Cantonese or cannot speak it well. They study in international schools in Hong Kong. Children communicate with their parents mainly in English, and the parents talk to them either in English or in Cantonese, or using code mixing and code switching, marking a language shift in the second generation of these returnees.

Putonghua

Table 16 shows the percentage of population using *Putonghua* as the primary language has remained quite stable – about 1% since 1961. This evidence means that only a very small percentage of the population speak *Putonghua* as a first language at home. However, *Putonghua* is becoming increasingly important because of the changing political and economic situation in Hong Kong since the early 1990s. Being pragmatic, Hong Kong parents with a middle class background also push their children to learn more *Putonghua* using a variety of measures including: e.g. employing native speakers of *Putonghua* as private tutors at home, sending children to *Putonghua* classes taught by native speakers of

Table 15.   Proportion of population aged 5 and over able to speak English, 1961–2006 (Census and Statistics Department, 1961, 1971, 1981, 1991, 2001, 2006a, 2006b).

	1961	1971	1981	1991	1996	2001	2006
English as the primary language	1.21%	1.04%	No record	2.2%	3.1%	3.2%	2.8%
English as another language	No record	No record	No record	29.4%	34.9%	39.8%	41.9%
Total				31.6%	38.0%	43.0%	44.7%

Table 16. Proportion of population aged 5 and over able to speak *Putonghua*, 1961–2006 (Census and Statistics Department, 1961, 1971, 1981, 1991, 2001, 2006a).

	1961	1971	1981	1991	1996	2001	2006
Putonghua as the primary language	0.99%	No record	No record	1.1%	1.1%	0.9%	0.9%
Putonghua as another language	No record	No record	No record	16.9%	24.2%	33.3%	39.2%
Total				18.0%	25.3%	34.2%	40.1%

Putonghua, or enrolling children in short *Putonghua* immersion programmes held in Beijing during the summer holiday. As a result, children and young people speak the majority language *Putonghua* much better than their parents.

Language attitudes of the younger generation

The 1980s saw the rising status of Hong Kong as an international city of trade and finance. The younger generation born in the 1980s and thereafter have a strong sense of Hong Kong identity. Consequently, their attitude towards Cantonese is very positive, unlike that of their parents or grandparents who experienced language hegemony prior to Chinese being made an official language in 1974. They think Cantonese can express their feelings much better than Modern Standard Chinese – the only accepted form of written Chinese. That is why the use of written Cantonese, which is not acceptable in formal writing, is becoming more popular in media like email, MSN, or Facebook. Written Cantonese gradually has spread to the media; for instance, it is being included in some newspaper articles and magazine articles.

The younger generation's attitude towards English is ambivalent. On the one hand, they are very positive about English because they know English as an international language is very important to their studies and their career development; on the other hand, their motivation to learn English is generally low. They find English difficult, and they do not want to put much effort into learning it.

Unlike their parents, who used to adopt a neutral attitude towards *Putonghua* because *Putonghua* did not have much practical value in Hong Kong prior to the 1990s, the younger generation have a more positive attitude toward *Putonghua*. Because of the economic amalgamation with Mainland China, they realize that one day they may need to work in the Mainland, so it is better to improve their *Putonghua*. Compared with English, *Putonghua* is much easier to learn because *Putonghua* is the spoken form of the sole recognised written Chinese – Modern Standard Chinese, which students learn at school. As a result, the younger generation is able to speak *Putonghua* much better than their parents.

Probable directions for change of language situation over the next generation

It is highly probable that the biliterate/trilingual policy announced in the aftermath of the handover in 1997 will be upheld as a government language policy in the next decade. Accordingly the statuses of written standard Chinese, English, Cantonese and *Putonghua* will remain as they are. Nevertheless, language use is always affected by the changing environment. As a rapidly changing society, Hong Kong is likely to see some changes in its language use, and the following sections outline a probable direction of change for the language situation in Hong Kong over the next generation.

Chinese and English

Chinese and English are the official languages of Hong Kong according to the Basic Law. English will not be replaced as long as Hong Kong remains as a metropolis and an international financial centre. In January 2009 the central government of the PRC announced a long-term development blueprint for economic co-operation and interaction in the Pearl River Delta region among Hong Kong, Macau and Guangdong. The Pearl River Delta is to become 'Globally competitive and the most vigorous area in the Asia-Pacific region by 2020' under the plan (Huang, 2009, January 9). Hong Kong will, therefore, continue to play the role of an international financial centre. To strengthen its competitive edge, in 2008 the Hong Kong government created a Task Force on Economic Challenges and announced on 10 June 2009 its plan to develop six economic areas where Hong Kong enjoys clear advantages, namely educational services, testing and certification, innovation and technology, medical services, cultural and creative industries and environmental industry (Task Force on Economic Challenges, 2009) in addition to its four traditional economic pillars (i.e. finance, tourism, logistics and import/export trade). The goal of educational services is to attract international students, especially students from Mainland China as well as from other Asian countries, to study in Hong Kong schools and universities. English is an obvious attraction to Mainlanders, and using English as a medium of instruction needs to be strengthened. Some universities in Hong Kong have actually changed their medium-of-instruction policy in this regard in recent years in order to attract more international students. Thus the importance of English is not likely to diminish in Hong Kong in the foreseeable future.

Chinese will continue to be the language used by the majority of the population. The written form of Modern Standard Chinese as used in Hong Kong has never been standardised by the Hong Kong government as there is no language planning for Chinese (Poon, 2000, in Part III). Hence different users adhere to the differing norms set by Taiwan or Mainland China, while some people simply follow the common usage in Hong Kong or use a mix of different norms. However, with the handover of sovereignty, a recent trend has developed shifting to the Mainland norm. Firstly, some terminology that has been used in Hong Kong for years has now been changed to conform to the Mainland norm by some users (see examples in Table 17).

Secondly, Mainlanders like to use the abbreviated form of a term, and the media in Hong Kong simply borrow their expressions (see Table 18).

Thirdly, apart from terminology, the translation of foreign names and countries follows Mainland practices. Traditionally, the media in Hong Kong have translated foreign names and countries themselves based on Cantonese pronunciation. After the handover, the Hong Kong SAR government issued some guidelines to the media urging them to adopt the official translation used in Mainland China, based on *Putonghua* pronunciation. That is why some newly changed translated names sound awkward to Hong Kong people – especially the traditional translated names that have been used in Hong Kong for a long time. Table 19 provides some examples.

Finally, the media plays an important role in the spread of translated terms as well as of new terminology. After the handover there was a language policy pertaining to the mention of such various persons and entities as Chinese leaders, state bureaux, state ministers, or state organizations on TV and in radio news (see Table 20).

These examples of changes in terminological usage indicate that some form of standardization pertaining to the use of Chinese is evident in Hong Kong after 1997.

The Chinese script used in Hong Kong remained the same after the handover, i.e. using traditional characters as in Taiwan. However, because of the influx of tourists from the

Table 17.   New Chinese terms used after 1997 in Hong Kong.

Traditional term	New term	Meaning	Remark
質素	素質	Quality	The order of the two characters is reversed.
新聞報導員	主播	News presenter	The characters used are totally different. It is not certain whether the new term is borrowed from Taiwan or the Mainland since they both use this term.
冷氣開放	空調	Air-conditioned	The characters used are totally different. The traditional term is based on Cantonese, which means 'cold air coming out', so it is more direct and lively. The new term is based on *Putonghua*, which means 'adjusting the air'.
改善	優化	Improve	The characters used are totally different.

Mainland, some advertisements, the notices for some shops, the pamphlets and notices issued by the Mass Transit Railway for tourists, etc. are written in simplified characters. At present, there is no call within Hong Kong society to change its script to simplified characters. On the contrary, the movement to resume traditional characters on the Mainland is gaining momentum. A series of TV documentaries entitled 'Chinese characters for five thousand years' highlighting the value of traditional Chinese characters was released on CCTV in Beijing in early 2009, and this move implies that the Beijing government is now seriously considering a reform in Chinese characters (Mao Feng, 2009). If this is the case, Hong Kong will not be under any pressure to change its script.

Table 18.   Abbreviated forms used after 1997 in Hong Kong.

The whole term	The abbreviated form	Meaning	Remark
神州七號	**神七**	The name of the Chinese spacecraft	The name is made up of two noun phrases '神州(China)' and '七號(number seven)', and the first character is taken out from each noun phrase as the abbreviated form.
非典型肺炎	**非典**	SARS (Severe Acute Respiratory Syndrome)	The Chinese term is made up of an adjective phrase '**非典**型' (atypical) and a noun phrase '肺炎' (pneumonia). The first two characters of the adjective phrase are used in the abbreviated form.
八十年代出生人士	八十後	Those born in the 1980s	The Chinese term is made up of: a noun phrase '八十年代' (1980s) + a verb '出生' (born) + a noun '人士' (people). The first two characters of the noun phrase plus an adverb '後' (thereafter) are used in the abbreviated form.

Table 19. New translations of place names used after 1997 in Hong Kong.

Traditional translation	New translation	Meaning	Remark
維珍尼亞州	弗吉尼亞州	State of Virginia (in the USA)	The new translation is totally different from the traditional translation. It is difficult to pronounce the characters in Cantonese.
和路**迪士尼**	華特**迪士尼**	Walt **Disney**	The translation of 'Disney' is the same in both translations. The sound of 'Walt' is more accurately translated in the traditional Cantonese-based translation (和路), but it is not accurately translated in the new translation (華特) *Putonghua*-based pronunciation.
肯亞	肯**尼**亞	Kenya	There are two syllables in 'Kenya' and the sound is accurately translated using Cantonese pronunciation in the traditional translation with two characters only (肯亞). The new *Putonghua*-based translation includes three characters (肯**尼**亞) (which means three sounds and the sound '**尼**' should be omitted). Obviously the name 'Kenya' is mispronounced.
杜拜	**迪**拜	**Du**bai	The sound of the first syllable 'Du' is more accurately translated in the traditional Cantonese-based translation (杜 /dou/) than in the new *Putonghua*-based translation (**迪** /di:/). The pronunciation of 杜 in *Putonghua* is /du:/, so it is in fact more accurate than **迪** /di:/.

Cantonese

If the biliterate/trilingual policy persists, Cantonese will remain as a majority language, used in all domains; i.e. in government administration, in the legislature, in education as a medium of instruction, in business, in the media and the like. Among these domains, education is the most critical because it involves the transmission of knowledge, thinking and culture. Since the handover, there has been a call from time to time for changing the medium of instruction of the Chinese language subject from Cantonese to *Putonghua*.

Table 20. New terms concerning Mainland China used after 1997 in Hong Kong.

Traditional term	New term	Meaning	Remark
中國國務院	國務院	The State Council **of China**	The term 'China' has been removed in the TV and radio news reports after 1997. It means that Hong Kong is part of China, and as in other parts of China when terms like 'The Premier' are mentioned, everybody should know who he is.
中國總理	總理	The Premier **of China**	
中國教育部	教育部	The Ministry of Education **of China**	

If this policy were to be implemented, the status of Cantonese would be seriously affected. Cantonese would be relegated to being a home language, and its development would be blocked, as has been the case in Quangdong where people are no longer able to use Cantonese in academic discourse.

A new direction in the changing use of Cantonese in Hong Kong has occurred among youngsters in recent years. A lot of new terms and expressions called '潮語' (trendy language) have been coined since 2000. They first appeared on the Web, in email, ICQ, MSN, Facebook, and online forums, and they are spreading very quickly. This topic of 'trendy language' even appeared in a Chinese Language paper in the public examination of HKCEE in 2008. It was severely criticized by the candidates and teachers, who were of the opinion that setting a question like this in a public examination would indirectly promote bad language; however, some scholars have argued that such a question would help students to think critically (Sing Tao Daily, 2008, April 27).

The 'trendy language' expressions draw on the pronunciation of some English or Cantonese sounds, the shape of some letters, the mouth or the body, mixing Cantonese sounds and English sounds, or taking part of an English word and mixing it with a Cantonese word (see Table 21).

Although the 'trendy language' is basically used among adolescents and young people, some terms have spread, and even adults are begining to use them; e.g. 'hea', 'level up' and 'O mouth'. The 'trendy language' is a new variant of Hong Kong Cantonese. On the one hand, youngsters are using Cantonese creatively and pushing it to the extreme of 'trendy language'; on the other hand, some scholars and teachers are trying hard to tackle the problem of young people's 'lazy articulation' of Cantonese, as mentioned previously. Sometimes the so-called accurate pronunciation of some Cantonese words is a bit awkward, as in Table 22.

Putonghua

Putonghua will remain the national language. Under the 'One Country Two Systems' policy, the official languages remained the same after the handover, i.e. Chinese and English, but Chinese is understood to consist of Modern Standard Chinese as the written form and Cantonese as the spoken form. Hence *Putonghua* is not stipulated as an official language. There have been calls to replace Cantonese by *Putonghua* as the medium of instruction at school for at least the subject of Chinese language, and the Education Bureau is doing a pilot study on this in some schools. Indeed, the Curriculum Development Council has stated in its Chinese Language curriculum consultation documents that using *Putonghua* to teach Chinese Language is the Council's long-term goal (Curriculum Development Council, 2000), and this policy was endorsed by SCOLAR as follows:

> We thus fully endorse the Curriculum Development Council's long-term vision to use *Putonghua* to teach Chinese Language. Nevertheless, in the light of the inconclusive findings of the local studies conducted so far, we recommend that more studies be conducted. The Government needs to better understand the conditions necessary for schools to make a successful switch to *Putonghua* and prevent possible negative outcomes, before formulating a firm policy and implementation timetable for all schools to adopt *Putonghua* as the MOI for Chinese Language. (SCOLAR, 2003, p. 36)

The Hong Kong government does not dare to push this too hard based on the tough lesson learnt in pushing through the compulsory Chinese medium-of-instruction policy about 10 years ago. As Hong Kong is gradually amalgamating with the Mainland, it is

Table 21. Examples of 'trendy language'.

Trendy language	English translation	Meaning	Example (All the examples are written in Cantonese.)	Remark
O 嘴	O mouth	Cannot help it; shocked; amazed	唔係啩?我哋咁嘅成績入唔到中大? **O 嘴** (Really? With such results like this, I won't be admitted to Chinese University? **O mouth!**)	It plays on the shape of the letter 'O'.
hea	N/A	Fooling around; killing time aimlessly	喂, 你一陣想去邊度 hea 呀? (Hey, where do you want to go and '**hea**'?)	It plays on the sound of Cantonese.
賣飛佛	賣(sell) 飛(fly) 佛(Buddha)	My favourite	我都唔喜唱 K 嘅,跳舞先係賣飛佛 (I don't like to go to Karaoke. Dancing is my favourite.)	It plays on the way the English words 'my favourite' are pronounced in Hong Kong English. The meaning of each of the Chinese characters '賣飛佛' does not count.
升呢	升 (raise) 呢 (a Chinese particle put at the end of a sentence and it has no special meaning)	Level up	我打敗咗隻怪獸後; 勁升呢!! (After beating this beast, I will raise a level.)	This term is originally used in computer games. Instead of pronouncing the full word 'level', the first syllable of the English word 'level' is taken out. Its pronunciation is similar to the Cantonese particle '呢'.

Source: Trendy language. Retrieved on 23 November, 2009, from: http://www.uwants.com/viewthread.php?tid=689308.

Table 22.   Awkward examples of accurate pronunciation of Cantonese.

Popular pronunciation	'Accurate' pronuncation	Meaning
彌(補) /nei/	/mei/	Patch up
糾(正) /dau/	/gau/	Correct
藉(口) /jih/	/jie/	Excuse

likely that *Putonghua* initially will be made a medium of instruction at school for the Chinese language subject, and its use may spread to other subjects in the future. In a similar vein, *Putonghua* is likely to become an official language in future.

Prospect of language planning

Prior to 1997, there was neither status planning nor corpus planning in Hong Kong; as a result, Poon put forward her argument that 'Hong Kong has no language planning, but it does have language policy' (2000, p. 116). The nature of language policy has changed since the changeover of sovereignty. It has been extended from language-in-education policy to language policy encompassing the education sector as well as other sectors such as the workplace, the media and the society at large. SCOLAR's 'Action Plan' (2003) signifies a further change in the policymaker's perception of language use and in the nature of language policy as practised in Hong Kong. Corpus planning was addressed for the very first time in this language policy document and *Putonghua* was formally endorsed as the medium of instruction for the Chinese Language subject as the government's long-term goal. Today, with corpus planning in place (e.g. the government's standardization of translation of names and places used in the media), the status of *Putonghua* has been greatly enhanced and *Putonghua* as a medium of instruction has been introduced. It is anticipated that language policy in Hong Kong will take a further major step into the area of status planning, i.e. to plan the status of *Putonghua* as an official language in Hong Kong. In that case Hong Kong will follow in the footsteps of Mainland China to have language planning.

Conclusion

Hong Kong has come a long way, evolving from a fishing village to an international financial centre over the past 167 years. Its language community started with two separate monolingual groups consisting of local Chinese speaking Cantonese and/or speaking other Chinese dialects (Luke & Richards, 1982), and British colonists speaking British English. Because of language spread and language shift as a result of political, economic and social changes, the monolingual group of Chinese speakers has become trilingual, speaking Cantonese, English and *Putonghua*, whereas the other monolingual group of English speakers has expanded to include native English speakers of such other varieties as Australian English, Indian English, North American English, and Singaporean English. In addition, there is a large group of bilinguals who speaks English and such south Asian languages as Filipino or the languages of Indonesia.

The development of language use in any setting is a natural process, but it can be influenced by the government's language policy and language planning. Hong Kong's prospects for a changing language situation depend on its political and economic development as well as on the PRC's policy. If the 'One Country Two Systems' policy persists and if Hong Kong is able to maintain its status of 'international city' and 'international financial centre', Hong Kong will stand a better chance of continuing to maintain the present language policy – i.e. the biliterate/trilingual policy – and thus maintaining the language situation consisting of Chinese (Modern Standard Chinese as the written form), English (both written and spoken), Cantonese and *Putonghua* as the majority languages. However, if the 'One Country Two Systems' policy should not be maintained and *Putonghua* were to be imposed on Hong Kong as the sole official language as is the situation in the Mainland, replacing Cantonese as the medium of instruction for all subjects at school, Cantonese would be downgraded to exist solely as the home language and the community language, and the standards of English would decline even further.

Acknowledgements

I would like to thank Professor Robert B. Kaplan and Professor Richard Baldauf for giving me this opportunity to write a monograph on the changing language situation of Hong Kong at this level of detail. The plan has been on my mind for some years and it is pleasing to see it realized after working round the clock on it for months. Thanks also go to the manuscript readers, without whose support the monograph would not have appeared in its present form.

Notes

1. Before July 2003, mainlanders could only visit Hong Kong in organised groups. The 'Visit Hong Kong as an individual traveller' policy initially allowed only the residents of five cities in Quangdong to travel to Hong Kong in their personal capacity. The policy has been gradually relaxed to include other parts of China. This policy has helped to double the number of tourists to Hong Kong.
2. Influenced by the Cultural Revolution on the Mainland, the local pro-Bejing leftists launched territory-wide struggles against the colonial government in Hong Kong in 1967. Demonstrations, strikes, and bombs were used as the means for their struggle. The lives of the entire Hong Kong population were affected.
3. A committee to promote Chinese education was set up in 1968. A recommendation on making Chinese an official language was sent to the British Colonial Secretariat in 1970. In order to give impetus to the movement, on 14 June 1970 various groups were united as the 'All Hong Kong Working Party to Promote Chinese as an Official Language'.
4. In 1978, 9-year free, compulsory education was implemented in Hong Kong. Starting from September 2008, free, compulsory education was extended to 12 years.
5. In the context of Hong Kong, if secondary school students' English standards reach the threshold level, that means students have acquired sufficient vocabulary in various fields as well as a variety of sentence structures enabling them to learn all content-based subjects through the medium of English.
6. Statutory holidays refer to the special holidays for labourers in Hong Kong according to the labour law. There are altogether 13 days a year, and they fall on some traditional Chinese festivals and western festivals. Office workers enjoy more public holidays than labourers.
7. The first cohort of students admitted to Senior Secondary 1 started in September 2009. At present both the old and new systems co-exist. The old British system will be completely phased out by September 2012.
8. According to Kloss (1969), 'status planning' focuses on the standing of a language 'alongside other languages or vis-à-vis a national government' whereas 'corpus planning' is concerned with 'the nature of the language itself' (p. 81), i.e. the structure and form of a language.
9. 'Acquisition planning' refers to the planning of acquisition of a language. The issues of medium of instruction, bilingual education, second language acquisition, and foreign language learning and literacy education are related to acquisition planning.
10. The debate pertaining to the declining standards in English started in the early 1980s and has persisted until the present time. An International Panel was invited in 1982 to review the

entire education system in Hong Kong. The Panel commented on two language-in-education issues in its report: 'Our concern is with two principal issues in relation to languages in the Hong Kong education system: quality of language teaching in all schools; and the use of English in Anglo-Chinese secondary schools [i.e. the medium of instruction in English-medium secondary schools] ... This has come about because of widespread concern with the alleged downward spiral in language competence of Hong Kong students. Given the complications of this situation (spoken Cantonese and English; and writing in English and modern Chinese), we are not surprised that, as the participation rate of the school age population has increased [because free, compulsory 9-year education began in 1978], so might the average level of performance have declined' (Llewellyn, Hancock, Kirst, & Roeloffs, 1982, p. 25). In response to the Llewellyn Report, the Education Commission of Hong Kong issued its first report and resolved 'there was general agreement that the emphasis on English in schools could not be reduced ... that the language standard of students in both Chinese and English must be improved; and that the teaching of Chinese and English must be strengthened at all levels' (Education Commission, 1984, p. 33). A number of measures to improve the language standards of students were subsequently taken: e.g. recruiting expatriate lecturers of English for Colleges of Education and local native speakers of English for secondary schools, revising the English and Chinese syllabuses, etc. The Education Commission Reports no. 2 (1986), no. 4 (1990) and no. 6 (1995, 1996) continued to explore measures that could help to raise the language standards of students. However, the declining trend could not be curbed although billions of dollars had been invested in language education. Some indicators of students' further decline in English standards after the handover will be reported subsequently.

11. The majority of secondary schools in Hong Kong used to be English-medium schools. When the compulsory Chinese-medium instruction policy was introduced in September 1998, only approximately 30% of secondary schools were granted an exemption to remain as English-medium schools. The details about changes in medium-of-instruction policy are elaborated subsequently (Poon, 1999).

12. Hong Kong students are categorized into three bands pertaining to their academic achievement, with Band 1 being the top and Band 3 the bottom. Schools claim to be Band 1 if the majority of their intake consists of Band 1 students.

13. There had been two syllabuses for the English Language paper in HKCEE until 2006. Syllabus A was easier than Syllabus B. The two syllabuses merged after 2007.

14. Language benchmarks were promulgated in 2000 because a significant segment of language teachers was not yet adequately subject-trained, since anyone with a university degree could join the teaching profession without any proper teacher training qualifications, and English teachers did not need to have a degree in English. The Benchmark Tests, when they were initially proposed in the Education Commission Report no. 6, were meant to provide an incentive to serving language teachers. Nonetheless, when the policy was translated into practice by the Advisory Committee on Teacher Education and Qualifications (ACTEQ) Task Force, the Benchmark Tests carried with them an implication of penalizing serving language teachers, who felt that their teaching career would be threatened if they failed the tests. That explained why, when the first live Benchmark Tests for both English and *Putonghua* teachers were announced, they were strongly resisted by the teaching profession and 6000 teachers took to the street in June 2000. Similar to the medium- (space)of-instruction policy, the language benchmark policy was politicized and rendered more than an educational issue. Subsequently the Hong Kong government made some concessions and granted exemptions to serving English teachers and to those new teachers who were English majors.

References

Appel, R., & Muysken, P. (1987). *Language contact and bilingualism*. London: Edward Arnold.

Axler, M., Yang, A., & Stevens, T. (1998). Current language attitudes of Hong Kong Chinese adolescents and young adults. In M.C. Pennington (Ed.), *Language in Hong Kong at century's end* (pp. 329–338). Hong Kong University Press.

Baker, C. (2006). *Foundations of bilingual education and bilingualism* (4th ed.). Clevedon, UK: Multilingual Matters.

Baldauf, R.B., Jr. (1990). Language planning and education. In R.B. Baldauf, Jr. & A. Luke (Eds.), *Language planning and education in Australasia and the South Pacific* (pp. 14–24). Clevedon, UK: Multilingual Matters.

Baldauf, R.B., Jr. (1994). 'unplanned' language policy and planning. *Annual Review of Applied Linguistics, 14*(1), 82–89.

Board of Education. (1973). *Report of the Board of Education on the proposed expansion of secondary school education over the next decade*. Hong Kong: Government Printer.

Board of Education. (1974). *Secondary education in Hong Kong over the next decade*. Hong Kong: Government Printer.

Bolton, K., & Kwok, H. (1990). The dynamics of the Hong Kong accent: Social identity and sociolinguistic description. *Journal of Asian Pacific Communication, 1*(1), 47–172.

Census and Statistics Department. (1961). *Report of the census 1961* (Vol. II). Hong Kong: Government Printer.

Census and Statistics Department. (1971). *Report of the census 1971*. Hong Kong: Government Printer.

Census and Statistics Department. (1981). *Report of the census 1981*. Hong Kong: Government Printer.

Census and Statistics Department. (1991). *Hong Kong 1991 population census summary results*. Hong Kong: Government Printer.

Census and Statistics Department. (May 30, 2000). Returnees to Hong Kong. Retrieved June 24, 2009, from http://www.censtatd.gov.hk/freedownload.jsp?file=publication/stat_report/social_data/B11301252000XXXXB0100.pdf&title=Social+Data+Collected+via+the+General+Household+Survey+%3a+Special+Topics+Report+-+Report+No.25&issue=-&lang=1&c=1

Census and Statistics Department. (2001). Proportion of the population able to speak Cantonese, English and *Putonghua*. Retrieved July 8, 2009, from http://www.censtatd.gov.hk/freedownload.jsp?file=publication/stat_report/population/B11200182001XXXXB0100.pdf&title=Hong+Kong+2001+Population+Census+-+Summary+Results&issue=-&lang=1&c=1

Census and Statistics Department. (2004). The Hong Kong population situation and its development trend for the number of emigration from 1981 to 2003. Retrieved June 24, 2009, from http://www.censtatd.gov.hk/FileManager/EN/Content_248/the_hong_kong_population_situation_and_its_development_trend.pdf

Census and Statistics Department. (2006a). Population by-census office. Proportion of the population able to speak Cantonese, English and *Putonghua*. Retrieved February 22, 2007, from http://www.bycensus2006.gov.hk/FileManager/EN/Content_962/06bc_summary_results.pdf

Census and Statistics Department. (2006b). Population by-census office. Population by nationality. Retrieved February 22, 2007, from http://www.bycensus2006.gov.hk/FileManager/EN/Content_962/06bc_summary_results.pdf

Census and Statistics Department. (2009a). Retrieved June 13, 2009, from http://www.censtatd.gov.hk/hong_kong_statistics/statistics_by_subject/index_tc.jsp?subjectID=1&charsetID=2&displayMode=T

Census and Statistics Department. (May 15, 2009b). Gross domestic product. Retrieved June 24, 2009, from http://www.censtatd.gov.hk/hong_kong_statistics/statisticaltables/index.jsp?tableID=030

Chao, Y.R. (1947). *Cantonese primer*. Cambridge, MA: The Harvard-Yenching Institute, Harvard University Press.

Cheng, N.L. (1979). *Issues in language of instruction in Hong Kong*. Hong Kong: The Cosmos.

Cheng, N.L., Shek, K.C., Tse, K.K., & Wong, S.L. (1979). [1973]. At what cost? – instruction through the English medium in Hong Kong schools. In N.L. Cheng (Ed.), *Issues in language of instruction in Hong Kong* (pp. 47–70). Hong Kong: Cosmos. [The report was originally published in 1973 and some chapters were included in Cheng's book published in 1979.].

Cooper, R. (1989). *Language planning and social change*. Cambridge University Press.

Curriculum Development Council. (1983). *Syllabuses for secondary schools: Syllabus for English (Forms I–V)*. Hong Kong: Government Printer.

Curriculum Development Council. (1999). *Syllabuses for secondary schools: English Language (Secondary 1–5)*. Hong Kong: Government Printer.

Curriculum Development Council. (2000). *Learning to learn: Key Learning Area Chinese Language Education. Consultation document*. Hong Kong: Printing Department.

Curriculum Development Council. (2001). *Learning to learn: Lifelong learning and whole-person development*. Hong Kong: Printing Department.

Curriculum Development Council. (2002). *English Language Education KLA curriculum guide (P1–S3)*. Hong Kong: Printing Department.

Education Bureau. (2009a). Speech of secretary for education delivered to the parent-teacher associations on 'fine-tuning policy' on 5 January 2009. Retrieved June 24, 2009, from http://www.edb.gov.hk/index.aspx?nodeID=133&langno=2&UID=103287

Education Bureau. (2009b). Legislative Council brief: Fine-tuning the medium of instruction for secondary schools delivered on 26 May 2009. Retrieved September 26, 2009, from http://www.legco.gov.hk/yr08-09/english/panels/ed/papers/ed0529-edbecp4802n-e.pdf

Education Bureau. (2001–2009). ELPAT results 2001–2009. Retrieved November 9, 2009, from http://www.edb.gov.hk/index.aspx?langno=2&nodeid=1365

Education Commission. (1984). *Education Commission Report no. 1*. Hong Kong: Government Printer.

Education Commission. (1986). *Education Commission Report no. 2*. Hong Kong: Government Printer.

Education Commission. (1988). *Education Commission Report no. 3*. Hong Kong: Government Printer.

Education Commission. (1990). *Education Commission Report no. 4*. Hong Kong: Government Printer.

Education Commission. (1994). *Report of the working group on language proficiency*. Hong Kong: Government Printer.

Education Commission. (1995). *Draft Education Commission Report no. 6*. Hong Kong: Government Printer.

Education Commission. (1996). *Education Commission Report no. 6*. Hong Kong: Government Printer.

Education Commission. (2005). *Report on review of medium of instruction for secondary schools and secondary school places allocation*. Hong Kong: Government Printer.

Education Department. (1989). *Report of the working group set up to review language improvement measures*. Hong Kong: Government Printer.

Education Department. (1997a). *Arrangements for firm guidance on secondary schools' medium of instruction*, Consultation paper. Hong Kong: Government Printer.

Education Department. (1997b). *Medium-of-instruction guidance for secondary schools*. Hong Kong: Government Printer.

Elliott, M. (2008, January 28). A tale of three cities. *Time*, 30–33.

Evans, S., & Green, C. (2007). Why EAP is necessary: A survey of Hong Kong tertiary students. *Journal of English for Academic Purposes, 6*(1), 3–17.

Evans, S., Jones, R., Rusmin, R.S., & Cheung, O.L. (1998). Three languages: One future. In M.C. Pennington (Ed.), *Language in Hong Kong at century's end* (pp. 391–415). Hong Kong: Hong Kong University Press.

Ferguson, C. (1959). Diglossia. *Word, 15*(3), 325–340.

Fishman, J.A. (1971). *Advances in sociology of language*. The Hague, the Netherlands: Mouton.

Flowerdew, J., Li, D., & Miller, L. (1998). Attitudes towards English and Cantonese among Hong Kong Chinese university lecturers. *TESOL Quarterly, 32*(2), 201–231.

Fu, G.S. (1975). A Hong Kong perspective: English language learning and the Chinese student (Dissertation, University of Michigan), *Comparative Education Series 28*.

Fu, G.S. (1987). The Hong Kong bilingual. In R. Lord & H.N.L. Cheng (Eds.), *Language education in Hong Kong* (pp. 27–50). Hong Kong: The Chinese University Press.

Gardner, R.C. (2001). Integrative motivation and second language acquisition. In Z. Dörnyei & R. Schmidt (Eds.), *Motivation and second language acquisition* (pp. 1–20). Honolulu: University of Hawaii Press.

Gardner, R.C., & Lambert, W.E. (1959). Motivational variables in second language acquisition. *Canadian Journal of Psychology*, *13*(4), 266–272.

Giles, H., & Byrne, J. (1982). An intergroup approach to second language acquisition. *Journal of Multilingual and Multicultural Development*, *3*(1), 17–40.

HKPISA. (2000). The first HKPISA report. Hong Kong: HKPISA Centre, The Chinese University of Hong Kong. Retrieved July 11, 2009, from http://www.fed.cuhk.edu.hk/~hkpisa/events/2000/files/HKPISA2000_Summary.pdf

HKPISA. (2003). The second HKPISA report. Hong Kong: HKPISA Centre, The Chinese University of Hong Kong. Retrieved July 11, 2009, from http://www.fed.cuhk.edu.hk/~hkpisa/events/2003/files/HKPISA2003_Summary.pdf

HKPISA. (2006). The third HKPISA report. Hong Kong: HKPISA Centre, The Chinese University of Hong Kong. Retrieved July 11, 2009, from http://www.fed.cuhk.edu.hk/~hkpisa/events/2006/files/HKPISA2006_Summary.pdf

Home Affairs Bureau. (2000). *Sample survey of the characteristics of the ethnic minorities in Hong Kong: Main findings*, Paper No. CB(2)590/00-01(01), Annex B, Table 6.

Hong Kong Examination and Assessment Authority. (2009). HKCEE statistics of entries and results over the years. Retrieved Nov 13, 2009, from http://www.hkeaa.edu.hk/tc/HKCEE/Exam_Report/Examination_Statistics/

Hong Kong Government. (1974). Official languages ordinance [no. 10/74]. Hong Kong: Government Printer.

Hong Kong Government. (1981). *The Hong Kong education system*. Hong Kong: Government Printer.

Hong Kong Government. (2008). *Hong Kong 2007*. Hong Kong: Government Printer.

Hong Kong Tourism Board. (2009). A statistical review of Hong Kong tourism 2008: Number of visitors to Hong Kong (p. 9). Retrieved July 24, 2009, from http://partnernet.hktb.com/b5/index.html

Huang, C. (2009, January 9). *South China Morning Post. Beijing reveals blueprint for delta's economic growth*, p. EDUT4.

Hughes, R. (1976). *Borrowed place, borrowed time: Hong Kong and its many faces* (2nd ed.). London: Andre Deutsch.

Hyland, K. (1997). Language attitudes at the handover: Communication and identity in 1997 Hong Kong. *English World-Wide*, *18*(2), 191–210.

Johnson, R.K. (1983). Bilingual switching strategies: A study of the modes of teacher-talk in bilingual secondary school classrooms in Hong Kong. *Language Learning and Communication*, *2*(3), 267–285.

Johnson, R.K. (1994). Language policy and planning in Hong Kong. *Annual Review of Applied Linguistics*, *14*(1), 177–199. 1993/1994.

Johnson, R.K., & Lee, P.M. (1987). Modes of instruction: Teaching strategies and student responses. In R. Lord & H.N.L. Cheng (Eds.), *Language education in Hong Kong* (pp. 99–121). Hong Kong: The Chinese University Press.

Kaplan, R.B. (1990). Introduction: Language planning in theory and practice. In R.B. Baldauf, Jr. & A. Luke (Eds.), *Language planning and education in Australasia and the South Pacific* (pp. 3–13). Clevedon, UK: Multilingual Matters.

Krashen, S.D. (1982). *Principles and practice in second language acquisition*. Oxford, UK: Pergamon Press.

Krashen, S.D., & Terrell, T.D. (1983). *The natural approach: Language acquisition in the classroom*. Oxford, UK: Pergamon Press.

Lai, E.F.K. (1999). Motivation to learn English in Hong Kong. *Language, Culture and Curriculum*, *12*(3), 280–284.

Lai, M.L. (2009). 'I Love Cantonese but I want English' – a qualitative account of Hong Kong students' language attitudes. *The Asia-Pacific Education Researcher*, *18*(1), 79–92.

Lam, S.F., Lau, I.Y.M., Chiu, C.Y., & Hong, Y.Y. (2007). *Executive summary of surveys on 'social identities of Hong Kong adolescents: Inter-group perceptions and orientations in political transition'*. Department of Psychology, The University of Hong Kong.

Lin, A.M.Y. (1991). *Teaching in two tongues: Language alternation in foreign language classrooms. Research Report no. 3*. Department of English, City University of Hong Kong.

Lin, A.M.K. (2008). Code-switching in the classroom: Research paradigms and approaches. In K.A. King & N.H. Hornberger (Eds.), *Encyclopedia of language and education, research methods in language and education* (Vol. 10, 2nd ed., pp. 273–286). New York: Springer.

Lin, A.M.Y., & Detaramani, C. (1998). By carrot and by rod: Extrinsic motivation and English attainment of tertiary students in Hong Kong. In M.C. Pennington (Ed.), *Language in Hong Kong at century's end* (pp. 285–301). Hong Kong University Press.

Llewellyn, Sir J., Hancock, G., Kirst, M., & Roeloffs, K. (1982). *A perspective on education in Hong Kong: Report by a visiting panel*. Hong Kong: Government Printer.

Lord, R. (1987). Language policy and planning in Hong Kong: Past, present and (especially) future. In R. Lord & H.N.L. Cheng (Eds.), *Language education in Hong Kong* (pp. 3–24). Hong Kong: The Chinese University Press.

Low, W.W.M., & Lu, D. (2006). Persistent use of mixed code: An exploration of its functions in Hong Kong schools. *International Journal of Bilingual Education and Bilingualism*, *9*(2), 181–204.

Lu, D., Li, Y., & Huang, Y.Y. (2004). Unpacking learner factors in L2 learning: A comparative study of students from Hong Kong and Mainland China. *Asian Journal of English Language Teaching*, *14*(1), 23–43.

Luke, K.K., & Richards, J.C. (1982). English in Hong Kong: Functions and status. *English World Wide*, *3*(1), 47–64.

Mao Feng. (2009). Chinese characters as used in Japanese reflects the debate on both sides of the strait about whether to use the traditional characters or the simplified characters. *The International Chinese Weekly*, June 28 (In Chinese).

Meisel, J.M. (2004). The bilingual child. In T.K. Bhatia & W.C. Ritchie (Eds.), *The handbook of bilingualism* (pp. 91–113). Malden, MA: Blackwell.

Ming Pao Daily. (1997, May 3). Publicity of mother tongue teaching can hardly change parents' minds.

Ming Pao Daily. (1997, May 30). Hong Kong federation of education workers supports mother tongue teaching.

Ming Pao Daily. (1999, September 3). Company directors visit schools.

Ming Pao Daily. (2001, November 16). Officials must use English at meetings.

Ming Pao Daily. (2008, November 1). Thirty percent of S3 students failed in basic English, p. A7.

Muysken, P. (2000). *Bilingual speech: A typology of code-mixing*. Cambridge, UK: Cambridge University Press.

Myers-Scotton, C. (1997). Code-switching. In F. Coulmas (Ed.), *The handbook of sociolinguistics* (pp. 217–237). Malden, MA: Blackwell.

Neustupný, J.V. (1968). Some general aspects of 'language' problems and 'language' policy in developing societies. In J.A. Fishman, C.A. Ferguson, & J. Das Gupta (Eds.), *Language problems of developing nations* (pp. 3–16). New York: Wiley.

Neustupný, J.V. (1974[1970]). Basic types of treatment of language problems. In J.A. Fishman (Ed.), *Advances in language planning* (pp. 37–48). (1). The Hague, The Netherlands: Mouton. First printed in *Linguistic Communications*, 1970.

Neustupný, J.V. (1983). Towards a paradigm for language planning. *Language Planning Newsletter*, *9*(4), 1–4.

Neustupný, J.V., & Nekvapil, J. (2006). Language management in the Czech Republic. In R.B. Baldauf, Jr. & R.B. Kaplan (Eds.), *Language planning and policy in Europe, Vol. 2: The Czech Republic, the European Union and Northern Ireland* (pp. 16–201). Clevedon, UK: Multilingual Matters.

Official Languages Ordinance. (1997, June 30). Chapter 5, Section 3. Retrieved 10 July 2008, from http://www.info.gov.hk/basic_law/facts/c-index.htm

Pennington, M.C. (1995). Pattern and variation in use of two languages in the Hong Kong secondary English class. *RELC Journal*, *26*(2), 80–105.

Pennington, M.C., Balla, J., Detaramani, C., Poon, A.Y.K., & Tam, F. (1992). *Towards a model of language choice among Hong Kong tertiary students: A preliminary analysis*. Research Report no. 18. City Polytechnic of Hong Kong.

Pennington, M.C., & Yue, F. (1994). English and Chinese in Hong Kong: Pre-1997 language attitudes. *World Englishes*, *13*(1), 1–20.

Phillipson, R. (1992). *Linguistic imperialism*. Oxford, UK: Oxford University Press.

Pierson, H.D., Fu, G.S., & Lee, S.Y. (1980). An analysis of the relationship between langauge atti-tudes and English attaining of secondary school students in Hong Kong. *Language Learning*, *30*(2), 289–316.

Poon, A.Y.K. (1999). Chinese medium instruction policy and its impact on English learning in post-1997 Hong Kong. *International Journal of Bilingual Education and Bilingualism*, *2*(2), 131–146.

Poon, A.Y.K. (2000). *Medium of instruction in Hong Kong: Policy and Practice*. Lanham, MD: University Press of America.

Poon, A.Y.K. (2001, 15 June). Don't learn English using the Chinese way. *Ming Pao*, p. A25.

Poon, A.Y.K. (2004a). Language policy of Hong Kong: Its impact on language education and language use in post-handover Hong Kong. *Journal of Taiwan Normal University: Humanities & Sciences*, *49*(1), 53–74.

Poon, A.Y.K. (2004b). Action research: A study on using narratives to teach L2 writing in a Hong Kong primary school. In G. Rijlaarsdam, H. Van den Bergh, & M. Couzijn (Eds.), *Studies in writing, 14, Effective learning and teaching of writing* (2nd ed., pp. 305–332). Dordrecht, the Netherlands: Kluwer Academic Publishers.

Poon, A.Y.K. (2009). Reforming medium of instruction in Hong Kong: Its impact on learning. In C.H. Ng & P.D. Renshaw (Eds.), *Reforming learning: Issues, concepts and practice in the Asian-Pacific Region* (pp. 199–232). Dordrecht, the Netherlands: Springer. [*Education in the Asia-Pacific Region: Issues, concerns and prospects*, Vol. 5].

Poon, A.Y.K., & Wong, Y.C. (2004). Governance in education in Hong Kong: A decentralizing or a centralizing path? In Y.C. Wong (Ed.), *One country two systems in crisis: Hong Kong's trans-formation since the handover* (pp. 137–166). Lanham, MD: Lexington Books.

Poon, A.Y.K., & Wong, Y.C. (2008). Education reform in Hong Kong: Through-road model and its societal consequences. *International Review of Education*, *54*(1), 33–55.

Poon, S.K. (1979). An investigation of the language difficulties experienced by Hong Kong primary school leavers in learning mathematics through the medium of English. In N.L. Cheng (Ed.), *Issues in language of instruction in Hong Kong*. Hong Kong: Cosmos.

Poon, W. (1988). Language ability, motivation and learning habits of business students. In V. Bickley (Ed.), *Language teaching and learning styles within and across cultures* (pp. 100–111). Hong Kong: Institute of Language in Education.

'Pre-School' Magazine. (2006). Helping children to learn phonics. *Vol. 49*.

Qiang, N., & Wolff, M. (2003). The Chinglish syndrome: Do recent developments endanger the language policy of China? *English Today*, *19*(4), 30–35.

Ren, D., Zhou, M., Wong, J., & So, P. (2009, March 26). Beijing backs Shanghai as finance hub. *South China Morning Post*, p. EDT1.

Rubin, J. (1984). Bilingual education and language planning. In C. Kennedy (Ed.), *Language plan-ning and language education* (pp. 4–16). London: George Allen & Unwin.

Schumann, J. (1978). The acculturation model for second language acquisition. In R. Gingras (Ed.), *Second language acquisition and foreign language teaching*. Arlington, VA: Center for Applied Linguistics.

SCOLAR. (2003). *Action plan to raise language standards in Hong Kong*. Hong Kong: SCOLAR, Education and Manpower Bureau.

Shek, C.K.W., Johnson, R.K., & Law, E.H.F. (1991). Survey of the language policy and practice in 193 Hong Kong secondary schools. *New Horizon, 32,* 1–10.

Sing Tao Daily. (1997, May 3). Many secondary schools were perplexed.

Sing Tao Daily. (2007, January 4). Infants learning foreign languages in playgroups.

Sing Tao Daily. (2008, April 27). *Trendy language fooled candidates*, p. A1.

So, D.W.C. (1989). Implementing mother-tongue education amidst societal transition from diglossia to triglossia in Hong Kong. *Language and Education*, *3*(1), 29–44.

South China Morning Post. (1997, September 19). Students voice fear on switch to Chinese.

South China Morning Post. (2000, February 29). 120 firms sign for English scheme.

Stone, R. (1994). English in Hong Kong: Word knowledge skills of science undergraduates. *Hong Kong Journal of Applied Linguistics*, *4*(2), 93–100.

Task Force on Economic Challenges. (2009). Press release, June 10, 2009.

The American Chamber of Commerce in Hong Kong. (2008). Business outlook survey. Retrieved November 14, 2009, from http://www.amcham.org.hk/hongkong/business_outlook_survey2008/2008_Report_FINAL.pdf

The Basic Law of the HKSAR. (1997, July 1). Retrieved 10 July 2008, from http://www.info.gov.hk/basic_law/facts/c-index.htm

The Hong Kong General Chamber of Commerce. (2007). Chamber press release, November 15, 2007.

The map of Hong Kong. Retrieved June 24, 2009, from http://www.wordtravels.com/Travelguide/Countries/China/Map

Tinker Sachs, G., & Mahon, T. (1997). Reading in English as a foreign language: Primary students' oral reading behaviour and comprehension. *Perspectives*, *9*(2), 78–109.

Trade and Industry Department. (2008). CEPA. Retrieved August 4, 2008, from http://www.tid.gov.hk/english/cepa/cepa_overview.html

Trendy language. Retrieved on 23 November, 2009, from: http://www.uwants.com/viewthread.php?tid=689308

Tsang, W.K. (2002). Evaluation on the implementation of the medium-of-instruction guidance for secondary schools report. Hong Kong: Hong Kong Institute of Educational Research, The Chinese University of Hong Kong.

Tsang, W.K. (2004). Further evaluation on the implementation of the medium-of-instruction guidance for secondary schools final report. Hong Kong Institute of Educational Research, The Chinese University of Hong Kong.

Tsang, W.K. (2008). *The effect of medium-of-instruction policy on education advancement.* Hong Kong: The Chinese University of Hong Kong.

Tung, P., Lam, R., & Tsang, W.K. (1997). English as a medium of instruction in post-1997 Hong Kong: What students, teachers, and parents think. *Journal of Pragmatics*, *28*(4), 441–459.

UNESCO. (2009). Human development report 2007/2008. Retrieved 10 July 2009, from http://hdr.undp.org/en/

Walters, S., & Balla, J. (1998). Medium of instruction: Policy and reality at one Hong Kong tertiary institution. In M.C. Pennington (Ed.), *Language in Hong Kong at century's end* (pp. 365–389). Hong Kong: Hong Kong University Press.

Wan, C. (2001, August 11). Law students face tough English requirements. *South China Morning Post*.

Wen Wei Po Daily. (1997, March 25). Many educators support the 'firm guidance'.

Wong, A. (2008, March 14). Hong Kong is falling short of greatness. *South China Morning Post*, p. EDT4.

Workplace English Campaign. (2009, October 30). Retrieved 30 October 2009, from http://www.english.gov.hk/eng/html/wec_hkweb_hkweb.htm

Yang, A., & Lau, L. (2003). Student attitudes to the learning of English at secondary and tertiary levels. *System*, *31*(1), 107–123.

Zhao, S.H. (2008). Chinese character modernization in the digital era: A historical perspective. In R.B. Kaplan & R.B. Baldauf, Jr. (Eds.), *Language Planning and Policy in Asia, Vol.1: Japan Nepal, Taiwan and Chinese Characters* (pp. 38–101). Bristol, UK: Multilingual Matters.

The language situation in Timor-Leste

Kerry Taylor-Leech

Division of Linguistics, Macquarie University, Sydney, New South Wales, Australia

Timor-Leste celebrated its formal political independence on 20th May 2002. The National Constitution of the new nation declared the endogenous lingua franca (Tetum) and the former colonial language (Portuguese) to be co-official. The remaining local languages were given the status of national languages. Indonesian and English were designated as working languages 'for as long as is deemed necessary'. In this monograph, I consider the origins and implications of these constitutional provisions. The paper consists of five parts.

1. A social and economic profile of the polity. This section also discusses migration, communications and the media in relation to language policy and practice.
2. A language profile of the country, followed by a discussion of diglossia, multi-lingualism, literacy and official language choice.
3. An account of the sociolinguistic consequences of language contact and an historical analysis of social policies and practices that have shaped the habitus.
4. A discussion and analysis of current language policy development in terms of goals, motives and orientations.
5. An assessment of the prospects for language maintenance with special reference to policy outcomes and options.

I advocate a rights-oriented approach to language management, arguing that in the absence of such an approach, *ad hoc* power relationships between languages will continue to dominate social discourse and language politics.

Keywords: Timor Leste; language policy; language practices; literacy; multilingualism; diglossia; official languages; national languages

Introduction

The East Timorese people have endured a long history of colonialism, underdevelopment, conflict, human rights abuse, civil unrest and dramatic political change. Although independence was originally declared in 1975, it was formally celebrated on 20 May 2002 when the United Nations (hereinafter the UN) handed over administration to the independent state after over four centuries of Portuguese colonialism and 24 years of occupation by Indonesia. The composition of the present population, the language profile of the country, language choice and patterns of language use, maintenance and spread can only be fully understood in the light of these experiences. For the purposes of analysis, I have turned to Bourdieu (1991), whose theories provide insights into the relationship between language policy, language use and power. Bourdieu's notions of *habitus* and *symbolic violence* identify the relations of power in the formation of language dispositions and the construction of identity. Following Freeland and Patrick (2004, p. 12), I define habitus as a set of embodied dispositions inculcated through socialisation into particular groups and milieus. Although these dispositions do not determine behaviour, they predispose people to respond in certain ways to familiar and unfamiliar situations. The term linguistic habitus embraces one important set of dispositions; as Freeland and Patrick (p. 12) point out, the term encompasses not only language structure but also the pragmatics of linguistic interaction. I use the Bourdieurian notion of symbolic violence to account for the kinds of symbolic and ideological domination used to legitimise and reinforce the prevailing social and linguistic order. Sometimes accompanying overt forms of violence, symbolic violence sustains domination by both institutional and interpersonal means (Thompson, 1991, p. 24). While Bourdieu's theories focus strongly on forms of state power, the concept of core cultural value (Smolicz, 1991) helps to explain why individuals and groups attach different values to the languages with which they come into contact. The notion of core value is based on the assumption that social groups subscribe to sets of cultural values considered essential to their existence. Where language has acquired the status of a core cultural value, it is elevated to a symbol of the survival of the group and the preservation of its heritage (Smolicz, 1991, p. 76). I have also made use of Cooper's (1989) accounting scheme, Skutnabb-Kangas' (2000) linguistic human rights framework and Ruiz' (1995) language policy orientations, in order to analyse the ideological tendencies in East Timorese language policy development. Each of these three frameworks is explained at the point where it is discussed in this article.

In this monograph, I draw on information from government bodies and academic research, aid agencies and non-government organisations (NGOs), journalistic accounts and my own academic research (Taylor-Leech, 2007). I have divided this monograph into five parts. Part I provides some social and economic background information about the polity. Part I also discusses migration, communication and the media in relation to language policy and practice. Part II presents a language profile of Timor-Leste supported by figures derived and computed from the Population and Housing Census conducted by the East Timorese government in collaboration with the United Nations Population Fund in 2004. Part III discusses the legacies of colonial and post-colonial policy, planning and practice with regard to language use and literacy. This diachronic account highlights the social, political and cultural variables that have combined and interacted to shape the habitus (Bourdieu, 1991). I aim to show how language ideologies have not just determined language use but have also played a key role in forming national and social identity.

Part IV presents a discussion and analysis of contemporary language policy development. Part V concludes this monograph by speculating on the prospects for language maintenance in light of the present language policy trajectory.

Part I: social and economic profile of the polity

Located on the easternmost tip of the Archipelago of the Lesser Sunda Islands (Figure 1), with a land mass of approximately 14,900 km^2 (Census Atlas, 2006, p. 16), the territory of Timor-Leste comprises the eastern half of the island of Timor; the Oecussi (Ambeno) exclave on the northwest portion of the island of Timor and the islands of Ataúro to the north and Jaco to the east (Figure 2). The country is a former Portuguese colony; it shares a border with Indonesia and it is a close neighbour of Australia. The sociopolitical

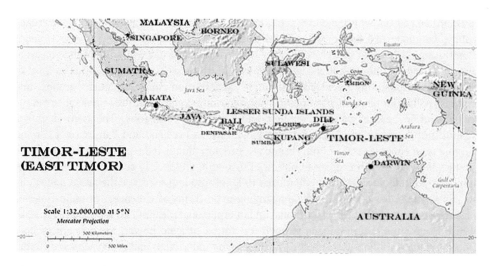

Figure 1. Map adapted from CIA Factbook (https://www.cia.gov/library/publications/the-world-factbook/).

agendas and linguistic ideologies of these three polities have shaped the course of modern East Timorese history.

Although Timor-Leste is often described as a small country, it is relatively large in size and population compared with some of the smaller Southeast Asian and Pacific maritime nations. Timor-Leste has a greater land mass and population than Brunei, Vanuatu and Samoa, for example. However, it is tiny in comparison to its powerful former occupier, Indonesia (Table 1).

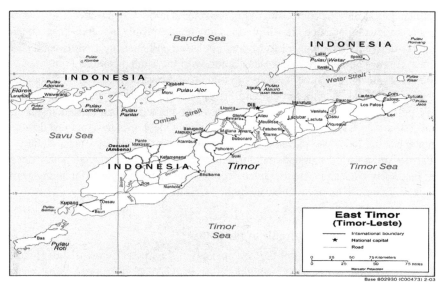

Figure 2. Map of Timor-Leste including the exclave of Oecussi, the East Timorese islands of Ataúro and Jaco and the Indonesian islands (*pulau*) of Roti, Semau, Flores, Pantar, Alor, Wetar and Kisar (United States Central Intelligence Agency, 2003). Map courtesy of the University of Texas Libraries, National University of Texas at Austin.

Table 1.   Comparisons of land area and population (CIA, 2008).

Nation	Land area (km^2)	Population
Timor-Leste	14,919	1,108,777
Samoa	2,944	217,083
Brunei	5,770	381,371
Vanuatu	12,200	215,446
Indonesia	1,919,440	234,693,997

Administratively, the country has recently been divided into 5 regions and 13 districts, 65 subdistricts and 442 *sucos* (*large settlements or clusters of villages*). In 2004, the population was 923,198 (Direcção Nacional de Estatística, 2006, p. 9), and in 2008, it was estimated to be 1,108,777 (CIA, 2008). The population is expanding rapidly. Estimated population growth is 3.2% or 31,000 people per annum, an average of 85 persons a day. If this annual growth continues, the population will double in about 22 years (Census Atlas, 2006, p. 29). The population is young, with an average age of 21. According to the *World Fact Book* (CIA, 2007), just over 35% of East Timorese people are under 14 years; some 60% are aged between 15 and 64 and only about 3% are aged 65 and over. There is also an intergenerational and urban–rural divide in terms of literacy, discussed later in this paper. The effects of conflict, population displacement, starvation, terror and human rights abuse have cast long shadows in Timor-Leste. Twenty-four percent of women aged 50–54 and 30% of women aged 55–59 are widows (CIA, 2007).

A few stark statistics from the 2004 Population Census indicate the scale of the development challenges facing this new and fragile democracy. Basic income, health and literacy indicators are among the lowest in Asia. The overall infant mortality rate is 98 per 1000 live births (Census Atlas, 2006, p. 84). Average life expectancy at birth is 55.5 years (Direcção Nacional de Estatística, 2006, p. 25). Literacy rates are extremely low. According to the Census Atlas (2006, p. 72), 54.2% (at least 400,000 people over the age of 6) cannot read or write in any of the official or working languages. Some 45% of the population aged 15 and older survive on subsistence labour, whereas at least 42% live below the poverty line. According to the *World Fact Book* (CIA, 2007), the per capita GDP (PPP[1] US$) was estimated at $800 per annum. This puts Timor-Leste on a par with Afghanistan and Burundi and makes its population only marginally better off than the populations of Somalia, Malawi and the Solomon Islands. In such situations, there are conflicting social and economic priorities and complex decisions to make about language and literacy planning for small ethnolinguistic communities most of which have no written tradition.

Migration and population change

As the authors of the Census Atlas (2006, p. 29) point out, population flux and movement in and out of Timor-Leste have been influenced by the tragic events of the last three decades. People tend to migrate in search of better economic opportunities and an improved standard of living but in Timor-Leste migration has largely been the result of conflict, population displacement and forced relocation. The demographic consequences of the Indonesian transmigration policy have not been fully researched but one can assume that they had significant sociolinguistic impact, as large numbers of Indonesian transmigrants moved into East Timorese speech communities in the 1980s. Conditions of war and intense repression led to an exodus of refugees and political exiles to places as far flung as Portugal,

Mozambique, Angola, Cape Verde, Australia, the USA, the UK and Ireland. Many East Timorese have also spent time living and studying in Indonesia. Since independence more East Timorese have gone to study abroad in Portugal, Australia, the USA and more recently, Cuba. In doing so, they have acquired international languages and transnational identities. Beneath these globalised identities, traditional values and ethnolinguistic ties remain strong, maintained through attachments to *fetsa humane* (*extended families*) and *uma fukun* (*ancestral homelands*).

The phenomenon of urban drift is particularly apparent in Timor-Leste. Having shown no change between 1990 and 2001, the population of Dili, the capital city, shot up by 12.58% a year between 2001 and 2004. Migration patterns show that older people are left behind in the country as younger people seek employment in the city (Census Atlas, 2006, p. 44). Urban drift has put pressure on infrastructure, goods and services and has created a large pool of young, urban unemployed. This situation exploded with the outbreak of the political '*crize*' (*crisis*) of 2006–2007 – violent political and civil unrest leading to huge numbers of internally displaced persons (IDPs). As of September 2007, at least 100,000 IDPs remained in camps in and around Dili because their homes were damaged or destroyed or because they were afraid to return. Another 70,000 or so remained in the outlying districts (Internal Displacement Monitoring Centre, 2007).

The East Timorese economy

The East Timorese economy shows all the signs of the underdevelopment that occurs when a traditionally rural economy is geared to the interests of the colonial metropolis (see Part III). To add to this legacy, in the upheaval that followed the referendum of 1999 most homes, water supply systems, schools and virtually the whole electrical grid were destroyed. Subsistence farming still dominates agriculture (the main food crops are rice, cassava and maize). As the authors of the Census Atlas (2006, p. 48) point out, this is the single most important feature of the economy and has major implications for development plans and policies. Insufficient food production and an underdeveloped local market have led to dependence on imports and key exports such as coffee (the main cash crop) and sandalwood have suffered from generations of underinvestment and mismanagement. The production of commodities such as vanilla, candlenut and palm oil await intensive, long-term investment and ecotourism is a potential growth industry. The official currency is presently the US$, which displaced the Indonesian rupiah and the Australian dollar. The East Timorese centavo is also used alongside US$ notes and coins. The currently depreciating US$ and rising oil prices are taking a toll on efforts to rebuild the economy. Although by the fiscal year 2004–05 economic growth in Timor-Leste had improved and there was some measure of economic stability, by mid-2006 economic activity in Dili had come to a virtual standstill while consumer prices had increased by about 13% (World Bank, 2007, p. 2). The World Bank (p. 2) estimates that in 2007, unemployment in Dili stood at 23% with youth unemployment at 40%, rising to 58% in the age bracket 15–19 years. According to the World Bank (p. 2), some 15,000 young people enter the labour market each year while only around 400 formal jobs per year are created. With such a large proportion of the population under the age of 18, urban youth unemployment and the problems associated with it are likely to increase unless vigorous economic growth can be promoted.

At present, the majority of the population survives in a rural, subsistence economy with few opportunities to access anything beyond basic education and literacy. The majority (78%) of the active labour force works in agriculture, fishing or forestry with the public sector a very distant second, employing only 6% of the active workforce. This tiny minority is currently obliged to use the co-official languages as the languages of public service. Less than 1% of the active work force is employed in industries such as mining, oil extraction, manufacturing, construction and electricity (Census Atlas, 2006, p. 51). There is also significant disparity between male and female employment patterns. Women are occupied predominantly in home industries. According to the authors of the Census Atlas (2006, p. 48), 8000 women said they worked in home industries compared with 686 men who said they worked in this sector. Nine percent of men currently work in the public sector compared with 4.5% of women. In the district of Dili, the UN and other donor agencies employ 14.3% of the active labour force, whereas for the nation as a whole only 3.8% are employed in this sector (p. 51). Most aid agencies and NGOs predominantly use English, as does the UN. I discuss the implications of this language distribution issue later in the monograph.

The most important determinant of the country's economic future is likely to lie in the way it manages the substantial revenues that are predicted to derive from oil and gas. In 2005, the National Parliament approved the establishment of a Petroleum Fund in order to manage petroleum revenue. While this action gives good cause for optimism, the effective utilisation of gas and oil resources will require major development of the country's human and institutional infrastructure. The development of literacy in the languages of wider communication will be essential for improved productivity and economic growth. In the not-so-distant future Timor-Leste will find itself in the position of having to avoid the 'resource curse', a term that describes the inability of resource-rich countries to convert wealth into sustainable development (Auty, 1993; Drysdale, 2007). The country will also have to manage the socioeconomic consequences of increasing contact with the outside world. For this increasing contact, it will need to draw on one of its richest resources – the multilingualism of its people.

Communications and language practices in the media

For the moment, Timor-Leste is still struggling with the effects of severe underdevelopment and conflict on its communications infrastructure. The telecommunications system was destroyed in 1999 along with most of the country's other infrastructure. While the cell or mobile telephone is widely used in the capital city and within about 2 km of district capitals, calls are expensive and coverage is patchy and unreliable. In the rural areas, at least 32% of the population and around 480 villages have never had effective telephone communications (Taylor, 2005, p. 136). Internet access is also expensive with limited availability outside Dili. A National Media Survey (NMS)[2] funded by US AID and conducted by the Hirondelle Foundation found that as few as 1 in 10 respondents owned a mobile telephone and 1 in a 100 had a computer at home while only half of these had Internet access (Mytton & Soares, 2007, p. 2). Moreover, Timor-Leste is one of the few countries in the world that does not have a domestic postal service. As Taylor states, the lack of communications contributes to 'an appalling neonatal death rate, a chronic lack of education facilities, difficulties with governance, isolation of communities and poor prospects for economic development' (2005, p. 136). Inadequate transport infrastructure and poor communications mean that communities are isolated and travel is difficult and time-consuming. Poor communications also slow down language spread. While this limitation on language spread might be a good thing as far as maintaining endogenous languages and sustaining local traditional culture are concerned, inadequate communications also impede the spread of standard official languages and literacy. The lack of contact between local communities and the outside world and the inability to communicate effectively in the languages of wider communication place communities at a disadvantage in a number of ways, including their ability to access good health care and economic opportunities (Grenoble & Whaley, 2006, pp. 102–103). Radio, television and newspapers play a critical role in keeping communities in touch, in enacting language reform, in promoting standardisation and in influencing public opinion. The following sections discuss the language practices in the media drawing attention to the way in which these practices not only mediate language policy but also reflect language attitudes and use.

Radio

With poor communications infrastructure and low levels of print literacy, the East Timorese rely on a combination of radio and interpersonal communication for their news. Far more people have access to radio than they have to television, mobile phones and the Internet. The state-owned *Radio Televizaun Timor-Leste* (*Radio Television Timor-Leste*) broadcasts in Tetum, Portuguese and Indonesian with retransmissions from Portugal, Radio Australia and the BBC World Service. Radio Timor-Leste (RTL) was the primary media source of information about the political crisis of 2006. The NMS confirms that radio is the most important source of information in Timor-Leste. Almost half the respondents in the survey had a radio at home, two-thirds of which were powered by batteries. Radio reaches about 146,000 people daily and about 243,000 people weekly (Mytton & Soares, 2007, p. 16). RTL was the single-most relied upon source of information for the respondents in the survey. The Catholic radio station, *Radio Timor Kmanek*, had the second greatest number of listeners, although at present it broadcasts mostly music due to lack of funding to pay presenters.

In its investigation of radio listening habits, the NMS produced useful and important findings about public language preferences. In the process, it also revealed some interesting information about language practices. The NMS found that radio listening appears to be a communal rather than a solitary activity in Timor-Leste. People listen to the radio in public places such as hotels, markets, at work, in the IDP camps or at friends' and neighbours' homes. This practice would indicate that the radio is a rich forum for community information, education and debate. An important finding was that nearly everyone in the survey listened to Tetum programmes on the radio. Respondents were asked which language they listened to on radio and all languages mentioned were recorded. The survey found that 98% of respondents said they listened to Tetum broadcasts but a slight majority (63%) also listened to Indonesian broadcasts. Half the respondents (50.9%) said they listened to Portuguese broadcasts and a few (just over 13%) listened to broadcasts in English. Respondents were also asked in what languages they *preferred* to listen and again all languages mentioned were recorded. The majority of respondents (92.3%) chose Tetum while a much smaller number (28%) expressed a preference for Indonesian with a mere 9.2% preferring Portuguese (Mytton & Soares, 2007, p. 25). The most popular international radio stations were Radio Australia and the BBC, both broadcasting mostly in English.

Community radio has a strong presence in Timor-Leste. There are six community radio stations in Dili and 13 district community radio stations which broadcast round the country in many of the national languages. These stations rely on funding, training and equipment from international agencies and lack of money has sometimes resulted in the interruption of services. Poor reception is also a problem for many listeners. Nonetheless, it seems that community radio is popular with local communities; to give an illustrative example, two-thirds of families in Lautém are estimated to listen in to *Labarik Nia Lian* (*Children's Voices*), a local radio programme with a focus on children's rights (UNICEF, 2005, p. 37) and similar programmes are planned for Maliana, Liquiçá, Oecussi, Aileu and Viqueque districts.

With such a large proportion of the population below the age of 24, the voices of youth are extremely important. In November 2006, the East Timorese Office for Promotion of Equality (under the auspices of the Office of the Prime Minister) in partnership with the United Nations Children's Fund (UNICEF) launched the Marta Communication Initiative (Accessed May 2, 2008, from http://www.unmiset.org/UNMISETWebSite.nsf). The character of Marta was created in 2003 through a radio melodrama series *Hakarak kaer ba fitun* (*I want to reach for the stars*). Marta is based on Meena, the South Asian animation character who has become a role model for promoting the rights of girls across South Asia. In a country where the media is starved of funds, this kind of initiative is important for attracting resources and improving the quality of programming but a valuable by-product is the contribution such local programmes make to language revitalisation and modernisation. Radio is clearly a powerful medium of language use, reaching as far as it does into local communities in languages they understand. However, the same cannot be said of television and the print media, which are restricted mostly to the capital city and urban areas.

Television

The NMS found that no more than one in five participants had a television at home (Mytton & Soares, 2007, p. 2). *Televizaun Timor Lorosa'e* (*Television Timor-Leste*) (or TVTL) appears to have large audiences only in Dili where 71% of survey respondents named it as a major source of information about current affairs (p. 13). In the remote districts of Covalima, Lautém and Manufahi not one respondent named television as a source of information, citing instead local radio stations and word of mouth as key sources of information (p. 14). TVTL broadcasts local programmes in Tetum and Portuguese as well as retransmissions from Portugal, ABC Asia Pacific from Australia and BBC World Service from the UK. The present television signal is confined to Dili with only taped broadcasts being available in the second city of Baucau. The NMS found that only two in five respondents ever watched television. No more than 45% watched television at home and the rest watched it at friends' or neighbours' homes or through various means of communal viewing – at least 103,000 people managed to watch at least some of the World Cup Football coverage by such means (p. 30). The respondents who watched television were also asked which languages they preferred to hear on television. All languages mentioned by respondents were recorded. Seventy-four percent of this small group said they most preferred to hear Tetum on television; just over 40% said they preferred to hear Indonesian; only 15.5% expressed a preference for Portuguese and a tiny 7.4% stated a preference for English. When asked which language they would prefer if there were only one language available on TV, 75% of television viewers said they would prefer Tetum while only 19.2% said they would prefer Indonesian; a mere 3.7% expressed a preference for Portuguese and as few as 0.4% stated a preference for English (p. 42). The most popular programmes among the television viewers were the news programme, *Telejornál* and a light entertainment programme, *Palku Muzikál.* Although many viewers watch Indonesian television programmes broadcast via satellite, the rate of television viewing in general is low and is restricted mainly to the affluent. The globalising influences of radio and television are still very new to Timor-Leste.

Newspapers

At present, there are two weekly newspapers and four dailies. *Tempo Semanal* (*Weekly Times*) and *Journal Nacional Semanário* (*National Weekly Journal*) are both published weekly. *Journal Nacional Diário* (*National Daily Journal*), *Timor Pos* (*Timor Post*),

Diário Tempo (*Daily Times*) and *Suara Timor Lorosa'e* (*Voice of East Timor*) are published daily. The pioneering bilingual Tetum-Portuguese newspaper *Lia Foun* (*New Words*), which ran a weekly Portuguese-Tetum course, was forced to cease publication due to lack of funding having run for less than a year. Newspapers are sold at US$0.50 a copy. In a country where the average daily wage is US$3, it is not surprising that circulation is low. *Suara Timor Lorosa'e* has the widest circulation at around 2000. *Timor Pos* has a circulation of approximately 1000. *Tempo Semanal* and *Diário Tempo* are new publications each with circulations of around 500.

The East Timorese press currently faces the challenge of providing information to a public with an enduring oral tradition as opposed to a much more recent literary one. Journalists have shown little enthusiasm for learning Portuguese and they have also shown some resistance to the official standard orthography of Tetum, available since 2004 (see Part IV). Steele, who favours Indonesian as an official language, claims that journalists have been marginalised by language policy (Steele, 2006; Steele & MacDonald, 2007). The fact that the majority of journalists were educated and trained in what are commonly referred to as 'Indonesian times' (1975 – 99) cannot fail to have influenced their language preferences, as the following paragraphs show but other sociolinguistic variables are also at play.

There is a complex blend of competing language ideologies and language attitudes behind journalistic resistance to top-down language planning. This complexity can be seen in the language practices of journalists, influenced by a combination of their target readership and their political orientations and sympathies. *Tempo Semanal* uses Tetum, English and Indonesian out of a desire to reach as wide a readership as possible, especially in the rural districts where circulation is extremely low. The paper also has close sympathies with veterans of the former resistance army, Forças Armadas para a Libertação do Timor-Leste (Armed Forces for the National Liberation of Timor-Leste) known as FALINTIL (Cheetham, 2005). *Journal Nacional Semanário* is a Portuguese language newspaper, which also uses some Tetum. The newspaper collaborates with and receives funding from the Portuguese *Instituto Camões* (*Camões Institute*). The Camões Institute is the principal agency for the promotion of Portuguese language, literature and culture in Timor-Leste. Prominent contributors listed on the *Journal Nacional Semanário* website include well-known East Timorese writer Ângela Carrascalão, former Prime Minister Mari Alkatiri, Bishop D. Ximenes Belo and President José Ramos Horta (Accessed December 17, 2007, from www.semanario.tp). *Timor Pos* publishes in Tetum and Indonesian. *Suara Timor Lorosa'e* (*STL*) once published in Indonesian but now publishes in all four state languages.

These language practices reflect the complex history of the East Timorese press. Under both the Portuguese and the Indonesians, it was subject to heavy censorship and surveillance. The Polícia International e de Defesa do Estado (International and State Defence Police) – the Portugese secret police, also known as PIDE – was established in Timor-Leste in 1959 in the aftermath of one of the most recent in a long tradition of local uprisings (see Part III), known as the *Viqueque rebellion*. In the late 1960s, a Catholic newspaper called *Seara* (*Harvest*) was published. As a Church publication, *Seara* was exempt from normal censorship laws. The paper published in Portuguese but it also ran a Tetum teaching programme. *Seara* served as a lively forum for progressive ideas and published the writings (in Portuguese) of some of the most renowned East Timorese nationalist leaders. PIDE closed the paper down in 1973 but by that time, like-minded nationalist activists were already in close contact.

The foremost grouping in the nationalist movement, *Frente Revolucionária do Timor-Leste Independente* (*Revolutionary Front of Independent East Timor*) – known as FRETILIN – was founded in 1974. It published its own newspaper known as the

Timor-Leste Journal do Povo Maubere (*Timor-Leste Journal of the Maubere people*). Contributors to the newspaper expressed criticism of colonialism and solidarity with African independence causes. Consistent with FRETILIN cultural policies (discussed further in Part III), the *Journal do Povo Maubere* published in Tetum and Portuguese. The newspaper published revolutionary nationalist poetry in Tetum and Portuguese as well as a series of articles written in both languages discussing its methods for teaching people how to read. FRETILIN initiated a literacy campaign at the beginning of 1975 using a Tetum-language reader entitled *Rai Timor, Rai Ita Nian* (*Timor, our Country*), which broke words into syllables and then placed them in different contexts of village life, together with associated words (Taylor, 1991, p. 34). The essence of the approach was its reflection of the East Timorese rural experience.

The role of *STL* during the Indonesian occupation has been the subject of some controversy. The newspaper's predecessor, *Suara Timor Timur* (*STT*) was founded in 1993. It was the first East Timorese newspaper to be published since the government-controlled publication of the late colonial years named *A Voz de Timor* (*Voice of Timor*), a weekly Portuguese-language newspaper, edited by José Ramos Horta, current President of the Republic (Nichol, 2002). The content of *STT* was written entirely in Indonesian. The East Timorese owner of *STT* was not only a member of the Indonesian legislative assembly but he was also a supporter of integration and a member of the powerful Indonesian political organisation, *GOLKAR*.[3] Steele argues that this fact has led scholars to overlook the contributions to the resistance struggle of journalists who worked for the newspaper. She claims that journalists who worked at *STT* during the occupation 'practised a kind of subterranean journalism that presented subtle challenges to the government's point of view' (Steele, 2007, p. 262). Steele claims that the newspaper's close connections with the Indonesian Information Department and the Indonesian publishing group *Kompas-Gramedia* were strategic and that its content was typical of Indonesian press culture during the Suharto years in that 'the paper was obliged to publish stories based on the statements of public officials and discouraged from reporting anything that undermined this positive view' (Steele, 2007, p. 266). However, although it is undeniable that there was intense pressure on *STT* journalists in the form of surveillance, phone calls, death threats and acts of violence from the Indonesian military, the pro-integrationist reputation of the paper still lingers. Its history has not only clearly coloured its journalists' attitudes towards the official languages but also shows the complex role that language plays in the forming of identity. The offices of *STT* were destroyed in the violence of 1999. The paper began publishing again under its new name (*Suara Timor Lorosa'e*) in 2000, at the request of the former resistance leader, Kay Rala, Alexandre (Xanana) Gusmão (Steele, 2007, p. 276), current Prime Minister of Timor-Leste.

Tensions between the press and the government have often arisen over journalistic language practices; one particular incident provides an illustrative example. Food insecurity is a recurrent problem in Timor-Leste. In 2005, *STL* ran a story about 53 tragic deaths resulting from lack of food in the subdistrict of Hatubuiliko (*Suara Timor Lorosa'e*, 2005). Then Prime Minister Mari Alkatiri evicted *STL* from its government-owned offices over the use of an Indonesian word *kelaparan* (meaning *hunger, starvation* or *famine*). The prime minister interpreted the word to mean *famine* and stated that the *STL* story was inaccurate and defamatory. Not only does this confrontation emphasise the urgent need for a standardised variety of Tetum in the print media but it also shows that the issue of press freedom in this young democracy is still sensitive and unresolved.

The controversy over language policy is further fuelled by the promotion of language ideologies in the English and Indonesian press, which continue regularly to attack East Timorese official language choice (see Cohen, 2002; Funnell, 2002; Khalik, 2007; Schulz and Freitas, 2002; Sheridan, 2006; Steele and MacDonald, 2007; *The Australian*, 2001, 2002, for only a few examples). Steele (2006) has criticised the use of Tetum in the press, claiming that 'it would be a tragedy if the journalists who helped build a sense of East Timorese identity were shut out by the language policy of the very nation they helped create'. Her claim is ironic given the circumstances in which most East Timorese acquired Indonesian (discussed in Part III). Such hostile discourses in the Australian and Indonesian press place tremendous pressure on the East Timorese government. In discussions with the international press concerning his plans for resolving the political crisis of 2006–2007, President José Ramos Horta suggested that Tetum, Portuguese, Indonesian and English might be placed on an equal footing (*Canberra Times*, 2007; Mali, 2007). The president's remark marks a significant shift from previous statements in which he has strongly supported Portuguese (Dodd, 2001). The relationship between the official and working languages is discussed in Part IV.

Part II: the language profile of Timor-Leste

Historians consider Timor-Leste to be one of the gateways for the movement of populations to Australia (Fox, 2003, p. 3). Austronesian and Trans-New Guinea or Papuan language speakers arrived on the island of Timor as a result of migration, trade and settlement. Glover's (1971) evidence indicates the presence of a hunter-gatherer population on the island dating from at least 11,500 BCE. First evidence of agricultural activity dates to 3000 BCE, data that are interpreted as evidence of the arrival of early seafaring Austronesian populations into the region (Fox, 2003, p. 5). It is thought that the Austronesian languages of Timor are related to the languages of eastern Flores and the islands of southern Maluku. The Trans-New Guinea phylum languages appear to form a subgroup with the languages on the Indonesian islands of Alor, Pantar and Kisar (Figure 2), which in turn appear to be related to languages in the Birdhead (Vogelkop) peninsula of West Papua.

Hull (1998a, pp. 2–4) lists the Austronesian language varieties spoken in Timor-Leste as:

- Tetum and its varieties (Tetum-Praça, Tetum-Terik and Tetum-Belu),
- Habun, Kawaimina (Kairui, Waima'a, Midiki and Naueti),
- Galoli,
- Atauran and Dadua dialects (belonging to the Wetarese language),
- Lóvaia (or Makuva),
- Mambae,
- Idalaka (Idaté, Isni, Lolein and Lakalei)
- Kemak,
- Tokodede,
- Bekais and
- Baikenu.

The non-Austronesian or Papuan language varieties are listed as Bunak, Makasae, Makalero and Fataluku. In 2007, the last speaker of a Papuan language related to Fataluku, known as Rusenu, was discovered (Noorderlicht, 2007). Hull's research (2001, pp. 98–99) shows that these languages form a linguistic area or *Sprachbund*, having over the course of centuries replaced their individual characteristics with Timorese forms and structures in a process of mutual assimilation. Figure 3 shows the geographical distribution of the endogenous languages.

Hull suggests that Tetum and the Austronesian languages of the islands of Timor and Roti descend from a single language (Old Timorese) introduced from the Buton region

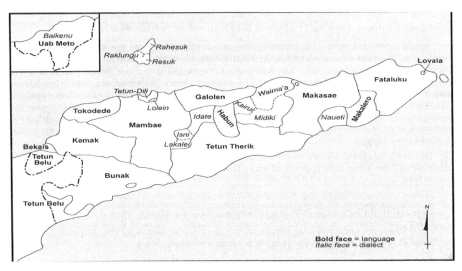

Figure 3.   Language map of Timor-Leste (Bowden & Hajek, 2007, p. 266). Reproduced with kind permission of the authors.

of southeastern Celebes. According to Hull (2001, p. 101), from about the thirteenth-century CE, the dialects of Timor were influenced by a central Moluccan language (probably from Ambon), and the impact of Malay, the regional lingua franca, began to be felt in the fifteenth century. The Papuan languages with the greatest numbers of speakers are Makasae and Bunak. The three largest Austronesian languages are:

- Baikenu (also known as Dawan, Atoni or Uab Meto), spoken in the East Timorese exclave of Oecussi and in West Timor;
- Mambae, spoken in eastern Timor and
- Tetum, spoken in the east and the west of Timor island.

The number of East Timorese languages

There are differences of opinion as to the precise number and classification of Timorese language varieties (Capell, 1944, 1972; Fox, 1997, 2003; Hull, 1998a; Thomaz, 1981). The most reliable figures may be drawn from *Ethnologue* (see Gordon, 2005), Hull (1998a) and the *Instituto Nacional de Linguística* (*National Institute of Linguistics*), known as the INL. Ethnologue listed 20 languages in Timor-Leste, 19 living and 1 extinct. The Linguistic Survey of Timor-Leste Project (see Hull, 1998a) at the INL identifies 19 distinct autochthonous language varieties in the whole of Timor and the offshore islands of Wetar, Ataúro, Semau, Roti (Figure 2) and Ndao (not shown). As Bowden and Hajek (2007, p. 265) observe, the differences between Gordon's list and the INL list are based simply on different ways of classifying languages and dialects. At least 16 language varieties are spoken in Timor-Leste compared with seven in West Timor. Baikenu, Tetum, Kemak and Bunak are spoken on both sides of the border with West Timor. The Wetarese and Galoli languages (and their dialectal varieties) are spoken on both sides of the border between Timor-Leste and Maluku (Hull, 1998a, p. 4). With one exception, the endogenous languages are considered to have high linguistic vitality. Only Lóvaia, also known as Makuva, is seriously endangered,[4] having only a small number of speakers with the

Table 2. Languages of Papuan origin reported as a first language according to the 2004 National Census (Direcção Nacional de Estatística, 2006, p. 80).

Language	Number of individuals	Percentage of population accounted for by the census ($n = 741,530$)	Main areas where used
Bunak	50,631	6.8	Central interior and Indonesia
Fataluku	28,893	3.8	Eastern tip of Timor-Leste around Lospalos
Makalero	5,981	0.8	South-east coast
Makasae	90,018	12.1	Eastern end of Timor island around Baucau

rest having shifted to Fataluku (Hajek, 2006, p. 719). As Hajek, Himmelmann, & Bowden (2003, p. 159) note, the Fataluku name of Lóvaia is considered by its speakers to be more respectful. In addition, the exogenous languages – Malay, Arabic, Chinese, Portuguese, modern Indonesian and English – are or have at some time been present in the ecology.

One of the main difficulties in studying multilingualism lies in the measurement of actual language use in society. It is always a challenge to enumerate language users in linguistically diverse polities such as Timor-Leste because research is limited by a lack of reliable statistical information. Robinson (1993, pp. 52–55) defines high language diversity as 'a situation where no more than 50% of the population speaks the same language' (see also Lopes, 1998, p. 445). As Tables 2 and 3 show, no language variety is spoken as a mother tongue in Timor-Leste by more than 18% of the population and most languages are used by far smaller numbers of speakers. It is also difficult to apply concepts such as *majority* and *minority* language in numerical terms. Indeed, as Skutnabb-Kangas (1990, p. 6) suggests, if the term *minority* is applied in terms of power rather than in terms of numbers of speakers, then all those groups whose mother tongues are not official in the countries where they live are linguistic minorities. In Timor-Leste, even Tetum is a minority language in certain parts of the country. According to Baker and Langeraar (2005) just over 78% of Dili residents use a variety of Tetum as a first language compared with 9% of residents in Baucau. Moreover, according to the 2004 Census estimates, no more than 1.4% of the populations of Lautém and Oecussi districts speak a variety of Tetum as a first language while in several districts less than 20% of the population can speak, read or write Tetum (Census Atlas, 2006, p. 70).

As *Ethnologue* points out (see http://www.ethnologue.com), given the difficulty of arriving at accurate counts of speakers of a given language, all figures (even census figures) are necessarily estimates. Definitions of what constitutes a language must be operationally stated and may differ from what speakers themselves consider a language. There is also the difficult problem of defining the difference between dialects and languages (Crowley, 2000a, p. 56). Many languages are known by more than one name. As in the case of Lóvaia, some names may not be used or may not be considered respectful by certain communities of speakers. There are also differences of opinion about how to measure both proficiency and literacy. Some of these difficulties are manifested in the language statistics in the 2004 National Census of Population and Housing for Timor-Leste.

Language data from the 2004 Population Census

The 2004 Census of Population and Housing was a magnificent achievement. The enumeration of the population in a mostly rural country without addresses and with a deficient land

Table 3. Languages of Austronesian origin reported as a first language according to the 2004 National Census (Direcção Nacional de Estatística, 2006, p. 80).

Language	Number of individuals	Percentage of population accounted for by the census ($n = 741,530$)	Main areas where used
The Ataúran varieties (Adabe, Atauran, Rahesuk, Raklungu, Resuk)	5,576	0.75	Ataúro Island
Baikenu, also known as Vaikenu/Atoni	45,705	6.16	Oecussi
Bekais	3,222	0.43	North of Balibó and Batugadé
Dadu'a	1,242	0.16	Around Manatuto
Galoli, also known as Galolen	10,998	1.4	North coast, Laklo, Manatuto, Laleia, Wetar island and Ataúro island
Habun	1,586	0.21	South of Manatuto and north-east of Laclúbar
Idalaka (Idaté, Isní, Lolein, Lakalei)	14,201	1.91	South-east of Dili
Kairui-Midiki	13,540	1.82	Central Timor-Leste
Kemak	51,057	6.88	The far west near the border with West Timor
Makuva, also known as Lóvaia	100	0.01	North-east tip of Timor island
Mambae	131,472	17.72	Mountains of central Timor
Naueti	11,321	1.5	South-east coast, around Uatolari
Tetum, in its rural varieties, also known as Tetum-Terik, Classical Tetum, Tetum-Loos	45,944 in Timor-Leste	6.1	The central south coast of Timor-Leste and its hinterland
Tetum-Dili, also known as Tetum-Praça	133,102	17.94	In and around Dili
Tetum (unspecified varieties)	45,362	6.1	
Tokodede	31,814	4.2	Bazar-Tete, Liquiçá, Maubara
Waima'a	14,506	1.95	North coast

cadastre was carried out using Global Positioning System (GPS) technology that was able to pinpoint every household in the country. Timor-Leste was the first country to complete a census using this satellite system (Direcção Nacional de Estatística, 2006, p. 19). Census Question 8 asked respondents to list their mother tongue. *Mother tongue* was defined in the census as 'the language usually spoken in an individual's home in his her early child-hood' (p. 46). The approximate numbers of speakers of Papuan and Austronesian languages

Table 4.   Exogenous languages reported as a first language according to the 2004 National census (Direcção Nacional de Estatística, 2006, p. 80).

Language	Number of individuals	Percentage of population accounted for by the census (n = 741,530)
Indonesian	2411	0.32
Portuguese	702	0.094
English	808	0.11
A variety of Chinese	511	0.068
Malay	146	Too small to be significant

as first or home languages and the main locations of those speech communities are listed in Tables 2 and 3. These figures were extracted by the present author from the 2004 National Census data which listed private household residents aged 6 years and over according to mother tongue. The languages are grouped according to the INL classification and percentages were calculated on the basis of a total of 741,530 people.

Census Question 8 asked respondents to name the language or dialect they spoke at home. Census Question 9 asked respondents if they could *speak, read or write* in Portuguese, Tetum, Indonesian and English. Neither question differentiated between the varieties of Tetum. Consequently, the number of respondents who declared they could speak or read or write Tetum included people who use Tetum-Praça, Tetum-Terik or other varieties (Census Atlas, 2006, p. 70). Table 4 shows the very small numbers of individuals who reported an exogenous language as a first or home language according to the 2004 National Census.

In order to collect data on language characteristics, the 2004 census employed the term *capability* – a term that was defined as 'the capacity to speak, read or write or any combination of the above as informed by the interviewee' (Direcção Nacional de Estatística, 2006, p. 47). Table 5 shows the numbers of individuals who reported capability (or lack of it) in the official and working languages.

However, national percentages alone are not very meaningful because capability and literacy vary greatly according to district. The census authors also measured language use in terms of literacy and they broke down the data according to district. The census authors considered anyone who was not able *both to read and write* in any of the official and working languages (Portuguese, Tetum, English and Indonesian) to be illiterate (Census Atlas, 2006, p. 72). In terms of the proportion of the population able to *speak, read and write* in any of the official and working languages, the most literate districts were Dili, Manatuto and Baucau whilst Oecussi and Ermera had the lowest literacy rates among the districts (Census Atlas, 2006, p. 66). As the authors point out, these numbers highlight the importance of local languages in districts outside Dili as well as the extent to

Table 5.   Capability in the official and working languages (Direcção Nacional de Estatística, 2006, p. 82).

Language capability (speak, read or write)	Number of individuals	Percentage of the population accounted for by the census (n = 741,530)
Tetum	634,458	86
Portuguese	272,638	36
Indonesian	435,255	59
English	160,160	21
None of these	96,703	13

Table 6. Literacy in the official and working languages (Census Atlas, 2006, p. 69; Direcção Nacional de Estatística, 2006, pp. 135–138).

Literacy (speak, read and write)	Number of individuals	Percentage of the population accounted for by the census ($n = 638{,}478^5$)
Tetum	295,033	46.2
Portuguese	86,917	13.6
Indonesian	276,199	43.3
English	37,136	5.8

which the educated elite are concentrated in and around the national capital. While Portuguese literacy rates tend to be higher in the eastern districts, Indonesian literacy rates are higher in the western districts where Indonesian influence was stronger. For example, the remote eastern subdistrict of Venilale had the highest literacy rates for both Portuguese and English. In terms of national literacy rates in the official and working languages, the census findings were far lower than those for capability. Table 6 shows the numbers of individuals who reported that they could speak, read and write in the official and working languages.

These figures stand in marked contrast to those for language capability. Moreover, the marked spatial variations in language use present a major challenge for language planners. For instance, although Tetum is an official language, less than 20% of the population speaks, reads or writes it in three of the four subdistricts of Oecussi. Throughout Oecussi and Lautém districts, more people could speak, read or write Indonesian than they could Tetum. The same is true of Atsabe subdistrict in the district of Ermera and Laclubar subdistrict in the district of Manatuto (Census Atlas, 2006, p. 70).

Previous estimates and census figures offer interesting comparison with the 2004 census. Basing his estimates on the Indonesian census of 1990, Hajek (2000, p. 409) esti-mated that between 60% and 80% of the population spoke some form of Tetum. He put the number of Portuguese speakers at anywhere between 5% and 20%. Indonesian census figures suggest that by 1991, some 60% of the population spoke Indonesian (Himmelmann & Hajek, 2001, p. 90). The Indonesian statistical system did not distinguish between native-born East Timorese and the children of non-East Timorese (e.g. the children of transmi-grants, government servants and the military). Consequently, statisticians approached estimates by dividing populations according to whether heads of household were born in the country (Hull, 2003, p. 31). Jones (2003, pp. 44–45) computed the 1990 Indonesian census data using this method and found that the proportion of males able to speak Indonesian where the head of the household was born in Timor-Leste was 56.4% while the proportion of females was 39.4%. The younger cohorts, who had been schooled in the Indonesian language, contained large proportions able to speak Indonesian – 85% of males and 77% of females aged 15–19 – but the numbers dropped off sharply to 35% for males and 17% for females at age 40–44 and even lower at more advanced ages (p. 48). At present, the younger generation is still more proficient in Indonesian. If one com-pares the figures for the same age groups in the 2004 census one finds that 82% (39,388 individuals) of males and 83% (38,288 individuals) of females aged 15–19 reported capa-bility in Indonesian (Direcção Nacional de Estatistica, 2006, p. 82). Among 40–44-year olds, 67% of males (15,034 individuals) and 36% of females (8545 individuals) reported capability in Indonesian (p. 82). It is reasonable to assume that those people who had been in the 15 to 19 year age group in 1990 would be in the 30–34 year age group in 2004. The members of this cohort (61,970 individuals) who reported capability in

Indonesian came to 84.6% for males (27,022 individuals) and 66% females (19,994 individuals). Overall, these figures indicate that knowledge of Indonesian is still high amongst the population below 35 years of age.

Diglossia and multilingualism in Timor-Leste

The study of diglossia is of great value in understanding processes of linguistic change in multilingual societies. Diglossia is an indication of change in the social functions of languages and in the social organisation of speech communities (Hudson, 1991, p. 1) as well as changing language attitudes as Hudson points out (p. 8). In Ferguson's (1959) definition, the term *diglossia* refers to two varieties of the same language that are functionally specialised and used in mutually exclusive domains by the same speech community. Fishman (1967) extended and elaborated the concept of diglossia to include the distribution of one or more language varieties to serve different functions in a society. Fishman suggested that diglossia exists not only in multilingual societies that officially recognise several languages but also in societies that use vernacular and classical varieties, registers or functionally different language varieties of whatever kind. Fishman distinguished diglossia from bilingualism, which he described as an individual's ability to use more than one language variety. Fasold (1984) also distinguished between bilingualism, which he described as an individual phenomenon and multilingualism, which is societal. Using these definitions, the current language situation in Timor-Leste is both diglossic and multilingual with varying levels of individual bi-, tri- and quadrilingualism. Some individuals, for example many Baikenu speakers, are monolingual. Indeed, in the 2004 Census, some 25% (192,692 individuals) reported capability in Tetum alone. Table 7 provides a selective indication of the numbers of individuals who reported capability in one or more of the official and working languages. Note that not all language combinations are reported and those combinations that are not reported contain numbers that are so low they are not considered significant.

It is also important to note that Indonesian itself is marked by diglossia. The varieties of Indonesian used and understood all over the archipelago vary along a continuum from the formal high (H) variety taught through the Indonesian education system to the highly informal, colloquial low (L) varieties used in everyday activities. Sneddon (2003, pp. 532−533) has observed that the difference in functions between H and L in Indonesian is not as strict as in Ferguson's model of diglossia (see also Wardhaugh, 1998, p. 88). Sneddon also notes

Table 7. Capability in one or more of the official and working languages (Direcção Nacional de Estatística, 2006, p. 84).

Language capability (speak, read or write)	Number of individuals	Percentage of the population accounted for by the census (n=741,530)
Tetum only	192,692	25
All four official and working languages	143,684	20
Portuguese, Tetum and Indonesian	113,008	15
Portuguese and Tetum	12,522	1.69
Tetum and Indonesian	158,001	21
Tetum and English	963	0.1
Indonesian and English	644	0.09
None of these	96,703	13

that while H and L Indonesian are associated with most formal and informal situations, there are a number of intermediate forms associated with semiformal situations. At present, Indonesian is still used in social life, in small businesses, in the daily work of NGOs and in secondary and tertiary education. The Portuguese language is undergoing revival in the education system, in the civil service and in the formal justice system. The dynamism and complexity of the language situation was enhanced by the sudden arrival of English in 1999. Tetum is also increasingly used in traditionally H domains such as the courts and parliament as well as in primary education. Even in traditionally non-Tetum speaking areas, its use appears to be increasing (Himmelman & Hajek, 2001, p. 93).

In both Ferguson's (1959) and Fishman's (1967; 1972a) discussions of diglossia, the languages in an individual's repertoire are highly compartmentalised, although Ferguson later revised his analysis to say that there is always a continuum between H and L. Even so, as Ferguson (1959, p. 337) notes, 'no segment of the speech community in diglossia regularly uses H as a medium of ordinary conversation and any attempt to do so is felt to be either pedantic or artificial [...] and in some sense disloyal to the community [...]'. Hudson (1991, p. 13) suggests that rigid compartmentalisation is a necessary requisite for the long-term maintenance of diglossia. While Ferguson and Fishman argue that this compartmentalisation in diglossic situations contributes to stable bilingualism and language maintenance, others claim that diglossia tends to be unstable when the changing balance of power between the two languages leads to language shift (Schiffman, 1993). Domain intrusion, as Appel and Muysken (1987, pp. 39–41) observe, is a clear sign of language shift. I suggest that the changing language situation in Timor-Leste has led to a form of unstable diglossia, reflecting the changing relationship and status of languages in society.

Tetum and Portuguese locales (domains) of use

As Ager (2005) notes, the status of a language in a particular society is defined by its position or standing in relation to other languages. The status of a language can also be measured by the number and nature of domains in which it is used. High status domains such as the elite, parliamentary, judiciary, educational systems and the forces of law and order represent the public domains. Low status domains include domestic and private situations and where powerless groups wish to distinguish themselves from those in power or where such groups are marked as powerless because they are unable to deploy linguistic skills in the high status language (Ager, 2001, p. 1040). For the purposes of this discussion, it is more appropriate to talk in terms of *locales* because they describe a less complex situation than does the term *domain* which in both Fishman's (1972b) and Romaine's (1995) definitions includes the parameters of reciprocal language choices by classes of interlocutors on kinds of occasions to discuss particular topics (Fishman, 1972b, p. 437). Tables 8 and 9 make rough classifications of the main locales of use for Tetum and Portuguese and the H or L registers of each language. It is important to point out, however, that speakers do not use these languages exclusively in these locales; rather, they tend to be reserved for these languages. There is a great deal of code switching and mixing in all locales. Tables 8 and 9, therefore, serve primarily as a guide for evaluating the vitality of Tetum and the extent of its repertoire.

As Tables 8 and 9 show, although Tetum is increasingly used in H locales, it is still used predominantly in L registers (or in a combination of H and L registers where it primarily plays an L role), whereas Portuguese is used in H locales for mainly H registers. A seemingly obvious conclusion is that for its standardisation to be successful and its status elevated, Tetum needs to extend its repertoire into locales such as the professions,

Table 8.   Tetum locales of use.

Tetum locales of use	H or L registers
The National Parliament. The majority of members of parliament use Tetum in debate and questions, in addition to Portuguese	H
The Police and Armed Forces	L
Church services	H
The District Courts	H
The Civil Service/public administration	L
Political meetings, speeches, conferences, rallies and other cultural events (Portuguese, Indonesian and English are also used when international audiences are present)	H and L
The press, radio and television (mainly news and public information programmes)	H and L
The marketplace	L
The home and family gatherings	L

the media, education and the sciences, high culture and refined social interaction. As previously stated, diglossia in which Indonesian dominates still exists in secondary and higher education, in many professions and in small businesses. The arrival of English has added another component because of its widespread use together with Indonesian in NGO activities and many working situations where foreign aid workers and volunteers are employed. English is also the working language of the Ministry of Foreign Affairs. Portuguese dominates the telecommunications and education sectors. The health sector is truly multilingual, being heavily reliant on international medical and health professionals. The language of technology (as elsewhere) is for the most part English.

Literacy

The management of literacy is one of the many complex challenges currently confronting the independent state. Fifty-eight percent of women and 50.2% of men are illiterate (Census Atlas, 2006, p. 72). Not surprisingly Dili district has the highest literacy rates with only 25.8% of the population over the age of 6 unable to read or write in any of the official and working languages. More than half the population in each of the other 12 districts is illiterate, and female illiteracy rates are consistently higher than those for males. The highest rate of illiteracy (i.e. 71.1%) occurs in the rural highland district of Ermera (p. 72).

The Census Atlas used a very specific definition of literacy. As stated earlier, the census authors, following the UN standard definition, considered anyone aged 6 and older who was

Table 9.   Portuguese locales of use.

Portuguese locales of use	H or L registers
The National Parliament, in the rubric of legislation and written documents	H
Pre-primary and primary education	H
The Court of Appeal	H
In church services in hymns and in funeral prayers and ceremonies	H
The Civil Service/Public Administration	H
Conferences, seminars and meetings	H
Customs and Excise	H
Diplomatic activities involving Portugal and other Portuguese-speaking countries	H
The press, radio and television (news and popular entertainment)	H and L

unable to *both read and write in any of the four official and working languages* to be illiterate (p. 72). According to the Census Atlas, 27% of people between the ages of 15 and 24 are illiterate. Very large numbers of people over the age of 40 are illiterate. Sixty-two percent (28,393 individuals) of 40–44-year olds and 76% (25,054 individuals) of 50–54 year olds cannot read or write (Direcção Nacional de Estatística, 2006, p. 133). Such high levels of illiteracy constitute a serious limitation to prospects for raising educational standards and improving socioeconomic development. The United Nations Development Program (UNDP) found that between 10% and 30% of primary-age children still do not attend school (UNDP, 2006, p. 1), a finding that raises two key issues concerning the role and function of literacy in East Timorese society that will need to be addressed:

(i) what kind of niche can be found for vernacular literacy and
(ii) what the current language policy and planning trajectory means for literacy in the languages of wider communication.

Figure 4 indicates by district the proportion of the population between the ages of 15 and 24 years who can read or write. It also highlights the urban–rural divide in terms of literacy. According to this map, 90% of 15–24-year olds in the relatively urbanised district of Dili are literate. In contrast, only 66% of this age group in the isolated and under-resourced district of Oecussi are literate The lowest rates of youth literacy occur in the highland districts of Ainaro (59%) and Ermera (49%).

Perceptions of literacy have shifted away from the view that it is an autonomous, value-neutral set of skills towards the view that literacy is inseparable from its social context (Street, 1994, 1995). As Grenoble and Whaley (2006, p. 110) point out, literacy is more than a bounded set of technical instructions on how to form letters, how to connect written symbols with words and how to derive meaningful utterances from text; rather literacy is a social practice embedded in social networks and in other cultural practices. Street (1984, p. 28) defines literacy as 'a social construction, not a neutral technology [whose]

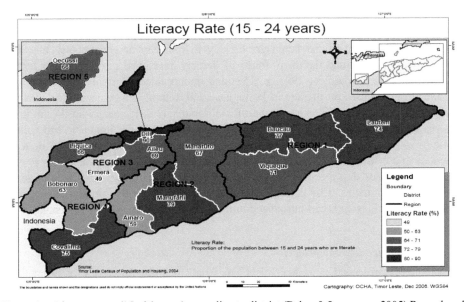

Figure 4. Literacy rates (15–24 years) according to district (Baker & Langeraar, 2005) Reproduced with kind permission of the authors.

uses are embedded in relations of power and struggles over resources'. Literacy also has an ideological dimension as I hope to show in the following discussion of the history of literacy education in Timor-Leste.

The parlous state of literacy in Timor-Leste reflects the fact that it has long been the instrument of colonialism. The consequences of Portuguese and Indonesian literacy planning and practices have shaped both the culture of Timor-Leste and the course of its history. Literacy has been seen as cultural missionary work (bringing the light of the gospel to the unenlightened and uncivilised natives), as a means of social exclusion and as a means of social control. In 'Portuguese times' literacy was a mechanism for bringing about the compliance of the indigenous leaders by incorporating them into the colonial enterprise and by excluding the vast majority of the population from the colonial elite. Under the Indonesians, literacy was a mechanism for the social and ideological control of the masses. Contemporary literacy rates in Timor-Leste and their distribution reflect both deep social inequality and alienation from an education system that has never reflected the needs and cultural realities of most of the population.

Yet ironically, literacy education has played a central role in shaping national identity in Timor-Leste. For the Indonesians in their independence struggle, literacy in the language of the coloniser (Dutch) had enabled wider communication and access to modernity. Increased educational provision in the Indonesian language under the Indonesian admistration offered greater numbers of East Timorese access to literacy. As far as the East Timorese were concerned, under Portuguese colonial administration, mass education was never a policy[6] and Indonesian literacy teaching on a national scale had the opposite effect to that which was intended. As Almeida (2001, p. 601) points out, while the spread of literacy in 'Indonesian times' failed to incorporate the East Timorese people into the Indonesian development project, literacy enabled new generations to make contact with each other and with the outside world and thus to agitate for support for national independence.

The failure to inculcate universal literacy in 'Indonesian times' serves to support the recognition that literacy is not merely the mechanical ability to read and write but rather is determined by social and political conditions. Language planning for literacy not only makes statements about perceptions of literacy but it also allocates status and functions to particular languages as languages of literacy. Where literacy is defined only in terms of the formal, written official language, literacy in minority or endogenous languages becomes marginalised and the many forms of literacy developed in other languages can be misrecognised (Bourdieu, 1991, p. 153) and undervalued. Current education policy in Timor-Leste focuses on literacy in Portuguese and Tetum. Where access to literacy is solely defined in terms of literacy in the official language(s), learners who do not know these languages are often regarded as deficient in some way. Their linguistic and cultural identities are 'remediated' through the process of education in the language(s) of wider communication (Manyak, 2004). An alternative perception of literacy is that it is a set of language processes that are independent of any particular language and can be carried over to other languages. This concept enables literacy skills to be initially developed in vernacular languages and then introduced in the official language(s) at a later stage.

Post-independence literacy projects

Among the few projects that produce literacy materials in Tetum for schools in Timor-Leste is a religious organisation known as *Mary MacKillop East Timor*. Its members have been working in Timor-Leste since 1994 (see http://www.mmiets.org.au). *Mary Mackillop East Timor* produces a Tetum literacy programme entitled *Mai hatene Tetum* (*Let's learn*

Tetum) that comprises books for children and literacy resources for teachers from Kinder-garten to Grade Six. *Mary MacKillop East Timor* is currently working with UNICEF to introduce Tetum readers that use the official orthography in all schools (Sister Irene Macinante, *Mary MacKillop East Timor*, personal communication, February 24, 2007). The children's educational magazine series *Lafaek Ki'ik* (*Little Crocodile*[7]) for children in Grades 1 and 2, *Lafaek Prima* for children in Grades 3 and 4 and *Lafaek* (*Crocodile*) for children in Grades 5 and 6 published in Tetum by the NGO *Care International* are shining examples of reading material in an endogenous language that go beyond the class-room. The *Lafaek* series is the main source of reading and learning material for some 300,000 students in schools across the country. *Care International* also runs a radio program (*Radio Lafaek*) and a pen pal programme in which some 6000 children participate (Accessed February 4, 2008, from http://www.careinternational.org.uk).

As far as adult literacy is concerned, there is a tradition of popular literacy campaigns that harks back to the days of the literacy campaign organised by FRETILIN in the 1970s. However, such projects have suffered from lack of coordination and aid dependency leading to a mixture of programmes being implemented with varying degrees of success. The government is heavily dependent on international donors for assistance with adult lit-eracy programmes. Multilateral aid agencies support and sponsor various literacy pro-grammes largely in partnership with government or local NGOs. Oxfam, for example, has a comprehensive adult education programme that includes adult literacy. UNICEF has also funded adult literacy activities for young mothers as part of its focus on maternal and child health and welfare. However, influenced by the World Bank's view that adult edu-cation was not a priority and that donor efforts in education should instead focus on primary schooling, UNICEF shifted its focus to life skills programmes for young people (Boughton & Durnan, 2007, p. 212).

In 2005, Cuba sent a small team of advisors with a model for a mass literacy campaign that had been used in several South American countries. They began planning for a pro-gramme known in Portuguese as *Sim eu posso* (*Yes I can*). In this programme, each Cuban advisor has an East Timorese counterpart. Four hundred and forty-two tutors have been recruited, one from more or less every *suco* (see Part I). Tutors also include volunteer university students. In June 2007, in the week before the elections for the National Parlia-ment, the first classes opened and by September, several thousand people had enrolled (Boughton, 2007). The classes follow a distance education format using televised classes shown on DVD. The classes are supervised by the Cuban-trained East Timorese tutors. By the end of the course of 65 lessons the learner is expected to be able to write simple sentences about themselves. The teaching manual is written in Portuguese and Tetum (Retrieved April 9, 2008, from http://www.sydney-acfs.org/news/Sydney-ACFS-News letter-June-2007.pdf). The programme appears to rely on support from the top-down through the establishment of a National Literacy Commission; this kind of literacy cam-paign has been successfully employed in North Korea (Yang & Chee, 1963), the former Soviet Union, the People's Republic of China and other socialist states (Bhola, 1984).

Important lessons can be learned about the need for local engagement from the experi-ences of one particular adult literacy project implemented with the aid of the *Agência Bra-sileira de Cooperação* (*Brazilian Cooperation Agency*) known as the ABC. In 2000, the Division of Non-Formal Education, within the Ministry of Education, coordinated a commu-nity literacy project known as *Alfabetização Solidária* (*Solidarity in Literacy*), after the Brazilian NGO that developed the methods with Brazilian adults. *Alfabetização Solidária* (also known as *AlfaSol*) works in partnership with Brazilian universities and local govern-ments, under the overall coordination of the ABC. The programme was designed to teach adults and young people over the age of 15 to read and write and to broaden provision of youth and adult education (*La'o Hamutuk [Walking Together] Bulletin*, 2003, p. 14). The pilot phase of the Community Literacy project began in Dili in October 2000. A team of 20 East Timorese teachers, coordinators and instructors undertook a short training course in Brazil. The project opened 11 classrooms in Dili, catering for around 275 students. The methodology and materials were the same as those used in Brazil and the project aimed to teach students to read and write Portuguese, as part of the ABC efforts to promote the Portuguese language in East Timor. The pilot phase ended in December 2001 and in January 2002, the second phase extended the project to the rest of the country. Community Literacy classrooms were opened in all 13 districts, each with 10 teachers, a coordinator and a pedagogic instructor, totalling 156 staff. Staff training was done in Dili by a team of Brazilian teachers. The second phase ended in December 2002. According to *La'o Hamutuk*, the implementation of *AlfaSol* was marked by problems flowing mainly from the fact that *Alfasol* used Portuguese and its early materials expressed Brazilian rather than East Timorese realities. In addition, the project was managed from Brazil. Consequently, East Timorese project officials located in the districts were responsible for implementing the project but had no decision-making powers. Teams of two Brazilian teachers came to East Timor every 2 months for periods of 10 days, to visit project sites, check project implementation and make decisions. Each team was responsible for three districts, alternating their visits so that each district was visited only approximately every 6 months for no longer than 4 days. According to *La'o Hamutuk Bulletin* (2003, p. 17), many East Timorese working in the project at the local level reported that they considered the Brazilian management too geographically distant and not well informed about the situation in East Timor. In the third and final phase, the management of the project was transferred to the Ministry of Education, which assumed administrative and financial responsibility, including the payment of staff salaries. The Ministry of Education modified the project so that the first 6 months of the classes were dedicated to teaching basic literacy in Tetum, before the teaching of Portuguese literacy was undertaken. In its current form, the project aims to initiate 205 classes, serving some 6000 students across all 13 districts. In this last phase, the role of the ABC was redesigned to concentrate on capacity building for the Ministry of Education team, developing teaching materials and supporting the writing of a curriculum for non-formal education in partnership with the Ministry of Education (*La'o Hamutuk Bulletin*, 2003, pp. 15–17).

Adult literacy programmes in Timor-Leste appear to focus on the provision of functional, print-based literacy with the long-term aim of poverty reduction and economic growth in line with the UN's *Education for All* policy. Aid-funded literacy programmes in Timor-Leste so far appear to have adopted an autonomous literacy approach with an emphasis on low-level text encoding and decoding. Autonomous models of literacy are characterised by a view of literacy as 'an autonomous set of skills which are considered separately from their contexts and literate practice is seen as mainly print-based' (Liddicoat, 2004, p. 7). To date, literacy programmes appear to have taken little account of the literacy needs and goals of the learners themselves. Bi and multiliteracies are not addressed. A further problem lies in lack of coordination across sectors leading to patchy and inconsistent provision. According to Boughton and Durnan (2007), at the first National Literacy Conference in September 2004, there was broad agreement between both government and non-government participants that literacy should be a priority but delegates expressed frustration at the uncoordinated nature of adult education programmes being delivered by a range of government, local and international agencies. As Boughton and Durnan assert, it is questionable whether these efforts can achieve the desired results in view of 'the tendency for different agencies and even different personnel within the same agencies to take new directions with little understanding of what has gone before or of what might already be underway in other agencies' (p. 212). Among other things, Boughton and Durnan question whether the total value of this effort contributes towards achieving national development priorities or indeed toward strengthening East Timorese national culture and identity. An effective and coordinated literacy strategy will require international agencies and NGOs to maintain their focus on this area rather than moving on to other priorities; operating organisations need to come to a shared understanding of the possible range and purposes of literacies that can be promoted in urban and rural communities.

Official, working and national languages

The National Constitution of Timor-Leste declares:

- *Tetum and Portuguese shall be the official languages in the Democratic Republic of Timor-Leste.*
- *Tetum and the other national languages shall be valued and developed by the State.*

National Constitution of the Democratic Republic of Timor-Leste. Section 13, p. 16 (Constituent Assembly, 2002).

In addition to the high status accorded to these languages, there is also a paragraph in a section entitled 'Final and Transitional Provisions' which declares:

- *Indonesian and English shall be working languages within the civil service side by side with the official languages for as long as deemed necessary.*

National Constitution of the Democratic Republic of Timor-Leste. Part VII, Section 159, p. 64. Working Languages (Constituent Assembly, 2002).

According to Faingold's (2004, p. 17) typology of provisions, the language provisions in the National Constitution of Timor-Leste conform to 'Type 17: Official language; national language; provisions for official language and national language' in common with the constitutions of Cameroon (1973), Ireland (1973) and Switzerland (1998). That is to say, the Constitution:

(a) designates one or more official and national languages and
(b) establishes provisions to protect these languages.

Via this set of constitutional provisions, Timor-Leste has also joined a small group of nations that have granted an endogenous language equal official status with a former colonial language. Other polities that have recently officialised an endogenous language include Malaysia, New Zealand, the Philippines, South Africa, Singapore, Tanzania and Vanuatu; India constitutes an important earlier example.

Skutnabb-Kangas (2000, pp. 511–512; 524–525) developed a framework that classified language policy types from a linguistic human rights perspective, broadly dividing the treatment of languages and the rights of their users into four tendencies, either implicit or explicit, termed:

(a) Assimilation-oriented elimination or prohibition of language use (which forces speakers to assimilate to the dominant language).
(b) Assimilation-oriented tolerance of language use (which describes a situation where the use of language(s) is neither explicitly nor implicitly forbidden).

(c) Non-discriminatory prescription (which describes a situation where people are granted permission to enjoy their own culture and to use their own language – overt or explicit non-discriminatory prescription forbids discrimination against people on the basis of language, a condition that also amounts to a form of implicit toleration).

(d) Maintenance-oriented permission or promotion of language use (which is aimed at maintaining and encouraging the use of a particular language or languages. Maintenance-oriented promotion of language use includes the provision of government resources for the use of minority languages in public domains, the prohibition of linguistic discrimination and the institutionalisation – in principle if not always in practice – of the use of minority languages in public domains. These goals may not be overt but may be implicit in equal rights or anti-discrimination laws[8]).

Provisions for official language status in legal covenants constitute an important dimension of linguistic human rights. The treatment of language rights makes a fundamental statement about how identity is perceived by the state. Following Skutnabb-Kangas (pp. 512–513), Section 13 of the East Timorese Constitution makes a definitive statement of national identity in officialising Portuguese and Tetum and privileging them over the national languages. In terms of the treatment of language rights, Clause One of Section 13 previously cited constitutes an example of *assimilation-oriented prohibition* (see also Lopes, 1998, pp. 460–461). It implicitly prohibits the use of languages other than Portuguese and Tetum for official functions and it requires all speakers to use Portuguese and Tetum for official purposes instead of their own languages or the shared use of all languages. Clause Two of Section 13 previously cited constitutes an example of *maintenance-oriented permission*. The national languages are not forbidden; rather their use is permitted and supported but not in official situations. Taken together, the two clauses amount to *assimilation-oriented tolerance* in that the endogenous languages are not forbidden but their use is restricted to non-official situations. The clauses that provide for international relations and language also privilege Portuguese. Although Section Eight (Constituent Assembly, 2002, p. 14) of the Constitution acknowledges Timor-Leste as an Asia-Pacific nation, 'proclaiming special ties of friendship and cooperation with its neighbouring countries and the countries of the region', Section Eight provides that 'the Republic shall maintain *privileged ties* with the countries whose official language is Portuguese'.

As Cooper (1989, p. 100) points out, there are three types of official language. *Statutory official languages* have been defined as legally appropriate languages for all politically and culturally representative purposes on a nationwide basis. Statutory official languages have been granted legal preference over other languages in given territories (see also Shohamy, 2006, p. 61). There are two other types of official language: a language (or languages) used for day-to-day activities in business and the workplace, known as *working languages*; and a language (or languages) used for symbolic purposes, i.e. as a symbol of the state, known as *symbolic official languages*. In Ireland and Israel, Irish and Hebrew are both statutory and symbolic official languages (Cooper, 1989, p. 103). In Timor-Leste, Portuguese is both a statutory and symbolic official language whereas Tetum is a statutory and symbolic official language as well as a national language.

Working languages hold powerful positions in polities. English is both a statutory and a working language in Ireland. English has also functioned as a working language in Israel since its independence. French is a *de facto* working language in former French colonies, such as Algeria, Morocco, Senegal and Tunisia (Cooper, 1989, p. 101). The UN has six working languages and the European Union has three. In Eritrea, although there are no official languages there are two working languages (Arabic and Tigrinya). Some working languages have special status and function as *de facto* official languages (Hailemariam, Kroon, & Walters, 1999, p. 486). Faingold (2004, p. 21) and Cooper (1989) assume the term *working language* to mean the same as *official language* in the context of the Ethiopian constitution, which declares Amharic to be the working language of the Federal Government because Amharic is the day-to-day language of the Ethiopian legislature, judiciary and administration. The positions of English and Indonesian are not as clear-cut in Timor-Leste. Indonesian is still widely used as a language of administration, business and education. As for English, although it is not the language of the judiciary or the civil service, it is used in certain formal legislative domains particularly in those where the UN is involved. English is also used in the Timor Sea Office and in the Ministry of Foreign Affairs. Moreover, both English and Indonesian are used on a daily basis in other professional domains.

The exact meaning and purpose of Section 159: 'Working Languages' in the East Timorese Constitution is a matter of some debate. The phrase 'as long as is deemed necess-ary' is understood by many people to imply that the language clauses are temporary and open to change. The 2004 Census National Priority Tables (Direcção Nacional de Estatística, 2006, p. 46) make the following statement regarding Section 159: 'The working languages of Timor-Leste are English and Indonesian. They have been approved in the Constitution to allow for working communication purposes until such time as the offi-cial languages [...] are fully integrated'. Following Skutnabb-Kangas (2000, p. 512), Section 159 can be interpreted as an example of *assimilation-oriented toleration*. While Indonesian and English are certainly not forbidden, the objective seems to be to contain them in this category until Portuguese and Tetum are established.

An official language is a language that a government uses for its activities in settings such as legislation, public administration, the courts, education, the military, law enforce-ment and so on, whereas a national language is a language (or languages) that a nation adopts as symbolic of its traditional heritage. According to the East Timorese Constitution, Tetum has both official and national status, while the other endogenous languages have only national status. At present, the national languages of Timor-Leste have symbolic rather than substantive status. Scholars from the INL and universities in the Netherlands and Australia are engaged in the study and documentation of several endogenous languages (Mambae, Naueti, Bekais, Lóvaia and Fataluku). However, I suggest that policymakers need to con-sider specific statutory provision to protect the linguistic rights of endogenous language users if their protection and promotion are to become substantive.

Three defining discourses serve to reconstruct national identity in the Constitution. The most central discourse is found in the 'Valorisation of Resistance' clause (Section 11, p. 15) commemorating the struggle for national liberation. As Leach (2002) notes, this clause embeds the official conception of East Timorese history in the statement: 'The Democratic Republic of Timor-Leste acknowledges and values the secular resistance of the People to foreign domination and the contribution of all those who fought for national independence' (Section 11, clause 1). This same clause valorises the Catholic Church for its role in uniting the different language groups and facilitating the emergence of Tetum as an expression of national identity (Section 11, clause 2). The admirably humane 'Solidarity' clause (Section 10, p. 15) declares solidarity with other national liberation struggles to be a guiding prin-ciple of the new State (Section 10, clause 1) and commits the Republic to providing asylum to all people persecuted in struggles for national liberation (Section 10, clause 2). These discourses invoke the memory of Indonesian occupation and the resistance struggle. The national anthem and flag deploy the emblematic symbols of *funu* (*resistance*), *patria* (*homeland*) and *solidariedade* (*solidarity*) against imperialism. Yet the national anthem, first used on 28 November 1975, at the original declaration of independence, is written only in Portuguese. The Indonesians prohibited this anthem during the occupation and it was readopted at the restoration of independence in 2002. To date, it is still sung in Portuguese, as there has been no translation into Tetum.

While the language clauses of the East Timorese Constitution acknowledge societal multilingualism and attempt to deal with its complexities, their provisions are more conservative than the provisions in the language clauses of the constitutions of Eritrea and South Africa, especially with regard to the maintenance and promotion of the endogenous languages. South Africa is one of the few nations in the world that recognises the linguistic rights of both individuals and groups. In the East Timorese National Constitution, the right to speak and understand a language of one's choice is an implicit component of individual freedom of speech and freedom from discrimination making the East Timorese Constitution one of the most progressive in the world. It enshrines the rights of freedom of speech and information (Section 40, clauses 1–2), along with the right to enjoy one's cultural heritage (Section 59: p. 5). It guarantees the right of freedom from discrimination on grounds of colour, race, marital status, gender, ethnic origin, language, social or economic status, political or ideological convictions, education and physical or mental condition (Section 16, clause 2). Unlike the South African Constitution, it does not mention the language rights of groups. The drawback of the East Timorese *laissez-faire* approach to language planning is that it stops short of the active promotion of language rights for minority or national languages – that is, it enacts a constraint that can effectively mean that the domination of certain language groups goes unchallenged. To understand the discourses of the Constitution, it is necessary to situate them in their historical context. In order to understand the symbolic power of language in Timor-Leste, this monograph now returns to the past to consider the influences that have shaped the habitus.

Part III: language contact and spread

As Thomaz (2002) attests, there has been a long association between the East Timorese and the Malays. The Tetum word *malae* used to describe all foreigners comes from Malay. Until the beginning of the nineteenth century, Malay words constituted the majority of loanwords in Tetum. Place names, numerals and occupational words, especially those having to do with fishing and agriculture, reflect a long and close relationship with the Malays. As Malay declined in use, Portuguese took its place as the primary lexifier language for Tetum until the Indonesian occupation – a time when words from modern Indonesian began to influence the language.

The Portuguese arrived on the island of Timor in 1514, attracted by the opportunity to exploit the island's sandalwood forests. Missionary work began after 1566 when the Dominicans erected a fortress-settlement on the island of Solor. The descendants of Portuguese sailors who married local women at the original settlement on Solor were known as the *Topasses*.[9] The *Topasse* population had two distinctive features: the first feature was its use of Portuguese in addition to Malay as well as the local languages; the second feature was its devout Catholicism. The *Topasses* allied themselves to the Dominicans and although they were reluctant to accept any outside appointee of the Portuguese crown, they were fiercely loyal to the language. After the Dutch attacked the settlement on Solor in 1613, they allowed the *Topasses* to leave. Thereafter the *Topasses* moved their base to Larantuka in Flores and from there they came to command the trade routes between Solor, Larantuka and Timor. In 1641, the Topasses established a settlement at Lifau in Oecussi, and in

1642, they attacked the Tetum-speaking kingdom of Wehali on the central south coast of Timor with the objective of gaining control of the sandalwood trade.

Although various scholars have described the history of Tetum (Fox, 1997, 2003; Hull 1998a, 1998b, 1999; Schulte Nordholt, 1971; Thomaz, 1981, 1994, 2002), very little is known about the process of language change and how or why the dialects of Tetum have diverged from one another. The expansion of Tetum-speaking people from their traditional place of origin on the central south coast to the north and along the south coast resulted in several distinct forms of Tetum (Figure 3). *Tetum-Terik* or rural Tetum (also known as Classical Tetum as well as *Tetum-Loos* or *True Tetum*) is the name given to the language variety spoken along the central south coast and its hinterland. The language variety spoken around the border region in a north–south strip from the Ombai Strait to the Timor Sea is known as *Tetum-Belu*. The variety spoken in the capital city of Dili and its surrounds became known as *Tetum-Praça*, the city being traditionally referred to by the Portuguese as a *praça forte* (*fortress*) and also as *Tetum-Dili* because it established itself as the vernacular of Dili as the area became urbanised.

According to Fox (2003, pp. 11–12), in 1777, the Portuguese regarded the island of Timor as divided into two provinces: the western province of *Servião*, consisting of 16 *reinos* (*kingdoms*) situated in the western part of the island of Timor and inhabited by the Vaiqueno (Baikenu or Atoni) people; and the eastern province of *Belu* (*Provincia dos Bellos*) dominated by the Tetum-speaking *datos* (*lords*) of Belu and comprising at least 46 kingdoms extending across the central eastern part of the island of Timor.[10] Thomaz (1981, p. 58) surmises that the spread of Tetum was the result of the influence of the powerful Tetum-speaking Belu kingdom of Wehali, traditionally known as the ritual centre of Belu. Dili was traditionally a Mambae-speaking area and this language is still spoken outside a four or five mile radius of the town. Thomaz (1981, pp. 58–59) suggests two plausible reasons for the spread of Tetum:

(i)   that Tetum-Praça spread in Dili because as the capital of the territory, it was a natural place for language contact;
(ii) that assisted by Catholic evangelism, Tetum came to play a unifying and differentiating role, similar to that of the national languages in Europe.

The combination of aggressive Topasse activities together with constant skirmishes with the Dutch eventually led the Portuguese to relocate from Lifau to Dili, where they established a settlement in 1769. As Fox (2003, p. 17) observes, European colonialists had difficulty in conceptualising the power of native rulers. The Portuguese used the royal designation of *rei* (*king*) and instituted a hierarchy of military ranks from colonel to lieutenant before they settled on the title *liurai* (*in its original meaning 'surpassing the earth'*), as equivalent to a local king. Most *liurais*, fearing Dutch domination but also influenced by the Dominican friars, who were anxious to prevent the spread of Calvinism, transferred their allegiance to the king of Portugal. The territory slowly came under colonial control from the 1860s onwards but the Portuguese found it very difficult to control the territory and there were constant local rebellions that have entered East Timorese historical discourse as 300 years of *funu* or resistance to colonial rule. While the details of the bitter rivalry, recurrent disputes, battles and negotiations between the Dutch and the Portuguese over the island of Timor from 1816 to 1916 make fascinating reading, they remain beyond the scope of this monograph. Nevertheless, it is essential to appreciate that this rivalry and the complex web of alliances between indigenous rulers and colonialists were fundamentally connected with the formation of identities. With the division of the island, the East Timorese were increasingly committed to the Portuguese colonial project and consequently increasingly disconnected from events that were to shape post-colonial Indonesia and Southeast Asia (Gunn, 1999, p. 156).

As Fox (2003, p. 11) notes, it was only after relentless incursions from Dili into the interior that the Portuguese were able to establish some degree of control over the native polities and their rulers. At least 60 military missions were sent to subdue the East Timorese between 1847 and 1913 (p. 16). It was only at the time of the 1913–14 *Manufahi rebellion*[11] (triggered by an increased poll tax), when the Portuguese succeeded in organising an alliance with several kingdoms, that they were able to effectively establish colonial domination and were able to spread their control gradually throughout eastern Timor. The seriousness of the *Manufahi rebellion* made it clear to the colonial powers that further rebellions could not be tolerated. The Portuguese practice of conferring military ranks on indigenous leaders was an effort to construct allegiances and exert some degree of control. A colonial army was raised from each kingdom and every *liurai* organised his own civilian militia or *Companhia de Moradores*. This system gave rise to a creolised variety of Portuguese in the Dili suburb of Bidau after 1851 (Albarran Carvalho, 2001; Baxter, 1990). This creole, which had become obsolete by the 1950s, had its origins in the form of Portuguese spoken by the Timorese troops who took the place of the Malay-speaking troops from Sika in Flores. The creole spoken by these troops came to be known as the *Portuguese of Bidau* (Thomaz, 1981).

Continuous wars maintained this colonial military system almost into the twentieth century and many Tetum words originate from this system (Thomaz, 2002, p. 112). By about 1845, the use of Tetum and Portuguese was well established and had begun to displace Malay. Tetum was used as a contact language throughout the colony. The use of Malay is presently confined to the Muslim community, the descendants of Arabs from Hadramaut who came to Timor via Java, in the *Kampung Alor* suburb of Dili, once also known as the *Campo Mouro* (*the Moorish area*). At present, this community is isolated and somewhat ostracised.

Japanese military occupation 1942–45: untold sociolinguistic history

The island of Timor became a part of the Pacific theatre of operations during the Second World War. The Japanese occupied Portuguese Timor between 1942 and 1945 – a period of extreme hardship for the East Timorese. Some 40,000 people died resisting the occupation and assisting Australian troops. By the time the Japanese surrendered, the East Timorese population was close to starvation. Women suffered particular abuses of their human rights through the system of sexual slavery (women enslaved as 'comfort women' by the Japanese) that existed throughout Timor-Leste during the 3.5-year Japanese occupation (CAVR, 2006; Turner, 1992). Gunn (1999, p. 226) mentions that, as in other parts of Japanese occupied Southeast Asia, the colonial education system was dismantled and Japanese language teaching was introduced (also see Kaplan & Baldauf, 2003). However, as Gunn comments, it is difficult to imagine this practice being enforced outside Dili given the instability of the situation. At present, there are no data that I am aware of concerning the sociolinguistics of the Japanese occupation of Timor-Leste. This aspect of the period can therefore only be treated as part of untold history.

Post-war Portuguese colonial policy, planning and practice: the promotion of Portuguese as the language of the elite

After the Second World War, Portugal began to invest more extensively in the social development of its colony. The development of an authoritarian, corporatist state under the dictator, António Salazar (1932–68), developed a colonial economic policy based on maximum wealth extraction coupled with autarchic trading policies that made the colonies captive markets for Portuguese goods. Foreign investment in the colonies was discouraged because commercial opportunities were reserved for the exploitation of the Portuguese alone. This strategy was accompanied by the compulsory production of raw materials in the colonies in order to support the industries of Portugal. Compulsory crop production was supplemented by forced labour and high taxation (Meijer & Birmingham, 2004; Smith, 1974). This process was accompanied by an ideology that emphasised Portugal's mission to bring civilisation to the benighted natives who inhabited the colonies. A conservative, triumphalist Catholicism was promoted by the State and propagated in its colonies. This ideological framework was elaborated into the discourse of *lusotropicalism*, claiming that Portugal had a special affinity with peoples of the tropics enabling them to fulfil a civilising mission free of racism (Almeida, 2001; Ellsworth, 1999; Ferreira-Mendes, 1940). Portugal continued to govern by means of a combination of direct and indirect rule, managing the population through traditional power structures rather than by using colonial civil servants as the British and Dutch had in their colonies. This Portuguese practice encouraged the ongoing incorporation of traditional society into the colonial system (UNDP, 2002, p. 71). Colonial policy permitted educated members of a small elite group to become full Portuguese citizens with Portuguese civil rights. In order to qualify for membership in the elite, an individual had to assimilate fully into the Portuguese way of life and faith, a practice requiring a shift to the Portuguese language.

In the aftermath of the Second World War, the Charter of the United Nations affirmed the right of subject peoples to independence and rejected colonialism, placing Portugal under intense pressure to relinquish its colonies (Retrieved February 28, 2008, from www.unhchr.ch/html/menu3/b/ch-cont.htm). In anticipation of admission to the UN, Portugal sought to bring about the integration of its colonies by amending the Portuguese Constitution in 1951. The amendment erased the word *colonies* and replaced it with the term *overseas territories*. Hence, there could be no justification for refusing Portuguese membership of the UN (Ferreira, 1974, p. 13). The Organic Law (Number 2066) of Portuguese Overseas Territories, enacted by the Salazar dictatorship in 1953, affirmed that all colonies were *províncias ultramarinas* (*overseas provinces*) of Portugal. Resolution 1542 of 15 December 1960, carried by the UN General Assembly listed territories then under the administration of Portugal as *non-self-governing territories* within the meaning of Chapter XI of the UN Charter (Article 73 Declaration regarding non-self-governing territories. Retrieved May 2, 2008, from http://www.unhchr.ch/html/menu3/b/ch-cont.htm). This designation persisted until as recently as the 1970s when the Portuguese Overseas Organic Law of 1972 designated all territories as *autonomous regions of the Portuguese Republic* (Ferreira, 1974, p. 38).

An essential component of this highly centralised colonial policy was the designation of Portuguese as the official language of instruction in all of Portugal's colonies. The acquisition of Portuguese was promoted through both the education system and the Church. Although the early missionaries in Portuguese Timor had used Tetum, the language used by the Church during this period was Portuguese. According to Aditjondro (1994, p. 40), by 1975, almost a quarter of the population had converted to the Catholic faith. In 1952, the first *liceu* (*high school*) opened in Dili and the first vocational school opened 4 years later. Staffing numbers indicate the small scale of the project. By the end of 1974, there were 200 teachers in Portuguese Timor, of whom 16 were Portuguese and the rest were East Timorese. According to Nichol (1978, pp. 21–22), only a small percentage of the group had any teacher training. Taylor (1991, p. 17) reports that the numbers of

East Timorese children attending primary school between 1954 and 1974 increased from 8000 to 57,000. These children were subjected to a classically subtractive model of schooling. Education – for those who completed primary school education and for the still smaller number who graduated from secondary school – required that children use Portuguese. As the person who was mainly responsible for education in the colonies, then Overseas Minister Silva Cunha stated in 1972:

> Education must [therefore] be eminently pragmatic in this sense. It cannot have as its objective the mere spreading of knowledge but rather the formation of citizens capable of feeling to the full the imperatives of Portuguese life, knowing how to interpret them and making them a constant reality in order to secure the continuation of the nation (English translation in Ferreira, 1974, pp. 80–85).

The Portuguese language was compulsory – the only one to be used in education. Elsewhere Silva Cunha asserted: 'We must be obstinate, intransigent and insatiable in the intensification and use of the Portuguese language' (English translation in Ferreira, 1974, p. 85). There was strict enforcement of the language in the classroom. As reported in Pinto and Jardine (1997, p. 35) and in my own interview data (Taylor-Leech, 2007), the punishment for speaking anything other than Portuguese in school could be a *palmada* (a slap in the face) or a beating with the *palmatória* (a thick piece of wood with a handle and a disc with holes in it so that there was no air to cushion the blows, raising painful welts on the hands). This is a classic feature of assimilation in which teachers act as its agents by punishing students for using their native languages. This type of punishment has been traditionally used to enforce linguistic assimilation in many colonial environments – e.g. Australia, the UK, the USA and across Latin America and Asia.

The small number of East Timorese who reached junior secondary school formed the core of the intellectual elite. There was a high school, a technical school and a teacher training college. The seminaries provided education for students who were destined to enter the priesthood or the civil service. A privileged few *assimilado* (*assimilated*) students obtained the opportunity to study in Portugal but by 1974 there were only a handful of university graduates (Taylor, 1991, p. 17). The irony of colonialism was that this tiny group of educated assimilados provided the leadership and momentum for its eventual defeat; this elite group emerged as the major actors in the movement for independence. Most graduates took up posts in government, administration, the health sector, education or the army. In this process, as Taylor (1991, p. 18) writes, 'they came up against the familiar realities of their childhood: rigid political control, colonial hierarchies, propaganda masquerading as education in poorly resourced schools and a rural sector where basic diseases were endemic'. In the 1960s, it began to seem possible that new political and social groups could emerge, having the ability to express their aspirations for national development within the framework of indigenous social values (Taylor, 1991, pp. 18–19). They used Portuguese and Tetum to express their awareness of the country's potential for independence. These developments mirror similar events in other colonised territories, including Portugal's African colonies (see Davidson, 1972; Ferreira, 1974). The Philippines is a neighboring case (see Gonzales, 1980).

Chinese as an immigrant language

Chinese speakers have been present on the island of Timor since at least 1699. Merchants from Macao and Taiwan were extensively engaged in the sandalwood trade and in import–export businesses. The Official Census of 1970 estimated the Chinese community at 6120 persons (Dunn, 1983, p. 8). According to Dunn (p. 8), in the early 1960s of the 400 or so wholesale and retail enterprises in the Portuguese colony all but three or four were in Chinese hands; however, as Dunn notes, since this figure omitted the large number of Chinese-Timorese (who considered themselves Chinese in cultural terms), the real figure was perhaps twice that number. The Chinese maintained a close-knit social group, remaining socially segregated from the endogenous communities. Even at the end of the Portuguese colonial period very few Chinese individuals held Portuguese citizenship, most of them holding Taiwanese passports. The Chinese established a separate Mandarin-medium schooling system (Hajek, 2000, p. 403). Following the Taiwanese curriculum, the students studied Mandarin, Chinese history and Chinese culture, a system that was tolerated by the Portuguese colonial administration on the proviso that all students also studied Portuguese. This schooling system produced a population that was literate in Mandarin and Portuguese. The children usually used Hakka at home (John Hajek, University of Melbourne, personal communication, 18 July, 2007). In addition, they commonly spoke Tetum and in some cases another vernacular language depending on the locality in which they lived. The links between China and Macao were important not only because of commerce but also as far as the Church was concerned. Indeed, Portuguese Timor was part of the diocese of Macao. In the Indonesian invasion of 1975, the invading forces killed many Chinese; some groups were deliberately targeted while others were killed in random attacks. Most survivors fled the country, abandoning their schools and businesses. At present, as the 2004 census data show, speakers of Chinese varieties constitute only a small minority in Timor-Leste (Table 4). The Census Tables do not specify which varieties of Chinese are spoken.

The Democratic Republic of Timor-Leste: the popularisation of Tetum as the language of the common people

The process of decolonisation in East Timor was initiated in 1974 following from revolution that overthrew the Salazar dictatorship in Portugal. In July 1975, the Portuguese government promulgated Constitutional law 7/75 providing for the formation of a transitional government in Timor-Leste in preparation for the election of a popular assembly in October 1976. The popular assembly was to be responsible for determining the future of the territory. Political groupings in Timor-Leste began to prepare for independence. In the 1970s, the *Associação Social Democrática Timorense* (*Timorese Social Democratic Association*) – known as ASDT – was the first political grouping to use local languages in addition to Portuguese at its meetings. As Taylor (1991, p. 42) notes, this strategy offered an effective means of reaching the mass of the population who spoke no Portuguese and were relatively unaffected by European culture. FRETILIN (see Part I) was the ASDT's successor organisation. FRETILIN used Tetum-Praça as the language of the *maubere* i.e. the common people; the term *maubere* being taken from the name of a character in Mambae mythology. Whereas the Portuguese had used the word in a derogatory sense, FRETILIN transformed it into a symbol of cultural identity and national pride using the phrase '*the Maubere people*' as an expression of solidarity. FRETILIN also promoted Tetum in its literacy campaigns in the rural areas, using volunteers to teach adults to read and write.

The founding declaration of FRETILIN in 1975 stated its intention to retain Portuguese as the official language, while establishing a programme for the study of Tetum and the vernacular languages. However as Jolliffe (1978, p. 335) notes, FRETILIN was not the only organisation to support the retention of Portuguese. Support for the officialisation of Portuguese was spread across the political spectrum. FRETILIN's political rival, the *União*

Democrática Timorense (*Timorese Democratic Union*) – known as UDT – advocated 'the integration of the Timorese people through the use of the Portuguese language' (p. 337). Even the party that supported integration with Indonesia, the *Associação Popular Demo-crática Timorense* (*Popular East Timorese Democratic Association*) – known as APODETI – stated that it would support the right 'to enjoy the Portuguese language' as well as the use of Indonesian as the language of instruction (p. 326). FRETILIN stood out from the other political parties in that, although it adopted Portuguese as its official language, it went even further in promoting traditional cultural forms, a feature evident in its literacy program, following the Freirean principles designed to change the conscious-ness of the oppressed through educational dialogue, praxis (or informed action) and *con-scientialização*, better understood as *awareness raising* (Freire, 1972). FRETILIN's founding programme declared the objective of fostering the literature and art of the various ethnic groups through cultural exchanges and 'the enrichment not only of East Timorese culture as a whole, but also as a contribution to universal culture' (Jolliffe, 1978, p. 335).

As Gunn acknowledges (1999, p. 267), the construction of the *maubere* identity was a masterstroke on the part of FRETILIN. Identification with the values of *mauberism* in no way weakened one's kinship or tribal alliances. Currently, the term *maubere* provokes mixed reactions (see Esperança, 2001, pp. 49–156). Some reject it because of its masculine, patriarchal connotations. Nevertheless, *mauberism* represents the construction of a unique ethnonational identity for the East Timorese, an identity that enabled a unified national resistance movement to come together as a force for change. The development of other such indigenous cultural forms as music, poetry and dance as well as the use of vernacular languages enabled FRETILIN to express their ideas in ways with which the common people could identify. FRETILIN first declared independence in 1975 after gaining the upper hand in the short civil war that followed a coup d'état by the UDT. This declaration was made in the hope that there would be UN support for a sovereign state. Following the norms of the time, FRETILIN opted for the former colonial language as the language of wider communi-cation. Ten days after the declaration of independence, the *Tentara Nasional Indonesia* (*Indonesian Armed Forces*) (or the TNI) invaded the territory. In the 24-year occupation that followed the linguistic landscape changed dramatically.

To this point, this monograph has followed the history of Malay, Tetum and Portuguese from the sixteenth to the late-twentieth century in order to explain their continuity and their place in the habitus. However, Timor-Leste then experienced a second very different form of colonialism. The following sections trace the impact of coercive language shift under Indonesian occupation.

Indonesian language planning 1975–99: coercive language shift

The Indonesian invasion of 1975 resulted in the integration of Timor-Leste into Indonesia as its 27th province, ushering in a long period in which the human rights of the East Timor-ese people were ignored – a period during which the linguistic landscape changed dramati-cally. Saturation bombing by the TNI during the invasion and in the pacification campaigns that followed caused massive loss of life among the East Timorese. The TNI conducted a series of encircling movements and annihilation campaigns in order to cut off and contain the resistance forces, which also caused great loss of civilian life. By 1980, an estimated 200,000 East Timorese out of a pre-invasion population of less than 700,000 had died (Robinson, 2003, p. 16). In 1975–76 some 4000 refugees fled to Portugal and Australia (Liddle, 1992, p. 22) and another 40,000 people fled over the border to West Timor

(CAVR, 2006, p. 75). Immediately after the invasion, most East Timorese took refuge in the mountains where they survived for 3 years outside Indonesian control behind FRETILIN lines. In these areas, FRETILIN organised its popular education programmes. After an intensive campaign of bombing and air attacks by the TNI, many of those East Timorese who had taken refuge in the mountains were forced down into the lowlands where they were met and killed by Indonesian soldiers. Those who survived were relocated by the TNI into the newly established resettlement villages, known as 'strategic hamlets'. This forced resettlement of East Timorese communities resulted in starvation because the strategic hamlets did not have accessible plots of land that could be cultivated. Forced resettlement also led to the dispersal of traditional speech communities. The Indonesian government designated Timor Timur, as they called the annexed territory, a *transmigrasi* (*transmigration*) area. The transmigration programme was an important vehicle for the spread of Indonesian among the highly concentrated East Timorese populations. By 1980, there were a reported 150 transmigration sites for incoming Javanese and Balinese (Hajek, 2002, p. 193).

The standardisation and modernisation of Indonesian has been rightly hailed as a monumental achievement in linguistic planning and reform, carried out over a relatively short period of time (see, e.g. Alisjahbana, 1975; Fishman, 1978; Sneddon, 2003). Indonesian represents what Gellner refers to as *high culture*. It is a school-mediated, academy-supervised idiom that has been 'codified for the requirements of a reasonably precise bureaucratic and technological communication' (1983, p. 57). Besides the official communicative functions that Indonesian now serves, it is also 'expressly the symbol of national pride and identity and a tool for the unification of Indonesia's diverse ethnic, cultural and language groups' (Lowenburg, 1992, p. 66). Indonesian language ideology in the annexed province of Timor Timur was propagated though the aggressive spread of the Indonesian language and the targeting of Portuguese and Chinese for elimination. The use of Portuguese was prohibited in schools, in administration and in the media and Portuguese was overtly vilified as a colonial language (Hajek, 2000, p. 406). A person who was heard using Portuguese risked arrest, torture and accusation of being *kepala dua* (*two-headed*), in other words, a FRETILIN sympathiser or a spy.

As part of their strategy of assimilation, the Indonesians increased the school population. As Nicolai (2004, p. 44) comments, despite the many criticisms that can be made of Indonesian education policy in Timor Timur, one thing that could be said in its favour was that it introduced the concept of education for all. By 1985, nearly every village had a primary school (UNDP, 2002, p. 48); however, as Nicolai (2004, p. 46) also observes, although on the face of it education was available from the early years through to university, the reality was that for most people basic education lasted only about six years. By 1990, even in the 15–19-year-old age group who grew up under Indonesian administration, less than half of both males and females had completed primary school or gone on to further education (Jones, 2001, p. 48). The proportion of East Timorese who had achieved senior secondary education did not exceed 23% for males and 9% for females (Jones, 2003, pp. 257–258).

Assimilation was important for the integration of Timor Timur into the Indonesian state structure. This integration also served as a means of social control since most Indonesians did not speak Portuguese or the local vernacular languages. According to Budiarjo and Liong (1984, p. 111) Indonesian was strictly enforced as the medium of instruction. In the early years of the occupation, the use of Indonesian in schools disqualified most East Timorese teachers who did not have proficiency in Indonesian. Indonesian military personnel served as teachers in the rural areas and throughout the occupation period, the majority of teachers in the province were Indonesian (Arneburg, 1999, p. 85); i.e. 427 out of 3698 teachers in the province were East Timorese (Jones, 2003, p. 49). The curriculum was devoid of information about East Timorese history and culture and the quality of the teaching was notoriously poor (Budiarjo & Liong, 1984, pp. 110–112). Student and teacher absenteeism were rampant (Jones, 2003, p. 50). Assimilation into the Indonesian language and state ideology were also promoted through compulsory membership of the scouting organisation, *Gerakan Pramuka*. In this regard, the Indonesians appeared to have learned the strategy of organising strenuous, time-consuming physical activities and military-style training in secondary schools from the Japanese (Murray-Thomas, 1966, p. 632). Between 1978 and 1981, the numbers of young people joining Pramuka more than doubled from 10,000 to 22,455 (CAVR, 2006). Youth martial arts groups were also encouraged. Such activities played an instrumental role in promoting a culture of gangs and militarism. Gangs and martial arts groups, often with political affiliations, have proved to be an intractable problem in East Timorese society; gangs of disaffected youth played a central role in the 2006–07 violence (Murdoch, 2006).

Events in the 1990s demonstrated that universal education had not succeeded in winning the hearts and minds of young people who by that time had begun to emerge as among the most vocal critics of the Indonesian regime. As Nicolai (2004, p. 50) remarks, many young people rebelled against the prescriptive and centralised education system, which ironically had been designed to assure the formation of good East Timorese Indonesian citizens. The imposition of the Japanese language in Korea immediately following the end of the Russo-Japanese war (1904–05) produced similar results (see Rhee, 1992). Parallels can also be found in the Norwegianisation of the endogenous languages of Sàmi and Finnish. Such policies exemplify the overt prohibition of native languages in order to promote assimilation (Kaplan & Baldauf, 2003; Skutnabb-Kangas & Phillipson, 1989, p. 25). By the 1990s, students' active rebellion and passive resistance in schools had become a serious problem. Indeed, as Jones (2003, p. 50) observes, an Indonesian education did not lead to improved employment prospects, as there were so few jobs for educated East Timorese people. In the 1990s, the schooling of young people suffered severe disruption because of increasing civil activism and the violent responses of the TNI. The visit of Pope John Paul II to Dili in October 1989 prompted the first of many demonstrations led by young people; 40 demonstrators were arrested, interrogated and tortured in the aftermath (Carey & Carter Bentley, 1995, p. 247). On 12 November 1991, Indonesian troops fired on young East Timorese demonstrators in the notorious Santa Cruz Massacre, the event regarded as setting the trajectory for independence and bringing the situation to world attention. According to popular estimates, 271 people (mostly in their 20s) died, 382 were injured and 250 simply disappeared (Retrieved October 12, 2006, from http://www.etan.org/timor/sntaCRUZ.htm). In the academic year before the 1999 referendum, students barely attended school as they took up an increasingly central role in the campaign for independence. The orchestrated violence that followed the referendum of 1999 destroyed the education sector. Most of the teaching force fled and large numbers of students became displaced persons.

By 1999, Indonesian was in common use in its 27th province. The use of Tetum as a medium of instruction was tolerated in Catholic primary schools by the 1990s (Aditjondro, 1994, p. 40) but as children progressed through school, they were forbidden to use Tetum in the schoolroom. Intensive borrowing from Indonesian further influenced and altered Tetum, compounding the process of grammatical simplification which had already been reinforced by the predominance of Portuguese as the prestige language used for all public written functions. By the 1990s, Portuguese was no longer openly spoken or taught in schools and transmission to new generations became virtually impossible. Despite – or perhaps because of – this phenomenon, Portuguese acquired deep symbolic value as the language of the clandestine resistance. According to Albarran Carvalho (2003, pp. 70–71), most resistance fighters' chose to write their correspondence in Portuguese rather than in Tetum. Members of the clandestine resistance used Portuguese for writing internal documents; for personal and external communication; for secret reports, coding and letters and for writing memorial texts and poetry (see also Cabral & Martin-Jones, 2008, for a discussion of Portuguese and Tetum literacy practices in the resistance between 1975 and 1999). In addition, the Church retained Portuguese as the language of external communication.

This monograph would not be complete without mentioning the human cost of social policies and practices in the Indonesian era. At least 102,800 East Timorese people are estimated to have been killed or to have died of hunger or illness directly attributable to the occupation of their country (CAVR, 2006). A study published in the British medical journal *The Lancet* (Modvig et al., 2000), based on a survey of 1033 East Timorese households, found that 97% of people in the sample had experienced at least one traumatic event during the occupation. The effects of torture and post-traumatic stress remain widespread. Overall, the occupation subjected the East Timorese habitus to sustained physical and symbolic violence.

Language planning for liberation: National Council of Timorese Resistance language planning discourses

The *Conselho Nacional da Resistência Timorense* (*National Council of Timorese Resistance*) (or CNRT) was formally established at a meeting in Portugal in 1998. This was the first broadly representative gathering of East Timorese nationalists since 1975. A key outcome of the convention was the acclamation, on 25 April 1998, of the charter of freedoms, rights, duties and guarantees for the people of Timor-Leste known as the *Magna Carta*. The *Magna Carta* was to serve as the basis for the future Constitution of the independent state. The *Magna Carta* stated that it was committed to the following (Walsh, 1999):

- upholding human rights and constructing a pluralistic, democratic society;
- respecting the environment;
- building relationships with other Portuguese-speaking nations;
- supporting the Association of East Asian Nations, Asia Pacific Economic Co-operation and the South Pacific Forum.

The CNRT adopted Portuguese as the official language and declared Tetum the national language of the future independent Timor-Leste (Hajek, 2000, p. 408). There appeared to be different opinions as to the status of Indonesian. José Ramos Horta, then roving ambassador for the CNRT, stated that English would be taught at school from primary level but that there would be no place for Indonesian. Other Indonesian-educated representatives argued that Indonesian should be maintained and that there should be multifaceted co-operation with Indonesia. At the CNRT Strategic Development Planning for Timor-Leste Conference held in Melbourne, Australia from 5 to 9 April 1999, East Timorese intellectuals, academics and professionals again discussed language policy issues. As part of the gradual transformation of the education sector, the CNRT conference recommended that Indonesian should be phased out of public administration and of the education system over a 10-year period. As Hajek (p. 408) comments, there is little doubt that the progressive elimination of Indonesian from all public domains was an important objective. Portuguese and Tetum would take its place and there would be space for English. Neither of these two documents or any subsequent documents gave any recognition to the endogenous languages. A 10-year timeframe was agreed upon to allow for the systematic replacement and retraining of Indonesian-speaking teachers. However, events after 1999 rapidly overtook the CNRT vision of orderly language planning for Timor-Leste (Hajek, 2000).

1999–2002: the UN Transitional Administration: the arrival of English and the revival of Portuguese

In 1997/98, the Suharto New Order collapsed in Indonesia, shaken by economic crisis leading to widespread protests in Jakarta and demands for political change. In a total break with previous policy, President B.J. Habibie declared that he no longer wanted to shoulder the burden of its dissident province and offered the East Timorese people autonomy within the Indonesian Republic. The Portuguese agreed on a referendum to be held in May 1999 under the auspices of the UN. On 30 August 1999, 78.5% out of a 98.6% turnout of a population of 450,000 voted for full independence from Indonesia (Hajek, 2002, p. 193). In retaliation, militia groups were actively encouraged by the TNI to perpetrate extreme violence against the population. Pro-integration militia gangs subjected the country to a frenzy of attacks, massacres, looting and burning, resulting in the deaths of at least 1200 East Timorese civilians (Robinson, 2003, p. 1). Some 60,000 people were forcibly displaced from their normal places of residence and 250,000 individuals were forcibly relocated to refugee camps over the border in West Timor (CAVR, 2006, p. 85). One effect of the violence and forced movements of populations was the further dislocation and disruption of speech communities. Fortunately, this dislocation appears to have been relatively short-term, as many people have returned to their original communities. At the present time, only a small number of people remain in militia-controlled camps in West Timor or have not returned for other reasons.

Under a veil of censorship and media silence, the events and abuses of the previous two decades had largely gone unreported in the international media. In contrast, the conduct of the militias, the TNI and the Indonesian authorities at the time of the referendum received worldwide media attention. In response to international pressure, the UN Security Council authorised a multinational peacekeeping force under Australian command to restore order. The UN established the *United Nations Transitional Administration of East Timor* (UNTAET), responsible for the administration of the country during its transition to independence. On 30 August 2001, on the anniversary of the referendum, elections were held for political representatives whose task was to draw up a new constitution. To date, the five UN missions in Timor-Leste have used English as an official and a working language. There are currently 15 UN agencies operating in Timor-Leste. Large numbers of English-speaking aid workers have come into Timor-Leste, creating a demand for interpreters and translators who are proficient in English. However, as the Census Atlas shows, this demand is concentrated in Dili. In the more remote areas, the use of English is far less widespread. The number of job opportunities for English speakers in the capital gives a somewhat misleading impression of the spread of English – in fact, English has fairly specific uses (mostly interpreting) in a limited range of urban locales. The census results should serve as a reality check on the strident calls in some circles for enhancing the status of English.

At the same, time the Portuguese began investing in the revival of their language. Portugal is the largest single contributor of foreign aid to Timor-Leste. Of all donors,

Portuguese annual disbursements for the education and training sector have been the largest (Nicolai, 2004, p. 101). In the main, this funding focuses on strengthening Portuguese as the language of instruction. Among its other initiatives, these funds have provided language training for teachers, procured textbooks and supported scholarships for the further education of East Timorese students. By 2004, the Camões Institute had sent 350,000 school-books, 650,000 textbooks and 410 cooperating teachers to Timor-Leste (da Cruz, 2004, p. 2). Portuguese aid has also funded the reconstruction of the education infrastructure. In the academic year 2001/02, some US$59,090 went into establishing a Portuguese Language Centre and US$156,407 was invested in Portuguese language and other forms of development training via the Dili Distance Learning Centre (DDLC),[12] located in the offices of the World Bank. Portugal also donated US$ 36,023 for teacher training (MECYS, 2004a, pp. 49–53). Brazil has also provided assistance based on its language ties with Timor-Leste. Its funds go primarily into non-formal education in the form of literacy teaching (see Part II) and vocational education.

On the occasion of East Timorese independence, an editorial in *Camões Revista de Letras e Culturas Lusófonas* (*Camões Journal of Lusophone Letters and Cultures*) declared:

> ... uma das principais tarefas que a nossa política cultural externa terá de prosseguir nos tempos vindouros: a consolidação do português como lingua official do futuro Estado de Timor-Leste. Este desafio enquadra-se nos objectivos que traçamos para a nossa política externa e para a futura acção do Instituto Camões: por um lado, preserver e promover uma iden-titidade lusófona, reforçando a ligação entre todos os que falam português no mundo, e, por outro, ser um dos instrumentos da nossa política externa, contribuindo assim para um novo recorte na afirmação de Portugal.
> ... one of the principal tasks that our foreign cultural policy will have to pursue in coming times is the consolidation of Portuguese as [the] official language of the future state of Timor-Leste. This challenge forms part of the objectives that delineate our foreign policy and the future action of the Camões Institute: on the one hand, to preserve and promote a Lusophone identity, reinforcing the connection between all those in the world who speak Portuguese[,] and on the other, to be an instrument of our foreign policy, contributing in this way to a new contour in the affirmation of Portugal (da Cruz, 2004, p. 2, author's translation).

As Kukanda (2000) notes, the existence of international organisations based on a common language is an important feature of post-colonial language planning. The *Comunidade dos Países de Língua Portuguêsa* or CPLP (*Community of Portuguese-speaking Countries*) was formed in 1996. Its function is to maintain links between Portugal and its former colonies. The CPLP member states are: Angola, Brazil, Cape Verde, Guinea-Bissau, Mozambique, Portugal, São Tomé and Princípe. Timor-Leste became a member of the organisation on 31 July 2002. Among the objectives of the CPLP are social, cultural, economic, legal, technical and scientific cooperation among its member states and the promotion of the Portuguese language. The discourse of *lusofonia* – or family of Portuguese-speaking nations – has also arisen as a grand theme for reconfiguring Portuguese identity in the post-colonial period and following Portugal's incorporation into the European Union (Almeida, 2001, p. 597). This discourse is nothing if not ambiguous in its oscillation between a neocolonialist ethos and a multinational political project, as Almeida (2001, p. 598) observes. Other former colonial powers – most notably France – have also promoted such discourses: the discourse of *francophonie*, the modern Francophone movement, serves to construct a useful bloc in the fight for markets and against English and American influence (Hagège, 1996). France is a major donor in Francophone initiatives and this nation is currently educating a greater number of Vietnamese than it did when it was a colonial power (Wright, 2004, p. 133). A similar phenomenon can be observed with the promotion of *lusofonia* and the teaching of the Portuguese language in Timor-Leste. The 2007–10 Indicative Cooperation Program, signed on September 3, 2007, by Portugal and Timor-Leste was estimated to have a total operating budget of 60 million euros. Forty-six million euros were allocated to the area of 'Sustainable Development and Combating Poverty' including the education sector and the reintroduction of the Portuguese language into the curriculum (Macauhub Economic Information Service, 2007, ¶5).

Language and religion

It is necessary to look again to history in order to understand how language and religion have interacted in Timor-Leste. Religion has played a fundamental role in the shaping of East Timorese identity. The 2004 Population Census affirms that the vast majority of the East Timorese people (715,285) identify as Catholic. There are 16,616 Protestants; 2455 Muslims; 484 Buddhists and 191 Hindus; 5883 people identified themselves as followers of what the census called 'traditional religions' (Direcção Nacional de Estatística, 2006, p. 78), a term referring to the highly spiritual Animist belief system still followed in Timor-Leste. The links between Catholicism and East Timorese nationalism have their origins in colonial history. The following sections discuss five important historical instances that highlight the role of the church and religious ideology in shaping the habitus.

One of the grand contradictions of Portuguese colonialism was that while the Catholic Church acted as its central ideological apparatus, the Church was also perhaps the most critical agency in shaping East Timorese national identity. The first Dominican missionaries established close and privileged relationships with the *Topasses*, for whom Catholicism and the use of Portuguese were marks of their identity. As local indigenous leaders converted to Christianity, they too formed close associations with Catholic priests. The Catholic missionaries appreciated that they needed to learn the local languages if they were to reach out to the native peoples. The early missionaries provided the first context in which endogenous languages were used as written languages. The seminary schools were at the heart of the early Portuguese evangelical, civilising mission and the Catholic schools formed the sole basis of the education system well into the twentieth century. Education was confined largely to the children of baptised *dato* and *liurai* families who were schooled in Portuguese literacy and Catholicism (see Part III). In the late-twentieth century, East Timorese church leaders strove to provide safe haven where they could against the depredations of the TNI (Smythe, 1998) but with tragic consequences, neither the TNI nor the militias respected the sanctity of the Church. Two of the worst massacres of civilian refugees occurred at Liquiçá Church in April and at Suai Cathedral in September of 1999. A number of priests and nuns gave their lives protecting and defending the East Timorese people, their culture and their spiritual values. East Timorese church leaders were also a vital source of information about human rights abuses despite relentless intimidation by the TNI; Bishops Martinho Costa Lopes and Carlos Ximenes Belo provide two well-known examples of such courageous leadership.

Missionary language activity

The promotion of Tetum by the Catholic Church was an important element in the establishment of Tetum as a lingua franca. According to Hull (2000), Tetum became so closely associated with Christianity that it was called *a lingua dos baptisados* (*the language of the baptised*). Although at first, the clergy seem to have used Galoli as much as Tetum (Fox, 1997, p. 14), according to Fox (p. 20), Tetum was only seriously taken up in the nineteenth century as the Portuguese territories in the region were reduced to the island of Timor. Crucial to the development and spread of Tetum was the establishment of the highly influential Jesuit seminary at Soibada in the Samoro district in 1898. The Soibada seminary was the only secondary school in Portuguese Timor; it was intended for the training of *mestre-escolas* (*schoolmasters*) who would teach basic literacy, numeracy and catechism in rural schools. These *mestres* were the only educated indigenous group in the country and they had great prestige (Thomaz, 1981, p. 67).

The Portuguese missionaries' decision to evangelise the population in their home languages led to the production of catechisms and liturgical and biblical texts in various vernaculars. Missionary priests also compiled dictionaries and grammars intended to assist newly arrived missionaries in communicating with the local peoples. The most notable dictionary was the work of Father Sebastião da Silva who produced a Portuguese-Tetum dictionary in 1889 (Hull, 1998a, p. 8). Father Manual da Silva wrote a grammar of Galoli in 1900 and a Portuguese-Galoli dictionary in 1905. Various priests prepared catechisms, prayer books and Gospel translations in Tetum, Galoli, Midiki and Mambae in the first decades of the twentieth century (pp. 8–9). As Hull observes, the Portuguese missionaries were enthusiastic lexicographers. Father Manuel Mendes and Father Manuel Laranjeira collaborated to produce a larger Portuguese-Tetum dictionary, printed in 1935, which contained some 8000 entries. Two important works by Fathers Conceição Fernandes and Campos were unfortunately destroyed during the Second World War (p. 10) and according to Hull (1998a, p. 8), dictionaries of Waima'a, Makasae and Baikenu have also sadly been lost. In 1937, Father Abílio Fernandes published a Portuguese-medium Tetum course for Europeans. Father Artur Basílio de Sá was the first trained linguist to take an interest in East Timorese languages. He studied the phonology of Tetum and his principles for an orthography of Tetum published in 1952 (see Hull, 1998a) laid the basis for a phonetic spelling system. Father Abílio Fernandes' Tetum primer (originally written in 1937) was reprinted for the use of Portuguese military officers to help them fraternise with the natives in order to spread the Portuguese language. The notice in the back of the soldiers' handbook made no secret of this policy:

> Na convivência futura, o soldado tem por dever, progressivamente, ir sustituindo o tétum por português [. . .] aproxima-te dos mais isolados e sé merecedor da sua confiança, para que depois eles te sigam (Fernandes, 1967/1937).
>
> (In our future co-existence, soldiers must consider it their duty progressively to replace Tetum with Portuguese [. . .] Approach only those most isolated and be worthy of their confidence so that later they will follow you) (Trans. Hull, 1998a, p. 15).

The Portuguese civilising mission

In 1940, a Portuguese Concordat with the Vatican established the Diocese of Dili, thereby ending its subordination to the See of Macao. The Concordat established the Catholic Church as the instrument of colonial policy. As the accord declared in grand colonial manner, 'Portuguese Catholic missions are considered to be of imperial usefulness; they have an eminently civilising influence' (Taylor, 1991, p. 13). Lundry (2000) takes a strong view of the acculturating influence of the Catholic Church on the East Timorese, arguing that becoming Christian and becoming culturally Portuguese amounted to almost the same thing. Indeed, as Cabral and Martin-Jones (2008, p. 154) observe, a Catholic education provided access to higher social status and the opportunity of higher education in Portugal. A significant number of the future leaders of Timor-Leste were educated at Catholic schools or seminaries. This was to be an important factor contributing to the emergence of East Timorese political elites in the 1950s and 1960s.

Catholicism and social justice

The Jesuit seminary of *Nossa Senhora de Fatima* was opened at Daré in 1958 with the aim of producing an indigenous clergy and providing secondary education for young men. Although Vatican II (1962–65) made social justice issues part of the call to evangelisation, as Lundry (2000) observes, the discourses of Vatican II had little impact in Portuguese Timor. In fact, during the 1960s, the East Timorese church had a reputation for being aloof and deeply conservative. Church leaders such as Bishop José Joaquim Ribeiro were suspicious of what they perceived as FRETILIN's communist sympathies. Yet as the atrocities during the occupation worsened, many priests and nuns came to identify with the suffering of the people and started to become more engaged with the struggle. The clergy distributed aid, provided refuge for the persecuted and sent information to the outside world about human rights abuses. In doing so, they made a substantial contribution to the nationalist movement. As Lundry (2000) suggests, perhaps the single most important element in the growth of nationalism in Timor-Leste was the enculturation of the clergy. A shared sense of betrayal at the withdrawal of the Portuguese administration and the departure of many Portuguese church officials after 1975 were instrumental in bringing the Church and Resistance together. Indeed, it is widely felt in Timor-Leste that without the support of the Catholic Church, the Resistance would have collapsed and the use of Tetum might not have withstood the pressure of Indonesian language ideology.

The prestige of liturgical Tetum

The evolution of Tetum into a language of national identity is inextricably linked with the evolution of the East Timorese Church. Portuguese suffered a severe blow when it was banned from public use in 1981. The Catholic Church established a form of liturgical Tetum or *Tetum-Ibadat* (Fox, 2003, p. 43). As Fox points out, this variety of Tetum is widely understood because of its use in church services but it is not what people speak in everyday communication. As Williams van Klinken (2002) observes, the religious register of Tetum was strongly influenced by the fact that most of its writers had been educated at the Soibada Seminary. Liturgical Tetum uses many Tetum-Terik forms and has fewer Portuguese loanwords than Tetum-Praça, making it more difficult to understand for Tetum-Praça speakers. Nonetheless, the use of Tetum as a religious language raised its status and made it prestigious in the eyes of its users. In acceding to East Timorese Church leaders' request for recognition as a diocese separate from Indonesia, the Vatican indicated its implicit disapproval of the occupation and Tetum was upgraded to a full liturgical language in 1981. Tetum as a medium of instruction in the lower grades was also introduced into Catholic primary schools in the Diocese of Dili. Aditjondro (1994, p. 40) reported that during the Indonesian occupation, the use of Tetum was spread substantially through Church activities.

Pancasila, Catholicism and identity

Pancasila is a set of guiding principles for the Indonesian state. Its philosophy emphasises consensus and group unity, particularly in its vision of democracy (Wright, 2004, p. 85). *Pancasila* consists of five principles:

- faith in one God;
- humanitarianism;

- national unity;
- representative government and
- the pursuit of social justice.

These principles form the basis of a contract between the citizen and the state in much the same way as the French state invokes liberty, fraternity and equality in its relationship with its citizens (Wright, 2004, p. 263). *Pancasila* requires that everyone must subscribe to one of five officially recognised religions: Islam, Hinduism, Buddhism, Protestantism or Catholicism – probably the main factor that led to the conversion of most of the remaining Animist population in Timor-Leste to Catholicism. The number of professing Roman Catholics rose from only 27.8% in 1973 to 81.4% in 1989 (Aditjondro, 1994, p. 34). The number of Catholics also increased as a result of the influx of Catholic transmigrants from West Timor. In fact, as Aditjondro (1994, p. 37) reported, other religions also saw an exponential growth in this period, mainly among Protestants and Muslims.

There are various explanations for the dramatic increase in the rate of conversion. Aditjondro (1994, p. 35) suggests that Catholic icons substituted for the *lulics* or sacred objects used in Animist ancestor worship, since it became difficult to conduct Animist rituals and celebrations for fear of their being seen as resistance gatherings. Smythe (1998, p. 154) suggests that given the anticommunist views of the Indonesian regime, it was safer to be a Catholic. While both these explanations are probably true, it is undeniable that the East Timorese Church stood by the people and supported them through a period of terrible repression and intimidation. As Smythe (1998, p. 158) suggests, Catholicism came to symbolise identity to the extent that Catholicism fused with nationalism. Aditjondro (1994, p. 37), himself an Indonesian, declared that he felt Catholicism served as an expression of East Timorese collective identity. The Church provided a form of cultural space for the East Timorese. It was almost the only place where people could associate freely and publicly in large numbers. Additionally, the translation of the liturgies into Tetum raised its prestige in the eyes of ordinary people. This combination of factors con-tributed to the transformation of Tetum into a core cultural value and ensured its survival.

The shaping of the East Timorese habitus

This preceding account of languages in contact has identified a combination of six social, political and cultural variables that have helped to shape the East Timorese habitus.

1. The first was the formation of an educated Portuguese-speaking leadership influ-enced by European culture and ideas.
2. The second was the deep symbolic value of Portuguese as the language of the resistance.
3. The third was the successful elevation of Tetum from a language and culture despised and denigrated in Portuguese colonial discourse into a symbol of indepen-dence and national identity.
4. The fourth was the exponential growth of the Catholic Church and its stance against human rights abuses, leading to its acquisition of core cultural value for the East Timorese people.
5. The fifth was the expansion of education and literacy under the Indonesian admin-istration and the spread of Indonesian through the education system, which facili-tated the growth of pro-independence sympathies and networks, especially among East Timorese youth frustrated by the lack of opportunities.

6. The last arose out of the terror tactics used by the Indonesian security forces together with appalling human rights abuses and disrespect for East Timorese religious and cultural values. These tactics, abuses and disrespect have entered collective memory and have, to use Anderson's (1983, p. 15) phrase, 'engendered particular solidarities'.

In order to describe and understand post-colonial language policy, it has been necessary to delve into social policies and practices that have had a direct influence on official language choice and public use. I now turn my attention to language policy development in the independent republic of Timor-Leste.

Part IV: language policy and planning

Language policy and planning theory is rich in frameworks with which to examine instruments of policy development. Two such frameworks are particularly helpful in contextualising these processes in Timor-Leste, i.e.:

(1) Cooper's (1989, p. 98) accounting scheme consisting of eight components indicating the variables that need to be attended to in the language planning process:
   (i)   what actors,
   (ii) attempt to influence what behaviours,
   (iii) of which people,
   (iv) for what ends,
   (v)   under what conditions,
   (vi) by what means,
   (vii) through what decision-making process,
   (viii) with what effect?

(2) Ruiz's (1984) framework for analysing the ideological orientations of language policy development suggesting that there are three possible orientations underlying language policies, particularly in multilingual settings:
   (i)   The first and most common orientation perceives linguistic diversity as a *problem*. The kinds of action taken to deal with the problem take the form of eradicating, minimising or alleviating the problem.
   (ii) The second orientation perceives language and multilingualism as a *right* and acknowledges legal, moral and natural rights to local identities (often these rights are more assumed than actual).
   (iii) The third and most progressive orientation perceives languages and their communities as social *resources*.

Ruiz' schema allows for the fact that a polity might adopt a combination of these ideological orientations. Using the frameworks outlined in this monograph, the following section analyses four key instruments of language policy development:

- The Language Decree (2004);
- The orthography of Official Tetum (2004);
- The Language Directive (2004) and
- Medium of instruction policy goals for 2004–08.

The Language Decree of 2004: language as right

On 14 April 2004, the Council of Ministers issued Government Decree No 1 of 2004, entitled 'Orthographical Standard of the Tetum Language', popularly known as the Language Decree. In the East Timorese legal context, the term used to describe sovereign laws enacted since independence is a *Decree Law*. In the preamble to the Language Decree, a *language as right* orientation to Tetum is discernable. In its English version, the preamble states . . .

> Tetum given its dual status as an official and national language must be used in a consistent manner in the entire administration of the State [and in other institutions] as well as by the mass media. Tetum is an essential element in the construction of the Nation and in the affirmation of East Timorese identity. For this reason, its utilisation is a constitutional imperative and its implementation a matter of urgency. To this end it is essential that its orthography be made uniform as part of the process of developing the language. Conscious of the strategic importance of the Tetum language in the cementing of national unity, the Government hereby decrees in the terms of paragraph 0 of Article 115 of the Constitution of the Republic, as a regulation with the force of law, the following: Adoption and Implementation of the Orthographical Standard for Tetum (Retrieved June 6, 2006, from www.asianlang.mq.edu.au/INL).

The Decree adopts the standardised spelling system developed by the INL (Article One). The Decree confirms that . . .

> The official and [first] national language is Official Tetum, a modern literary form of the vernacular, most widespread in the country and based on Tetum-Praça with the proviso that this choice is made without prejudice to those varieties of Tetum circumscribed to particular regions, which the State preserves and fosters as national languages. (Article Two, English version).

The Decree provides that the orthographical standard of Official Tetum must be used in three high status public domains: in the general education system, in official publications, and in social communication. It further provides that . . .

> English and Indonesian, as simple working languages, must not be used in public images and priority must be given to Official Tetum and to Portuguese in public images and signs unless they are accompanied by texts in Tetum and Portuguese with greater visual prominence (Article Three, English version).

The Language Decree enacts three measures to reinforce the status of the official languages:

(i) It reaffirms Tetum as a defining symbol of East Timorese identity. The preamble makes the status of Tetum as a nation-building tool very clear.

(ii) The Decree legitimates the joint co-official status of Tetum and Portuguese.

(iii) The Decree adopts the official orthography of Tetum.

The decree requires that the co-official languages should take priority in public images and signs. Reflecting a *language as problem* orientation towards English and Indonesian, the Language Decree addresses the issue of the ongoing and widespread use of English and Indonesian by many NGOs. The Decree contains a mixture of sanctions and incentives to enhance the status of Official Tetum and Portuguese. Articles One through Three institutionalise Tetum and Portuguese, implying a *language as right* view of the official languages. The Decree legitimates the acrolectal or high form of Tetum as the prestige variety or standard. The three articles have the effect of ensuring space for the official languages. The symbolic uses of language in forms such as bilingual public signage, in street and place names, on public formal occasions, in education and in the arts creates space in which a limited range of language can be used to achieve great impact on community perceptions and revive a sense of cultural identity. Article Four establishes the INL as the Language Academy – the authority on standardisation. The INL also has the task of producing orthographies for the other national languages. In general, language academies are also established to preserve language purity. Part of their rationale is to keep the language free from foreign and politically undesirable influences. The INL has acquired some sweeping powers in order to achieve this remit. Breach of these provisions can lead to the cancellation of a researcher's visa. Among other provisions concerning linguistic research, Article Four sets out the role and function of the INL as follows:

- The INL is the scientific custodian of Official Tetum;
- The INL must develop the scientific activities necessary to the preservation and protection of the other national languages, devising orthographical standards for each of them (English version).

Article Four also charges the INL with responsibility for maintaining and preserving the endogenous languages. As Bowden & Hajek (2007, p. 268) observe, the Constitution provides a rare degree of recognition for the national languages. The Language Decree is an example of the *maintenance-oriented promotion* of Tetum. It charges the INL specifically with developing Official Tetum as the national language. The goal is to prescribe the use of English and Indonesian and consolidate the status of Official Tetum in the public domain. Politically, Official Tetum is a powerful symbol of national identity and potentially an equally powerful symbol of national unity. The appointment of a language-planning agency is important for the development of a modern lexicon, requiring the investment of significant resources over the long term.

The orthography of Official Tetum, 2004: language as resource

The new orthography of Official Tetum is an instance of the *maintenance-oriented promotion* of a language. The INL aims to achieve the standardisation of Official Tetum through a set of four principles for renovating the lexicon (Hull & Eccles, 2001). These principles are powerful statements of identity:

(i) Tetum-Praça will form the basis of the literary language.
(ii) Indonesian loanwords are to be avoided and eventually eliminated.
(iii) There is to be a distancing from Indonesian-influenced idiom in favour of Tetum-Terik and Portuguese-based higher vocabulary.
(iv) All loanwords are to conform to the rules of the orthography.

The standard orthography unifies previous systems into a more linguistically coherent one. The removal of Indonesian words is a first step in returning Tetum to its authentic endogenous origins. A contiguous aim is to devise a system that avoids the imposition of ethnocentric Portuguese or Indonesian-influenced spelling onto Tetum sounds. Hull and Eccles (2001, p. 222) declare that the orthography of Official Tetum aims to be true to the work of earlier orthographers while avoiding ethnocentric, Portuguese-influenced and macaronic spelling. The principles of renovation also aim to establish a systematic approach to word formation, establishing three key conventions:

(i) A clear set of rules for hyphenation of words (there are many hyphenated words in Tetum).

(ii) A set of rules for the use of accents to mark regular and irregular stress.
(iii) The Tetum-Terik phoneme /w/ is replaced by /b/ so that, for example, the Tetum-Terik word *lawarik* (*child*) becomes *labarik* in Official Tetum.

The orthography follows spelling principles introduced by FRETILIN in 1974, when it launched its national literacy campaign and the reforms introduced by the Catholic Church when it adopted Tetum as the liturgical language. These involved the simplification of Portuguese words. To give some illustrative examples, *educação* (*education*) is transliterated as *edukasaun* and *colonialismo* (*colonialism*) as *kolonializmu*. However, in other respects, the orthography departs from these traditions. One innovation that has proved controversial to a public schooled in Portuguese orthographic conventions is the transliteration of the Portuguese sequences *lh* and *nh*, which were imposed onto Tetum sounds, into *ñ* and *ll* as found in Galician, a language closely related to Portuguese. To give two illustrative examples, *senhor* (sir) as written in Portuguese is written as *señor* and *trabalhador* (worker) as *traballadór*. These conventions were previously completely unknown in Timor-Leste. Another reform that departs from Portuguese orthographic conventions is the consistent replacement of the grapheme *c* and the digraph *qu* with *k* as in *kareta* (car), *kaneta* (pen) and *kolega* (friend), although place names such as Bacau and Viqueque have not changed their spelling. A further change consistently transliterates the *ch* combination in Portuguese as *x*. Hence, *cha* (tea) is written *xá*. Actual pronunciation is closer to *sá*. A final reform occurs with the replacement of the diphthong *ou* with *o* so that, for example, *mouris* (*to live*) is spelt *moris* (Hull & Eccles, 2001, p. 222).

In a situation in which literacy levels are low and the concept of spelling rules is new, some people find the rules for hyphens complex while others find the functions of accents difficult to perceive. Indeed, there are many examples from other languages showing that not all attempts at orthographic reforms are successful (see Kaplan & Baldauf, 2003, p. 216, for a discussion of successful and unsuccessful reforms of Malay spelling). In short, the long-term adoption of the orthography depends on the willingness of users to change and the degree of fit between the orthography and concurrent popular notions of identity.

The Language Directive of 2004: language as problem

In the civil service, the reintroduction of Portuguese and the introduction of Tetum are already in progress. Law 8/2004, which came into force on 16 July 2004, established a number of requirements including the obligation of public servants to use the official languages as the languages of the public service. Article 2 (3) of this law specifies that the law applies to:

- Civil servants of the Defence Forces.
- The Police and administrative staff of the office of the President of the Republic.
- The National Parliament.
- The courts.
- The Public Defenders Unit.
- The Prosecution Unit (JSMP, 2004, p. 23).

The current language issues in the formal justice sector are a legacy of three drastic system changes in the formal justice sector. Indonesian public policy imposed a shift from a Portuguese to an Indonesian justice system. To complicate matters further, UNTAET Regulation 2000/11 (as amended by Regulation 2001/25, Article 35) had allowed for the use of four working languages (Portuguese, Tetum, Indonesian and English) in the courts during what was known as the Transitional Period, referring to the period between 1999 and 2002.

On 27 February 2004, the Superior Council of Magistrates adopted the Directive on the Use of Official Languages in the Judicial System, known as the Language Directive (the term *Directive* refers to a lower-level class of laws passed by UNTAET). The Language Directive established that after an interim period of seven months, all court documents were to be written in the official languages (JSMP, 2004, p. 4). One of the main justifications given by the Superior Council of Magistrates for its decision was the need for the courts to follow developments in other institutional areas such as public administration and the ministries, where Portuguese is currently in use.

The Language Directive reflects a *language as problem* orientation in the formal justice sector. It requires every court actor to use the official languages. The directive instructs all court actors[13] to use Portuguese in *actos procesuais* (*procedural acts*), correspondence, requests, official documents and letters (JSMP, 2004, p. 13). The directive allowed for the use of working languages in documents concerning sentences and appeal submissions up to September 30, 2004; after that date, judicial secretaries and other court officials were instructed not to accept documents that were not written in Portuguese. The judicial secretaries and other court officials would be subject to disciplinary action if they failed to follow this directive. According to the directive, all documents not submitted in the official languages must be returned to their authors and given eight days for translation to be completed before resubmission. To understand the full significance of the Language Directive, it is necessary to know something of the impact of several previous changes in the formal justice system.

The Judicial System Monitoring Program (JSMP) is a national NGO (funded by a number of English-speaking donors: Aus Aid, US Aid, The Asia Foundation, New Zealand Aid and the International Commission of Jurists. It is also funded by the Finnish Embassy) set up to monitor the courts, provide legal analysis and produce thematic reports on the development of the justice system. In 2004, the JSMP produced a report on the use of language in the formal justice system. The report was produced as an argument against the Language Directive and for retaining the use of working languages in the justice system until such time as court actors become fully bilingual. Although the report reflects the language attitudes of its writers, it also provides a glimpse into the realities of language change and shift. During the UNTAET period, regulations in the district courts were written in English with translations, mostly into Indonesian (JSMP, 2004, p. 8). Court actors in the district courts used Indonesian in hearings and for administrative purposes. UNTAET adopted 72[14] regulations, all written in English; 63 of these were translated into Indonesian and nine into Tetum. The Special Panel for Serious Crimes (set up by the UN and disbanded at the end of 2005) used English. From 2003 to 2004, the JSMP stated that it did not see a single case from the district courts where the court actors spoke Portuguese in hearings. During the same period in the district courts, the JSMP observed a gradual shift from Indonesian to Tetum, although Indonesian was still used for writing. The JSMP noted that in the district courts more hearings were conducted in Tetum in 2004 than in the previous year. However, in practice, the JSMP observed that court actors used Indonesian when writing long documents. Prosecutors still tended to use Indonesian for reading out indictments and sentencing. Appeal statements up to April 2004 were written in Indonesian.

In the Appeals Court too, the effect of multiple system changes on language practices was chaotic. Up to April 2004, the JSMP noted that only two written court decisions were issued in Tetum. According to the JSMP, during appeal hearings originating from the districts, the court actors used Tetum when they spoke. The JSMP noted that after April 2004, in compliance with the Language Directive, every document from the Court of Appeal had been written in Portuguese, although as the JSMP pointed out, these documents are all based on a set form that does not require high levels of linguistic ability to complete. The majority of indictments were written in Tetum. The JSMP observed that court clerks were complying with the Language Directive but for documents that were more complex, they usually made use of Indonesian. After 2004, according to the JSMP, two out of the three appeal judges who were fluent in Tetum had started to write decisions in Portuguese. On the other hand, the JSMP also noted some reluctance on the part of certain international judges to allow the translation of documents into Tetum from Portuguese, indicating an expectation that court actors should function fully in the Portuguese language. As the Appeal Court judges invariably work under international contract, there is also frequent turnover of personnel that leads to a lack both of continuity and consistency of practice.

There are two equally important sets of competing issues in the debate over language reform in the formal justice sector, neither of which have quick nor easy resolutions. On the one hand, the right to a fair trial implies that it is imperative to avoid any injustice arising out of errors of linguistic interpretation or delays caused by translation, possibly resulting in loss of public confidence in the system. On the other hand, the use of official languages in the judicial system enhances their prestige. Tetum does not yet possess a full set of legal terms that could be used in the formal justice system; this is due not only to the imposition of the Indonesian system but also to the fact that East Timorese communities have used an informal justice system based on oral traditions, known as *Lisan*, so no formal source of legal reference has existed for legal terms in Tetum. The INL produced a glossary of legal terms in Tetum in early 2005; in mid-2005, the first cohort of 23 students graduated from a course in legal translation and court interpreting using Official Tetum. The Asia Foundation, a US-funded NGO, also set up a project to develop and clarify legal terms in Tetum. Only a very small number of laws and decrees have been officially translated into Tetum. One of the tasks of the translators on completion of their training is to translate the applicable laws into Tetum. Simultaneous translation facilities have been available (although not always fully operational) in the Appeals Courtroom since April 2004.

This period of linguistic transition in the East Timorese justice system is likely to continue for quite some time. As Powell (2004, p. 111) points out, some 25 years after independence, Malaysia still ran its judicial system in English. Despite decades of sophisticated, well-resourced terminological development, there was still reluctance to shift to the full use of Malay in the Malaysian courts system (p. 109). Language shift in such a powerful domain is never straightforward. Moreover, the legal system in most countries is deeply linguistically conservative because words that have been tested in previous legal decisions have a known meaning and force whereas new wording may not be deemed to have the same connotations (Kaplan & Baldauf, 2003, p. 120). The delicate matter of the relationship between language and justice remains an important human rights issue. As Powell states of the legal profession in Malaysia, it has a long way to go before it operates in a language most people know best but that does not mean it is less just (2004, p. 126). The sentiment may be applied with some confidence to the legal system in Timor-Leste, which still faces a massive task of reconstruction and linguistic renovation. Indeed, the numerous sound and valid criticisms of the East Timorese legal system made by the JSMP since its inception have not so far included any serious miscarriages of justice on account of language.

The Language Directive, like the Civil Service Law of 2004, is an example of *assimilation-oriented prohibition* in placing an obligation on all court actors to use the official languages, in an effort to carve out a niche for the official languages in this high-status domain. The implicit objective is to eliminate Indonesian and English from the legal domain. The longer English and Indonesian dominate in such key domains, the greater the threat they continue to pose to the successful reintegration of the official languages. This has important implications with regard to the work of NGOs and aid agencies.

Medium of instruction policy goals for 2004–08: language as problem

A few brief statistics illustrate the scale of the task of rebuilding education in post-conflict Timor-Leste. According to the World Bank (2004, p. xvii), in 2001, 57% of the adult population had little or no schooling. Only 23% of the population had received primary education, 18% had received secondary education and a mere 1.4% had received tertiary education. Following the violence of 1999, most buildings had been burnt to the ground and a great number of non-East Timorese teachers had left the country, precipitating the collapse of the education system. The system was not operational again until the start of the October 2000 school year. From 2002, enrolment increased rapidly across the whole education sector in spite of the lack of adequate buildings, furniture and equipment, in spite of unsanitary, unsafe conditions in most classrooms and in spite of a severe shortage of both teachers and teaching materials. Between 2001 and 2003, the number of primary school teachers increased from 2992 to 4080 and the pupil–teacher ratio dropped from 67:1 to 45:1. At junior secondary level, the number of students increased from 29,586 to 38,180 and the number of teachers rose from 884 to 1103 (World Bank, 2004, p. xviii). Although this growth implies an improvement, the situation is still far from ideal. According to the development indicators published in the Education and Training Sector Investment Program (MECYS, 2004a, p. 1), net enrolment (i.e. the percentage of all children of primary age) in 2001 was 75%. This compares poorly with 99% net enrolment in Indonesia. Net enrolment of children of secondary age was 26%, compared with 43% in Indonesia and 67% across East Asia and the Pacific. The mean youth literacy rate (i.e. the percentage of the population aged between 15 and 24 who can read or write in any official language) is 73% compared with 98% for Indonesia. The Ministry of Education currently employs more than 7825 teachers, all recruited after 1999 (MECYS, 2004a, p. 20). Most of these are primary school teachers who were educated under the Indonesian system. At secondary level, a significant percentage of teachers are drawn from among university students who have not completed teacher training (UNDP, 2002, p. 52). A large segment of university teachers do not hold basic teaching qualifications let alone postgraduate qualifications. Many recently recruited teachers were employed simply on the strength of being able to speak Portuguese.

The negative outcomes of two assimilation-oriented education systems have left a legacy of low-level, low-quality educational, personal, social and economic development along with confusion, anger and controversy over the issue of national identity. Education remains in a state of crisis. It is estimated that at least a quarter of all students currently fail the school year in which they are enrolled and at least 10% abandon their studies at each year of primary and pre-secondary education (World Bank, 2004, p. 25). A significant number of parents still do not see education as a worthwhile investment. Rural parents in particular remain unconvinced of the value of education for their children. The World Bank Education Report of 2004 provides an index of the level of parental disengagement. This document reported that 32% of the poorest families and 26% of the richest families had 'no interest' in sending their children to school (World Bank, 2004, p. xix), citing poor educational quality (including in this category, instruction in a language that children did not understand) and lack of access to schools as the main deterrents. The World Bank (2004, p. xix) has predicted that only 47% of those who enter Grade 1 will complete Grade 6, while 53% will drop out. Dropout rates are consistently higher among boys than among girls (p. 25) and they are generally higher in the poorest social quintiles. On average, school dropouts will only complete 4 years of schooling, leaving school with very low levels of basic literacy and numeracy. The outcomes of this situation are low levels of skill and productivity in the workforce. Such high levels of school dropout and repetition also increase the costs of education. However, a much greater challenge to achieving universal basic education is the evidence that both parents and children remain alienated from two successive education systems that failed to acknowledge or respect East Timorese languages and culture or to meet educational needs.

Educational language reform in Timor-Leste is being phased in through the formal primary school system. The structure of the East Timorese education system consists of:

- 2 years of non-compulsory preschool or kindergarten, known in Portuguese as *escola pre-primária* (*pre-primary school*);
- 6 years of *escola primária* (*primary school*);
- 4 years of *escola pre-secundária* (*lower secondary school*); and
- 2 years of *escola secundária* (*upper secondary school*).

Upon completion of this structure, pupils sit for the *Ensino Secundário Diploma* (*Secondary School Diploma*). Curriculum and language planning for the pre-primary years takes place outside the formal school system. Currently, there are 70 preschools catering for around 4700 children. Only eight of these pre-schools are public and they are mostly situated in the urban areas. Not more than 2% of children between the ages of 3 and 5 years attend any sort of preschool programme (UNICEF, 2005, p. 18). Consequently, crucial opportunities for early language and literacy development are lost. In the first instance, the medium of instruction policy focused exclusively on the reintroduction of Portuguese. In 2000, UNTAET updated the primary school curriculum and Portuguese was designated as the language of instruction. This reform moved up a grade every year after that, reaching Grade 5 in the academic year 2003–04. This curriculum model delivered Portuguese as a subject for 4 hours a week. However, the practical difficulties caused by the fact that so few teachers spoke the language let alone wrote it led the Ministry of Education (under the FRETILIN government it was designated the Ministry of Education, Culture, Youth and Sport) to relax its policy and allow teachers to use Tetum to explain things to the children. Following intense debate over the issue of early literacy in the child's first language, in 2005 the Ministry accepted Tetum as the medium of instruction in the first 2 years of schooling, i.e. from Grade 1 in primary school.

The Education Policy Framework for the years 2004–08 set out a vision, goals and priorities for education. Education policy objectives include hastening the reintroduction of Portuguese as well as hastening the revival of Tetum in all schools. Under the new national curriculum framework, policy mandated the use of Portuguese as the medium of instruction from Grades 1 to 6 (World Bank, 2004, pp. 28–29). The new curriculum framework was introduced into each grade, commencing from September 2005 with Grades 1 and 2, with the objective of instituting the framework in all primary schools by 2009.

The new curriculum designated:

- 4 hours a week of Tetum and Portuguese as subjects in Grades 1–3;
- 5 hours a week of Portuguese and 3 hours a week of Tetum in Grade 4 and
- 6 hours a week of Portuguese and 2 hours a week of Tetum by Grade 6.

The new syllabus framework was introduced through the *Hundred Schools Parent-Teacher Association Project*, a pilot programme set up to encourage parent and community involvement in schools.

Colonial legacies continue to pose significant problems in the curriculum. Although Portuguese was introduced as a subject in the junior secondary grades from 2005, at the time of writing, the curriculum in junior high schools and senior high schools still runs on the Indonesian model. Indonesian is the most common language of instruction in the universities and high schools. Moreover, textbooks are still largely in Indonesian. At the National University, the degree structure, syllabi and methods of assessment remain predominantly Indonesian. By 2003, Indonesian was no longer taught as a subject in schools or in the national university; however, junior secondary and secondary school students have continued to use Indonesian books, while learning Portuguese up to the time of writing (World Bank, 2004, p. 29). In this educational context, a *language as problem* orientation is inevitable.

A key goal of the Education Policy framework was to reintroduce Portuguese and Tetum as languages of instruction (MECYS, 2004b, p. 10). The Ministry also committed itself to developing teaching materials for the official languages in addition to improving the educational standards and qualifications of its teaching staff. This improvement included:

- language development in Portuguese;
- the development of bilingual Portuguese/Tetum teaching materials;
- the development of parent–teacher associations and
- the reinforcement of the role of parents and of communities in school life (MECYS, 2004b, pp. 20–24).

One particularly striking statement in the MECYS Policy Document for 2004–08 stands out as an indicator of attitudes towards the use of Tetum and the national languages as medium of instruction:

> Overall, since Tetum is at a preliminary stage of development, the implementation of Portuguese will have precedence, and Tetum may be used as a pedagogic aide in the teaching of disciplines related to the environment, social sciences, history and geography (MECYS, 2004b, p. 11, English version).

Despite its co-official status, this statement firmly places Tetum in the role of junior partner to Portuguese and effectively states that it is an inferior medium for educational purposes. An educational policy containing the implicit assumption that endogenous languages are deficient contributes to the low esteem in which people tend to hold their native languages. This phenomenon frequently fosters a downward spiral of underachievement among their speakers; moreover, in this policy document, the national languages are not even mentioned.

The high level of multilingualism in Timor-Leste means that first language-based or vernacular medium schooling presents a major challenge. In almost all cases, the first language is unwritten. Appropriate terminology for education purposes is yet to be developed in Tetum, let alone in the national languages. School-based educational materials in the national languages are simply not available. Another logistical challenge lies in the employment and placement of adequately trained teachers who speak the local languages in the appropriate communities. To date, the medium of instruction policy appears to combine *maintenance-oriented promotion of Portuguese* with *assimilation-oriented toleration of Tetum*. Timor-Leste is not unique in encountering this kind of dilemma; the country shares such problems with small island states across the South Pacific faced with managing the continuing influence of colonial languages. As Lotherington (1998, p. 65) notes in the context of these small island states, 'postcolonial education policies continue to oscillate between the security of instituted colonial models and the pressing need to shelter and nourish [. . . indigenous] cultures and languages'.

As the draft curriculum framework for 2004–08 (MECYS, 2004b, p. 8) affirms: 'Portuguese and Tetum are the languages of instruction'. The framework describes one of the curriculum objectives for the teaching of languages as: 'the development of two languages at the same time in a process of mutual enrichment' (p. 9) and it goes on to state that early literacy will be taught in Tetum under the assumption that the transfer of literacy skills to Portuguese will occur, although it does not state clearly how such a transfer will be achieved. This position indicates that the new curriculum has shifted from a submersion model of bilingual education to a transitional one. At a policy level, it would appear that children are intended to acquire basic skills in Tetum while building up a threshold level in Portuguese sufficient to cope with the demands of schooling (World Bank, 2004, p. 29). After the introduction of Tetum in Grade 1, the emphasis changes gradually to Portuguese by the end of Grade 6. In reality, practice varies from school to school and teachers seem to be using a variety of language and content teaching strategies. Nevertheless, according to policy, children are learning to read in Tetum, which is a second language for many children and in Portuguese, which is an unknown language for the majority of children. A further issue lies in the reality that teachers are working in a low or no resource situation.

The Curriculum Framework states that its literacy goals are:

- to ensure the effective mastery of both national languages, both oral and written skills and
- to develop good habits of reading and writing in practical and recreational situations (MECYS, 2004b, p. 9).

These policy goals focus on literacy in the co-official languages. However, the goals do not address the many forms that literacy can take. As observed earlier, these forms include local literacies or literacy practices associated with local or regional identities (Street, 1994, 1995) as well as vernacular literacies. As Hornberger (1994) argues, literacy planning needs to engage with different forms of literacy and with the uses to which literacy will be put. Decisions concerning these options have important implications for the wellbeing of those citizens for whom literacy is being planned. In a situation in which teachers cannot give sufficient oral support for the second language and in which there is inadequate support for children's first language or lingua franca, transitional bilingual education can become submersive in effect. Moreover, if children's first languages are educationally and socioculturally devalued through continued emphasis on the colonial language, one potential long-term outcome could be continuing deficient mass literacy and poor home and community support for children's literacy acquisition. As Lotherington (1998, p. 72) advises, bilingual education requires careful attention:

- if it is to avoid failing to acknowledge the importance of maintaining and facilitating the languages of the home and community;
- if it is successfully to enrich and maintain children's linguistic repertoires; and
- if it is to value their first languages.

There is a substantial evidence to support the view that providing children with educational support for cognitive and social development in their first language enhances the acquisition and development of the second language by augmenting general language development, increasing language awareness and sharpening a sense of cultural identity. Such reinforcement is especially important for children in low-status speech communities (Baker, 2001; Cummins, 2000). Providing education in the home language also helps to enhance opportunities for increased community participation in education. Siegel (1997) reports that in Papua New Guinea, vernacular medium literacy programmes for children in community preschools resulted in substantial benefits for children when they entered formal education (see also Crowley, 2005, p. 36). However, such a goal is far from realisation in Timor-Leste, where print material in the vernacular languages is virtually non-existent and where the absence of graphisation for the majority of the national languages makes vernacular literacy education impossible to implement at present.

The use of a language as the medium of instruction provides a powerful tool for maintaining and reviving that language and its culture. The use of a language as the medium of instruction is also an important instrument for intergenerational language transmission (Fishman & Fishman, 2000). The prestige enjoyed by colonial languages together with the low status accorded to endogenous languages have jointly resulted in a universal lack of confidence in endogenous languages as being adequate and suitable for schooling. Like many former colonies, Timor-Leste has fallen victim to this popular interpretation. Its extreme poverty and aid dependency have worked to slow down corpus planning efforts and to impede serious commitment to literacy in the national languages. As Alidou (2004, p. 209) asserts, the absence of standardisation frequently becomes a convenient delaying tactic serving to maintain the power of colonial languages since little meaningful effort is devoted to the use of national languages as the medium of instruction. Although the World Bank (2004, pp. 89–90) has advocated the teaching of literacy in the first language in the early grades as a policy option, there is little evidence of a practical commitment to making this a reality in Timor-Leste. This situation is by no means unique to Timor-Leste. As Alidou (2004, p. 205) observes, the World Bank demonstrates continuing reluctance to embark on programmes to promote comprehensive bilingual education in Africa.

In summary, the medium of instruction problem in Timor-Leste is the legacy of two colonial powers, which imposed their own languages as medium of instruction for economic, political and cultural reasons. In the post-colonial era, the search for effective solutions to the problem has been constrained not only by inadequate physical and human resources and by the hesitancy of the Ministry of Education to promote the instructional use of East Timorese languages but also by the economic power of western agencies to influence development policies. Table 10 attempts to synthesise the goals, motives and orientations of language policy development using Cooper's (1989, p. 98) accounting scheme to draw the activities together into a process. The instances of language policy development discussed in this paper are classified according to:

   (i) their societal or linguistic focus (Haugen, 1983),
  (ii) their treatment of language rights (Skutnabb-Kangas, 2000; Skutnabb-Kangas & Phillipson 1989) and
 (iii) their ideological orientations (Ruiz, 1984).

The implications of this state of affairs for the maintenance of the national languages are discussed in Part V of this monograph.

Part V: language maintenance and prospects

The Democratic Republic of Timor-Leste came into existence in 2002 at 'ground zero'. Since then there has been a massive drive for the reconstruction of:

- basic infrastructure, governance, civil society and the economy;
- the formal legal system and the judiciary;

Table 10. Five instruments of language policy development classified by focus, activity type, goals, treatment of multilingualism and policy orientation.

Who?	Does what?	To whom or what?	By what means?	To what ends?		With what effects?	
Language planning agents	Statutory instrument	Focus: societal or linguistic	Activity type	Policy goals (the formal role of language in society)	Planning goals (the function of languages in society)	Treatment of multilingualism and linguistic human rights	Policy orientation
Constituent Assembly	National Constitution of 2002	Societal focus: Directed at the *uses of* language(s)	Status planning	Officialisation of Tetum and Portuguese as co-official languages Officialisation of English and Indonesian as working languages Nationalisation of 16 endogenous languages including Tetum	Revival of Portuguese	Maintenance/promotion of Tetum and Portuguese Tolerance of endogenous languages	Language as right
Council of Ministers	Language Decree of 2004	Societal focus: Directed at the *uses of* language(s)	Status planning	Prescription of language use	Tetum reinvigoration and spread	Maintenance/promotion of Tetum	Language as right

INL	Orthography of Official Tetum 2004	Linguistic focus: directed at the *structure* of language(s)	Corpus planning	Standardisation of Tetum Praça	Renovation of Tetum	Maintenance/promotion of Tetum	Language as resource
Superior Council of Magistrates: Ministry of Justice	Language Directive of 2004	Societal focus: directed at the *image* of language(s)	Prestige planning	Reversal of language shift	Extension of repertoire: modernisation and stylistic development of Tetum	Maintenance/promotion of Portuguese and Tetum	Language as problem
Ministry of Education	Medium of Instruction Policy Goals 2004–08	Societal focus: directed at language *users*	Acquisition planning	Redistribution of languages in society	Language revival and (re)acquisition through schooling	Promotion of Portuguese Tolerance of Tetum Elimination of Indonesian	Language as problem

- agriculture, information and communications and
- health, education and human resource development.

The government has had to manage the process of social reconciliation and building diplomatic relationships with Portugal, Australia and Indonesia as well as with the rest of the international community. The East Timorese have also had to manage their relationship with the UN and the international aid industry. Although in some quarters it has been called a potential failed state, modest progress has been made, particularly in the field of education (for a more detailed discussion, see Anderson, 2006). Despite the recent upheavals, Timor-Leste is still an independent democracy, albeit a somewhat precarious one. The development challenges and achievements of the period between 1999 and 2006 have been described and evaluated in detail elsewhere (Anderson, 2006; Kingsbury & Leach, 2007; Nicolai, 2004). In this final part, I discuss the prospects for language maintenance and some possible future directions for language policy and planning.

Language revival efforts

Language revival efforts like other social reforms have been impeded by political instability and lack of funding. Competing language ideologies that disparage Tetum while promoting Portuguese, Indonesian and English have also hampered language revival and reform. At present, the languages of Timor-Leste coexist in an uneasy, hierarchical relationship. Language politics and *ad hoc* language practices on the part of NGOs aid agencies and peacekeeping forces contribute to a situation of *assymetrical multilingualism* (Clyne, 1997, p. 306) in which:

- Indonesian and English compete with the official languages;
- Portuguese has greater prestige than Tetum in most formal domains and
- the endogenous languages have a lower sociolinguistic profile than do all four official and working languages.

While the constitutional provisions for language allow for the development of scientific activities to protect and preserve the national languages, the main focus has been on reintroducing the co-official languages as quickly as possible. As Bowden and Hajek (2007, p. 272) point out, if the experience of other countries may be taken as providing some guidance, the concentration of resources on developing Portuguese and Tetum may prove to be economically of only short-term benefit. As the following examples show, current language revival projects are small scale and dependent on outside funding. There is still a long way to go for the endogenous languages actually to be maintained and promoted.

Three projects have achieved modest success in the face of funding constraints, lack of local expertise and political instability.

(1) The Linguistic Survey of East Timor, a collaborative project between the INL at the University of East Timor and the University of Western Sydney, was launched in 1995. It aimed to produce language profiles of selected vernaculars in East Timor. The East Timor language profiles are a series of basic descriptions of the national languages intended as introductions for linguists and non-linguists working in Timor-Leste. Language profiles have been published for Tetum-Praça, Waima'a, Southern Mambae, Baikenu and Galoli (Accessed February 4, 2008, from www.asianlang.mq.edu.au/INL/profiles.html).

(2) The Waima'a Documentation Project (see http://rspas.anu.edu.au/linguistics/ projects/waimaha/eng/team.html) focuses on developing and documenting Waima'a and on investigating the effects of its contact with a neighbouring language, Makasae. In addition to producing an orthography for Waima'a, the project participants have prepared two collections of children's stories, an alphabet book and a Waima'a–Tetum–Portuguese–English–Indonesian glossary for local distribution. The investigators report that the proposed orthography (based on the INL official orthographic conventions) and materials have been well received by the local community.

(3) Lastly, the Fataluku Language Project has produced a dictionary, a proposed orthography and recordings of songs and stories in Fataluku. The only written text ever published in Lóvaia is published on its website (Available April 30, 2008, at www.fataluku.com).

Potential policy outcomes

To return to the models used in my analysis of language-policy development, policy approaches in Timor-Leste combine non-discriminatory prescription, assimilation-oriented tolerance and maintenance-oriented promotion. A mixture of language-as-problem, language- as-resource and language-as-right orientations is discernable and no clear picture of a coherent overall orientation emerges. Mixed language-policy orientations are a product of deferential attitudes towards colonial languages, which are associated with modernity and progress while endogenous languages tend to be associated with backwardness and tradition (Fishman, 1990; Pattanayak, 1986; Ruiz, 1995). There are three potentially negative outcomes from this kind of policy approach.

The marginalisation of the national languages

According to the provisions of the Constitution, the national languages are not forbidden. Their use is permitted and supported but not for functions that are performed in an official language. The best outcome that can be expected from this policy approach is that the national languages will continue to be restricted to oral usage in rural domains. However, the worst outcome could be that as language shift begins to occur on a wider scale, the national languages might be expected to decline or even to start to disappear, an outcome that has occurred to a number of smaller languages in Indonesia (Florey, 1991; Hajek, 2006).

The failure of Tetum to thrive in higher domains

The orthography of Official Tetum, the Language Decree and the Language Directive are all examples of maintenance-oriented promotional language policies; however, in view of the overall policy approach and without evidence of greater support and engagement from social actors at both community and individual levels together with the cooperation of international donors, these maintenance-oriented promotional policies are unlikely to fully achieve the desired outcome of ensuring that Tetum thrives in the designated domains.

Subtractive language learning and lack of teacher/parent support

Initially, the medium of instruction planning followed a typical submersion model of language instruction. The recent change to a transitional model including an early shift to Portuguese is encouraging but it is still likely to result in subtracted competence in both Portuguese and Tetum in later grades. Submersion education not only affects the self-esteem of learners but also that of teachers and parents, who are themselves often survivors of such systems. The experience of being socialised into considering their own language to be inferior can lead teachers and parents to take a negative view of the use of first languages in the classroom. Parents also often want their children to learn the colonial language because they realise that it is the language of opportunity. Lack of parental support and understanding has been the cause of bilingual education policy failure in a number of contexts where the former colonial language is regarded as the only language of opportunity and upward mobility (Hornberger, 1987; Kamwangamalu, 2001).

Future directions

In view of the issues raised in this monograph, I would like to discuss four final recommendations, based on linguistic research and on the experiences of many small countries struggling with the legacies of colonialism that might underpin a more proactive, rights-oriented approach to language management in Timor-Leste.

Additive bilingualism offers the best model for valuing endogenous languages

The literature provides convincing international evidence that early immersion in the first language rather than in the former colonial language has educational, psychological, social and cultural benefits (UNESCO, 2003). The results from such immersion programmes have been positive in many parts of the world (Romaine, 2001, p. 529). The model of additive bilingualism, promoted through the education system, is widely regarded as the best model for valuing not only the official languages but also the endogenous languages and cultures and for exploiting the potential of those languages as resources for development and growth. An additive approach to language teaching and learning would demonstrate the value of Tetum by granting it equal status with Portuguese as a language of instruction and, as Alidou (2004) and Lopes (1998) suggest, would allow for vernacular-medium schooling at least as an oral medium through the early primary years. Such an approach can facilitate the transfer of literacy to the official language(s) at a later stage in education as has been demonstrated to be ideally the case with the 'Three Language Formula' in India (Khubchandani, 1978; Schiffman, 1996).

Lopes (1998, p. 31), writing in the context of Mozambique, has recommended an 'initial bilingualism model'. Applied to Timor-Leste, the initial bilingualism model would mean that the changeover to Portuguese would only occur after a period of at least 3 years in which Portuguese and Tetum were used as joint medium of instruction. This recommendation resembles the current Ministry of Education policy goals. However, I contend that policymakers should place greater emphasis on Tetum as a language of instruction and literacy. Such emphasis would not only validate Tetum but would also reduce the risk of underproficiency in Portuguese in the later grades. There is abundant evidence that the Tetum language has become an overarching core cultural value for the East Timorese people, suggesting that the young people and newly literate adults who emerge from an additive bilingual and biliteral education will do so with a good command of both Portuguese and Tetum. Young people and newly literate adults will also have the self-respect that comes from the knowledge and affirmation of their own linguistic and cultural identity and from the awareness that it is genuinely valued in society and by the state.

While schools cannot be expected to bear exclusive responsibility for language maintenance and revival, they can play an important role in forging links with parents and local communities to raise awareness and encourage cooperative engagement in language planning. It is vital that parents be convinced of the value of additive bilingual education. The Hundred Schools Parent-Teacher Association Project in Timor-Leste presents a golden opportunity to engage with parents on the issues of bi and multilingual education. In an additive approach to language teaching and learning, parents can play a useful role as models of the local languages. Parents and children can be more involved in the life of the school when the school validates the language that is used at home.

Successful literacy is indigenised into peoples' cultures

While the promotion of vernacular literacy cannot protect endogenous languages against possible threats from languages of wider communication, there are other very good reasons for encouraging literacy in the endogenous languages. In addition to the positive psychological and educational benefits, speakers of such languages can be informed about their own histories, cultures and traditions as well as empowered to make informed choices about their place in the world. Developing literacy can imbue a language with prestige and make it suitable for use in modern social domains. Dictionaries and grammars also enhance the status of languages in the eyes of their users. At the same time, however, as Grenoble and Whaley (2006, p. 102) point out, it is important to understand that the pursuit of vernacular literacy is not an end in itself. Local literacies require contexts of use. Ideally, the emergence of local literacies should increase the social and economic advantages of local languages for literate speakers. In addition, the objective should be to develop multiple literacies including literacy that:

(1) empowers people in their activities outside their immediate environment and
(2) emboldens people to use a local language by creating social spheres where reading and writing the local language is expected (Grenoble & Whaley, 2006, p. 118).

However, as Grenoble and Whaley warn, it is important to be cautious when it comes to introducing literacy to an endogenous, oral culture. As they point out (p. 103), literacy has a complex relationship with other aspects of culture and inevitably its introduction initiates changes in a traditionally oral culture. The introduction of literacy also implies that there is a literate group within the culture who can act as teachers and the creation and emergence of this group invariably calls for outside expertise and funding. The influences of external expertise and funding as well as the creation and emergence of a literate elite add another level of complexity. It is essential to assess the costs and benefits to a community that may accompany the introduction of literacy. Most unsuccessful attempts at literacy implantation occur when outsiders impose orthographies and prescribe forms of the language or reading materials that are unacceptable to those being asked to adopt them. Ideally, as Grenoble and Whaley suggest, literacy develops best from grassroots movements within the communities themselves.

According to Crowley (2000b, p. 379), the experience of literacy projects in many Pacific island populations demonstrates that literacy should be incorporated into people's cultures in order to permit them to be successful. This experience implies that while literacy has been introduced from outside, successful literacy becomes indigenised into the language ecology. A critical issue in Timor-Leste will be the production in both Tetum and the endogenous languages for both children and adults of literacy materials that go beyond the classroom and reflect East Timorese culture, values and realities so that literacy can have a purpose and can flourish. As Crowley (2000b, p. 384) has observed in the context of literacy teaching in Vanuatu, language policymakers should be encouraged to promote vernacular literacy in such a way that it promotes local rather than exclusively national or international interests. Crowley (2005, pp. 31–49) wisely recommends a very gradual introduction of initial vernacular literacy, over a period of at least 15 years in order to avoid losing public support through errors in implementation or poor planning.

Language policy success grows from changes in perceptions of language and from community decision-making

As I have discussed at length in this monograph, colonial language planning has fostered the impression that endogenous languages are inferior and as a consequence less suitable for use at higher levels of national life. Successful planning for language revival needs to grow from community changes in the perception of language and from community involvement in decision-making processes. Such processes can make a positive contribution to reconciliation and social reconstruction. Community engagement through the multitude of networks and NGOs that exist in Timor-Leste could yield rich lexical resources and encourage interest in the standardisation of Tetum.

Language policy can promote social inclusion

As Almeida (2001) observes, the era of post-colonial studies has been marked by the revelation of the dependency of post-colonial societies on representations of their identity by the colonisers. A language policy approach that invites an inclusive and accommodating view of identity should be able to incorporate the different narratives that have grown out of the experience of occupation and diaspora. Following May (2001, p. 311), I suggest that through the recognition of the collective language rights of all language groups, the nation state can be re-imagined (Anderson, 1983) to accommodate greater diversity, while still acknowledging the historical and cultural forces that have shaped the identities and the habitus of its speech communities.

On a final note, I suggest that successful nation-building in the present political climate makes social inclusion in Timor-Leste not so much an ideal as an imperative. A language policy that moves towards the maintenance-oriented promotion of language rights needs to acknowledge that language planning is a *niched* activity (i.e. it states unequivocally what languages should be used for which purposes). In closing, I suggest that such a rights/resource orientation to language management can avoid a situation in which *ad hoc* power relationships between languages continue to dominate social discourse and language politics. It can also enable the speakers of all East Timorese languages to participate in the nation-building process and to confront the challenges of social reconciliation and national development on their own terms.

Acknowledgements

My sincere thanks to Professors Robert Kaplan, Richard Baldauf Jr, John Hajek and an anonymous reviewer for their close reading and helpful comments on this monograph. All responsibility for the findings and any errors rest with the author.

Notes

1. PPP (Purchasing Power Parity) designates a rate of exchange that accounts for price differences across countries, allowing comparisons of real output and incomes. PPP US$ rate has the same purchasing power in the domestic economy as $1 has in the USA.

2. The survey was conducted over 2.5 years (August 2003 to December 2006). The representative sample of 1272 adults (aged 15 and over) was selected using random methods from all districts.

3. *GOLKAR (Sekretariat Bersama Golongan Karya or Joint Secretariat of Functional Groups)* was the ruling party during the Suharto regime (1966–98). It is the biggest party in the current ruling coalition in Indonesia.

4. The last surviving Lóvaia speakers live in Porlamano in the Mehara *suco* in the district of Lautem. They are surrounded by the Fataluku language, which is used for daily communication across all generations. Fataluku linguistic vitality is very high. Although intergenerational transmission of Lóvaia has long been in decline, particularly since the Second World War, it is thought that 'cultural concealment' has contributed to its demise (Hajek et al., 2003, p. 165). Cultural concealment is a process in which subordinate ethnic groups mask their linguistic identity outside certain physical boundaries. Severe population loss in the Indonesian period and the advancing age of speakers also account for the drop in the number of Lóvaia speakers. It has recently been suggested that Lóvaia is not so much moribund as 'in a coma' because its speakers are only introduced to the language by someone who wants to transfer their knowledge of Lóvaia. This usually implies that the recipient will be in their 60s (Engelenhoven & Cailoru, 2006).

5. The figures for literacy appear to have omitted the data for the age group 6–9 years. In other words, the percentages for language use shown in Table 18 of the Census Atlas are for the population over the age of 10 and are based on the ability to speak, read and write in any of the official languages.

6. The constriction of mass-education policy was the same throughout Portugal's colonies. To illustrate, vernacular education was outlawed in Angola in 1921 and by 1950, all schools in Angola were Portuguese-medium (Powell, 2002, p. 271).

7. The crocodile is an important symbol in East Timorese mythology and culture.

8. Note, however, that such provisions may create conflict or violate other legal conditions (Youmans, 2007).

9. The word *topasse* is derived from *tupassi*, a Dravidian word, meaning interpreter. They were also called *os casados (lit. the married ones)* because they were the product of mixed race marriages, a practice originating in Goa and Malacca where there are many people of Eurasian origin (Albarran Carvalho, 2003, p. 74).

10. For an interesting discussion of the historiography of the island of Timor, see Hägerdal, 2006.

11. The *Manufahi rebellion* was a serious challenge to Portuguese control. It has been invested with nationalist sentiments, and the liurai *Dom Boaventura*, who led the rebellion, has gone down in the discourses of East Timorese history as a nationalist hero.

12. The DDLC is supported by the German Agency for Technical Cooperation and the Portuguese National Parliament. The Calouste Gulbenkian Foundation in Portugal and the Portuguese government also provide funding (see Timor Links, Accessed February 4, 2008, from www.worldbank.org/WBSITE/EXTERNAL/COUNTRIES/EASTASIAPACIFICEXT/TIMORLES TEEXTN/O).

13. Court actors include judges, prosecutors, lawyers and court clerks.

14. The figures given in the JSMP report are mathematically inconsistent. The figures quoted here must therefore be regarded as approximate.

References

Aditjondro, G. (1994). *East Timor: An Indonesian intellectual speaks out*. Melbourne: Australian Council for Overseas Aid.

Ager, D. (2001). *Motivation in Language Planning*. Clevedon: Multilingual Matters.

Ager, D. (2005). Prestige and image planning. In E. Hinkel (Ed.), *Handbook of research in second language teaching and learning* (pp. 1035–1054). Mahwah, NJ: Erlbaum.

Albarran Carvalho, M. (2001). Características das línguas crioulas e do Português conservado na zona. Contribuicão para a língua official [Characteristics of the creole languages and the

Portuguese conserved in the zone. A contribution to the official language.]. *Studies in Languages and Cultures of East Timor*, *4*, 20–36.

Albarran Carvalho, M. (2003). Panorama linguístico de Timor. Identidade regional, nacional e pessoal [Linguistic panorama of Timor: Regional, national and personal identity.]. *Camões: Revista de letras e culturas Lusófonas [Camões: Journal of Lusophone letters and Cultures*, *14*, 65.

Alidou, H. (2004). Medium of instruction in post-colonial Africa. In J. Tollefson & A. Tsui (Eds.), *Medium of instruction policies: What agenda? Whose agenda?* (pp. 195–214). Mahwah, NJ: Lawrence Erlbaum.

Alisjahbana, S. (1975). *Language planning for modernisation: The case of Indonesia and Malaysia*. The Hague: Mouton.

Almeida, M. (2001). Epilogue of empire: East Timor and the Portuguese post-colonial catharsis. *Identities: Global Studies in Culture and Power*, *8*(4), 583–605.

Anderson, B. (1983). *Imagined communities: Reflections on the origin and spread of nationalism*. London: Verso.

Anderson, T. (2006). Timor-Leste: The second intervention. *Journal of Australian Political Economy*, *58*, 62–93.

Appel, R., & Muysken, P. (1987). *Language contact and bilingualism*. London; Baltimore, MD: Edward Arnold.

Arneburg, M. (1999). Education and human capital. In J. Pederson & M. Arneburg (Eds.), *Report on social and economic conditions in East Timor* (pp. 83–103). Oslo: Fafo Institute of Applied Social Science.

Auty, R. (1993). *Sustaining development in mineral economies: The 'resource curse' thesis*. London: Routledge.

Baker, C. (2001). *Foundations of bilingual education and bilingualism* (3rd ed.). Clevedon: Multilingual Matters.

Baker, D., & Langeraar, W. (2005, February 3–4). *Timor-Leste 2004 Census mapping and GPS operations*. First Asia and Pacific Forum on Statistics. Retrieved January 29, 2008, from www.unescap.org/STAT/apex/1/apex1_session2_UNFPA.pdf

Baxter, A. (1990). Notes on the creole Portuguese of Bidau. *Journal of Pidgin and Creole Languages*, *5*(1), 1–38.

Bhola, H. (1984). *Campaigning for literacy: Eight national experiences of the twentieth century, with a memorandum to decision-makers*. Lanham, MD: UNIPUB.

Boughton, B. (2007, November 14–15). *East Timor's national adult literacy campaign and its contribution to social transformation*, Paper presented at the CRAMS Symposium, NSW: University of New England.

Boughton, B., & Durnan, D. (2007). The political economy of adult education and development. In D. Kingsbury & M. Leach (Eds.), *East Timor: Beyond independence* (pp. 209–221). Clayton, Victoria: Monash University Press.

Bourdieu, P. (1991). *Language and symbolic power*. Cambridge: Polity Press.

Bowden, J., & Hajek, J. (2007). Not just Tetum: Language development and the case of Waima'a. In D. Kingsbury & M. Leach (Eds.), *East Timor: Beyond independence* (pp. 263–274). Clayton, Victoria: Monash University Press.

Budiarjo, C., & Liong, L. (1984). *The war against East Timor*. London: Zed Books.

Cabral, E., & Martin-Jones, M. Writing the resistance: Literacy in East Timor. 1975–1999. *The International Journal of Bilingual Education and Bilingualism*, *11*(2), 149–169.

Canberra Times (Australia) (2007, July 7). Ramos Horta's new directions for East Timor. Retrieved June 28, 2008, from http://www.etan.org/et2007/july/07/07jrnew.htm.

Capell, A. (1944). People and languages of Timor. *Oceania*, *14*(3), (1943), 191–219; *14*(4), (1944), 311–337; *15*(1), (1944), 19–48.

Capell, A. (1972). Portuguese Timor. Two more non-Austronesian languages. *Oceania Linguistic Monographs*, *15*, 96–104.

Carey, P., & Carter Bentley, G. (1995). *East Timor at the crossroads: The forging of a nation*. London: Cassell.

CAVR. (2006). *Chega!* Final report of the Commission for Reception, Truth and Reconciliation in East Timor. Dili, RDTL: *Comissão de Acolhimento, Verdade e Renonciliação de Timor-Leste* [Commission for Reception, Truth and Reconciliation in East Timor].

Census Atlas. (2006). *Timor-Leste Census of Population And Housing 2004*. Dili, Timor-Leste: Direcção Nacional de Estatística [National Statistics Directorate] and UNFPA. Dili: RDTL. Retrieved April 11, 2008, from http://dne.mopf.gov.tl/latestrelease/publications/ATLAS/ATLAS%English.pdf

Cheetham, J. (2005). A weekly newspaper – East Timor's hope [Electronic Version]. *Union Aid Abroad Overseas Projects*. Retrieved October 29, 2007, from www.apheda.org.au/projects/east-timor/pages/1187140447_22841.html

CIA. (2007). *The CIA world fact book: Timor-Leste*. Retrieved December 10, 2007, from https://www.cia.gov/library/publications/the-world-factbook/geos/tt.html

CIA. (2008). *The CIA world fact book: Timor-Leste*. Retrieved June 8, 2008, from https://www.cia.gov/library/publications/the-world-factbook/geos/tt.html

Clyne, M. (1997). Multilingualism. In F. Coulmas (Ed.), *The handbook of sociolinguistics* (pp. 301–314). Oxford: Blackwell.

Cohen, M. (2002). A tangle of tongues. *Far Eastern Economic Review, 165*(14), 50–52.

Constituent Assembly (2002). *The Constitution of the Democratic Republic of Timor-Leste*. Dili: RDTL.

Cooper, R. (1989). *Language planning and social change*. Cambridge University Press.

Crowley, T. (2000a). The language situation in Vanuatu. *Current Issues in Language Planning, 1*(1), 47–132.

Crowley, T. (2000b). The consequences of vernacular (il)literacy in the Pacific. *Current Issues in Language Planning, 1*(3), 368–388.

Crowley, T. (2005). Competing agendas in indigenous language renewal: Initial vernacular education in Vanuatu. *International Journal of the Sociology of Language, 172*, 31–49.

Cummins, J. (2000). *Language, power and pedagogy: Bilingual children in the crossfire*. Clevedon: Multilingual Matters.

da Cruz, A. (2004). Editorial. *Camões: Revista de letras e culturas Lusófonas [Camões: Journal of Lusophone Letters and Cultures], 14*, 1.

Davidson, B. (1972). *In the eye of the storm: Angola's people*. London: Longman.

Direcção Nacional de Estatística (National Statistics Directorate). (2006). *National priority tables: Census of Population and Housing 2004*. Dili: RDTL, Direcção Nacional de Estatística and United Nations Population Fund (UNFPA).

Dodd, M. (2001, August 25). Timor fighting a war of words. *The Age*. (Australia). Retrieved June 28, 2008, from http://www.etan.org/et2001c/august/19-25/25tfight.htm.

Drysdale, J. (2007). *Sustainable development or resource cursed? An exploration of Timor-Leste's institutional choices*. Unpublished doctoral dissertation, Australian National University, Canberra ACT.

Dunn, J. (1983). *East Timor: A rough passage to independence*. Double Bay, NSW: Longueville Books.

Ellsworth, K. (1999, February 19). *Racial and ethnic relations in the modern world-system: A comparative analysis of Portuguese influence in Angola and Brazil*, Paper presented at the 1999 Conference of the International Studies Association.

Esperança, J. (2001). *Estudos de Linguística Timorense [Studies of Timorese Linguistics]*. Aveiro: SUL Associação De Cooperação Para o Desenvolvimento.

Faingold, E. (2004). Language rights and language justice in the constitutions of the world. *Language Problems & Language Planning, 28*(1), 11–24.

Fasold, F. (1984). *The sociolinguistics of society*. Oxford: Basil Blackwell.

Ferguson, C. (1959). Diglossia. *Words, 15*, 325–340.

Fernandes, A. (1967). *Metodo pratico de aprender o Tetum [Practical method for learning Tetum]*. Macao: Escola tipografica do orfanato de Macau, (Original work published 1937).

Ferreira, E. (1974). *Portuguese Colonialism in Africa: The End of an Era*. Paris: UNESCO.

Ferreira Mendes, F. (1940). Portugal and her colonial empire. Part 1. *Journal of the Royal African Society, 39*(156), 225–230.

Fishman, J. (1967). Bilingualism with and without diglossia; diglossia with and without bilingualism. *Journal of Social Issues, 23*(2), 29–38.

Fishman, J. (Ed.). (1972a). Advances in the sociology of language: An interdisciplinary social science approach to language in society. *Advances in the sociology of language* (Vol. 1, pp. 217–404). The Hague: Mouton.

Fishman, J. (1972b). Domains and the relationship between micro and macro sociolinguistics. In J. Hymes & D. Hymes (Eds.), *Directions in sociolinguistics: The ethnography of speaking* (pp. 435–553). New York: Holt, Rinehart & Winston.

Fishman, J. (1978). The Indonesian language planning experience: What does it tell us? In S. Udin (Ed.), *Spectrum: Essays presented to Sultan Takdir Alisjahbana on his 70th birthday* (pp. 332–339). Jakarta: Dian Rakyat.

Fishman, J. (1990). What is reversing language shift (RLS) and how can it succeed? *Journal of Multilingual and Multicultural Development, 11*(1), 5–36.

Fishman, J., & Fishman, G. (2000). Rethinking language defense. In R. Phillipson (Ed.), *Rights to language: Equity, power and education* (pp. 23–27). Mahwah, NJ: Lawrence Erlbaum.

Florey, M. (1991). Shifting patterns of language allegiance: A generational perspective from Eastern Indonesia. In H. Steinhauer (Ed.), *Papers in Austronesian linguistics No 1* (pp. 39–47). Canberra, ACT: Pacific Linguistics.

Fox, J. (1997). *The historical position of Tetum among the languages of the Timor area,* Paper presented at the Tetum language conference, Mirambeena Tourist Resort, Darwin.

Fox, J. (2003). Tracing the path, recounting the past: Historical perspectives on Timor. In J. Fox & D. Babo Soares (Eds.), *Out of the ashes: Deconstruction and reconstruction of East Timor* (pp. 1–27). Canberra, ACT: ANU E Press.

Freire, P. (1972). *Pedagogy of the oppressed.* Harmondsworth: Penguin.

Funnell, A. (2002). Poverty-stricken – A divided nation struggles to cope [Electronic Version]. *ABC News Online,* Retrieved January 5, 2007, from www.abc.net.au/news

Gellner, E. (1983). *Nations and Nationalism: New Perspectives on the Past.* Oxford: Basil Blackwell.

Glover, I. (1971). Prehistoric research in Timor. In D. Mulvaney & J. Golson (Eds.), *Aboriginal man and environment in Australia* (pp. 158–181). Canberra, ACT: The Australian National University.

Gonzales, A. (1980). *Language and nationalism: The Philippine experience thus far.* Quezon City, Metro Manila: Ateneo de Manila University Press.

Gordon, R. (2005). *Ethnologue: Languages of the world* (15th ed.), [Electronic Version]. Retrieved December 11, 2005, from www.ethnologue.com

Grenoble, L., & Whaley, L. (2006). *Saving languages.* Cambridge University Press.

Gunn, G. (1999). *Timor Lorosa'e: 500 years.* Macao: Livros do Oriente.

Hagège, C. (1996). *Histoire d' un combat [History of a conflict].* Paris: Michel Hagège.

Hägerdal, H. (2006). Servião and Belu: Colonial conceptions and the geographic partition of Timor. *Studies on Asia, 3*(1), 49–64.

Hailemariam, C., Kroon, S., & Walters, J. (1999). Multilingualism and nation-building: Language and education in Eritrea. *Journal of Multilingual and Multicultural Development, 20*(6), 475–493.

Hajek, J. (2000). Language planning and the sociolinguistic environment in East Timor: Colonial practice and changing language ecologies. *Current Issues in Language Planning, 1*(3), 400–413.

Hajek, J. (2002). Language maintenance and survival in East Timor: All change now? Winners and losers. In D. Bradley & M. Bradley (Eds.), *Language endangerment and language maintenance* (pp. 189–202). New York: Routledge and Curzon.

Hajek, J. (2006). Timor Lorosa'e: Language situation. In K. Brown (Ed.), *Encyclopedia of languages and linguistics.* London: Elsevier.

Hajek, J., Himmelmann, N., & Bowden, J. (2003). Lóvaia: An East Timorese language on the verge of extinction. *International Journal of the Sociology of Language, 160,* 155–167.

Haugen, E. (1983). The implementation of corpus planning theory and practice. In J. Cobarrubias & J. Fishman (Eds.), *Progress in language planning* (pp. 269–290). Berlin: Mouton.

Himmelmann, N., & Hajek, J. (2001). A report on the current sociolinguistic situation in Lautém (East Timor). *Studies in Languages and Cultures of East Timor, 4,* 88–97.

Hornberger, N. (1987). Bilingual education success but policy failure. *Language in Society, 16*(2), 205–226.

Hornberger, N. (1994). Literacy and language planning. *Language and Education, 8*(1–2), 75–86.

Hudson, A. (1991). Toward the systematic study of diglossia. *South West Journal of Linguistics, 10*(1), 1–22.

Hull, G. (1998a). The languages of Timor 1772–1997: A literature review. *Studies in Languages and Cultures of East Timor, 1,* 1–38.

Hull, G. (1998b). The basic lexical affinities of Timor's Austronesian languages: A preliminary investigation. *Studies in Languages and Cultures of East Timor, 1,* 97–202.

Hull, G. (1999). Towards a language policy for an independent East Timor. *Studies in Languages and Cultures of East Timor, 2,* 1–7.

Hull, G. (2000, August 25). *Identity, language and educational policy.* Paper presented at CNRT Congress, Dili: Instituto Camões.

Hull, G. (2001). A morphological overview of the Timoric Sprachbund. *Studies in Languages and Cultures of East Timor, 4,* 98–205.

Hull, T. (2003). From province to nation: The demographic revolution. In J. Fox & D. Babo Soares (Eds.), *Out of the ashes: Deconstruction and reconstruction of East Timor* (pp. 29–40). Canberra, ACT: Australian National University E Press.

Hull, G., & Eccles, L. (2001). *Tetum reference grammar.* Winston Hills: Sebastiao Aparicio da Silva Project and the Instituto Nacional de Linguística [National Institute of Linguistics]. Dili: National University of Timor-Leste.

Internal Displacement Monitoring Centre (2007). *Timor-Leste: Unfulfilled protection and assistance needs hamper the return of the displaced,* Retrieved January 29, 2008, from www.internal-displacement.org.

Jolliffe, J. (1978). *East Timor: Nationalism and colonialism.* St Lucia: University of Queensland Press.

Jones, G. (2001). Social policy issues in East Timor: Education and health. In H. Hill & J. Saldanha (Eds.), *East Timor: Development challenges for the world's newest nation* (pp. 256–271). Canberra, ACT: Asia Pacific Press.

Jones, G. (2003). Education and human resource development. In J. Fox & D.B. Soares (Eds.), *Out of the ashes: Destruction and reconstruction of East Timor* (pp. 41–52). Canberra, ACT: Australian National University E Press.

JSMP (Judicial System Monitoring Program) (2004, August). *The impact of the language directive on the courts in East Timor,* [Electronic Version]. Retrieved February 10, 2005, from www.jsmp.minihub.org.

Kamwangamalu, N. (2001). The language planning situation in South Africa. *Current Issues in Language Planning, 2*(4), 361–445.

Kaplan, R., & Baldauf, R.B., Jr. (2003). *Language and language-in-education planning in the Pacific Basin.* Dordrecht: Kluwer.

Khalik, A. (2007). Indonesian yes, English yes, Portuguese, sorry, no. *The Jakarta Post, 3.*

Khubchandani, L. (1978). *Language, education and social justice.* Pune, India: Centre for Communication Studies.

Kingsbury, D., & Leach, M. (Eds.). (2007). *East Timor: Beyond independence.* Clayton, VIC: Monash University Press.

Kukanda, V. (2000). Diversidade linguística em África [Linguistic diversity in Africa]. *Africana Studia, 3,* 101–117.

La'o Hamutuk [Walking Together] Bulletin (2003). Brazilian cooperation in East Timor, *4*(3/4), 14–17. Retrieved April 9, 2008, from http://www.laohamutuk.org/Bulletin/2003/Aug/bulletinv4n 34b.html

Leach, M. (2002). Valorising the resistance: National identity and collective memory in East Timor's Constitution. *Social Alternatives, 21*(3), 43–47.

Liddicoat, A. (2004). Language planning for literacy: Issues and implications. *Current Issues in Language Planning, 5*(1), 1–7.

Liddle, R. (1992). *Pemilu-Pemilu orde baru: pasang surut kekuasan politik [New Order elections: The ebb and flow of political power].* Jakarta: LPPPES.

Lopes, A. (1998). The language situation in Mozambique. *Journal of Multilingual and Multicultural Development, 19*(5–6), 440–486.

Lotherington, H. (1998). Trends and tensions in post-colonial language education in the South Pacific. *International Journal of Bilingual Education and Bilingualism, 1*(1), 65–75.

Lotherington, H. (2004). Bilingual education. In A. Davies & C. Elder (Eds.), *The handbook of applied linguistics* (pp. 695–718). Oxford: Blackwell.

Lowenburg, P. (1992). Language policy and language identity in Indonesia [Electronic version]. *Journal of Asian Pacific Communication, 3*(1), 59–77.

Lundry, C. (2000, February 19–20). *From passivity to political resource: The Catholic Church in East Timor (revised version),* Paper presented at the Seventeenth Annual University of

California, Berkeley Conference, 'Religion, Civil society and NGOs in Southeast Asia', Retrieved September 29, 2004, from www.etan.org/etreligious/2001a/polresrce.htm

Lundry, C. (2004, October 6–8). *The success of tradition: Lisan and the reintegration of East Timorese militia members.* Paper presented at the Twentieth Annual Wisconsin Institute for Peace and Conflict Studies Conference, 'Challenges and Paths to Justice', Marquette University.

Macauhub Economic Information Service (2007). *Portugal signs 2007–2010 co-operation program with East Timor*, [Electronic Version]. Retrieved September 3, 2007, from www.macauhub. com.mo

Manyak, P. (2004). Literacy instruction, disciplinary practice and diverse learners: A case study. *Journal of Early Childhood Literacy*, 4(1), 129–149.

Mali, A. (2007, June 6). Ramos-Horta to announce plans to end E. Timor military crisis. *Kyodo News.*, Retrieved June 28, from http://www.etan.org/et2007/june09/06ramos.htm

May, S. (2001). *Language and minority rights. Ethnicity, nationalism and the politics of language.* Harlow: Pearson.

MECYS (Ministry of Education, Culture, Youth and Sports) (2004a). *Education and training: Priorities and proposed sector investment program.* Dili: RDTL.

MECYS (Ministry of Education, Culture, Youth and Sports) (2004b). *Education policy 2004–2009.* Dili: RDTL.

Meijer, G., & Birmingham, D. (2004). Angola from past to present. *Accord, 15*, Accessed October 16, 2007, from http://www.c-org/accord/ang/accord15/02.shtml

Modvig, J., et al. (2000). Health and human rights: Torture and trauma in post-conflict East Timor. *The Lancet, 356*(9243), 1763.

Murdoch, L. (2006, October 31). Dili gangs linked to political players. *Sydney Morning Herald* (Australia), Retrieved June 10, 2008, from http://www.smh.com.au/news/world/dili-gangs-linked-to-political-players/2006/10/30/1162056926759.html

Murray Thomas, R. (1966). Educational remnants of military occupation: The Japanese in Indonesia. *Asian Survey, 6*(11), 630–642.

Mytton, G., & Soares, E. (2007). *Timor-Leste National Media Survey: Final report*, Fondation Hirondelle [Hirondelle Foundation], Media for Peace and Human Dignity.

National Geographic Atlas of the World (2004). *Timor-Leste*, [Map]. Retrieved May 21, 2007, from http://www.nationalgeographic.com/xpeditions.atlas.etimor/etimor-d.pdf

Nichol, B. (1978). *Timor: The stillborn nation.* Melbourne: Visa.

Nichol, B. (2002). *East Timor: A nation reborn* (2nd ed.). Jakarta: Equinox Publishing.

Nicolai, S. (2004). *Learning independence: Education in emergency and transition in Timor-Leste since 1999.* Paris: International Institute for Educational Planning.

Noorderlicht (2007). *Sprankje hoop voor talenvorsers. Nieuw ontdekte taal Rusenu alweer bijna uitgestorven*, [Electronic Version]. Retrieved January 24, 2008, from www.noorderlicht.vpro.nl/ artikelen 336635727.

Pattanayak, D. (1986). Educational use of the mother tongue. In B. Spolsky (Ed.), *Language and education in multilingual settings* (pp. 5–15). Clevedon: Multilingual Matters.

Pinto, C., & Jardine, M. (1997). *East Timor's unfinished struggle.* Boston: South End Press.

Powell, R. (2002). Language planning and the British Empire: Comparing Pakistan, Malaysia and Kenya. *Current Issues in Language Planning*, 3(3), 205–279.

Powell, R. (2004). Terminological creation and language shift in Malaysia's legal system. *Current Issues in Language Planning*, 5(2), 109–129.

Rhee, M. (1992). Language planning in Korea under the Japanese colonial administration, 1910–1945. *Language, Culture and Curriculum*, 5, 87–97.

Robinson, C. (1993). Where linguistic minorities are in the majority: Language dynamics amidst high linguistic diversity. *AILA Review*, 10, 52–70.

Robinson, G. (2003). *East Timor 1999: Crimes against Humanity: Report commissioned by the United Nations Office of the High Commission for Human Rights (OHCHR).* High Commission for Human Rights.

Romaine, S. (1995). *Bilingualism.* Oxford: Blackwell.

Romaine, S. (2001). Multilingualism. In M. Aronoff & J. Rees-Miller (Eds.), *The handbook of linguistics* (pp. 512–532). Oxford: Blackwell.

Ruiz, R. (1984). Orientations in language planning. *NABE Journal*, 8(2), 15–34.

Ruiz, R. (1995). Language planning considerations in indigenous communities. *Bilingual Research Journal*, 19(1), 71–81.

Schiffman, H. (1993). The balance of power in multiglossic languages: Implications for language shift. *International Journal of the Sociology of Language, 103,* 115–148.

Schiffman, H. (1996). *Linguistic culture and language policy.* London: Routledge.

Schulte Nordholt, H. (1971). *The political system of the Atoni of Timor.* The Hague: Martinus Nijhoff.

Schulz, D., & Freitas, F. (2002, August 16). East Timor's tower of Babel. *Sydney Morning Herald,* p. 9.

Sheridan, G. (2006, June 1). Downhill all the way since Habibie let go: Australian policy towards East Timor has failed since 1998. *The Australian,* p. 012.

Shohamy, E. (2006). *Language policy: Hidden agendas and new approaches.* London: Routledge.

Siegel, J. (1997). Formal versus non-formal vernacular education: The educational reform in Papua New Guinea. *Journal of Multilingual and Multicultural Development, 18*(3), 206–222.

Skutnabb-Kangas, T. (1990). *Language, literacy and minorities: A minority group report.* Brixton, London: Minority Rights Group.

Skutnabb-Kangas, T. (2000). *Linguistic genocide in education or worldwide diversity and human rights?* Mahwah, NJ: Lawrence Erlbaum.

Skutnabb-Kangas, T., & Phillipson, R. (1989). *Wanted! Linguistic human rights.* Roskilde: Roskilde University Centre.

Smith, A. (1974). António Salazar and the reversal of Portuguese colonial policy. *The Journal of African History, 15*(4), 653–667.

Smolicz, J. (1991). Language core values in a multicultural setting. *International Review of Education, 37*(1), 33–52.

Smythe, P. (1998). The Catholic Church in East Timor. In T. Retbøll (Ed.), *East Timor: Occupation and resistance,* (WGIA Document No. 89, 153–176). Copenhagen: International Work Group for Indigenous Affairs.

Sneddon, J. (2003). Diglossia in Indonesian. *Journal of the Humanities and Social Science of Southeast Asia and Oceania, 159*(4), 519–549.

Steele, J. (2006, April 3). Timor-Leste Press essential in building identity. *Pacific Media Watch,* 12.

Steele, J. (2007). The voice of East Timor: Journalism, ideology and the struggle for independence. *Asian Studies Review, 31*(3), 261–282.

Steele, J., & Macdonald, J. (2007, June 11). Timor-Leste needs Indonesian language more than others. *The Jakarta Post Online.*, Retrieved June 18, 2007, from http://www.thejakartapost.com

Street, B. (1984). *Literacy in theory and in practice.* Cambridge University Press.

Street, B. (1994). What is meant by local literacies? *Language and Education, 8*(1–2), 9–17.

Street, B. (1995). *Social literacies: Critical approaches to literacy in development, ethnography and education.* London: Longman.

Suara Timor Lorosa'e. (2005, February 7). *53 warga Hatubuiliko mati kelaparan (53 citizens die of starvation in Hatubuiliko).*

Taylor, J. (1991). *Indonesia's forgotten war. The hidden history of East Timor.* London: Zed Books.

Taylor, A. (2005). Rural communications development in Timor-Leste. *Development Bulletin, 68,* 136–139.

The Australian. (2001, July 5). Timor deal closes the revenue gap. p.010.

The Australian. (2002, December 6). Tough tasks ahead for East Timor. p.010.

Taylor-Leech, K. (2007). The ecology of language planning in Timor-Leste: A study of language policy, planning and practices in identity construction. Brisbane, Queensland: Griffith University, Unpublished doctoral dissertation.

Thomaz, L. (1981). The formation of Tetum-Praca, vehicular language of East Timor. *Cahiers d'archipel 13.* Paris: Association Archipel.

Thomaz, L. (1994). *De Ceuta a Timor [From Ceuta to Timor].* Alges, Portugal: Carnaxide, Difel – Difusao Editorial S.A.

Thomaz, L. (2002). *Babel Lorosa'e. O problema linguistico de Timor-Leste [Babel Lorosa'e. The linguistic problem of Timor-Leste].* Instituto Camoes [Camoes Institute].

Thompson, J. (Ed.). (1991). *Language and symbolic power, Pierre Bourdieu.* Cambridge: Polity Press.

Turner, M. (1992). *Telling East Timor: Personal testimonies 1942–1992.* Sydney: New South Wales University Press.

UNDP (2002). *Ukun rasik a'an: East Timor – The way ahead: East Timor Human Development Report 2002.* Dili: RDTL, Author.

UNDP (2006). *The path out of poverty*. Dili: RDTL, Author.

UNESCO (2003). *Education in a multilingual world*, UNESCO Education Position Paper.

UNICEF (2005). *UNICEF in Timor-Leste*. Dili: RDTL, Author.

United States Central Intelligence Agency. (2003). *East Timor* [Map]. Perry Castañeda Map Collection: East Timor Maps. TX: University of Austin. Retrieved June 22, 2007, from http://www.ulib.texas.edu/maps/east.timor.html

van Engelenhoven, A., & Cailoru, J. (2006, June 2–3). *The Makuva enigma*, Paper presented at the Second Conference on Austronesian Languages and Linguistics, Oxford.

Walsh, P. (1999). *From opposition to proposition: The National Council of Timorese Resistance (CNRT) in transition*, Retrieved February 21, 2006, from www.pcug.org.au/~wildwood/CNRTPat.htm

Wardaugh, R. (1998). *An introduction to sociolinguistics*. Oxford: Blackwell.

Williams van Klinken, C. (2002). *High registers of Tetum-Dili: Portuguese press and purist priests*, Paper presented at the Australian Linguistics Society, Retrieved June 22, 2007, from http://www.als.asn.au

World Bank (2004). *Timor-Leste: Education since independence. From reconstruction to sustainable improvement*, (Report No. 29784-TP). Human Development Sector Unit East Asia and Pacific Region.

World Bank (2007). *Timor-Leste: Economic and social development brief.*, World Bank Group and the Asian Development Bank in consultation with development partners.

Wright, S. (2004). *Language policy and language planning: From nationalism to globalisation*. Basingstoke: Palgrave Macmillan.

Yang, K., & Chee, C. (1963). North Korean educational systems: 1945 to present. *The China Quarterly, 14,* 125–140.

Youmans, M. (2007). *Chicano-Anglo conversations: Truth, honesty and politeness*. Mahwah, NJ: Lawrence Erlbaum.

The language planning situation in Sri Lanka

Sandagomi Coperahewa

Department of Sinhala, Faculty of Arts, University of Colombo, Colombo 3, Sri Lanka

This monograph examines the language planning situation in Sri Lanka with particular emphasis on the planning of Sinhala as an official language of the country. It explores the historical, social, ideological and political processes, changes in language policy decisions, as well as the complexities of the language policy and planning situation in the country. After a general account of the language profile of Sri Lanka, the sections that follow examine both *status* and *corpus* planning that have occurred in Sri Lanka since the country became independent in 1948. This monograph investigates the spread of Sinhala in education, literacy and the media and the role of English in the wider context. The final section describes some important recent developments in language planning in Sri Lanka and suggests some ideas for continuing research on language policy planning. This monograph demonstrates the linguistic, political and ethnic character of language planning in a South Asian post-colonial setting.

Introduction

Language is fundamental to the ethnic identity of each community and is intimately bound up with the community's distinctive culture and way of life. It is the main factor in the formation of groups as well as a major barrier between groups. Different linguistic groups wish to see their language identities and interests maintained and may actively campaign for recognition (Crystal, 1997). These groups have their own language practices, beliefs, and ideologies (Spolsky, 2004). Differences in the social and political relationship between languages relate to the nature of the society and the political structure of the country. Most nations in the world are multilingual, and disputes over language policy are part of the political life of communities around the world. It is a well-known fact that 'developing nations' show a wide range of complex language problems in almost all spheres of national and social activities (Fishman, Ferguson, & Das Gupta, 1968). It has become evident that such problems have far-reaching implications for political mobilization and nation-building on the one hand and for planning for the development of linguistic resources on the other. Many South Asian countries raise a number of important issues of concern for those interested in language policy and planning (LPP): issues of multilingualism, linguistic nationalism, language conflict, and linguistic rights (Annamalai, 2003; Brown & Ganguly, 2003; Das Gupta, 1970; Dharmadasa, 1996; Fishman, 1974;

Fishman et al. 1968; Rahman, 1996; Simpson, 2007). At independence, the successor states of the British empire in South Asia confronted the critical issue of deciding which language – or languages – should replace English as the official language(s). In the first decade after independence, all three nations – India, Pakistan, and Sri Lanka – faced language problems that arose in the formulation of language policies especially with reference to the question of official/national language(s).[1]

Sri Lanka is a tropical island in the Indian Ocean showing a composite physical pattern. It is a land of much natural beauty, especially world famous for sunny beaches, diverse landscapes, and historical monuments. Scholars are still in the process of assessing the significance of recent archeological excavations relating to Sri Lanka's pre-history. The Democratic Socialist Republic of Sri Lanka (known as Ceylon before 1972)[2] is an island nation with an area of 65,610 km^2 (25,332 square miles) off the southeast coast of the Indian subcontinent lying between latitudes 5°55′–9°51′N and longitudes 79°41′–81°53′E. It is separated from the peninsula of India by the Gulf of Mannar and a narrow strip of shallow water, the Palk Strait. Its nearest neighbours besides the Indian subcontinent are the Maldives Islands to its west and the Nicobar and Andaman Islands to its east and north east, respectively. The island is centrally located in the Indian Ocean. As a result, it has been a focal point of sea routes for many centuries. The island is pear-shaped, 435 km from north to south and 225 km from east to west. For administrative purposes, Sri Lanka is divided into 9 provinces and 24 districts (Figure 1).

Over the past few decades, the country has moved away from a traditional reliance on agriculture to a more liberalized open economy. Based on the regional distribution of annual precipitation, the island is divided into a Wet Zone and a Dry Zone. Geographically, the island may be divided into five major regions: the central highlands, the well-watered south-west, the drier east and southeast, the northern lowland, and the coastal belt. The country's climate is tropical, with heavy monsoon rains and average temperatures around 28–30°C in the lowlands and 10–20°C in the central highlands.

Sri Lanka belongs to the cultural region of South Asia, and it is a member of the SAARC (South Asian Association for Regional Cooperation). With a total population of 19.8 million (15% urban) and a per capita income of US$1320 (World Bank, 2006), Sri Lanka is considered a middle-income country. Despite a very low per capita income, Sri Lanka has achieved remarkably high levels in quality of life indices such as life expectancy, infant mortality, and literacy. According to World Development indicators in 2001, Sri Lanka has a very highly educated labour force displaying the lowest labour cost per worker. Many scholars believe that such statistics reflect the benefits of sustained government intervention in social welfare (Gunatillake et al., 1992).

The growth of modern political consciousness and activity in Sri Lanka can be traced to a cluster of religious and social reform movements that appeared in the late nineteenth and early twentieth centuries (K.M. De Silva, 1981; Dharmadasa, 1992; Kearney, 1967, 1973; Malalgoda, 1976). Universal suffrage was introduced to the island by the British in 1931, and Sri Lanka claims a democratic tradition of governance since its independence in 1948. From the 1970s, the democratic political system and the territorial integrity of Sri Lanka came under threat due to:

(1) an armed struggle by a youth group of the Sinhala community known as JVP (*Janatā Vimukti Peramuna*, i.e. People's Liberation Front) in 1971 and again in 1988–1989 to capture state power and
(2) the Tamil militant activities in the north of the island.

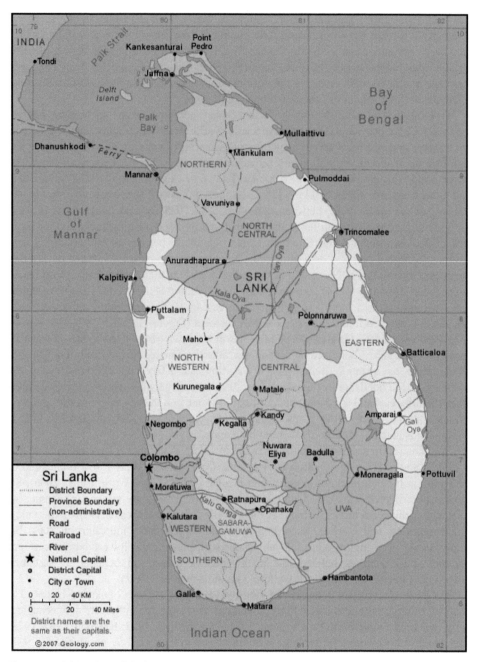

Figure 1.   Sri Lanka political map.
Source: http://geology.com/world/sri-lanka-map.gif.

As a South Asian state, Sri Lanka constitutes a very important 'case study' of the politics of LPP in colonial societies on the brink of independence and in post-colonial situations (Canagarajah, 2005; K.M. De Silva, 1993a, 1993b, 1996; Dharmadasa, 1981, 1992, 1996, 2007; Kearney, 1967). In Sri Lanka (as in most South Asian states), the language issue has historically been what Tollefson (1991, p. 13) calls an 'arena for struggle', where the majority of the country's population has sought to exercise power over minority ethnic groups. The attempt to ensure the primacy of the majority language by legal enactment disturbed the civil peace of the country for five decades. Language has been used as a weapon in the power struggle, and so the selection of an official language(s) for nations in the region has proved to constitute a controversial and emotional policy decision.

In a multilingual country divided by a plurality of major languages, language acts as an important means of individual identification: i.e. people's access to their own cultural tradition and their distinctive religious and political representation (Das Gupta, 1969). Language – of the Sinhalese[3] majority (70%) and the Sri Lankan Tamils (13%) – is at the root of the present ethnic conflict in Sri Lanka, a conflict that originated in the mid-1950s over the selection of an official language after the country obtained independence from the British. Language planning as a practical activity came into being in the 1950s when Sinhalese replaced English as the official language. However, the language planning aspects of Sri Lanka's language problem have not yet been explored in detail, and there are only a few scholarly studies related to this issue (Coperahewa, 2004; Dharmadasa, 1996; Goonetilleke, 1983; Musa, 1981). A review of the existing literature on the subject reveals a noticeable gap in studies related to language planning in Sri Lanka, a gap which this monograph fills. I will look into the language planning situation in Sri Lanka in this study – more specifically, the planning of Sinhala as an official language of the country. I examine the political, ideological, and ethnolinguistic dimensions of the language planning situation in the post-colonial society of Sri Lanka. In order to understand the theoretical context of the situation, I will, in my discussion, refer to various LPP theories and models.

Language policy and planning

Language is a 'social institution', and speakers of a language control and adapt their language for a variety of non-linguistic purposes: political, literary, economic, educational, religious, nationalistic, or social. As a medium of communication, language is considered a 'societal resource' which should be put to maximum use, and its allocation has to be planned (Fishman, 1980; Jernudd & Das Gupta, 1971). According to this view of language, measures can be taken to influence, or attempt to influence, a language situation (Cooper, 1989). At the present time, there are instances in which language has been systematized and planned for specific purposes. Generally speaking, language planning is a 'decision-making' process seeking to solve 'language problems, typically at the national level' (Fishman, 1974; Jernudd & Das Gupta, 1971). Thus, language planning has become an integral part of modern nation building worldwide (Wright, 2004). In a recent review of the field, Kaplan and Baldauf (1997, p. 3) provide a broad definition of language planning: 'a body of ideas, laws, and regulations (language policy), change rules, beliefs, and practices intended to achieve a planned change (or to stop change from happening) in the language use in one or more communities'. As implied by this definition, the scope of activities covered by language planning is rather broad. The *Oxford International Encyclopaedia of Linguistics* offers the following definition: '[t]he term language planning generally denotes a deliberate response to language problems – systematic, future-oriented, and based on a theoretical framework' (Clyne, 2003, Vol. II, p. 409). Therefore, as pointed out by Daoust (1997, p. 440), 'the devising of a language planning policy implies a vision of a future sociolinguistic situation that should be brought about'.

This study will refer to Haugen's (1983, 1966 [1972]) 4-fold model of language planning and Kloss's (1969) distinction between *status planning* and *corpus planning* in order to discuss relevant issues related to the language planning situation of Sri Lanka. In the practice of language planning, *status planning* deals with the initial choice of language, including attitudes toward alternative languages and the political implications of various choices. On the other hand, *corpus planning* is concerned with the internal structure of the language and involves activities such as coining new terms, reforming spelling, and standardizing a language (Cooper, 1989); in short, it refers to efforts to change the internal structure or corpus of a language. However, in many instances, it is difficult to separate *corpus* from *status* planning issues (Baldauf, 1990). As pointed out by Bourhis (1984, p. 3) 'a coherent co-ordination of corpus and status language planning is vital for the success of both limited and broad language planning goals'. Cooper (1989) adds another dimension, *acquisition planning*, referring to efforts to enable individuals or groups to learn a language, either as a first, as a second or as a foreign language. In summary, language planning refers to a deliberate change in the corpus, status, or acquisition (or in all or any combination of these changes) in a language or languages. More recently, another dimension has been identified: *prestige planning*. It is directed towards creating a favourable psychological background that is crucial for the long-term success of language planning activities (Haarmann, 1990). Therefore, language planning normally covers four major aspects: status planning (about society); corpus planning (about language); language-in-education (or acquisition) planning (about learning); and prestige planning (about image) (Baldauf, 2006). However, it should be noted that the goals or functions of language planning programmes vary across the world. Nahir (1984) directs attention to 11 specific goals that can be related to the language planning programme.[4] Some of these goals are relevant to the Sri Lankan situation.

On the other hand, all language planning takes place within a *language policy* and is the result of political choices that attempt to regulate the relationships between languages and societies. Language policy is most commonly developed and applied at the national level. According to Spolsky (2004, p. 9), language policy may refer to 'all the language practices, beliefs and management decisions of a community or polity'. Moreover, LPP decisions are power related and always 'socially situated and continually evolving' (Ricento, 2000, p. 2). Hence, language policies represent the interests of those in power and authority. As Tollefson (1991, p. 10) puts it, '[l]anguage policy is one mechanism available to the state for maintaining its power and that of groups which control state policy'. Therefore, in any language planning situation, the planner must take into account the linguistic and non-linguistic variables in that society (Rubin, 1971). According to the notion of *language ecology*, Kaplan and Baldauf (1997, p. 13) explain:

> Language planning [...] is a question of trying to manage the language ecology of a particular language to support it within the vast cultural, educational, historical, demographic, political, social structure in which language policy formulation occurs everyday.

Moreover, LPP is a domain for language ideological debates in a society (Blommaert, 1999). In a multilingual society such as Sri Lanka, the role of each language is parallel to the importance of the community that speaks it; any change in power relations between groups is linked to modifications in the status of their language. Therefore, Sri Lanka provides a typical example of a situation wherein the different types of language planning are combined. The history of language planning in

Sri Lanka can be divided into two major phases and five subphases, each associated with the particular socio-political context.

The first phase: Language planning in the colonial period (1505–1948)

   (I) Language planning in the Portuguese era
   (II) Language planning in the Dutch era
   (III) Language planning in the British era

The second phase: Language planning in the post-independence period (1948 to the present)

   (IV)   Independence to Sinhala-only policy
   (V)   Aftermath of Sinhala-only policy.

Outline of the monograph

This monograph is divided into five main sections, looking into the language-planning situation in Sri Lanka with particular attention to the planning of Sinhala as an official language of the country and exploring the historical, ideological, and political processes and the changes in language policy decisions, as well as the complexities of the LPP situation in the country. After a general account of the language profile of Sri Lanka, the sections that follow provide the following:

   (i) an examination of the language planning activities related to both *status* and *corpus* planning, that have happened in Sri Lanka since the country became independent in 1948.
   (ii) Moreover, this monograph investigates language spread in education, literacy, and media and the role of English in the wider context.
   (iii) The final section describes some important recent developments in language planning in Sri Lanka related to language rights and the globalization process.

This monograph provides a sociolinguistic understanding of the socio-cultural and linguistic issues and demonstrates the linguistic, political, and ethnic character of the language planning situation in this particular South Asian post-colonial setting.

Having set out the broad theoretical framework and outline of the study, the following section provides a general account of the ethnolinguistic and socio-historical context under which the planning activities have taken place. As Ferguson (1977, p. 9) puts it 'all language planning activities take place in particular sociolinguistic settings, and the nature and scope of the planning can only be fully understood in relation to the settings'.

Part I: the language profile of Sri Lanka

Socio-historical background

Sri Lanka is an ethnically, linguistically, and religiously diverse country, and its historical and cultural heritage spanning more than 2000 years. From the earliest times, Sri Lanka has had a multi-ethnic pluralistic society. Each ethnic group is marked by some distinctive characteristics including language, religion, and historical antecedents. Consequently, ethnic and religion divisions continue to be of considerable social, political, and cultural importance. A striking feature of Sri Lanka's long and complex 2000-year-old recorded history springs from the island's proximity to India. While its close proximity brought the island within range of a wide variety of Indian influences, its separation enabled it to retain a distinct identity in religion, culture, and language. Its main component elements have a common Indian origin, one North Indian and Indo Aryan, the other South Indian and the Dravidian. The majority groups in ancient times, as it is today, were the Sinhalese, a people of Indo Aryan origin who first came to the island from northern India about 500 BCE.[5] From about the third-century BCE, there appear to have been trade relations between Sri Lanka and South India. As a result, the Tamils came as traders and subsequently as invaders, but until the tenth century CE these Tamil settlements were not very substantial. From about the third-century BCE until 1017 CE, Anuradhapura was the capital of Sri Lanka.

The most important socio-historical event of this period was the introduction of Buddhism to the island from India by Mahinda, the emissary of the great Buddhist emperor, Asoka, during the third-century BCE. The introduction of Theravada Buddhism to the island influenced many aspects of the life of the people. Buddhism expected its adherents to be literate, and from very early times, the Buddhist monks developed the custom of recording events connected with the institution to which they were attached and the sacred objects which they held in honour and worshipped (Godakumbure, 1955, p. 105). The most significant feature of this tradition is the literary genre known as *vamsa*, and 'the Sinhalese can claim a special place in the South and Southeast Asian region as the earliest people to keep such historical records' (Dharmadasa, 1992, p. 3). The two chronicles, the *Mahāvamsa* (possibly compiled about the sixth-century CE) and its continuation the *Culavamsa* (compiled in the thirteenth-century CE), provide a remarkably full account of the island's ancient and medieval history. The Sinhalese ethnicity and Buddhism are closely linked, and together they paved the way for the Sinhala-Buddhist identity in the society. In explaining the historical and social basis of Sinhala nationalism, several scholars have pointed out the ethno-religious character of the community (Dharmadasa, 1992; Malalgoda, 1976). According to Dharmadasa (1992), a Sinhala sociolinguist, 'the term *Sinhalese-Buddhist*, although it came into [common] parlance in the early twentieth century, reflects an ethnic cum religious identity, the origin of which can be traced to very early times' (p. 2). Therefore, the question of group identity among the Sinhala people has engaged the attention of scholars in recent times (Dharmadasa, 1989; Gunawardana, 1979). However, according to Harvard anthro-pologist Thambiah (1986, p. 73), language has been a more important issue than religion in the Sinhalese–Tamil conflicts.

Few countries of the Third World have felt the influence of Western colonialism for a longer period than has Sri Lanka. The sixteenth-century CE saw the first impact of European languages on the Sinhala language and society. The island's coastal region fell under Portuguese influence in 1505, but within 60 years the Portuguese were displaced by the Dutch, and finally, the Dutch were replaced by the British in 1795–1996. With the fall of the Kandyan Kingdom in 1815, the last native kingdom, the British managed to bring the entire country (which was then called Ceylon) – both coastal regions and interior – under their control. Sri Lanka gained independence from British colonial rule in 1948, when it adopted a parliamentary system of government. The country was declared a republic within the British Commonwealth in 1972.

Sinhala, an Indo-Aryan language, the language of the majority population, has its roots in classical Indian languages but is spoken nowhere else in the region. Thus, it is related to such modern Indian languages as Hindi, Bengali, Gujarati, Marathi, Punjabi, and Kashmiri. Moreover, Maldivian, or *Divehi*, an offshoot of Sinhala, separated from the latter around the tenth-century CE (M.W.S. De Silva, 1970; Geiger, 1902). Sinhala and Divehi are the only two Indo-Aryan languages that are geographically and linguistically separated from the main Indo-Aryan linguistic area (Disanayaka, 1994). Geiger and Jayatilaka (1935, p. xxiv), the editors of the *Dictionary of the Sinhalese language*, divided the history of the Sinhala language into four major periods:

(1) Sinhala Prakrit – from second-century BCE to third- or fourth-century CE (Ancient Brahmi inscriptions)
(2) Proto Sinhala – from the fourth-century to the eighth-century CE (Later Brahmi inscriptions)
(3) Medieval Sinhala – from the eighth century to the middle of the thirteenth century (inscriptions of that time and the most ancient literature)
(4) Modern Sinhala – from the middle of the thirteenth century to the present time (the whole of the classical literature and modern works).

However, Sinhala has been geographically separated from the rest of the Indo-Aryan languages by a wide belt of Dravidian languages. Owing to its close contact with Tamil, Sinhala shares some linguistic features of the Dravidian, thus providing an excellent example of linguistic convergence[6] in a 'linguistic area' (Coperahewa, 2007). The influence of Tamil on Sinhala vocabulary has been a topic of much interest among language scholars (Coperahewa & Arunachalam, 2002). The structure of the Sinhala language has also been influenced considerably by the Dravidian. Examining the position of Sinhala in the South Asian linguistic area, Gair (1982) remarks that Sinhala is 'an Indo-Aryan isolate'. Geiger and Jayatilaka (1935) – founding editors of the *Sinhalese Dictionary* – remarked:

It is, no doubt, a splendid proof of the proud national feeling of the Sinhalese people that they were able to preserve the Aryan character of their language in spite of their geographical isolation. (pp. xviii–xix)

As a South Asian language, Sinhala has its own script, the origins of which go back to the ancient Indian script known as 'Brāhmi'. Masica (1991) describes this script as a 'unique cursive script of South Indian type' (p. 443). Writing was first introduced to the island in the third-century BCE, when Buddhism was brought to Sri Lanka. The present Sinhala alphabet has 60 letters; however, some of these letters are confined to writing words of Pāli and Sanskrit origin.[7] Recently, a new letter was added to the Sinhala alphabet to represent the English sound '/f/'. The earliest records of the Sinhala language are found in the cave and the early rock inscriptions dating to the third-century BCE. These are either lithic records of grants caves (to the *Sangha*) or royal decrees and proclamations.[8] Written literary works are available from the tenth century. The composition of literary works in ancient Sri Lanka appears to have been largely in the hands of religious dignitaries, especially Buddhist *bhikkhus*. Although the bulk of the early inscriptions were recorded in caves and on pillars (i.e. on rock surfaces), the common material used for writing seems to have been the leaf of the Palmyra palm, dried and prepared in a special manner for the purpose of writing. Palm-leaf manuscripts of most of the early Sinhala literary works are still available in temple libraries. The earliest extant grammar of Sinhala, *Sidat Saṅgarāva*, was compiled during the thirteenth century. This early grammar dealt largely with the language of poetry, although later grammarians interpreted the rules of *Sidat Saṅgarāva* as suitable for prose work as well.

Sinhala, which has a long and unbroken tradition of writing and literature spanning over a millennium, suffered a major setback during the period of colonial rule. However, the

Sinhalese language continued to be spoken and written by the vast majority of the people and also used in spheres other than those of the colonial administration. *Bhikkhus* and lay scholars used it for literary, religious, and philosophical discussions. During the Portuguese, Dutch, and British occupation of Sri Lanka, large numbers of words entered the Sinhala language from those European languages (A.M. Gunasekera, 1891; Sannasgala, 1976). The Sinhalese of the low country have adopted and still retain Portuguese surnames: de Silva, Fernando, Perera, and de Mel. Since Portuguese and Dutch rule did not extend beyond the coastal areas, there do not appear to be vestiges of other European names. During the period of western colonization, beginning during the first part of the sixteenth century, prestige was naturally accorded to the languages of the rulers. As Sannasgala (1976) points out, at the time that the Dutch occupied the coastal areas of Sri Lanka a large number of Sinhala words of Portuguese origin were in current use (p. 51). British rule, on the other hand, brought the people into closer association with the English language and its literature, and also with the thought of the West. English was the official language of Sri Lanka from 1815 to 1956 and still exerts a tremendous influence on both the vocabulary and the structure of Sinhala.

As a language with a fairly long history of written literature, Sinhala is a 'diglossic' language; that is, two different varieties are used for spoken/colloquial (*bhāshana*) and written (*lēkhana*) purposes. During the sixteenth century, classical Sinhala written usage lost some of its original purity due to the interference from the spoken language, but in the eighteenth century a movement began to revive the classical literary tradition. This movement was heightened during the British period due to the literary activities of Sinhalese scholars. Sinhala diglossia has been extensively studied from the perspective of the grammatical differences between written (H) and spoken (L) varieties, based on Ferguson's notion of 'high' and 'low' varieties (M.W.S. De Silva, 1967, 1974, 1976; Gair, 1968, 1985; Paolillo, 1997). Commenting on diglossia and literacy, Gair (1983, p. 56) remarks 'widespread literacy, though it has been considered a possible threat to diglossia, has clearly had no great effect in that direction so far'. Gair (1968) also identifies a third register, 'Formal Spoken Sinhala', used for public speaking purposes; it has colloquial grammar with literary lexical items. In contrast to spoken Sinhala, the grammatical structure of literary Sinhala is more complex; its structure is closer to the classical literary idiom and its vocabulary has more Sanskrit and Pali words. Moreover, it has classical words (or *Elu* lexical items) that are no longer in common use. The functional distribution of Sinhala diglossic situation is illustrated in Table 1.

The written language is regarded as the 'correct' language, and the teaching of Sinhala grammar in schools has always been confined to the literary variety; many of the 'modern' grammars of Sinhala have been written on the model of the *Sidat Saṅgarāva*, the earliest extant Sinhala grammar compiled in the thirteenth century (M.W.S. De Silva, 1979, pp. 32–33). Sinhala has a rich literary tradition that is intimately bound up with the community's ethnic identity and 'historical past'. According to a Sinhala sociolinguist '[t]he classic linguistic heritage appears to possess a symbolic significance which keeps the archaic idiom strongly entrenched in the value system of the community' (Dharmadasa, 1977, p. 29).

Table 1. Sinhala diglossic situation.

Variety	Status	Function
Written Sinhala	High (H) variety	Formal written purposes
Spoken Sinhala	Low (L) variety	Informal speech

The Sinhalese community forms a large majority of the island's population, a fact of great political and ethnic significance. According to one anthropologist, the Sinhalese are a 'majority with a minority complex' (Thambiah, 1986) in that Sri Lanka is the only country where the Sinhala language is spoken, whereas Tamil is the language of Sri Lanka's close neighbour – South India. The Sinhala ethnic identity has strong connections with Buddhism. The majority of the Sinhalese are Buddhists, and Buddhism has been given the foremost place in the island's socio-political culture. On the other hand, the Sri Lankan (Jaffna) Tamils and Indian (Up-country) Tamils are predominantly Hindus and speak Tamil. But the two communities retain separate and distinct group identities. Tamil is a Dravidian language also spoken in South India and comes from the same linguistic source of such modern South Indian languages such as Malayalam, Telugu, and Kannada. The Tamil script also developed from the South Brāhmi writing system of Asokan inscriptions. Tamil has had a long history in Sri Lanka. It played a key role in trade and business along the Indian coasts as well as along the Sri Lanka coasts, as it was a main language used for commercial communication.

From a geo-linguistic point of view, the nearest relatives of Sinhala are the Dravidian languages, i.e. Tamil, Malayālam, Telugu, and Kannada. The geographical proximity led to cultural contact between Sinhalese and Tamil communities for many centuries. In spite of ethnic differences, both Sinhalese and Tamils share similarities, especially in social customs, manners, practices, beliefs, and linguistic patterns. From a historical point of view, Tamil enjoyed a 'prestige' status in Sri Lanka after the thirteenth century, for political reasons, and it influenced both Sinhala language and culture. For instance, after the thirteenth century, there was a huge influx of Tamil vocabulary into Sinhala, mainly connected with daily life, warfare, arts, and administration (Coperahewa & Arunachalam, 2002). The Sri Lankan Tamil community is concentrated in the north of the island and along the east coast and consists mainly of descendants of settlers who arrived from South India 1000 or more years ago. Geographically, the Jaffna peninsula lies very close to South India, and this proximity enabled Jaffna to become one of the earliest parts of Sri Lanka to receive settlers from India and also to have continual contact with the subcontinent. Nevertheless, due to isolation from India, the Sri Lankan Tamils have, over the centuries, become a distinct people and have developed a dialect that exhibits certain peculiar linguistic features that are not found in South Indian spoken Tamil (Kailasapathy & Sanmugadas, 1976; Thanajayarajasingham, 1975). As a diglossic language, Tamil also shows two distinct varieties – literary and colloquial. In Tamil, the H variety is referred to as *centamil* and the L variety as *kotuntamil* or *koccai-t-tamil*. The rise of Tamil nativistic movements in the twentieth century promoted the notion of the superiority of the Tamil language through the H variety (Thanajayarajasingham, 1978). Tamil traditional grammarians have always given prominence to the written form or literary Tamil. There are several usages reflecting the social hierarchies in the Spoken Tamil in Sri Lanka (Suseendiararajah, 1970). On the other hand, most of the Indian Tamils live in the tea-estate areas of the central hill country. They are descendants of migrants from South India who have been coming to Sri Lanka since the nineteenth century and have generally been employed as labourers on the tea estates.

Another minority ethnic group consists of the Sri Lankan Muslims. They are traditionally divided into five subgroups, namely, Sri Lanka/Ceylon Moors, Coast/Indian Moors, Malays, Memons, and Borahs. The Ceylon/Sri Lanka Moors are the largest Muslim community in Sri Lanka constituting 8% of the total Sri Lankan population (Nuhuman, 2004). The early Muslim settlers were Arab traders from the Persian Gulf. Therefore, Muslims have been in the island from pre-colonial times, but it was under the Portuguese and the

Dutch that 'they were brought into sharp focus as a distinctive social group' (Samaraweera, 1977, p. 89). For most Sri Lankan Muslims, the language of the home has been Tamil, although there is a significant tendency at the present time for Muslims living in the Sinhala speaking areas to adopt Sinhala as their first language and to educate their children in that language. As Raheem says, 'though Tamil is important to the Moor in his daily life, it is not as important as it is to the Tamil speaker who has tended to make the language the focus of his loyalties' (quoted in Suseendirarajah, 1980, p. 351). Muslims who settled in Sinhala areas developed a proficiency in both languages. Therefore, the ethnicity of Sri Lankan Muslims is not defined by language – as in the case of Sinhalese and Tamils – but rather by religion, i.e. they give greater importance to their religion than to their language (Nuhuman, 2004, p. 11). More importantly, the Koran had been translated into Tamil and Sinhala.

The Burghers are a Eurasian ethnic group living in Sri Lanka. In the Census of 2001, the Burgher population of the Sri Lanka was enumerated at 35,300 persons. The Burghers were originally Dutch settlers who worked for the Dutch East India Company. However, there is an important distinction between the Portuguese Burghers and the Dutch Burghers. In modern times, English has been the language of the home for most Burghers. The Burghers became a leading community during British colonial times because of their command of the English language, and they dominated in government employment. Moreover, they had greater social contact with British offices. However, after independence, most of the Dutch Burghers began emigrating to Britain and Australia.

Ethnic differences between the Sinhalese and the Tamils have become more marked in the country since the mid-1950s, resulting in communal and political rivalry (Kearney, 1967). For more than two decades, Sri Lanka has been the scene of an escalating civil war between the government forces and the Liberation Tigers of Tamil Eelam (LTTE), a separatist militant organization of Tamils. The LTTE puts forward claims for a 'separate state' based on the territorial concentration of the community in the northern and eastern parts of the island, areas Tamils describe as the 'traditional homeland' of the community. More than 70,000 people have been killed in Sri Lanka since the LTTE launched its campaign for a separate state in the north and east of the country in 1983. As a result, ethnic conflict has been a central feature of the politics of Sri Lanka for most of the past decades. However, in February 2002, the government and LTTE signed a permanent ceasefire agreement, paving the way for talks to end the long-running conflict. The peace initiative was sponsored by Norway. But recently, the violence has erupted again. The LTTE has been banned as a terrorist group in many Western countries and also in neighbouring India.

The official languages

Sinhala and Tamil

English was the official language of the country from 1815 to 1956, and it is still widely used in government, administration, and higher education. As a colonial language, English continued to be the official language even after Sri Lanka (then Ceylon) gained independence in 1948. Fifty years (1956–2006) have passed since Sinhala was made the official language, and 18 years (1988–2006) have elapsed since the Tamil language was declared as the other official language of Sri Lanka by the 13th amendment to the constitution. The dispute over whether Sinhala and Tamil or Sinhala only should be the country's official language became a controversial socio-political issue in the years immediately following Sri Lanka's independence (K.M. De Silva, 1996; Dharmadasa, 1981).

At present, Sri Lanka has two official languages, namely Sinhala (sometimes referred to as Sinhalese) – the language of the majority Sinhalese, and Tamil – the language of the major minority group, the Tamils. Sinhala, the language of the majority, has enjoyed 'official' status since 1956; in 1988, Tamil was also declared an official language of the country. The demand to raise the 'status' of Sinhala, the language of the majority of Sri Lankans, to that of the official language became one of the most crucial demands of the post-independence official language movement. In 1956, 8 years after independence, the *Official Language Act of 1956* (popularly known as the 'Sinhala-only' Act) made Sinhala, 'the sole official language' of Sri Lanka (then Ceylon), replacing English (Government of Sri Lanka (Ceylon) [GOSL], 1956a). This language law was certainly one of the most important socio-political events in the post-independence period of Sri Lanka, and it had both immediate and long-term consequences (K.M. De Silva, 1993a, 1993b; see ensuing discussion). In 1988, as a part of the 13th amendment to the present constitution, Tamil was raised to the status of an official language, with English given the position of a 'link language'. The most striking features of modern Sinhala are, first, 'the enormous and impressive functional elaboration, and secondly, the very substantial influence of English on Sinhala' (Fernando, 1977, p. 358). All public sector documents are published in Sinhala, Tamil, and English and these languages are used in the media.

Lesser known languages, dialects and creoles

In Sri Lanka, there are only a few minority languages and dialects. Most of these lesser-known languages and creoles are spoken by a small group of tiny communities living in remote areas of the island. Most of these lesser-known languages are considered to be 'endangered languages' by linguists, and some foreign scholars have launched projects to provide documentation of these languages. However, it should be noted that there is no government policy or programme for the comprehensive documentation of these languages.

Vedda creole

The creole of the Veddas, the so-called aboriginals of the Island, is used by them in addition to Sinhala. The Veddas are regarded as the descendants of an aboriginal tribe living in Sri Lanka prior to the advent of the Aryans[9] (M.W.S. De Silva, 1964; Geiger, 1935). Geiger (1935) observed:

> Only [a] few words have been preserved from the original non-Aryan language of the Veddas, because they gradually adopted the Sinhalese colloquial language. In the pre-Aryan period the Veddas also possessed a code language of which they made use in their migrations and in hunting [...] and a number of Sinhalese expressions have likewise penetrated into this language. (p. 515)

Modern Vedda includes many words and some grammatical features from Sinhala, but the non-Sinhala vocabulary relates to the traditional Vedda way of life and is assumed to have survived from the original language which has many shared forms and traits with Sinhala and was sometimes (incorrectly) classified as a dialect of Sinhala. The speech of the Veddas has aroused much debate in learned circles ever since the early twentieth century when detailed records of their speech were published. In his research, M.W.S. De Silva (1964, 1972) concludes that modern Vedda is a creole based on an original Vedda language with Sinhala as the second contributing base. Therefore, the creole appears to be based on the grammar of Sinhala with a vocabulary derived from the original language of the Veddas. According to Dharmadasa (1974), Vedda reflects a 'creolization of an aboriginal language' as the result of language contact. During the past few decades, the Veddas have largely lost their traditional identity, and most of them have been assimilated into the Sinhalese population.

Portuguese creole

The arrival of the Portuguese in the island in 1505 for the first time introduced a European language. Some parts of the island were under Portuguese domination for a century and a half beginning from the dawn of the sixteenth century. After the Portuguese rulers departed from the island, the Portuguese language continued to be spoken in the maritime areas during the Dutch occupation and also in the first few decades of the British occupation as well. The first Portuguese settlements were in the coastal Sinhala speaking areas. As a result, a large number of Portuguese words entered the local languages. There are many Portuguese loan words still in common daily use in Sinhala (A.M. Gunasekera, 1891; Perera, 1922). The interaction of the Portuguese and Sri Lankans led to the generation of a new dialect, Sri Lanka Portuguese creole, which flourished as a *lingua franca* in the island from the sixteenth to the mid-nineteenth century. It falls within the group of Indo-Portuguese creoles. Today this creole is facing extinction and it is spoken in the Eastern towns of Batticaloa and Trincomalee and in the Northwestern province, in Puttalam. However, it is now fairly well documented in the literature of linguistic convergence and creole studies (Bakker, 2006; De Silva Jayasuriya, 1999; 2001; Smith, 1979). Sri Lanka Portuguese creole had been the solution to the intercommunication problems that arose when the Portuguese and Sri Lankans, who did not speak each other's first languages, came into contact (De Silva Jayasuriya, 1999; 2001). According to Hettiaratchi (1969) 'the richest source of Ceylon [Sri Lankan] Portuguese is Batticaloa'. Commenting on the Portuguese creole community in Vahakotte, Matale district, Hettiaratchi (1969, p. 747) says: 'a few hundred Portuguese descendants live there; they have completely Sinhalized, and hardly anybody possesses any knowledge of Portuguese'. However, Bakker (2006, p. 137) states that 'Portuguese in Sri Lanka first creolized and then Tamilized. The language makes use of Portuguese elements to express Tamil grammatical categories'. However, De Silva Jayasuriya (1999) argues that not Tamil but Sinhala is the main source of Sri Lanka Portuguese.

Sri Lanka Malay

Sri Lanka Malay is used by a small community of people of Malay origin. Sri Lanka Malay speakers are only about 0.3% of the population, and the language is no longer a home language for the younger generation of Sri Lankan Malays. The majority of Malay speakers are concentrated in the Colombo district, while the next highest population grouping is to be found in the Hambantota district of southern Sri Lanka. Scholars differ in their views as to the earliest date of the arrival of the Malays in Sri Lanka. According to historical evidence, there was a Malay presence in Sri Lanka in the thirteenth century (De Silva Jayasuriya, 2003). However, the large numbers of Malays migrated to the island during the eighteenth and nineteenth centuries from Java when the western coastal areas of Sri Lanka were under Dutch rule, since the Dutch had their headquarters in Batavia in Java. During the Dutch period (1656–1796), many Malays and Indonesians were brought to Sri Lanka both as constituents of the work force and as soldiers. The Sinhalese use the term *Jāminissu* ('people from Java') to refer to the Sri Lankan Malays. In Sri Lanka, Malay is at present only a spoken dialect. Being a small community living in areas where the majority population is Sinhala or Tamil, the Malays conduct their affairs in English, Sinhala, or Tamil, depending upon their own social status. Sri Lanka Malay is characterized by its own peculiarities of phonology, grammar, lexis, and semantics (Kekulawala, 1982). Hussainmiya (1987, p. 168) considers it to be a language consisting of Malay lexicon with a syntactic surface structure of Sri Lanka Tamil. Its phonology is thoroughly influenced by Tamil (Bakker, 2006). Moreover, Ansaldo (2005, 2008) argues that, though often presented as creolized, Sri Lanka Malay varieties do not meet any current criteria for creole status but may be better viewed as 'mixed languages' resulting from typological convergence.[10]

Rodi

The creole of the 'Rodi' community, who call themselves 'Gādi', is used by that population in addition to Sinhala. The *Rodiyas* are a so-called low-caste group, initially isolated through social ostracism, but eventually progressively assimilated into the general population. Raghavan (1957) believes their language to be connected to the Munda language spoken to this day by primitive tribes in Orissa and Bihar in India. He says: 'most of the words in the *Rodiya* dialect bear very little affinity to Sinhalese, being of non-Aryan and non-Dravidian origin' (1957, p. 105). M.W.S. De Silva (1969) says *Rodiya* is a 'secret language' in which non-Sinhalese lexical items are used in Sinhalese structures.

Sri Lanka: Telugu or 'ahikuntika'

The Sinhalese used the term *ahikuntika* – which means those who play with the mouth (*tunda*) of serpents (*ahi*), or who sport with serpents or make them dance – to refer to a group of isolated communities (also known as Sri Lankan gypsies) living in Sri Lanka (Bell, 1916). The male members of these groups are primarily snake charmers, and the female members are soothsayers by profession. According to Karunatilake (1982), a survey of their language definitely attests to its being a dialect of Telugu, one of the major Dravidian languages spoken in the Andra Pradeh area of India. However, this variety of Telugu is used by the community members only when they communicate among themselves, while Sinhalese and Tamil are used when communicating with the Sinhalese and the Tamils, respectively. The language has been considerably influenced by these two languages.

Dialects of Sinhala and Tamil

With regard to the dialect studies of modern Sri Lanka, some work has already been done on Vedda creole, but other lesser-known dialects and creoles need further investigation. Moreover, Sinhala and Tamil both exhibit some regional variations. All Sinhalese dialects are mutually intelligible. However, as M.W.S. De Silva (1979, p. 37) points out 'there are some phonological – particularly intonational – differences [between various dialects], and some dialects show morphological peculiarities too'. Standard spoken Sinhala differs from various 'regional varieties' mostly in its stock of words and their nuances of meaning (Disanayaka, 1976, 1977). According to Tamil scholars, Sri Lanka Tamil can be considered a 'major hypersystem of a number of sub-dialects' (Kailasapathy & Sanmugadas, 1976). There are six sub-dialects of Sri Lanka Tamil:

(1) North variety or Jaffna Tamil with Jaffna as centre of prestige,
(2) North eastern variety with Trincomalee as centre
(3) North-western variety with Chilaw as centre
(4) South-eastern variety or Batticaloa Tamil with Batticaloa as centre
(5) Muslim variety and
(6) Plantation variety (Kailasapathy & Sanmugadas, 1976, p. 3).

Muslims in Sri Lanka who speak Tamil have a unique dialect of that language, namely the Muslim dialect of Tamil, which 'differs remarkably from all other dialects of Tamil and marks [the speakers] as a different community' (Suseendirarajah, 1980, p. 351).

Religious and classical languages

There are four classical languages spoken in Sri Lanka which are used mainly for religious purposes. In terms of religion, Sri Lanka has four major religions of the world: Buddhism, Hinduism, Islam, and Christianity. Table 2 shows the distribution of the population by religion. Each of these religions has a classical language that is used to conduct religious transactions, including traditional rites and rituals. Moreover, these classical languages are also used in coats of arms of educational institutions, as mottos and in other traditional symbols. For instance, Buddhist schools use mottos in Pali, universities use mottos in Sanskrit and old public schools and Christian schools use mottos in Latin. In the eighteenth and nineteenth centuries, Christian missionaries promoted local languages for religious purposes.

Pali

Pali is the classical language used in Buddhist religious activities. According to historical linguists, Sinhala appears to be connected with the Pali language.[11] Pali is also a member of the Indo-Aryan family, its origins going back to the ancient Indian language called Magadhi, which was spoken in the state of Magadha where the Buddha spent the greater part of his life. Most of the Theravada Buddhist scriptures (e.g. the *Tripitaka* (The Three Baskets) are written in Pali. In fact, these were committed to writing for the first time in Sri Lanka in the first-century CE. Pali was the medium of communication in the ancient Buddhist world. The Buddhist kings of Sri Lanka communicated with the Buddhist kings of Siam (modern Thailand) in Pali. It is a language close to Sanskrit in terms of grammar and lexicon. Sri Lanka is also famous as a stronghold of Pali learning. Scholars in ancient Sri Lanka were well versed in both Pali and Sanskrit. The Oriental Colleges known as *Pirivenas* attach much importance to the teaching of Pali in the traditional manner. Moreover, the Sunday Dhamma Schools (*Daham Pāsala*) conduct lessons on the Pali language for school children, and Pali is also offered as a subject in schools. In the higher education sector, the Buddhist and Pali University of Sri Lanka, as well as some other university departments, offer Pali as a subject of study for undergraduate and graduate students. Buddhist religious activities are carried out in the Sinhala and Pali languages; Buddhist sermons are preached in Sinhala, but the language of the sacred texts is Pali. Buddhist monks use Pali stanzas (*gāthās*) in their religious rites, and lay Buddhists also recite Pali stanzas when they worship Buddha at the temple or at home. Most Buddhists recite these Pali *gāthās* and *sutras* without actual comprehension. However, Pali has no script of its own; consequently, it is written in

Table 2. Population by religion – 1981.

Buddhists	10,288,300	69.30%
Hindus	2,297,800	15.48%
Muslims	1,121,700	7.55%
Christians	1,130,600	7.61%
Others	8,300	0.06%

different parts of the Buddhist world in different scripts. In Sri Lanka, it is written mainly in Sinhala, but the Roman script is also used occasionally. The Pali Text Society of London uses the Roman script in its publications. The island's ancient chronicles were written in Pali, a language that plays an important role in the Buddhist culture and civilization of the island. Pali quotations are used as mottos in some government schools and *pirivenas*.

Sanskrit

Sanskrit is the classical language of Hinduism. It is one of the official languages of modern India. It has its own script – known as *Devanāgari* – that is shared by both Sanskrit and Hindi, the principal official language of India. Some ancient Buddhist texts were also written in Sanskrit. The study of the Sanskrit language is also part of Oriental Studies in the *pirivenas*. However, knowledge of Sanskrit and Pali provides an advantage for traditional Sinhala grammatical studies, and it is also considered a part of oriental scholarship. To write Pali and Sanskrit words, Sinhalese use the 'mixed Sinhala' alphabet that has 60 characters. Those who study indigenous medicine (*Āyurveda*) still consult works in Sanskrit. Sanskrit is also offered as a subject in some universities in the country and also as a part of the oriental education. In Hindu religious functions, Sanskrit and Tamil are employed. Sanskrit quotations are used as mottos of some higher educational institutions, such as the universities.

Arabic

Arabic is the classical language of Islam. In Sri Lanka, the Muslims use Tamil for their daily communication both at home and in the mosque, but they use classical Arabic to recite the *Koran*, their most sacred religious text. Classical Arabic is taught in Muslim schools as a subject and also as a part of religious education. But the majority of the worshippers do not understand Arabic. Muslims use a good number of Arabic words and phrases in their formal Tamil writings on Islam and Islamic culture. Moreover, the Sri Lankan Muslims (Moors) usually select Arabic personal names.

Latin

Latin is the classical language of the Christian Church. It is still used in the chanting of certain hymns, although there is a trend to replace Latin with the national languages. However, the religious activities of the Christian churches in Sri Lanka are conducted in both English and the national languages. Latin quotations are used as mottos of some educational institutions; for example: *Esto perpetua* (St Thomas' College, Mount Lavinia), *Disce aut Discade* (Royal College, Colombo).

Linguistic demography and literacy

Sri Lanka has an estimated population of 19.8 million, of which 91% (92.6% of the male population and 89.7% of the female population) were literate in 2001, and more than 60% were reported to reside in rural areas (Department of Census and Statistics, 2006). This population consists mainly of three ethnic groups: the Sinhalese, the Tamils and the Muslims (Moors).[12] The percentage of each group according to the last all-island census[13] of 1981 is indicated in Table 3. Although four different ethno-religious linguistic communities live in Sri Lanka, more than 92% of the inhabitants identify themselves with one of two distinct ethnic groups, Sinhalese and Tamils. The Sinhalese, who constitute about 74% of the total population (about 16 million), speak Sinhala and are primarily Buddhists. Tamil is spoken by Tamils and Muslims who form 25.5% of the total population. Tamils are largely Hindus; the country's Christian population (predominantly Roman Catholic) includes both Sinhalese and Tamils. Table 4 provides a description of the population by languages.

For administrative purposes, Sri Lanka is divided into 9 provinces and 24 districts. Each of the major ethnic groups displays a clear pattern of regional concentration. The majority of the Sri Lankan Tamils and Sinhalese have been geographically separated from each other for several centuries. The majority of the Sinhalese are concentrated in the densely populated southwest; the northern and eastern parts of the island are Tamil-speaking areas (Figure 2). As Sarkar (1957, p. 201) observes, 'one of the factors that perpetuates the racial distinctions in Ceylon [Sri Lanka] and prevent their [the two populations] amalgamation, is the distinct geographical location of the races'. According to Peiris (1996), a Sri Lankan geographer, 'the historical ties that bind the main ethnic groups to different parts of the country is a subject that has loomed large in the controversies associated with the current ethnic conflict' (p. 23).

More than half of all Sri Lankan Tamils lived in the northern districts, but the concentration of Tamils in the north and east declined slightly over the past twenty years as Tamils sought employment and educational opportunities in the Sinhalese southwest and as a result of the civil war. It should be noted that 52% of Tamil-speaking people live outside the north and east. A considerable proportion of Tamils who live in predominantly Sinhala-speaking areas speak Sinhalese bilingually with Tamil. The Indian (Up-country) Tamils are concentrated in the Tea plantation areas of the Kandyan highlands.

The Moors of Arabic and Indian Muslim descent live in the eastern part of the island, in small pockets on the west coast, around the central parts and are also scattered across the island. There is a concentration of Muslims in the capital city, Colombo. However, there is no district where the Muslims constitute a majority. Moreover, the Muslims who live in Sinhala-speaking areas use Sinhala as their working language and speak Tamil in their homes. According to Suseendirarajah (1980, p. 346), 'religio-cultural distance of the Muslims from other groups helped them to adopt Tamil in a rather peculiar and exclusive manner'.

Literacy rates

Sri Lanka ranks among the nations that have the highest levels of literacy in Asia, considered in the context of its low per capita income. According to figures estimated by

Table 3.   Ethnic composition of the population of Sri Lanka (Department of Census, & Statistics, 1981).

Ethnic Group	Number	Percentage
Sinhalese	10,985,666	74.0
Sri Lanka Tamils	1,871,535	12.6
Sri Lanka Moors	1,056,972	7.1
Indian Tamils	825,233	5.6
Malays	43,378	0.3
Burghers	38,236	0.3
Others	28,981	0.2

Table 4. Population by languages – 2001 (Based on 2001 Census).

District	Sinhala speaking (%)	Tamil speaking (%)
Colombo	76.59	21.30
Gampaha	91.08	7.36
Kalutara	87.09	12.73
Kandy	74.03	25.51
Matale	80.24	19.48
Nuwaraeliya	40.03	59.76
Galle	94.33	5.60
Matara	94.16	5.80
Hambantota	97.09	1.47
Mannar[a]	0.68	99.27
Vauniya[a]	8.45	91.52
Batticaloa	0.78	98.43
Ampara	3.35	96.24
Trincomalee	40.08	59.54
Kurunegala	91.74	8.09
Puttalam	9.36	25.90
Anuradhapura	90.78	8.99
Polonnaruwa	90.30	9.63
Badulla	70.57	27.59
Monaragala	95.60	4.31
Ratnapura	86.62	13.27
Kegalle	85.61	14.30

[a]Incomplete.

UNESCO, in 2001 the literacy rate in Sri Lanka was 91%. The adult illiteracy rate is 9.8% in Sri Lanka, but it is 36.6% for South Asia (UNESCO, 2000). Many factors contribute to this state of affairs; one of these is the position literacy occupies in the historical and cultural life of Sri Lankans in general and of Sinhalese in particular (Disanayaka, 1990). Literacy is closely linked to a number of issues and aspects related to language and education. The colonial educational system introduced two kinds of school-based literacy to the island: first literacy in a Western language – English – and second literacy in the vernacular. The growth in literacy reflects a rapid expansion of educational opportunity commencing during the late nineteenth century and accelerating during the twentieth century. Education in government schools has been tuition-free from the primary level through the university level since 1945. The standard literacy rate among the local population in the early years of modern censuses had been very low, but a steady improvement in literacy standards has been recorded in the subsequent censuses. The literacy rate increased progressively from 17.4% in 1881 to 57.8% in 1946, the progress in literacy becoming really significant only after 1911. As Sarkar (1957, p. 203) correctly points out, this was also the period of nationalist and religious revival when large numbers of Buddhist and Hindu schools were opened and when they began to compete with the Christian mission schools. As observed by Panditaratne and Selvanayagam (1973, p. 301), the difference in literacy between males and females is, however, significant; in the early years, the low literacy standard among females was expected in view of the peasant social structure. However, conditions changed in the 1940s, and the 1946 census recorded a substantial increase in the percentage of literate females in the population. Sri Lanka reached independence with one of the highest levels of education and literacy in Asia. The granting of free education facilities to the entire

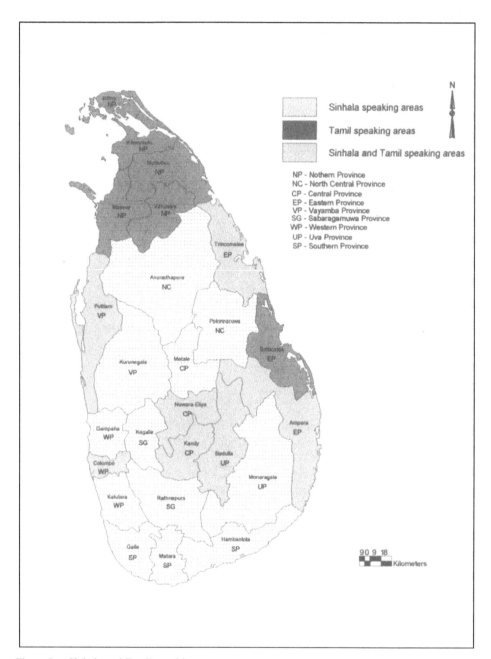

Figure 2.   Sinhala and Tamil-speaking areas.

population has expedited a rapid growth in literacy levels. Within the past 40 years, literacy levels have reported a remarkable increase of nearly 20%. The districts of Western province, Gampaha (95.4%), Colombo (94.7%), and Kalutara (93.2%) show the highest literacy rates. Table 5 shows the growth in literacy in Sri Lanka, in census years between 1881 and 2001.

Table 5.   Percentage of first language literacy in Sri Lanka in census years between 1881 and 2001 (computed from the Census Reports).

Year	All	Male	Female
1881	17.4	29.8	3.1
1891	21.7	36.1	5.3
1901	26.7	42.0	8.5
1911	31.0	47.2	12.5
1921	39.9	56.4	21.2
1946	57.8	70.1	43.8
1953	65.4	75.9	53.9
1963	71.9	79.4	63.8
1971	78.1	85.2	70.7
1981	87.2	86.6	67.3
2001	90.7	92.2	89.2

Part II: language spread

Languages in the educational system

The system of education in Sri Lanka evolved over centuries, originating with an indigenous system of education provided in Buddhist temples (*pansala*) and *pirivenas*.[14] A prominent place was given to the promotion of literacy under the curriculum of monastic education, no doubt accounting at least in part for the high literacy rate among the population. The *sanghas*, or Buddhist monks, were the custodians of education and literary activity. At the village level, literate monks taught students in the temple school. However, colonialism brought European style 'school education' to Sri Lanka in the seventeenth century. Its momentum sustained, during the early nineteenth century, the tradition of literacy and scholarly activity that had undergone a revival in the mid-eighteenth century. The *pirivenas* were reorganized during the early nineteenth century, but they were never integrated into the modern education system. In the early twentieth century, *pirivena* education provided training in Buddhist doctrine and oriental languages, mainly Pali, Sanskrit, and Sinhala.

In the nineteenth century, as a result of British colonial rule, English was introduced as a medium of instruction. The British rulers set up an English education system which paved the way for a new class of bilingual professionals. Moreover, the establishment of a University College in Colombo in 1921 laid the foundation for tertiary-level education in the island. The first three decades of the twentieth century saw a steady expansion in the educational structure and in the growth of education in national languages. The problem of medium of instruction and the concept of *mother tongue* became live issues in the early twentieth century as a result of the *swabhasha* (i.e. own language) movement. The colonial pattern of education began to change in the 1930s due to various legislative reforms, and the Ministry of Education came under the control of elected representatives. The most far reaching educational reforms came after 1943, following the publication of the *Report of the Special Committee of Education* in 1943. The Committee recommended that education should be in the student's first language – Sinhala or Tamil, instead of in English. In 1942, the University of Ceylon was established as the main centre of higher education. At independence (in 1948), Sri Lanka had a well-developed education infra-structure. According to Kearney (1967, p. 55) '[m]ass education in Ceylon [Sri Lanka] has been synonymous with vernacular education'. As a result, by 1953, 65% of the population 5 years of age and over was literate, compared with 17% in 1881. Since independence, the government has

179

assumed a larger role in education, and state control over education is visible in all aspects of educational reform and development. Formal school education is free in all government schools, and the medium of instruction is the first language of the pupil. The essential textbooks are provided free to all students up to the senior-secondary level (Year 11).

English is the most important 'second language' in the Sri Lankan educational system. In 1954, the Commission on Higher Education in National Languages also mandated that 'as a transitional measure at least, pupils in the Junior Schools should achieve a reasonable standard of proficiency in English' (GOSL, 1954, p. 4). However, during the last decade there has been growth among the 'International Schools' in major towns, and the medium of education in these schools is English. There are also a few fee-levying private schools in the country which offer both first-language education and English education. Proficiency in English is tested at the G.C.E. (Ordinary Level), and in 1999, English was made compulsory for students at the advanced level final school examination who wish to pursue higher education (Wijesinha, 2003). In higher education in general, the predominant language of instruction is Sinhala, but in the faculties of Medicine, Dentistry, Veterinary Medicine, Science, Engineering, and Law, English serves as the medium of instruction. However, the poor level of English is a severe problem in higher education – especially in the faculties of Social Sciences and Humanities. Universities have their own English programmes – namely Intensive and Foundation English Courses – to enhance the standards of English of their undergraduates. Apart from the academic teaching areas, there has been an unprecedented demand for English by business companies and the general public. Many private and government institutions conduct various English programmes at certificate and diploma level.

Language use in the media

Sri Lanka's media channels are divided along linguistic and ethnic lines, with state-run and private stations offering services in the main languages. The internet is a growing medium for news and current affairs, and many newspapers have online editions.

Newspapers and magazines

At the beginning of the British period in Sri Lanka (1815–1948), there were a few printing presses maintained by various missionary societies for the purpose of publishing pamphlets and books of religious instruction. The first Sinhalese printing press was established by the Dutch government about 1734. In connection with the subject of education, the British Colebrooke Commission (1832) noticed the deficiency in the means of diffusing information through the medium of the press (G.C. Mendis, 1956, p. 75). The *Ceylon Government Gazette* was started in 1802, and in 1832, the first newspaper, the *Colombo Journal*, was started under government authority. At about 1860, the three English newspapers in the country – the *Observer*, the *Times of Ceylon*, and the *Examiner* – were being published twice a week. The earliest Sinhala periodicals appeared in the 1830s as a part of the religious propaganda launched by Christian missionaries (Dharmadasa, 1998). Controversies between the Buddhists and the Christian missionaries were published and discussed in these journals, which, in addition, performed a useful function by publishing a large number of articles of social, religious, and literary interest. The first Sinhalese newspaper, the *Lankā Lōkaya*, was published in 1860; the first Tamil newspaper, the *Uthayathāraki*, was published by missionaries in 1841. Most of the early Sinhalese newspapers and periodicals were devoted to religious and literary debates. That period also contributed to the development of a suitable prose style for modern Sinhala. As pointed out by Sarathchandra (1950, p. 52), 'newspapers were also chiefly responsible for fostering and feeding to some extent, the taste for fiction' at the beginning of the twentieth century. Moreover, the Sinhala press was involved in the Buddhist revival movement in the late nineteenth century. Later, in the early part of the twentieth century, due to various socio-economic and political changes, there was a rapid growth in the Sinhala press. Most of the Sinhala newspapers of the early decades of the twentieth century were owned by various associations and prominent persons. The expansion of Sinhala journalism in this period went hand in hand with the commercialization of the press. In 1928, D.R. Wijewardene established 'Lake House' as a large, commercial organization to publish Sinhala, Tamil, and English newspapers.

After Sri Lanka gained independence in 1948, there was an 'enhancement of the importance of party politics in the affairs of the country, with political leaders becoming more aware than ever before, of the crucial role of the press in moulding public opinion' (Disanayaka & Coperahewa, 1998, p. 171). It is a generally accepted view that the language of newspapers has a strong influence on people's language in general. The language used in Sinhalese newspapers (and also on radio and in television programmes) is probably fundamental for the future development of the Sinhala language. The Sinhala press has, over the years, made a significant contribution to the development of the Sinhala language and influenced Sinhala vocabulary, orthography, style, and usage. In the print media certain linguistic styles gained the acceptance of the reading public, while others were marginalized. As pointed out by Disanayaka (1999), 'the Sinhala press, in particular, helped not only to mould different styles of writing but also to produce a simplified grammatical structure suitable for practical communication' (p. 268). However, certain grammarians attached to puristic groups have pointed out that journalists often pay scant attention to the correct usage of Sinhala.

At present, *Divayina*, *Lankādeepa* and *Lakbima*, owned by private firms, and *Dinamina* of the state sector, cater to the Sinhala readership of the daily press. The major Tamil newspapers are *Virakesari, Thinakkural*, and *Thinakaran*. There are three private daily English newspapers, (namely *The Island, Daily Mirror*, and *Morning Leader*) providing an alternative coverage of news and opinions. Table 6 presents a list of national newspapers in Sri Lanka according to the languages in which they are published, and Table 7 presents the number of newspapers in circulation from 1998 to 2003.

Table 6.   National newspapers in Sri Lanka – 2006/2007.

Sinhala	Tamil	English
Dinamina (d.)	*Virakesari* (d., w.)	*Daily News* (d.)
Divaina (d., w.)	*Thinakkural* (d., w.)	*The Island* (d., w.)
Lakadeeapa (d., w.)	*Thinakaran* (d., w.)	*Daily Mirror* (d.)
Lakbima (d., w.)	*Sudar Oli* (d., w.)	*The Morning Leader* (d.)
Silumina (w.)	*Tinamurusui* (w.)	*Sunday Observer* (w.)
Ravaya (w.)	*Uthayan* (d., w.)	*The Sunday Times* (w.)
Lanka (w.)	*Navamani* (d., w.)	*The Sunday Leader* (w.)
Irudina (w.)		*The Nation* (w)
Satdina (w.)		*Lakbima News* (w.)
Rivira (w)		
Lak Janatha (w)		

Note: d., daily; w., weekly.

Table 7. Number of newspapers in circulation (Department of National Archives).

	1998	1999	2000	2001	2002	2003
Sinhala	119	112	119	122	110	109
English	35	34	39	45	46	46
Tamil	23	22	22	22	33	28
Bilingual	4	–	–	–	–	4
Total	181	168	180	189	189	187

TV and radio

The history of radio broadcasting in Sri Lanka dates back to 1925. Launched just 3 years after the BBC began broadcasting, Colombo radio was the first radio station in Asia. At present, state-owned Sri Lanka Broadcasting Corporation (SLBC) broadcasts nationwide on six regular programme channels, and those six 'national' channels account for the major proportion of its domestic broadcasting. The six channels are:

(1) Sinhala Swadeshiya Sēvaya (Sinhala National Service),
(2) Tamil National Service,
(3) English Service,
(4) City FM (Sinhala),
(5) Velenda Sēvaya (Sinhala Commercial Service), and
(6) Thendral (Tamil Commercial Service).

According to SLBC sources, the first three channels are dedicated to public service, broadcasting in the three languages: Sinhala, Tamil, and English; the fourth channel (City FM) is maintained as a channel dedicated for youth. The last two channels, while representing 'an adult contemporary' genre, accommodate a certain amount of commercial content (SLBC, 2004).

Television was introduced to Sri Lanka in April 1979, and the Independent Television Network (ITN) pioneered television transmission throughout the country. Sri Lanka Rūpavāhini Corporation (SLRC), the national television network of Sri Lanka, is a gift from the people of Japan to the people of Sri Lanka. It was established under Act No. 6 of 1982 to carry out national television broadcasting service, commencing operations in April 1979. State-owned SLRC and the ITN broadcast TV programmes in all three languages, but Sinhala is widely used in many programmes. As a public service broadcaster, SLRC operates two programme channels namely 'Rūpavāhini' (in Sinhala and English) and 'Channel Eye' (in Tamil and English). MTV Channel (Pvt) Limited, a premier private television network in Sri Lanka, telecasts in the three main languages with separate channels for each of them: namely, Sirasa TV in Sinhala, Shakthi TV in Tamil, and Channel 1-MTV in English. Shakti TV is the only privately owned Tamil TV channel available to viewers across the entire island including the Jaffna Peninsula and most parts of the North Eastern Province. Sirasa FM, a privately owned Sinhala radio station, enjoys the greatest listenership across the country; this channel has taken FM radio to new heights of mass popularity in Sri Lanka. (See Table 8 for a list of radio stations and TV Channels). Sinhala dominates radio and TV broadcasting; indeed, it is used for some 60% of total TV broadcasting time, while English dominates all foreign-produced movies and documentaries. There is also dubbing for some English documentaries and movies, and some English and Hindi movies are subtitled in Sinhala.

Table 8.   Number of radio stations and TV channels in Sri Lanka (2007).

Language	Radio		Television	
	State	Private	State	Private
Sinhala (S)	8	12	3	6
Tamil (T)	1	2	1	1
English (E)	1	4	2	4
Total	10	18	6	11

Language spread in the wider context

English language in Sri Lanka

Sri Lanka inherited the English language from its colonial past. English was introduced into Sri Lanka at the beginning of the nineteenth century by the British rulers as the medium of instruction and the language of administration; in other words, it was the official language, and knowledge of it was essential for any position of importance. It was also associated with the evangelical zeal of the Christian missionaries. In fact, it is, at present, the third language in use on the island along with Sinhala and Tamil. From the beginning, it has been intertwined with the two key issues: employment and education. The recommendations of the Colebrooke–Cameron Commission in 1833 paved the way for the establishment of English as a medium of administration and education (G.C. Mendis, 1956). The Commission further noticed the importance of diffusing knowledge of the English language through the schools. The Colebrooke–Cameron Commission believed that knowledge of English would lead to the enhancement of the people of the island, and consequently, the Commission showed little interest in the local languages. The introduction of English education in the nineteenth century had a profound long-term impact on the socio-cultural life of the island. During colonial times, English was the medium of education from secondary level onwards. Discussing the English language situation at the beginning of the twentieth century, Passé (1943), a former professor of English at the University of Ceylon, provides the following account:

> .at the beginning of the present century the vernaculars began to lose ground seriously to English ... English was adopted by many educated people as their first language. The vernaculars were used chiefly by simple and illiterate folk, and by the educated only in the simplest and most familiar intercourse, and were even then freely mingled with borrowings from English. The spoken languages adapted themselves to the needs of the new life that Westerners brought with them chiefly by the rough and ready method of borrowing largely from the English vocabulary. (p. 54)

The teaching of English in premier English schools during the colonial period was quite successful. In English schools, textbooks and timetables were in English, and the vernaculars were strictly forbidden (Samarakkody & Braine, 2005). However, the standard of teaching English in schools was uneven. Over more than 100 years of British rule, English proficiency gradually increased; in 1921, 3.7% of the population were literate in English, and in 1946, 6.5% were literate. Table 9 shows the English language competence in the last years of British rule. From time to time, the alleged deterioration in the standard of English in schools has become a topic for educationists of English schools (Passé, 1949).

According to the Census reports, in 1946, 84.9% of the population were monolingual but by 1953 this had fallen to 80.7%. In 1946, a total of 6.5% spoke English; in 1953, 9.6% did. This increase occurred between the last census under British rule and the first

Table 9.   Language proficiency in English – 1946.

Ability to speak English only	0.2%
Ability to speak English and Sinhala	2.9%
Ability to speak English and Tamil	1.9%
Ability to speak English, Sinhala and Tamil	2.4%
Total	7.4%

Source: Department of Census and Statistics (1952).

census after independence (Coates, 1961). In 1943, the Special Committee of Education recommended that English be taught in the vernacular schools as a compulsory second language from Grade 3 onwards – that is from the age of 8. In 1954, the Commission on Higher Education in National Languages also recognized the value of teaching English as a 'compulsory second language' and observed that 'the objective of learning English will be very different from what it used to be in the past' (GOSL, 1954, p. 4). Moreover, the *Report of the Ceylon University Commission* in 1959 also pointed out that the use of Sinhala and Tamil as the media of undergraduate instruction in the university should 'not lead to the elimination of English', and added that 'such a situation [i.e., elimination of English] would be quite disastrous'. This report further recommended:

> . . .that while the principle of the use of the Swabasha languages [Sinhala and Tamil] in teaching up to the first degree must be implemented without any unnecessary delay, the great importance of adequate knowledge of secondary international language must always be recognized. Special provision must be made for the intensive training in English of those undergraduates who feel the need of it. (GOSL, 1959b, p. 232)

In 1957, a Committee of Inquiry into the teaching of English was appointed by the Minister of Education; its report recommended that English should be compulsory, taught to all up to and including the 8th standard (age 14 plus), and thereafter it should be optional. With reference to the aims and objectives of teaching English as a second language, the Committee suggested that the general aims should be the acquisition of competence in speaking, reading and writing (GOSL, 1960).

At present, English is taught as a second language in schools. It is spoken mainly by the educated and upper middle class. According to the Census data of 2001, 17% of the population were able to read and write English and 14% of the population had proficiency in speaking English (Department of Census and Statistics, 2006). English is almost exclusively an urban language. Among the urban areas, Colombo has much the largest English-speaking population. English remained the official language of the country even after independence (in 1948), and it was used in all official domains until 1956. The official status of English underwent a dramatic change with the introduction of the Sinhala-only Act in 1956. In 1987, as a result of the 13th amendment to the Constitution, English was declared to be a 'link language', although no further definition or clarification of its use and status in relation to Sinhala or Tamil was provided. The use of English has declined since independence, but at present it is commonly viewed as a gateway to international communication and knowledge. As a result, those learning English have increased in large numbers in the past few decades and the public use of English has spread to a wider population. On the other hand, due to the fact that education is provided in the national languages and also because of the lack of competent English teachers in rural schools, the standard of English has fallen considerably over the past two decades. In the 1980s, District English Language Improvement Centres were set up round the country to help potential teachers with the language (Wijesinha, 2003). The role and status of English in contemporary Sri Lanka raises some significant issues related to the politics of language policy and language power. English is the most empowering language in contemporary Sri Lanka because it gives access to both the most lucrative jobs and social prestige. According to a survey of opinions and attitudes toward English conducted by Raheem and Gunasekera, 'English is the official language of the private sector; [its use] is increasingly becoming a requirement for recruitment in the public sector' (cited in Raheem & Ratwatte, 2004, p. 99). It has been difficult, however, to dislodge English from many other domains, including higher education, commerce, science, and technology.

At present, English serves as a link language, and Sri Lankan society maintains a kind of 'love–hate relationship' with English (Goonetilleke, 1983). However, that relationship applies effectively only within a minority group whose members have adequate proficiency in English. Investigating language policy in Sri Lanka, Raheem and Ratwatte (2004, p. 103) point out '[t]he associations which English was identified with seem to have changed over time due to a variety of complex visible and invisible factors'. Discussing the post-imperial status of English in Sri Lanka, Fernando (1996, p. 508) concludes:

> Currently, the place of English as a second language in Sri Lanka is secure; what is uncertain are its benefits for the majority, for if genuine social justice is to prevail in today's Sri Lanka, reform has to go beyond the measure taken in 1946 to teach English to everybody and the continuing measures to improve ELT to an overhaul and restructuring of the country's colonial-style education system.

In 1997, the Presidential Task Force on General Education recommended that English should be used as a means of communication from Grade 1 onwards, while the formal teaching of English should commence at Grade 3 (GOSL, 1997). In April 2008, the government launched a major programme titled 'English as a life skill' for the enhancement of spoken/communicative English language skills in the country. This initiative by President Mahinda Rajapaksa seeks within three years to provide 50,000 persons with job-oriented spoken/communicative English skills for employment in services such as the IT and other service industries (Daily News, 2008).

At present, leading government schools in Colombo as well as private schools in major towns offer English medium classes as part of the local curriculum. Major universities in Sri Lanka offer English as a subject at both undergraduate and postgraduate level. Moreover, there are many university diploma level courses on academic, business, and professional English for careers. The British Council offices in Colombo and Kandy conduct various English language courses for both adults and young learners and also for preparation to sit the IELTS and other English language examinations. In most of the major towns, one can see posters for various private 'tuition classes' teaching spoken English. English is a popular subject, and there is a great demand for it. Apart from English, other foreign languages such as French, German, and Japanese are also popular among language learning centres and their clients. Foreign language learning, however, is not encouraged in the school educational system. On the other hand, due to the lack of English teachers, children from rural areas and small towns are not receiving adequate English language training. Even in the major towns, only a few schools teach effective and functional English language skills. While fluency in English is the desired goal of many parents for their children, there is strong evidence that English is gaining momentum as a dominant language because of the current language practices of higher levels of administration and commerce (see discussion in Part IV).

Bilingualism in Sri Lanka

The idea of bilingualism was taken up by some politicians and educationists and, by the 1940s, a few schools in various parts of the island had made Sinhala/Tamil bilingual instruction available. For example, as early as 1926, speaking at a Legislative Council debate, bilingual Tamil politicians such as Ponnambalam Ramanathan pressed for the promotion of bilingualism in education.

> I for one cannot condemn the deeper study of the English language. I would say that the local language, Tamil or Sinhalese, should be taught to the same extent . . . that sort of bilingual facility is essential and should be developed. I should like a Tamil or Sinhalese man born here to know English as well as his own language. (GOSL, 1926, p. 375)

In 1929, the report of the Macrae Commission, which inquired into the system of education in the country at that time, paid particular attention to the difficulties of bilingualism. Having examined the problem of the medium of instruction in a 'multilingual country', the Commission concluded that 'a bilingual system has greater advantages for Ceylon than a unilingual system of education' (GOSL, 1929). During the pre-independence era, most of the political leaders promoted the value of learning each other's language. In 1944, R. S. S. Gunawardena, who represented the Gampola district in the State Council, stated: 'I think it would be a happy day for this country if in every Sinhala school Tamil was made [a] compulsory subject and in every Tamil school Sinhala was made compulsory and both sections understood each other's language' (GOSL, 1944, p. 760). However, when legislation was enacted in 1956 to make Sinhala the 'only' official language of the country, the Tamils saw this as a move by the Sinhalese to 'dominate them through language'. As a result, their attitude towards the Sinhalese language also underwent change. As pointed out by Kasyanathan and Somasundaram (1981):

> Though politicians including those in power have often declared that Sinhala and Tamil students should be taught each other's language and even made some attempts to do this, the inhibiting factors have been effective for the most part in preventing the adoption of any large scale institutionalized plan for the promotion of bilingualism. (p. 57)

After the formation of the new government in 1977, the Ministry of Education implemented a 'link language' programme in schools to teach Tamil to Sinhala students and Sinhala to Tamil students. Attempts at bilingualism in past decades have not been successful. As the Sinhalese and Tamils are being educated in their 'respective compartmentalized mother tongues, they have no common language linking them' (Wilson, 1988, p. 47). The status of English as a 'link language' applies effectively only within a minority group whose members have sufficient proficiency in English (Fernando, 1996).

The spread of English language teaching as a result of secondary school expansion paved the way for the rise of a new bilingual intelligentsia in the late 1950s and in the 1960s (Fernando, 1977). Fernando (1977) identifies three 'main patterns of bilingualism':

> Group one bilinguals show a highly Anglicized life style and speak a virtually uniform variety of English whatever its racial origin [. . .] Such bilinguals are typically members of the legal, medical and educational professions, civil servants, commerce executives, etc. [. . .] Group two bilinguals, generally of peasant, lower-middle or working class origin, would regard English very much as a foreign language unlike the bilinguals of Group one [. . .] Group three consists of bilinguals whose fluency in English is small but who are typically of the same background as those of Group two. (pp. 348–356)

However, most Sinhala speakers – even monolinguals – inevitably use a relatively high proportion of English words in their everyday speech. According to Disanayaka (1976, p. 26), 'the use of English words as parts of compound words, though more frequent in the speech of bilinguals, is not uncommon even among ordinary folk'. The impact of English on the Sinhala vocabulary is immense. Bilingualism resulting from this language contact situation has also given birth to a variety of English that may legitimately be called 'Sri Lankan English' (SLE). Studies pertaining mainly to SLE highlight a number of characteristics of Sri Lankan and have identified it as a distinct variety of English (M. Gunasekera, 2005; Kandiah, 1981; Parakrama, 1995). In the linguistic literature, SLE has been mainly characterized as a spoken variety though written elements, and particularly elements of creative writing, have been analysed for distinctive features as well (M. Gunasekera, 2005; Kandiah, 1979) . Kandiah (1979) argues that SLE is 'an independent distinctive and fully formed linguistic system adequate for the communicative and expressive needs of its users' (p. 102). Discussing the 'postcolonial identity' of SLE, M. Gunasekera (2005) says 'it is the not the English of the colonizer, it is the English of the once colonized' (p. 20). Sinhala–English bilinguals enjoy high status in the society, and English is symbolized as *Kaduwa*[15] (i.e. sword) by the monolingual youth majority (Kandiah, 1984). As M. Gunasekera (2005) observes, 'the fact that English is referred to as a sword is indicative of its power in Sri Lankan society' (p. 33). As a result, from a functional point of view, the adulation of English shows the nature of language inequality in the community (Fernando, 1987; Kandiah, 1984). On the other hand, a majority of speakers believes that English should be learnt and used purely as English with no borrowings from Sinhala or Tamil (M. Gunasekera, 2005). In November 2007, Meyler published the first ever dictionary of SLE as an attempt 'to define SLE, and to promote the acceptance of SLE as one of the many established varieties of English as an international language'. According to Meyler (2007) 'Sri Lankan English (SLE) is the language spoken and understood by those Sri Lankans who speak English as their first language, and/or who are bilingual in English and Sinhala or Tamil'.

Sinhala/Tamil bilingualism is also a rare phenomenon in Sri Lanka, because it is uncommon for both languages to be taught to the same child through the educational system. Sinhala/Tamil bilingualism is commonest in the up-country tea plantation areas and along the provincial borders of the Sinhala-speaking and Tamil-speaking areas. Presently, the government encourages the teaching of Tamil to Sinhala students and *vice versa*. Though the government promotes a trilingual policy, the majority of the population is monolingual; perhaps not more than 14% of the population can command the English language in Sri Lanka. Moreover, it should be noted that the vast majority of the vernacular Sri Lankans live under the large linguistic ecology of Sinhala and Tamil. Table 10 shows the percentage distribution of population (10 years and over) by ability to speak, read, and write Sinhala, Tamil, and English.

Table 10. Percentage distribution of population (10 years and over) by ability to speak, read and write and Sinhala, Tamil and English – Census 2001.

Sinhala		Tamil		English	
Ability to speak	Ability to read and write	Ability to speak	Ability to read and write	Ability to speak	Ability to read and write
92.9	81.8	20.3	14.9	14.4	17.1

Source: Department of Census and Statistics (2006).

Part III: LPP

LPP in colonial Sri Lanka

English education and language policy

According to Powell (2002) in order to discuss postcolonial language planning it is necessary to look into policies that had a direct influence on language during colonization. The history of language policy in Sri Lanka dates back to the nineteenth century. With the fall in 1815 of the last Sinhalese kingdom – the Kandyan kingdom – the British managed to bring the entire country – both coastal regions and the interior – under their control. In 1829, the British Colonial Office sent a Royal Commission of Eastern Inquiry – the Colebrooke–Cameron Commission – to assess the administration of the island. In 1833, this Commission made some far reaching recommendations in relation to the administrative, economic, educational, and social organization of Sri Lanka, and seeing the need for a common language for administrative purposes, the Commission made explicit the position of English in Sri Lanka. Although the Commission's purpose was mainly focused on economic reforms, its recommendations extended to language policy planning as well. The first official pronouncement relating to language policy in colonial Sri Lanka is to be found in the Colebrooke–Cameron Commission Report, which offered proposals on language status planning and also commented on acquisition planning. Many of the proposals were adopted, and they helped to set a pattern of administrative, economic, judicial, and educational development that continued into the next century (G.C. Mendis, 1956; Samaraweera, 1973). As a result of the work of the Commission, during the years 1830–1833, English was introduced as a medium of instruction, and the use of English as the language of administration, education, and of the courts of law in Sri Lanka was determined. Commenting on the 'employment of natives', the Colebrooke, report on administration stated: 'A competent knowledge of the English language should however be required in the principal native functionaries throughout the country' (G.C. Mendis, 1956, p. 70). A regulation had been enacted in 1828 to the effect that, in future, no native headman should be appointed who could not read and write the English language. Since the majority of the population was not proficient in English, the use of indigenous languages was permitted in a limited way. Colebrooke and his colleagues observed the education provided by 'the native priesthood in their temples and colleges' and expressed the opinion that the continuation of that practice was a matter to be dismissed as one that 'scarcely merits any notice' (G.C. Mendis, 1956, p.73). Commenting on the education in government schools in that period, this Commission's report remarked:

> The schoolmasters are not required to understand the English language, of which many are wholly ignorant, and they are often extremely unfit for their situations. Nothing is taught in schools but reading in the native languages, and writing in the native characters. (G.C. Mendis, 1956, p.72)

The Commission's report made note of the importance of diffusing knowledge of the English language through the schools. In his proposals for the establishment of English schools, Colebrooke was influenced by the view held by Englishmen at the time, i.e. that 'oriental' learning was of little value and that knowledge of English would lead to the moral and intellectual improvement of the Eastern people (G.C. Mendis, 1956). Indeed, this proposal anticipates by only a few years the publication of Thomas Babington Macaulay's 1835 'Minute'.[16] Macaulay had been sent to Calcutta in an official capacity (as 'advisor' to the government), knowing nothing about any of the South Asian languages – actually, he appears to have despised them. His 'minute' or 'message' concerned the intent of colonial education and language policy in India, dealing particularly with the use of English in the education of Indian people. The wide adoption of his advice introduced the future leaders of India to English literature and history, providing a common language in multilingual India and laying the groundwork in the traditions of English law. Thus, Colebrooke Commission's Report actually anticipated developments in India just 2 or 3 years later and was in accord with imperial thought.

Colebrooke placed education in the hands of the Christian clergy who pioneered the introduction of Western educational forms in Sri Lanka.[17] Approving the Colebrooke–Cameron Commission's proposals, the Secretary of State for the Colonies wrote in 1833 to the governor in Colombo: '[t]he dissemination of the English language is an object which I cannot but esteem of the greatest importance, as a medium of instruction and as a bond of union with this country' (cited in Jayaweera, 1971, p. 156). Colebrooke also commented that '[t]he English missionaries have not very generally appreciated the importance of diffusing a knowledge of the English language through the medium of their schools, but I entertain no doubt that they will co-operate in this object' (G.C. Mendis, 1956, p. 73). The Commission laid down the policy of imparting Western knowledge through English, but only to a minority of the population.[16] A system of English schools was introduced for the purpose of creating a loyal, westernized native elite, who could be employed cheaply in the lower echelons of the colonial bureaucracy. The English schools provided a curriculum that led to lucrative employment opportunities and higher education, while the vernacular schools led to low levels of employment and to no opportunities for higher education. Commenting on language and colonial education policy in nineteenth century Sri Lanka, Jayaweera (1971, p. 162) states:

> There was agreement that vernacular education should be confined to the masses and that English schools were to provide an exclusively English education, divorced from all local traditions, and influences, for future administrators and social elite. Each type of school would operate in its own medium to the complete exclusion of other languages.

Since cultural imperialism was another determinant of the colonial language policy, colonial language policy promoted British culture via the English language. As Phillipson (1992, p. 110) points out '[t]he significance of language was understood from the early expansionist phase of imperialism'. The introduction of English created two classes of people based on education – the English educated and the vernacular educated. The vernacular educated students were prepared for few careers more rewarding than that of a teacher in the vernacular school. Education in the English medium, on the other hand, opened the door to more lucrative and prestigious professions (Dharmadasa, 1992; Ryan, 1961). During the latter part of the colonial period, the language issue arose from dissatisfaction with the privileged position occupied by those Sri Lankans who had acquired an English education.

During the century and half when English enjoyed the prestige of being the official language, the two local languages of the country, Sinhala and Tamil, were demoted to the lower status of vernaculars; the higher functions of social, political, and economic life were conducted in the medium of the English language, while the vernaculars – Sinhala and Tamil – were confined, in terms of the dominant value system, to lower significance (Dharmadasa, 1992). The Westernized English educated Sinhalese and Tamil elites adopted English as their home language and so became deficient in the national languages. At this time, despite his Christianity and English education, the language loyalist and bilingual scholar James De Alwis (1823–1878), stressed the value of Sinhala as the 'national language' and Buddhism as the 'national religion'. In 1852 he translated the thirteenth-century Sinhala grammar, the *Sidat Sañgarāva*, into English. His main aim in undertaking such a work was 'the dissemination of the Sinhalese language amongst Europeans' (De Alwis, 1852, p. vi). Writing a long introduction to this book, De Alwis pointed out the value of learning Sinhala literature and language for the English educated (Dharmadasa, 1992, pp. 47–85).

Missionaries and corpus planning activities

The establishment of the printing press by the Dutch (1734) was a landmark in the history of modern Sinhala. During the eighteenth century, the Dutch missionaries used the printing press mainly to publish translations of the Bible, catechisms, and prayer books for use in schools and churches. According to information available at present, the first book to have been printed in Sinhala – and the first book ever printed in Sri Lanka – was a Sinhala prayer book published in 1737 (Wickramasuriya, 1978). From the beginning of the nineteenth century, British missionaries carried out various corpus-planning activities such as compiling dictionaries, wordbooks, grammars, and textbooks for educational and mission-ary purposes.[18] The translation of the Bible was of utmost importance to all missions. It was a challenging task, and the Bible translators faced various difficulties with regard to the grammar, syntax, and spelling of Sinhala. The Bible was translated many times, in search for a proper linguistic norm (Sarathchandra, 1950; Somaratne, 1990). The question of language became an important one for missionaries in the context of their main purpose, conversion to Christianity. They learned local languages in order to spread Christianity. For example, the first Baptist missionary in the island, the Rev. J. Chater, learned Sinhalese and compiled a grammar of the Sinhalese language. The linguistic work of missionaries also played an important role in the development of modern Sinhala prose. The Christian publications of the early decades of the nineteenth century occupy a prominent place in the annals of modern Sinhala literature. The language of some of the Christian literature exercised a powerful influence upon Sinhalese prose writers. The publication of tracts, periodicals, and text books necessitated a systematic and scientific knowledge of the language, providing an impetus for the compilation of grammars and dictionaries. The devel-opment of dictionary-making in the modern sense, however, took place when Europeans began to compile dictionaries of Sinhala. In 1759, the Dutch published a Sinhalese dictionary. In the first half of the nineteenth century, several such compilations were undertaken by English missionaries with the assistance of native scholars. The first Englishman to undertake the task of compiling a Sinhalese dictionary was a civil servant named Samuel Tolfrey; this task was finally completed by Rev. Benjamin Clough in 1830. He had already published the English–Sinhalese part of his dictionary in 1821. These works were followed by:

- *A School Dictionary, Singhalese–English and English–Singhalese* (1845–1847) by W. Bridgnell,
- *An English–Sinhalese dictionary* (1891) and *Sinhalese–English dictionary* (1924) by Charles Carter,
- *An English–Sinhalese dictionary* (1905) as well as *Sinhalese–English dictionary* (1915) by A.M. Gunasekera.

As early as 1881, Sir Charles Bruce, who was then the Director of Education, stressed the need for a scientifically compiled dictionary of the Sinhalese language and referred to that need as 'the greatest need felt in Ceylon' (Geiger & Jayatilaka, 1935).

Indeed, western influence on the Sinhala and Tamil languages began during the seventeenth century through the work of missionaries. Two important contributions were:

(i) the introduction of printing and
(ii) the development of a new prose, which had formerly been employed only for commentaries on classical works.

The printing press, originally introduced for the propagation of Christianity, became a crucial weapon in the revivalist movement. The classical works were edited and published for both educational and scholarly pursuits. In the early years of the nineteenth century, the press was used mainly for printing Christian literature, simple grammars, and vocabularies of Sinhala for foreigners. The introduction of printing in vernacular languages aided in both the 'standardization' of such languages and the growth of literacy in those languages. As a result, vernaculars attained their modern forms as media of communication. The growth of print Sinhala, on the other hand, paved the way for reforms in orthography, grammar, and lexicon. The addition of punctuation marks, the hyphenation of words and the use of para-graphing are other innovations found in modern Sinhala language that arose as a result of Sinhala printing. Moreover, with the expansion of journalistic activity at the end of the nine-teenth century, many new writers appeared on the literary scene. In addition, the educational system created by the British served later as a major agent of the language standardization process. Thus, language planning, in the sense in which the term is used at the present time, may have had its inception during the colonial period.

The official/national language movement

Language revitalization and the growth of language loyalty

Ethnic and linguistic revival movements are sometimes associated with nationalism and nationalist movements. Fishman (1973) suggests that, in modern nationalistic movements, language loyalty and ethnocentrism are intimately and essentially related. He notes that the single, most pervasive factor in modern nationalism is the absolute and essential need of a unique language that will express the authenticity of a speech community. The awareness of the greatness of one's own culture and language seems to play some part in the *revitaliza-tion* and *development* of languages, especially those that have 'great traditions' of language and culture. Language revitalization refers to 'the new-found vigor of a language already in use', and also it reflects 'the firm and solid desire for independence and political freedom from a superstrate power' (Paulston, 1994, pp. 97–100). A clear example of *language revitalization* can be found in relation to Sinhala between 1920 and 1956.

The second half of the nineteenth century was a period of literary and religious controversies that saw the growth of considerable literary and religious activity. Social changes in operation in the second-half of the nineteenth century resulted in a steady increase in the size of the *elite* (Roberts, 1973). By the end of the nineteenth century and the beginning of the twentieth century, there had emerged a nativistic revival, namely the Sinhala-Buddhist revival, which, like similar movements in other colonial settings, aimed at promoting the indigenous language and religion (Dharmadasa, 1992; Malalgoda, 1976). One of the concerns expressed by the leaders of the Sinhalese-Buddhist revival was the growth of English education and the patronage it received from the state as well as from the Christian missionary organizations.

The literature that was created in the twentieth century was very much a product of the new urban and western educated *elite* that had been emerging from about the middle of the nineteenth century (Sarathchandra, 1973, p. 193). During that period, Oriental scholars – mainly Buddhist clergy – campaigned in favour of classical usage. Moreover, vernacular school-teachers were also dedicated to the classical tradition (M.W.S. De Silva, 1976, pp. 96–97). Although the writers did not revert to early literary models, it should be emphasized that the first half of the twentieth century was a period of resurgence of classical Sinhala literature. During that renaissance period, writers took special care to adhere to the literary language that had been in use in an earlier time. On the other hand, the second and third decades of the twentieth century saw notable changes in the island's political structure. The expansion of modern education, the growth of literacy and the development of Sinhala journalism also contributed to the advancement of Oriental learning and literary activity in Sinhala – particularly in the form of the printed word (Dharmadasa, 1992, p. 167). Print helped in the standardization of Sinhala and introduced new discursive styles, modes of punctuation, and syntax and genres of literature. The growth in the number of printing presses and publishing houses after 1920 catered to the needs of the newly literate public. According to Anderson (1983), it is 'print capitalism', manifested most clearly in the novel and the newspaper, that 'provided the technical means of 'representing' the kind of imagined community that is nation' (p. 30). With the popularization of literature, the Sinhala reading public as well as the number of writers who served the expanding literate population increased tremendously. The writers, scholars, and poets made their thoughts and work public through this print medium. Moreover, the contact with Western literature introduced new genres such as the novel and the short story, but also a 'new set of values which seem to have been attractive to the new lay writer' (Sarathchandra, 1973, p. 344). As Dharmadasa (1992, p. 116) notes 'this social mobilization through new channels of mass contact is one of the most noteworthy features in the growth of modern Sinhalese nationalism'. When literary activity radiated into new areas of knowledge in the twentieth century, Sinhala intellectuals looked to language use and literary form for additional signs of ethnic identity.

During that period, as a result of ethno-nationalist ideologies, language loyalty pressures increased, largely in the political and educational systems. The *revitalization* and *modernization* of Sinhala as a goal of language planning constituted a new trend. Many Sinhala scholars and language loyalists propagated Sinhala language and literature by publishing various newspapers, periodicals and creative works. For example, Munidasa Cumaratunga (1887–1944), an outstanding scholar of Sinhala and the foremost language loyalist and grammarian of twentieth century Sri Lanka, launched a campaign for the study of the Sinhala language and its purification (Dharmadasa, 1972). He made an attempt to standardize, refine, and correct the Sinhala language in accordance with classical Sinhala. In many instances, Cumaratunga (1938) complained about the 'linguistic decline', and in 1938, he pointed out the importance of grammatical rules to safeguard the language:

> The scientific rules and regulations dealing with the elegant and the correct usage is grammar. Civilized society is safeguarded by social rules. Likewise the elegant language is protected by the rules of language called grammar. The uncultured people break social rules. But the cultured people do not go by that type of instructions and make an attempt to convert them as cultured ones. The illiterate ones break the rules of language. The scholars without taking that account make an attempt to peruse the illiterate ones to assume the form of the literate ones. (p. 1)

Cumaratunga was more interested in language as a maker of ethnicity and nationalism. In place of the slogan 'Country, Nation and Religion' (*rata, jātiya, āgama*), he adopted 'Language, Nation and Country' (*basa, räsa, desa*) placing language as the foremost nationalist element. These three words became the main slogan of the *Hela* movement in the 1940s. According to Wimal Dissanayake (2005, p. 48) 'Cumaratunga also conceived of language as a spiritual force that can exercise a deep and far-reaching impact on a given community'.

By editing classical Sinhala works of the thirteenth and fourteenth centuries, he discovered the 'pure' and 'genuine' Sinhala usage and grammatical rules of classical Sinhala. Cumaratunga attempted to renovate literary Sinhala according to the usage found in the classical texts from the thirteenth and fourteenth centuries.[19] As M.W.S. De Silva (1974, p. 79) pointed out:

> the adoption of the classical language of the thirteenth and fourteenth centuries for literary purposes was motivated by the belief that the revival of the 'golden age' of Sinhalese culture would only be possible in the language of that period.

During that time, Cumaratunga – through his editorials in his newspaper – generated a nationalist self-consciousness and 'prestige' for the Sinhala language within the Sinhalese community. Thus, 'prestige planning' became a 'prerequisite for status planning' (Mesthrie, Swann, Deumert, & Leap, 2000, p. 388). As an individual language planner, he led a struggle on behalf of the position of Sinhala in government activity, education and promoted the 'purity' of Sinhala usage. Cumaratunga considered that independence in the sphere of language was a prerequisite for political independence. He also argued that only those who promised to speak exclusively in Sinhala should be elected to the State Council. He considered language the symbol of freedom from British colonial rule. In 1941, he founded one of the most dynamic language associations of the time, *Hela Havula* (Pure Sinhala Fraternity), in order to bring together all the language loyalists. *Hela Havula* purists opposed the use of Sanskritic lexis and advocated the use of pure Sinhala (*Hela*) vocabulary. At that time, oriental scholars who had pirivena education promoted a mixed Sinhala (*miśra Sinhala*) usage in their writings. As a reaction to this linguistic practice, Cumaratunga and his followers criticized the linguistic policy of oriental scholars and *launched* a purification programme for Sinhala. The *Hela* ideology was constructed solely on a language foundation, but it was used to designate race, land, music, and so forth (Dharmadasa, 1992, p. 283). According to Nahir's (1984) classification of language planning goals, the role of Cumaratunga in colonial Sri Lanka can be discussed in terms of language purification, language revitalization, language reform, language standardization, and lexical modernization. Examining the language situation in that period, Dharmadasa (1992, p. 281) also observed the impact of *Hela Havula* on language planning:

> It gave forceful expression to the sense of ethnolinguistic uniqueness of the Sinhalese community, and with it was reached the ideological pinnacle of Sinhalese nationalism. It had a profound impact on the corpus planning activities in Sinhala, and more important, it inspired hopes and strategies for status planning endeavours in the cause of the Sinhala language.

However, after the demise of Cumaratunga in 1944, the *Hela* movement failed to obtain wider societal attention for its programmes. That period saw the beginning of various language planning activities and linguistic research to cultivate the Sinhala language. Systematic historical studies of the Sinhala language carried out by such European and local scholars, as D. M. De Z. Wickramasinghe, Wilhelm Geiger, S. Paranavitana, and D.E. Hettiaratchi helped to identify the linguistic character of the Sinhala language. More importantly, Geiger's (1938) grammar on Sinhala – *A grammar of the Sinhalese language* was considered as a pioneer effort in the study of the historical aspects of the Sinhala language. On the one hand, these studies made a valuable contribution towards expanding the domains of Indo-Aryan linguistic research on Sinhala (M.W.S. De Silva, 1979). On the other hand, these discoveries also led to many language controversies among scholars. One such controversy was the Indo-Aryan/Dravidian debate about the origin of the Sinhalese language (see Note 6). The most important linguistic project of this period was the dictionary. In 1927, the compilation of the *Sinhala Etymological Dictionary* began, as a project of the Royal Asiatic Society of Ceylon Branch and with government patronage, under the direction of Prof. Wilhelm Geiger, a German professor of Indology, with Sir D.B. Jayatilaka, a statesman and scholar, as Editor-in-Chief. In connection with the *Sinhala etymological dictionary*, De Lanerolle documented the principles of Sinhala spelling in a paper, published in 1934, and entitled *The uses of n,n and l,l in Sinhala orthography*. The work on the Sinhala dictionary proceeded slowly, its first part appearing in 1935. This work laid the foundation for the study of Sinhala from a historical linguistic perspective. The foundation of first the University College (1921) and then the University of Ceylon (1942) also contributed to the systematic study of Sinhala. The reorganization of the Faculty of Oriental Studies at the University of Ceylon into three departments of Sanskrit, Pali, and Sinhalese in 1943 was a significant event in the history of language studies in Sri Lanka. It was only in 1944 that a separate Chair for Sinhala was established along with a separate department for Tamil.

The decade of the 1930s had also witnessed the rapid growth of Sinhala journalism and publishing, as an aid to the development of Sinhala language and literature. According to Dharmadasa (1992, p. 183), a 'neoclassical' form was established as the 'standard language' for the mass media while more erudite scholars utilized a 'literary form with a highly classical flavour'. As a result, the Sinhala language was transformed into a vibrant medium of expression and comment.

The swabhasha[20] *movement*

Pressure for the replacement of English as the official language by Sinhala and Tamil began in the 1920s. This pressure gained momentum with the Donoughmore reforms and the introduction of 'universal suffrage' in 1931; these actions set the stage for the demand for the *swabhasha* (or the people's 'own language') as a political cause (K.M. De Silva, 1981; Dharmadasa, 1992; Kearney, 1973). The two decades beginning in the 1930s were a crucial period in the evolution of Sri Lanka's modern education system; they also marked the emergence of language policy as a major national political issue. The *swabhasha* movement included both Sinhalese and Tamils who campaigned for their respective languages to replace English as the language of administration and education (De Votta, 2004; Dharmadasa, 1992; Kearney, 1967). The *swabhasha* movement reflected the frustrations of vernacular speaking Sri Lankans being governed in a language they did not understand. The *swabhasha* movement, largely a Sinhalese movement (Kearney, 1967, pp. 59–69), was, in its origins, a protest against the privileges enjoyed by those who constituted the English-educated and English-speaking elite, and it was also a protest against the control of all important positions in public life, and in the bureaucracy, by the English language. In 1946, the Select Committee of the State Council also reported that '[t]he present Government of this country is … a Government of the Sinhalese or Tamil-speaking 6,200,000, by the English-speaking 20,000 Government servants, for the 400,000 English-speaking public' (GOSL, 1946, p. 10). As pointed out by Kearney (1967, p. 59) '[w]ith English as the language of administration, the people unacquainted with English increasingly found themselves brought into contact with a government functioning in an alien tongue.' In this period, Sinhalese and Tamil legislators realized the problems of vernacular speakers and started to support the *swabhasha* demands.

From the 1920s, education and the law courts became the most important arena of the language issue. Accordingly, the national language issue moved onto the political agenda of the State Council; for example, in 1926, A. Cangaratnam, a Legislative Council member from the Northern Province, introduced a motion that cited the disparities between the English and vernacular schools and called for 'English, Sinhalese and Tamil [to] be made language subjects in all schools, the mother tongue of the students being gradually adopted as the medium of instructions in all schools of all grades' (GOSL, 1926, p. 317). In 1932, G.K.W. Perera, a Buddhist member of the State Council, presented a resolution for the 'functional expansion' of vernaculars – in administration and the legal system (GOSL, 1932, p. 3118); however, this resolution failed to secure the necessary two-thirds majority. In the mid-1930s, Marxist politicians stressed the value of national languages in the field of the administration of justice; for example, Philip Gunawardhana, a member of the State Council, presented a resolution in July 1936, addressing two issues:

(i) the use of the first language in recording police entries and
(ii) the use of the first language in the Municipal and Police courts.

That motion was approved but was not implemented. As noted by K.M. De Silva (1993b, p. 275), in Sri Lanka, the main policy decisions on changes in language and education policy had been taken in the late 1930s and early 1940s, in the last decades of British rule. At that time, language was a central issue in the controversies surrounding educational reform. In the early years of the 1940s decade, this *swabhasha* demand was transformed into a national or official language question. The political influence of *swabhasha* teachers – mainly Sinhalese – was a common feature of the language politics of that time. Following the recommendation of a State Council committee, but amidst enormous opposition from some elite groups, a decision was taken in 1943 to require that primary education be in the 'mother tongue/vernacular' of the student, but permitting the introduction of English at a later stage (GOSL, 1943; Sumathipala, 1968).

In June 1943, J.R. Jayewardene, a Member of the State Council, introduced a motion in the State Council, stipulating the opinion of the Council:

... with the object of making Sinhalese the official language of Ceylon within a reasonable number of years this Council is of the opinion –

(a) That Sinhalese should be made the medium of instruction in all schools;
(b) That Sinhalese should be made a compulsory subject in all public examinations;
(c) That legislation should be introduced to permit the business of the State Council to be conducted in Sinhala also;
(d) That a Commission should be appointed, to choose for translation and to translate important books of other languages into Sinhalese;
(e) That a Commission should be appointed to report on all steps that need be taken to effect the transition from English into Sinhalese (GOSL, 1944, p. 1024).

The motion was taken up for consideration in May 1944, and this language debate, as Russell (1981) aptly points out, 'brought together the correlated issues of language, education and nationalism' (p. 38). The most salient feature of Jayewardene's original proposal was the absence of Tamil as an official language. Jayewardene believed that there was a need 'to protect the Sinhala language' from the South Indian Tamil influences.

The great fear I had was that Sinhalese being a language spoken by only 3,000,000 people in the whole world would suffer or may be entirely lost in time to come if Tamil is also placed on an equal footing with it in this country. The influence of Tamil literature, a literature used in India by over 40,000,000 and the influence of Tamil films and Tamil culture in the country, I thought, might be detrimental to the future of the Sinhalese language (GOSL, 1944, p. 748)

At the request of several Tamil politicians, Jayewardene accepted an amendment to revise 'Sinhala' to read 'Sinhalese and Tamil'. This amendment passed 29 votes to 9. The argument of those who voted against the amendment was that national unity could be forged only by the adoption of one language. Dudley Senanayake, as a member of State Council, pointed out that Sri Lanka was 'too small [a] place' to have two official languages. He insisted: 'It is very essential that there should be only one official language. And, I ask, what could that language be other than Sinhalese? (GOSL, 1944, p. 769). Speaking to that debate, Jayewardene argued:

... Language, Sir, is one of the most important characteristics of nationality. Without language a nation stands a chance of being absorbed or of losing its identity. With language, it has a chance of living for centuries. It is because of our language that the Sinhalese race has existed for 2400 years, and ... composed as we are in this House, on the eve of freedom as a free country, we should prepare for a national official language. (GOSL, 1944, p. 748)

However, many Tamil politicians criticized this resolution. Speaking to this language resolution, G.G. Ponnambalam, the principal leader of the Tamils Ponnambalam, said that underlying the motion was the idea of 'one official language and one medium of instruction' in all schools. He strongly opposed Jayewardene's original motion and said: 'it is merely one of the first steps that one would take to advance the theory of one race, one religion and one language.' (GOSL, 1944, p. 764). He further said it would be better to retain English as the official language. He pointed out that 'English is a world language'; therefore, he said, English is 'accepted by other linguistic communities outside Ceylon, and its use as a lingua franca between the different linguistic communities makes it virtually indispensable' (GOSL, 1944, p. 766).

The 1944 language resolution was more fundamental than all the previous attempts and led to a final decision by the State Council to make the 'national languages' – Sinhala and Tamil – the official languages of the country. The Council saw the first political support for a move to declare the country's languages to be its official languages. However, the State Council was divided into three groups on the issue of official language:

(i) the first group was against the demotion of English (mainly European and Burgher members and some Tamil members);
(ii) the second group sought to declare Sinhala as the sole official language (a group of Sinhalese councillors), and
(iii) the third group supported the adoption of both Sinhala and Tamil as official languages.

The language resolution being debated also mentioned that a Commission should be appointed to effect the transition from English into Sinhalese and Tamil. Accordingly, a Select Committee was appointed by the State Council on 20 September 1945, with a brief 'to consider and report on the steps necessary to effect the transition from English to Sinhalese and Tamil with the object of making Sinhalese and Tamil the official languages of the country'. Jayewardene was appointed chairman of the Committee. The Committee, through notices in the newspapers published in Sinhala, Tamil, and English, invited the public to send their written memoranda on the above task. In the course of the evidence given before this Select Committee and in the correspondence columns of the daily press, several Sinhalese witnesses advocated the use of Sinhala as the one official language (Daily News, 1946). The Select Committee Report – published in December 1946 as *Sinhalese and Tamil as official languages – Sessional Paper (SP) XXII of 1946* – was considered as an 'important landmark in the evolution of language policy in the country' (R.G.O. Gunasekera, 1996, p. 19). This Committee Report viewed the language of nation as one of its 'most precious assets', and in the case of Sri Lanka that precious asset had been 'neglected for centuries'(GOSL, 1946, p. 11). It then provided a comparative picture of the two national languages, Sinhala and Tamil.

> if we consider its present state particularly that of Sinhalese, we realize how it has suffered almost irreparable damage. Tamil is more fortunate than Sinhalese, for nearly 20 million speak it in South India and it is one of the best developed and most copious of Indian languages. (GOSL, 1946, p. 11)

This lengthy Report dealt with the scope of the national languages and their future development, focusing in addition on some of the corpus planning work relating mainly to Sinhala language. Focusing on the impact of English on national languages, it pointed out:

> In the face of this very natural demand for English, natural as long as it remains the official language, Sinhalese and Tamil find it very difficult to develop. From generation to generation the national languages have been relegated further and further to the background – a subtle and sinister process that threatens to oust these languages, and to reduce Sinhalese, once an elegant and forceful speech, to an insignificant patios. (GOSL, 1946, p. 11)

The report listed the seven more serious defects that needed immediate rectification:

(iv)   Disregard of idiom,
(v)   Absence of a modern prose style,
(vi)   Absence of literary criticism,
(vii)   Lack of training in literary discipline and of instruction in composition,
(viii)   Neglect of the formative apparatus,
(ix)   Faulty translations, and
(x)   Absence of suitable textbooks.

Discussing the future official languages of the country, the Additional Secretary of the above Select Committee and a well-known Sinhala scholar, De Lanerolle (1945), pointed out that, if 'one finds greater prominence given to Sinhalese than to Tamil, it is not because Tamil is considered less important, but because the case of Sinhalese is more complicated' (p. 35). It should be noted, however, that the committee report was published during a period when Sinhala language loyalty was high, and many Sinhala scholars and language loyalists expressed their satisfaction with this report and its proposals. The Select Committee chaired by Jayewardene, recommended that:

(1)   Sinhala and Tamil should become the languages of administration with effect from 1 January 1957.

(2) A Commission for National Languages should be appointed and a Department for National Languages should be established, and

(3) A Translation Bureau and a Research Institute should be established (GOSL, 1946).

The committee, having studied the language issue, realized that the problem of making Sinhala and Tamil the official languages of the country required close investigation of contemporary conditions and careful planning, both long and short term. Many reasons have been advanced for the delayed implementation of Sinhala and Tamil as official languages. The 'inadequacy of the national languages for immediate official use' was the main issue that confronted the Committee (GOSL, 1946, p. 10). The committee also recommended a 10-year transition period (from 1947 to 1957), at the end of which English would cease to be the language of government. In this report, the two languages (Sinhala and Tamil) are referred to as the 'national' languages, as distinct from English, which is not mentioned as a 'national' language, but which is rather designated as an 'official language'. The committee's report concluded:

> We trust that our efforts will remove the gulf that now divides the people into two classes, and thus not only afford the vast majority of our countrymen better opportunities of participating fully in the life of the nation, but also create a cultural and literary renaissance equalling the golden ages of Lanka's historic past. (GOSL, 1946, p. 48)

According to models of language planning, the committee report can be considered as an *initial fact-finding* activity, offering timed recommendations on how to introduce the two languages into the various public domains, i.e. educational, legislative, judicial, and administrative. In the language-planning context, the report is considered to be a pre-planning activity – an input into policy formulation (Rubin, 1971). Moreover, this committee report became 'a major landmark in the evolution of the country's new official language policy of bilingualism, when its recommendations were adopted in the early years of independence' (K.M. De Silva, 1996, p. 19). On the eve of independence, the understanding was that both Sinhala and Tamil would be made official national languages, thus giving both languages 'parity of status'. The situation changed dramatically within a few years after independence.

Post-colonial language policy and language conflict

Planning of Sinhala and Tamil as official languages

According to Spolsky (2004), 'the transition from colonial status to independence provided an opportunity for a country to decide or recognize its language policy' (p. 133). In many South Asian countries, the 'language conflict became acute immediately following national independence' (Das Gupta, 1970, p. 20). The on-set of independence in 1948 led to far-reaching political, social, and linguistic changes in Sri Lankan society. The most important change was in the position of the vernaculars. By the time of independence, a considerable expansion had occurred in vernacular education. The growing number of youths educated in the vernacular, however, found few careers open to them. At independence, government affairs were conducted in English, and government officers were educated in that medium. As Canagarajah (2005, p. 423) points out 'though Sri Lanka was granted independence in 1948, the English-educated local elite who took over power were not interested in changing the status of the language from which they themselves profited'. The vernacular-educated were excluded from the bureaucracy, because English remained the language of government after independence, and public service employment remained a monopoly for the English-educated. Sinhalese politician I.M.R.A. Iriyagolla, pointed out the problem in 1949.

> The ordinary people, the masses of this country, do not feel that they have obtained freedom at all. We do not deny that we have secured political freedom to some extent, but we cannot feel that we have any freedom at all until and unless our national languages become the State languages. (GOSL, 1949, col. 184)

Sinhala received greater attention after independence because electors without any knowledge of English were eligible to enter the Parliament. On the other hand, political independence after nearly four and half centuries created a psychological atmosphere suitable for literary activities. As Fernando (1977, p. 345) noted, 'the linguistic situation in post-independent Sri Lanka is naturally very different and infinitely more complex than it was before'. Independence allowed a new choice of official language. However, as Das Gupta (1970, p. 21) observed, 'the task of replacing the former colonial language by national languages is not easy.' Status planning also becomes an important activity when a country achieves independence (Spolsky, 1998, p. 68).

Accordingly, in the period immediately following the achievement of political independence, a comprehensive and systematic programme of language planning was introduced and implemented under the direction of Jayewardene, as Minister of Finance in the first post-independent government. On 23 May 1951, a three-member Official Languages Commission (OLC) was appointed by the Governor General to inquire into, report on, and make recommendations about matters relating to the proposed transition from English to Sinhala and Tamil with the objective of making Sinhala and Tamil the official languages of the administration and of government:

(1) The procedure that should be adopted in taking such steps recommended by the Select Committee of the State Council as are considered necessary and practicable;
(2) any further steps that should be taken for the purpose of achieving that object, and the procedure that should be adopted in taking such further steps; and
(3) *any changes, whether by way of policy* or otherwise, that should be effected in the administration of all government departments or of any one or more of such departments for the purpose of achieving that objective (GOSL, 1951, p. 1, emphasis added).

The Commission published press notices in an attempt to gather information about the public needs and wishes and their views in regard to these matters. The Commission gave much attention to the Railway, the Post and Telecommunications, the Police and Pubic Trustee's departments with which the public have frequent dealings. The Commission started work in 1951, and it issued five interim reports and one final report. The interim reports dealt with the measures related to all government departments in general for the smooth transition from English to Sinhala and Tamil as the languages of administration. Accordingly, the government began to implement the recommendations of the reports from 1951. In the first interim report, the Commission looked at similar situations in South Asia and reported the language planning situation in Sri Lanka as follows:

> As regards the time necessary for the change from English into the national languages, we found that a speedy transition was possible in a country like Burma (though not altogether without sacrificing efficiency) because English-educated Burmans had never ceased to use their national language for all domestic, economic, social or spiritual purposes. To the

Burmans, Burmese has always been a living language, whereas Sinhalese, for more than a century, has been almost a dead language to most of the English-educated Sinhalese. Consequently, many people at present who are government clerks and staff officers who, though they posses a fairly good knowledge of Sinhalese, would never write even a single sentence, for fear of making some mistake. In point of fact, however, a good many of them could do much of their official business in Sinhalese, if only they were shown how to overcome the linguistic differences. The Tamils, though they are in a somewhat better position, seem to be in need of similar assistance. (GOSL, 1951, p. 4)

Investigating the language situation in that period, the OLC in its first interim report recommended:

(i) that an Official Terms Committee be set up, immediately, to make a systematic collection of current terms and phrases, to supply new ones where necessary, and to standardize the new terms with a view to compiling an authoritative glossary and
(ii) that all necessary arrangements be made, immediately, to provide instruction in Shorthand and Typewriting in Sinhalese and Tamil, at an institution or institutions to be opened or adopted for the purpose by the Government (GOSL, 1951, p. 5).

The fourth interim report of the OLC (February 1953) proposed the establishment of a new 'Department of National Languages' for the general supervision, control and direction of the necessary steps:

(a) the preparation of a glossary of official terms and phrases;
(b) the training of the present members of the Public Service in the use of Sinhalese and Tamil as the official languages of administration;
(c) the translation of legislative and administrative publications into Sinhalese and Tamil;
(d) the instruction of pioneer classes of selected pupils in Shorthand and typewriting in Sinhalese and Tamil (GOSL, 1953a, p. 14).

In the fifth interim report, published in October 1953, the Commission made recommendations on Sinhala typewriters, shorthand writers, typists, Sinhala monotype/linotype printing presses, official literature, glossaries of official terms, and phrases. The Commission also devoted considerable time and attention to the improvement of Sinhala and Tamil. The final report of the OLC enumerated the following language planning activities:

(1) the compiling of official glossaries in Sinhalese and Tamil;
(2) the training of shorthand writers and typists in Sinhalese and Tamil;
(3) the training of 'pilot teachers' as instructors at departmental centres;
(4) the organizing of district centres designed to provide rapid courses of instruction to departmental officers who need such instruction (GOSL, 1953b).

The 2.5-year period of the Commission's work marked some very imaginative achievements in language planning (R.G.O. Gunasekera, 1996). In 1954, the Commission on Higher Education in National Languages, in its interim report, recommended the creation of an organization for obtaining and publishing a sufficient number of textbooks and background literature glossaries and translations for the use of Senior Secondary schools (GOSL, 1954, p. 5). In October 1955, the Official Languages Bureau, which had been organized under the Ministry of Finance, was converted into a separate department to be known as the Department of Official Languages. While this department was expected to attend to all the duties relating to official languages in administration, a *Swabhasha* department was set up in addition, under the Ministry of Education, to attend to the educational needs in national languages. However, in the final report (1953), Sir Arthur Wijewardene, the Chairman of the OLC, asserted:

> In my opinion the replacement of English by *swabhasha* would have been very much easier if instead of two *swabhasha* languages as official languages one alone had been accepted in terms of the motion introduced by Mr J.R. Jayewardene in the State Council on 22 June 1943. (GOSL, 1953b)

In the following year (1954), Wijewardene repeated this same opinion in a rider to the *Report of the Commission on the National Languages in Higher Education* (SP XXI of 1954). The developments that took place thereafter in regard to the language policy of the country were largely in accord with the rider. At the same time, the Tamil quest for parity of status was supported by the Lanka Sama Samaja Party (LSSP) and the Communist Party (CP). In October 1955, N.M. Perera of the LSSP introduced a motion supporting parity in the legislature. This motion specifically called for 'the Ceylon (Constitution) Order in Council ... [to] be amended forthwith to provide for the Sinhalese and Tamil languages to be state languages of Ceylon with parity of status throughout the island' (GOSL, 1955, Vol. 30, col. 1280).

Linguistic nationalism and politicization of the language problem

Political aspirations and nationalist motivations have been found to underlie numerous goals of language planning (Bourhis, 1984; Fishman, 1971). The work of the Commission on the Official Languages was carried out against the background of significant political changes. The most important socio-political incident was the crossover of S.W.R.D. Bandaranaike (1899–1959), a prominent campaigner for *swabhasha* and a charismatic Sinhalese politician, to the opposition in 1951, and the establishment of the Sri Lanka Freedom Party (SLFP). From the 1952 general election, the question of *swabhasha*/official languages became an election issue. The *swabhasha* teachers showed a marked interest in this issue since it affected them very directly. According to Weerawardana (1952), in the general election of 1952, '[s]ome took it [the language issue] to mean a merely nationalistic propaganda vehicle. Others saw it as a cultural or linguistic problem' (p. 123). The language issue did not become a predominant campaign issue in the 1952 elections, and all the major parties campaigned in favour of two native languages as official languages. Moreover, in 1953 Prime Minister Senanayaka mentioned that Sinhala and Tamil would be given their place in the government 'within a reasonable period of time' (Kearney, 1967, p. 64). In the early 1950s, sentiment grew to make Sinhala the sole official language, and by 1955, the SLFP, led by Bandaranaike, emerged as an amalgam of the largest number of opposition groups advocating the replacement of English by 'Sinhala only'. Although the question of national language had been under consideration, Premier Sir John Kotalawela's policy (1952–1956) when he was the leader of the United National Party (UNP), seems to have been rather vague and undecided', as Pakeman (1964, p. 182) puts it. The UNP made little effort to elevate the status of local languages, and because of this neglect, 'a mass social group became increasingly alienated from the UNP' (Woodward, 1969, p. 120). Accordingly, Bandaranaike took up the language issue in an attack on the UNP. Moreover, Bandaranaike and other supporters of the SLFP recognized the power of language as an aspect of group identity and used that fact effectively in their political campaign.

During the period from 1951 to 1953, the SLFP stood for Sinhala and Tamil as the official languages. However, in early 1955, a powerful wing of the SLFP, led by prominent *bhikkhus* and laity, proposed a motion that sought to amend the Constitution of the SLFP on the language issue.[21] The motion demanded that Sinhala be made the only official language. Discussing the language issue and the *bhikkhu* pressure groups of that time, Phadnis (1976) has pointed out that 'such a status to Sinhala automatically meant greater support to the Pirivenas and further recognition of the Bhikkhus's expertise in Sinhala' (p. 250). In October 1955, the LSSP's N.M. Perera moved a resolution that called for 'the Ceylon (Constitution) Order-in-Council [to] be amended to provide for the Sinhalese and Tamil languages to be state languages of Ceylon with parity of status throughout the island' (GOSL, 1955). During that time, Bandaranaike complained about the slow progress of the transition from English to Sinhala and Tamil with respect to the recommendations of the 1946 Select Committee. In 1955, as the leader of the opposition, Bandaranaike said that the people should force the government to declare Sinhala alone to be the state language before the then present parliament was dissolved. He further pointed out that.

> the Tamils with their much more developed culture will dominate us. Tamil even as a regional language is not desirable as Tamils are insatiable and they will not rest until the whole of Ceylon is given parity. (Times of Ceylon, 1955)

At the general election of 1956, Bandaranaike claimed that, if returned to power, he would affect a switchover from English in 'twenty four hours' (Wilson, 1979, p. 127). However, the leaders of the UNP at first resisted the 'Sinhala-only' policy, then in 1956 abruptly reversed their policy, but the left-wing parties continued their policy towards parity of status for Sinhala and Tamil as national languages. Discussing the political events of this time, historian K.M. De Silva (1981, 1986) aptly labels the period immediately after 1956 as a period that saw 'the triumph of linguistic nationalism'. By this time there were two opposing propositions: 'Sinhala-only' and 'Parity of Status for Sinhala and Tamil'. During that time, all English language newspapers opposed the idea of 'Sinhala-only', all Sinhalese newspapers supported it, and all Tamil newspapers called for 'parity of status' for Sinhala and Tamil.

As Kearney (1967) pointed out, in 1953 80% of the population of Sri Lanka spoke only one language (see Table 11); nearly 60% were monolingual speakers of Sinhala and more than 20% were monolingual speakers of Tamil. In 1953, only 9.4% of the population (5 years of age and older) were literate in English. Only about 13% of the population were bilingual speakers of both Sinhala and Tamil (Table 2). The size of the population, however, is only one of the elements determining the national/official language of the country.

From about that time, the medium of education was also changed to the national languages. However, the Sinhala-educated groups found that rewarding careers were closed to them by the pervasive dominance of English as the language of administration. For many years before independence and until the 1956 election, 'the passport to influence and wealth, with exceptions, was knowledge of English' (Wriggins, 1959, p. 33). As Tollefson (1991, p. 16) points out 'language policy is one mechanism for locating language within the social structure, so that language determines who has access to political power and economic resources'.

Shortly after independence, however, a national resurgence among the Sinhalese 'with roots extending back to the late nineteenth century, burst onto the political arena' (Kearney, 1978, p. 527). Accordingly, the demand among the majority Sinhalese community turned

Table 11. Languages spoken by Sri Lankan population – 1953 (Kearney, 1967).

Languages spoken	Number	Percentage of population
Sinhala only	4,289,957	58.9
Tamil only	1,570,084	21.6
English only	14,066	0.2
Sinhala and Tamil	719,194	9.9
Sinhala and English	307,570	4.2
Tamil and English	146,549	2.0
Sinhala, Tamil and English	233,567	3.2
	7,280,987	100.0

from '*swabhasha*' (Sinhala and Tamil) to 'Sinhala-only'. During that period, the official language movement shifted from an attack on the privileged position of the English elite, to a clash between ethnic communities. On the other hand, the Tamil demand for 'parity of status' was not understood by the Sinhalese masses, and Sinhala politicians mislead the Sinhalese people by making out that the Tamil claim meant that the Sinhalese should become *bilingual* (Wilson, 1988, p. 43). Moreover 'a shift in leadership at the village level gave impetus to the language movement' (Kearney, 1964, p. 127). As a result, the language issue became the 'focal point of a new ethnic consciousness of two rival nationalisms' (K.M. De Silva, 1993b, p. 282). At that time, those who talked of making both Sinhala and Tamil official languages became 'the enemy of the Sinhalese' (Arasaratnam, 1964, p. 27). Describing the political situation in 1954–1955, K.M. De Silva (1981) states:

The Prime Minister [Sir John Kotalaweal], while on an official visit to the Tamil north, made a public pronouncement that he would make constitutional provision for parity of status for the Sinhalese and Tamil languages. The thunderstorm of protests against this that arose in the Sinhalese areas took every section of opinion by surprise. Nobody had anticipated such a profoundly hostile reaction. The SLFP which like the UNP and all other national parties, stood for Sinhalese and Tamil as the official languages of the country, capitalized on the situation by declaring itself in favour of Sinhalese as the only official language – with a provision for the 'reasonable use' of the Tamil language. (p. 501)

In the decades preceding 1956, there had emerged a 'rural elite' educated in the Sinhala language. The members of this new elite consisted of, among others, Sinhala school teachers, *ayurvedic* physicians (those who practiced indigenous medicine), Sinhalese writers, traders, and newly rich merchants (*mudalālis*). Issues related to religion, language, and culture became central topics in the public sphere. The cultural protest, combined with opposition to Western values, manifested itself effectively in the political arena during the 1956 elections. In that way, the 'Sinhala-only' movement had developed and, under the influence of the *bhikkhus*, had become linked to the issue of state support for Buddhism. Moreover, the celebration of *Buddha Jayanthi*, the worldwide commemoration of the 2500th anniversary of the death of Buddha, coincided with the election year, and it paved the way for a Buddhist revival across Sinhalese society. More importantly, at that time Buddhist pressure groups – mainly *bhikkhus* organizations – campaigned for the adoption of Sinhala as the sole official language, and for the restoration of the rightful status of Buddhism (Dharmadasa, 1988; Phadnis, 1976). With the triumph of Buddhist activities, linguistic nationalism also gained wide attention. According to K.M. De Silva (1986, p. 164) 'linguistic nationalism was a populist nationalism, in contrast to the elitist constitutionalism of the early years after independence'. In this revivalist atmosphere, Sinhala language and Buddhism enjoyed a priority over other languages and religions; the Sinhalese masses strongly believed that this marked a new era in the history of Sinhalese Buddhists.

From linguistic parity status to the 'Sinhala-only' policy

The general election of April 1956 marked a dramatic transformation in Sri Lanka's social and political history, and the question of the official language was a key issue in that election campaign. Most Sinhala newspapers and magazines became deeply involved in the official language controversy. On the eve of the election, a coalition formed under the name *Mahajana Eksath Peramuna* (People's United Front) for the purpose of organizing anti-UNP votes and defeating the Government. It was composed of Bandaranaike's SLFP, the *Viplavakari Lanka Sama Samaja Paksaya* of Phillip Gunawardena, and the *Bhāshā Peramuna* (Language Front), an organization, led by W. Dahanyake and S. Chandrasiri, advocating 'Sinhala-only' (Woodward, 1969, p. 114). During the election campaign, Bandaranaike coined the popular slogans 'Sinhala-only' and in 'twenty four hours'. Along with the *bhikkhus*, the Sinhala language activists provided an energetic support to Bandaranaike. In that election, Bandaranaike was elected Prime Minister at least in part based on his main election promise to establish Sinhala as the *only* Official language of the country, replacing English, and indeed, his first official action after his election was to fulfil his promise. In June 1956, the *Official Language Act No. 33 of 1956* (popularly known as the 'Sinhala-only' Act) declared that Sinhala was to be the sole official language of Sri Lanka (GOSL, 1956a). Pieter Kueneman of the CP described the official language act of 1956 as doing 'grievous wrong to the Tamil-speaking people' (GOSL, 1956b, col. 1689). After the passage of that Act in Parliament, Dr Colvin R. De Silva, a Marxist Politician, prophesied:

Do you want *two languages and one nation or one language two nations*? Parity, Mr. Speaker, we believe is the road to the freedom of our nation and the unity of its components. Otherwise two torn little bleeding states may arise of one little state, which has compelled a large section of itself to treason, ready for the imperialists to mop up that which imperialism only recently disgorged'. (GOSL, 1956b, Vol. 24, col. 1917, emphasis added)

As Uyangoda (2001, p. 56) pointed out, on the one hand, this act was 'a policy measure aimed at correcting an injustice to a people who had suffered in the past under colonial rule' and, on the other hand, the act was a demonstration 'that justice done to the Sinhalese masses turned out to be an immense injustice to ethnic and linguistic minorities'. This language legislation certainly was one of the most important events that drove the two communities asunder in the post-independence period. As Kearney (1978, p. 528) succinctly explained:

For the Sinhala people, the Sinhala-only demand reflected their aspirations to retrieve their cultural heritage, which they felt was endangered by the incursions of the West, and to reassert their position and prerogatives as the majority of the island's population. To the Tamils, the language dispute epitomized the dangers of political domination by the Sinhala majority, which could lead to the undermining of Tamil language and culture in Lanka.

According to Bourhis (1984, p. 174), language planning can be quite 'a controversial enterprise when it involves the promulgation of a single language as the only official language of a society or nation state'. With respect to designating one language as an official language, Kaplan and Baldauf (1997, p. 16) also stated that the language selected is sometimes assumed to be the one spoken by a majority of people in the nation, but in reality 'it is more likely to be a language associated with a powerful group'. In the Sri Lankan situation, Sinhala was the majority language and it was also associated with power groups. Thus, the passing of the 'Sinhala-only' act of 1956 was bitterly resented by the Tamils (Kearney, 1967, 1978; Wriggins, 1960). These worries were aggravated when a peaceful demonstration (*satyagraha*) organized by the Federal Party against the 'Sinhala-only' act was disrupted by a counter-demonstration of pro-Sinhala elements in Colombo. Soon after the Official Language Act was passed, the Federal Party stressed the importance of the Tamil language and called on the Tamil people:

- to refuse to transact any business with the government in Sinhalese,
- to refuse to teach and study Sinhalese and
- to communicate with the government only in Tamil or in English.

In an appeal to the Tamil people, Ponnambalam – the Federal Party leader – declared, 'it is our bounden duty to continue the struggle for the preservation of our language rights lest we disintegrate and lose our national identity'(quoted in Kearney, 1967, p. 97). Tamils were also deeply concerned that the official language policy would destroy their language and distinctive culture, which they zealously cultivated from the time of their arrival from South India in ancient times (Manogaran, 1987, p. 46).

The ethnic riots that broke out in the wake of the introduction of this bill in Parliament underlined 'the combustible nature of linguistic nationalism in a plural society' (K.M. De Silva, 1986, p. 181). In addition, this language legislation was noted for its 'stark brevity' (K.M. De Silva, 1993a). It had only three clauses:

- the first clause served as the citation, or short title;
- the second clause indicated that the 'Sinhala language shall be the one official language of Ceylon', with a proviso that, if immediate implementation is 'impracticable', 'the language or languages [currently in use] may be continued ... until the necessary change is effected as early as possible before the thirty-first of December 1960;
- the third and final clause enabled the Minister to make regulations 'for the purpose of giving effect to the principles and provisions of this Act'.

No provisions were made in the Act for the use of the Tamil language for official purposes inTamil-speaking districts. The Act was not followed by subsidiary legislation in the form of regulations, as was the normal practice; the implementation was based solely on policy statements and cabinet circulars. Commenting on this, one administrator remarked:

The practical advantage was that this enabled greater manoeuvrability and flexibility in the implementation of the language policy. In a sense this was due to a realization of the complex difficulties involved in changing the language of administration from English to Sinhala, amidst opposition especially from the Tamil minority. (R.G.O. Gunasekera, 1996, pp. 25–26)

Discussing the politics of language in that period, K.M. De Silva (1996, p. 26) stated:

Bandaranaike and the SLFP ignored the substantial achievements in systematic language planning in the period 1946–1955, and created problems for the future in raising expectations of more rapid change than the Sri Lankan political and administrative system was capable of handling.

However, Prime Minster Bandaranaike realized the difficulty of implementing this language act overnight and therefore postponed, by Gazette notification, its full implementation to January 1961, thereby guaranteeing that there would be no immediate implementation of 'Sinhala-only' policies. [The Act specified 31 December 1960; January 1961 is merely one day (or at best 31 days) later.].

On 10 September 1956, Prime Minister Bandaranaike presented a Cabinet Memorandum on the status of public officers in relation to the Official Language Act. According to R.G.O. Gunasekera (1996, p. 26) 'this [memorandum] formed the basis of implementation of the new language policy in the public service'; it categorized public officials into two groups, namely *old entrants* (those who were in service prior to 7 July 1956) and *new entrants* (those who were recruited after that date). In order to encourage the 'new entrants' to the Public Service to learn Sinhala, the Cabinet laid down the following conditions of service:

Conditions of service for new entrants

(I) The period of probation/trial of new entrants shall be 3 years;
(II) (a) These officers should acquire proficiency in Sinhala during their period of probation/trial;
  (b) Their confirmation, at the expiry of the period of probation/trial, will depend *inter alia*, on the passing of a proficiency test in Sinhala.

Those who fail to reach the prescribed standard of proficiency in Sinhala during their period of probation/trial are liable to be discontinued, but discontinuance may be deferred if the appointing authority is satisfied that a genuine attempt had been made to acquire proficiency in the official Language. (GOSL, 1958a)

In accordance with that decision, arrangements were made to conduct language-training classes for public servants in all major towns. With the passage of Language Act No. 33 of 1956, work connected with official language affairs became a matter under the responsibilities of the Prime Minister. The Department of Official Language Affairs, under the Ministry of Finance and the Department of Swabhasha under the Ministry of Education were brought under the purview of the Prime Minister from 1 October 1956. A separate Ministry of Cultural Affairs also established in that year. The official language act was gradually implemented in the field of public administration (R.G.O. Gunasekera, 1996). At that time, with regard to the implementation of the official language policy, the following activities were carried out by the Official Languages Department:

(1) The publication of the *Government Gazette* in Sinhala.
(2) The Franking of official letters in Sinhala.
(3) The Issuing of Circulars in Sinhala.
(4) The Printing and use of official terms.
(5) The Compilation of Glossaries of Technical Terms.
(6) The creation of Language Training classes for government servants.
(7) The Training of Stenographers in Sinhala and Tamil.
(8) The Translation of text books into Sinhala and Tamil.

(GOSL, 1957)

According to the reports of the Official Language Affairs Commissioner, there has been a steady increase in the number of Departments corresponding with one another in the Sinhala medium.

In summary, the language policy decisions moved by Sri Lankan politicians in the national legislation from the 1930s to the 1950s occurred in this order: 1932 – Sinhala and Tamil; 1936 – Sinhala and Tamil; 1943 – Sinhala (later amend to include Tamil);1951 – Sinhala and Tamil; 1956 – Sinhala only.

Language planning and policy implementation

This section deals with the activities and some of the issues related to *status planning* and *corpus planning* of Sinhala as an official language. First, the aftermath of the 'Sinhala-only' policy and relevant status planning issues – particularly the change of language policy and the problems of policy implementation – are discussed.

From a *language ecology* perspective of language planning,

> Anything done to one language in a polity is likely to have effects on that language in all the other places it may be spoken and is likely to have an impact on all the other languages spoken in that polity. (Kaplan & Baldauf, 1997, p. 361)

It should be amply clear that language planning has significant social, political, and psychological consequences. Instrumentally, the use of language in government activity – in the public administration, in the courts of law and in education – becomes one of the most important areas of socio-political life.

Problems of policy implementation and the rise of Tamil separatism

Historically, the principle cause of most language-based conflicts has been 'the *denial* of legitimate minority-language rights rather than their recognition' (May, 2001, p. 224). The purpose of language legislation should be to resolve such conflicts and differences by legally defining the status of and use of coexisting languages (Turi, 1994). After the passage of the 'Sinhala-only' legislation, the 1956 government – and successive governments – made various legislative and other attempts to allay the grievances of the Tamil-speaking community. Kearney (1967), who has discussed the communalism and language of politics in Sri Lanka, observed, 'the official language issue posed profound communal implications and great potential for mobilizing communal support' (p. 138). Those most affected by the Sinhala-only Act were Tamil monolinguals. Discussing the language policy and the public service, Vamadevan (1996, p. 121) stated:

> In the area of promotion, In the area of promotion, Tamil public officers were adversely affected by the Sinhala-only Act. Those who did not acquire the necessary proficiency in Sinhala within the prescribed period were not made permanent. As a result their seniority in the service was affected.

Tamil citizens have argued that, due to the Sinhala-only policy, they have been 'treated as aliens in their own land' (Kearney, 1978). In August 1956, the Federal Party outlined its main demands on behalf of the Tamils.[22] First among these was autonomy for the Northern and Eastern provinces under a federal constitution; next came the 'parity of status' for the Sinhala and Tamil languages (Ponnambalam, 1983, p. 106).The party was prepared to accept a 'federal' system of government, with Sinhala as the official language, but in which Tamil would be the language of administration and the medium of instruction in the Northern and Eastern provinces.

Since the passage of the 'Sinhala-only' Act in 1956, two major attempts were made to resolve the issues arising from this language legislation: one attempt, in 1957, designated the Bandaranaike–Chelvanayagam (B–C) Pact, and another attempt in 1965–1966, designated the Senanayaka–Chelvanayagam Pact. According to the provisions of the B–C Pact, two important steps were to be taken in order to recognize the linguistic rights of Tamils. First, a Regional Council Bill was drafted with the purpose of transferring powers to regional units. Secondly, the *Tamil Language (Special Provisions) Act* was introduced, intended to provide for the use of Tamil in prescribed administrative activities in the Northern and Eastern provinces, without infringing on the position of the Official Language Act. This pact recognized Tamil as the 'national language' of a minority. However, there was strong opposition from Sinhalese extremist groups and from the main opposition party (UNP) to this pact. Both groups accused Bandaranaike of 'betraying the Sinhalese and seeking to divide the country' (Wilson, 1979, p. 128). Due to the massive protest against the pact, in April 1958 Prime Minister Bandaranaike had to abrogate it.

In March 1958, state-owned buses were transferred to the North with the Sinhala letter representing *Sri* on their number plates; the Tamils viewed this act as another Sinhalese attempt to dominate minorities. Tamils in the Northern Province protested against the Sinhala *Sri* symbol and demanded that the Tamil *Sri* symbol be substituted for the Sinhala symbol. In retaliation for this anti-*Sri* campaign by the Tamils, the signboards written in Tamil in Colombo were tarred over (De Votta, 2004, pp. 108–111; Kearney, 1967, p. 86). The Federal Party, disappointed by Bandaranaike's refusal to implement the pact, launched a mass civil disobedience campaign in northern district of Vauvniya. As a result, ethnic riots erupted once again in May 1958. Shortly after the 1958 Sinhala–Tamil ethnic riots, the government enacted the *Tamil Language (Special Provisions) Act No. 28 of 1958* to assure 'reasonable use' of Tamil. The Act provided for the use of Tamil as a medium of instruction and required public examinations in Tamil, official correspondence in Tamil and the additional use of Tamil for 'prescribed administrative purposes' in the Northern and Eastern provinces in the country 'without prejudice to the use of the official language [Sinhala]'. During the parliamentary debate of this Act in 1958, Prime Minister Bandaranaike elucidated the government's understanding of the term 'official language':

> Many people do not understand what is meant by the term 'official language.' That is interpreted in various ways. The official language conception is a Western conception. In our country, we had no official language as such. Even in many Western countries they have no legal official language today; it has grown up by practice. When you have a language declared by law as an official language, what does it mean? It only means that you recognize that language for necessary official acts. That is the meaning of the term 'official language.' For instance, if I send a letter to a foreign country, it should really go in the official language, with a suitable translation. In due course, official records and things like that should be kept in the official language. Documents that a court would recognize would have to be in the official language, though there may be, for purpose of convenience, a translation. That is what an official language means. An official language does not mean a language that is thrust down the throats of everybody for every purpose. Most of these troubles arise out of a misconception of the term 'official language'. (GOSL, 1958b, col. 1968)

The Act hardly satisfied the aspirations of Tamils. Their arguments were:

- first, it did not recognize Tamil as a national language;
- second, there was no follow-up strategy to implement it; and
- third it was too late and too little.

The political instability of the last phase of Bandaranaike's administration, and his assassination in September 1959, prevented the taking of necessary measures for the implementation of the bill. It took 8 years before the regulations envisaged under the act were eventually approved by the Parliament. As pointed out by R.G.O. Gunasekera (1996, p. 36), '[i]f this provision had been immediately put into effect, it would have had far reaching consequences on the implementation of the official language policy'. The first phase of implementation ended on 31 December 1960, but the switchover to the official language did not happen. In his *Administration Report* (1962), the Commissioner of Official Languages identified the main difficulties experienced by government departments for the wider use of Sinhala as an official language:

(1) the lack of enthusiasm for the wider use of Sinhala as an official language;
(2) the absence, in certain departments, of an adequate number of officers proficient in the official language;
(3) the lack of Sinhala typewriters in the offices;
(4) the absence of the necessary forms in Sinhala for use in suboffices (GOSL, 1962).

From 1956 to 1960, the SLFP, which had legislated the language act, was in power (except for few months). In 1960, after winning the general election, the SLFP government implemented its original 'Sinhala-only' language policy and ignored the provisions of the Tamil Language (Special Provisions) Act of 1958. In the history of language status planning, another landmark was the *Language of the Courts Act No. 3 of 1961* which was repealed by the Constitution of 1972. The Language of the Courts Act had been enacted in response to nationalist pressures that Sinhala be made the language of judicial administration. The Official Language Act of 1956 took effect in January 1961,[23] and in February 1961, the Federal Party launched, in the Northern and Eastern provinces, another *satyagraha* or passive resistance movement aimed at preventing the implementation of the official language and Language of Courts Acts in Tamil-speaking areas. As a result, on 30 January 1961, a majority of Tamil public servants in the North and West provinces ceased working in the official language in response to a letter appealing to each of them to boycott implementation of the official language act. Furthermore, in 1964 the Federal Party leaders launched a 'Tamil-only' letter-writing campaign intended 'to embarrass the government' and to 'slow-down the bureaucratic machinery' (Wilson, 1988, pp. 113–115).

During the general election of 1965, the UNP election manifesto promised 'a Round Table Conference to discuss ways and means of unifying the nation within the framework of Sinhala as the official language of the state' (cited in Loganathan, 1996, p. 34). The agreement between Prime Minister Dudley Senanayaka of the UNP and S.J.V. Chelvanayagam, leader of the Federal Party in 1965, (known as the Dudely–Chelva Pact) acknowledged the previous failures. This pact mentioned that action would be taken early under the *Tamil Language Special Provisions Act* to make provision for the Tamil Language to be the language of administration and record in the Northern and Eastern Provinces. As Loganathan (1996) states, this pact contained 'distinct advantages to the Tamil polity in relation to land alienation and a language policy that could be constructed as a viable interim alternative to "parity"' (p. 36). Though the Tamil Language (Special Provisions) Act had been passed under Bandaranaike's government, due to political instability the regulations needed to implement the bill were not approved. However, in January 1966 Senanayake and his government approved the *Tamil Language (Special Provisions) Regulations of 1966* to give effect to the Tamil language in administration. In 1966 Tamil became the language of the administration and courts in the North and East. The SLFP and its left-wing allies, however, opposed this language legislation.[24]

Manogaran (1987, p. 54) describes the language situation and the reaction of Tamils towards the enactment of the Tamil language regulations Act:

> Soon after the enactment of the language regulations into law, public servants in Tamil areas sought Sinhala training and accepted Sinhala as the official language. More than seven hundred Sinhalese teachers assumed duties in Tamil schools on invitation from the Tamils of the Northern and Eastern provinces. The number of motor vehicles with Sinhala licence plates proliferated in the Northern and Eastern provinces, and signs in government departments and public places were posted in both Tamil and Sinhala.

In the 1960s, the Official Languages Department continued to pursue its activities 'to accelerate the progressive transition' from English into Sinhala in all government departments, state corporations and institutions (GOSL, 1967, p. 3). Special efforts were made to overcome the day-to-day difficulties encountered by various departments in their endeavours to affect a complete switch over to the use of Sinhala in the transaction of official business.

The 1972 constitution and language policy

In 1972, with the adoption of the first Republican constitution, the official language policy was given constitutional recognition. However, the Constitution of 1972 also explicitly consolidated the 'Sinhala-only' policy of the 1950s, emphasizing the essentially subordinate role of the Tamil language. The *Official Language Act No. 33 of 1956*, and the *Tamil Language (Special Provisions) Act of 1958* were incorporated into Chapter III of the 1972 Constitution. Section 7 of the 1972 constitution provided for Sinhala as the official language of Sri Lanka. Section 8(1) provided for the use of the Tamil language in accordance with the *Tamil Language (Special Provisions) Act of 1958*. However, Section 8(2) provided that regulations for the use of the Tamil language 'shall not in any manner be interpreted as being a provision of the constitution but shall be deemed to be subordinate legislation'. As pointed out by Wilson (1979, p. 22), 'the Tamils felt indignant that it was specifically stated in the constitution that the provisions relating to the Tamil language could be amended by ordinary legislation whereas the provisions relating to the Sinhalese were constitutionally entrenched'. In addition, the new constitution conferred a special status on Buddhism, the religion of the majority of Sinhalese, and declared 'it shall be the duty of the state to protect and foster Buddhism' (GOSL, 1972, p. 4). According to Kearney (1978, p. 529), 'the swift growth of sentiment for separation was fuelled by the adoption of a new constitution in 1972'.

During the 1970s, the Sinhalese community also complained about the position of Sinhala. They expressed the opinion that, between 1965 and 1970, little had been done to consolidate the position of Sinhala as the official language (R.G.O. Gunasekera, 1996). The Official Languages Department also lost much of its status and influence in the early 1970s (Samarasinghe, 1996). In 1973, the obligations and the responsibilities of the Official Languages Department were transferred to other government ministries and departments. A separate division was set up in the Ministry of Public Administration to undertake:

- implementation of the official language policy,
- teaching of Sinhala to public officers,
- training external students in Sinhala shorthand and typewriting,
- assisting government departments in the translation of important documents into Sinhala and Tamil, etc.

However, during the period 1970–1977, many language planning programmes were not implemented, and there was 'an apparent set-back in the implementation of the language policy' (Samarasinghe, 1996, p. 101). As in many other language planning programmes, the lack of an evaluation component is a common feature in the Sri Lankan situation.

As Manogaran (1987, p. 57) points out, 'the official languages controversy in the 1950s drove a deep wedge between the communities, but no major Tamil parties proposed a total separation prior to the 1970s'. In 1972, the formation of the Tamil United Front (TUF) clearly manifested the unity of Tamil parties. Moreover, from the early 1970s, Tamil youths began civil disturbances in the North, and in 1975 the LTTE was formed to carry out an armed struggle for the establishment of a separate state on the island. In May 1976, at the first national convention of the TUF (recast as the Tamil United Liberation Front (TULF)) a political resolution (the Vaddukodai Resolution) was unanimously adopted for the 'restoration and reconstruction of the Free, Sovereign, Secular Socialist, State of Tamil Eelam based on the right of self-determination'. The TULF manifesto stated that Eelam would be ultimately established 'either by peaceful means or by direct action or struggle'. This resolution mentioned that the Sinhalese people have used their own political power to the detriment of Tamils by 'making Sinhala the only official language throughout Ceylon thereby placing the stamp of inferiority on the Tamils and the Tamil language' (Ponnambalam, 1983, p. 192).

New official language policy: 1978–1988

The year 1978 marked the beginning of a new phase in the implementation of language policy in Sri Lanka. The new government, under the leadership of President J.R. Jayewardene, appointed a select committee of the National State Assembly to draft a new constitution. As K.M. De Silva (1996, p. 37) points out, 'the framers of the constitution of 1978 deliberately sought a more conciliatory language policy and gave it a very high priority'. According to the Report of the National State Assembly Select Committee, 'the Draft constitution preserves unimpaired the status of Sinhala as the 'Official Language of Sri Lanka', but 'the Committee unanimously agreed that both Sinhala and Tamil should be the National Languages of Sri Lanka, and that the status of Tamil should receive constitutional recognition, especially by incorporating in the Constitution the relevant provisions of the existing law' (Second National State Assembly, 1978). Accordingly, Chapter IV of the new 1978 Constitution, while maintaining the status of Sinhala as *the* official language of Sri Lanka (Article 18), recognized Tamil as a 'national language' along with Sinhala (Article 19), a significant modification of the 'Sinhala-only' policy pursued by all governments since 1956 (GOSL, 1978). A prominent Tamil lawyer, N. Satyendra, assessed the significance of this policy change thus:

> . . .for the first time in the political history of this country the new constitution recognizes the existence of the Tamil community as [a] distinct nationality with a separate language, and Section 19 provides that the national languages of Sri Lanka shall be Sinhala and Tamil. This is a step which previous governments have been unable [or] unwilling to take, and the status afforded to Tamil as a national language in the new Constitution is by itself a significant step forward in the attempt to bring about a unity of purpose amongst the members of the Sinhala and Tamil communities in this country and thereby foster the growth of a truly national awareness and consciousness. (cited in K.M. De Silva, 1986, p. 297)

According to Dharmadasa (1981, p. 63), 'this recognition has more to it than mere symbolic value'. Moreover, all the rights assured to the Tamil-speaking people of Sri

Lanka by regulations under the *Tamil language (Special Provisions) Act* have been incorporated into the Constitution so that they cannot be altered except by way of a constitutional amendment. With the introduction of a new language policy, the government took an important policy decision to re-establish the Official Languages Department in 1979 to implement a policy of bilingualism instead of the 'Sinhala-only' policy. It marked a new phase in the implementation of the official language policy in Sri Lanka.

Moreover, the Constitution guarantees the freedom to use one's own language, and puts down as a principle of state policy 'that no citizen shall suffer any disability by reason of language'. According to Article 20 of the new constitution, a Member of Parliament or of any local government authority is entitled to function in any of the national languages. Article 21(1) of the constitution guarantees the right of an individual to be educated through the medium of either of the national languages. According to Article 22(1), the Tamil language shall be used as a language of administration in all business conducted by public institutions in the Northern and Eastern provinces. According to Article 22(2), a person anywhere in Sri Lanka is entitled to 'receive communication and communicate and transact business with any official in his official capacity in either of the national languages'. In addition, Article 22(4) lays down that all proclamations, all by-laws, and all official publications shall be published in both languages. The Article repeats the requirement that all laws have to be published in Sinhala and Tamil with a translation in English (Article 23). However, the inadequacy of state officers to transact business in Tamil depressed the Tamil -peaking population (Theva Rajan, 1995). For example, in 1983 the Home Affairs Minister, K.W. Dewanayagam, stressed the delayed implementation of the Tamil language provisions: 'of course, there is very little left to be fulfilled because of the lack of implementation of the Constitution. I must say that the root cause for the entire dissatisfaction of the minority is the lack of implementation' (cited in Theva Rajan, 1995, p. 63).

The ethnic riots in July 1983 and the subsequent civil war conditions have further complicated the problem of arriving at an amicable solution to the linguistic rights of Tamils. Discussing the period he entitled 'linguistic nationalism to civil war', De Votta (2004, p. 157) says: 'while economic rivalry and ethnic jealousies partly lay behind the 1983 riots, the major reasons were the Sinhala-only policy and the culture of ethnic outbidding and institutional decay that the language issue initiated, enculturated, and legitimated'. During the early 1980s, the notion of Tamil as a minority language had been used as a justification for separatist aspirations. However, the Indo-Sri Lanka Accord, signed by Sri Lankan President J.R. Jayewardene and Indian Prime Minister Rajiv Gandhi in July 1987, declared that Sri Lanka is 'a multi-ethnic and multilingual plural society'. Underlining this designation, Tamil and English were proclaimed to be official languages along with Sinhala. Accordingly, in 1988, as a part of the 13th amendment to the constitution, Tamil was raised to the status of an official language, while English was assigned the position of a 'link language'. This part of the 13th amendment to the constitution stated, 'Tamil shall also be an official language'. However, the legality of the word 'also' was not explained in the relevant constitutional provision. As K.M. De Silva (1993b, p. 299) observed, '[a]lthough there is some ambiguity about the position of English, its legal position appears to be almost equal to Sinhalese and Tamil in many areas'. The provisions of the 13th amendment were clarified and indeed consolidated by the 16th amendment. However, as De Votta (2004, p. 164) explains, 'Jayewardene government's accommodative language policies were too little and too late'. The benefits of the 13th amendment to the Constitution have not, in fact, percolated down to the Tamil-speaking population in the country due to the lack of policy implementation. The Tamil language was afforded parity status only after Tamil youths mobilized militarily seeking a separate state, *Eelam*.

Shortly after the enactment of the 16th Amendment, the Commissioner of Official Languages and the International Centre for Ethnic Studies, Colombo, together organized a conference to examine the implications of bilingualism and the effective implementation of the language policy. This conference adopted twenty proposals, in three stages – 'immediate', 'transitional', and 'long term' – for the successful implementation of the new official language policy in administration:

Immediate.

(1) Working out [a] reasonable time frame for the phased implementation of the policy.
(2) Setting out guidelines, strategies, and incentives for implementation.
(3) Displaying name boards and informative signs in all three languages in all government offices.
(4) Arranging that service counters in all government offices would have bilingual facilities.
(5) Providing that all official circulars, forms, and documents would be in all three languages.
(6) Assuring that inter-departmental meetings, interviews and public functions would be conducted in the official languages. Further, assuring that all records of the same would be maintained in the official languages (Sinhala and Tamil).
(7) Establishing, by an Act of Parliament, an independent OLC to monitor the implementation of the official language policy.
(8) Enact a National Languages Charter, embodying the rights of citizens with respect to language in their relations with the state, and the obligation of both the central Government and Provincial Councils in this regard.
(9) Upgrading the Department of Official Languages and streamlining its activities.
(10) Requiring new entrants to the important All-island Services/Cadres (such as the Sri Lanka Administrative Service) to acquire a prescribed level of proficiency in Sinhala/Tamil within a specified period of time or before reaching a stipulated salary point.
(11) Creating an advisory body, representative of government and non-government institutions, and including writers and scholars, to assist the Commissioner of Official Languages.
(12) Initiating a programme of public advocacy of bilingualism through the media.

Transitional.

(1) Providing a staff capable of working in both official languages in the crucial geographical and administrative sectors.
(2) Ensuring that security forces can communicate with members of the public in both official languages.
(3) Conducting a national survey to do empirical ground-work for implementation of policy.
(4) Identifying required resources for completion of the official languages policy in stages – through staff development, staff training and equipment.
(5) Developing curricula for language training relevant to the context of administration.
(6) Printing forms and documents in the two official languages.

Long-term.

(1) Setting up comprehensive training and orientation programmes to make all government servants bilingual.
(2) Extending the implementation of the new language policy to those departments and regions not covered during the transitional period (International Centre for Ethnic Studies, 1989).

In 1989–1990, the UNP government, under President Premadasa, took an important policy decision to establish an OLC with legislative powers to supervise the implementation of official language policy (see the ensuing discussion).

The activities of the several governments discussed so far can be described as instances of *status language planning*. The discussion highlights the complex interactions of language status and use. Status planning, referring to the allocation of new functions to a language, affects the role a language plays within a given society (Deumert, 2000). As the Sri Lankan situation demonstrates, most of the language planning undertaken by the government is intended to solve complex socio-political problems at the national level, and political changes had major implications on the implementation of the official language policy.

Language standardization and modernization

If a language is used for new communicative functions that it has not previously served, then the corpus or 'body' of that language may need to be adapted or elaborated to make it suitable for the new functions, and standardization and modernization of the language become necessary. In 1956, the Sinhala language entered a new phase in its history, ushering in changes not only in its 'status' as the official language, but also changes in its structure. As the official language, Sinhala was now required to cope with a variety of new roles, in effect, as the medium of official communication in the Parliament, in state departments, and in the courts of law. This era also saw the resurgence of Sinhala and Tamil as the mediums of instruction in education. The shift to *swabhasha* media inevitably increased the functional load of these languages. During the fact-finding period in the 1950s, the Official Languages Department had identified four especially important obstacles:

(a) Lack of personnel, i.e. insufficiency of staff proficient in the national languages.
(b) Lack of funds, i.e. all applications for financial provision for the purchase of Sinhala and Tamil typewriters, for the replacement of name boards, etc., were not approved.
(c) Lack of technical terms in Sinhala or Tamil and the lack of printed forms in these languages.
(d) Absence of legal enactments in the national languages (based on R.G.O. Gunasekera, 1996, pp. 24–25).

In order to implement the official language policy during the transitional stage, the Official Languages Department carried out various language corpus planning activities related mainly to Sinhala but also to Tamil. Its programme included a range of activities such as:

(i) the coinage of new technical terms in Sinhala to facilitate government administration and academic instruction,
(ii) the teaching of Sinhala as a second language for public workers,

(iii) the designing of a Sinhala typewriter keyboard and a system of short-hand in Sinhala, and

(iv) the translation of official documents of other departments.

In addition, the Official Languages Department issued many reference documents and booklets related to use of Sinhala (and also Tamil) in governments departments; for example, in 1955 the Official Languages Department issued a booklet entitled *Aid to the use of Tamil in government departments* in order to resolve difficulties related mostly to routine correspondence and reporting on various matters.

Language corpus planning and linguistic purism

Many aspects of corpus planning are primarily linguistic and hence internal to language. However, as Baldauf (1990, p. 7) points out 'corpus planning operates in real world contexts in conjunction with social, historical, cultural, and political forces'. The period during which modern Sinhala arose was characterized by interconnected and fundamental changes in the socio-cultural organization of Sri Lankan society. The planning of Sinhala for new functions became an important issue during the 1950s in response to the changing status of the language. Language 'corpus planning' has traditionally been considered the work of grammarians and language scholars, of linguists working on their own behalf or under commission, and of language academies. In Sri Lanka, from the colonial period onward, many individual language planners undertook various efforts to 'modernize' Sinhala as a medium of communication. Especially during the twentieth century, the scholarly activities of Munidasa Cumaratunga (1887–1944) and of Martin Wickramasinghe (1897–1976) influenced the structure of Sinhala in terms of terminology and style. For example, without any official or popular support, Cumaratunga carried out such corpus planning activities as the production of normative grammars, the coining of new words and the standardization of Sinhala usage. He made a special effort to constrain what is considered 'bad language' (*dubasa*) and to encourage what is considered 'good language' (*subasa*). He took meticulous care to use the 'good language' in his writings and also encouraged others to work along the same path. For Cumaratunga, the approved language was one associated with 'civilized' society. As a language reformer in the 1930s, Cumaratunga used the metaphor of law and society in defining the relation of grammar and language, and he struggled to purify the Sinhala language.[25] He said 'signs are appearing that Sinhala will become an uncivilized language ... Need it be said that a people who use an uncivilized language are themselves uncivilized' (quoted in Dharmadasa, 1992, p. 274). Cumaratunga's writings were mainly focused on the promotion of Sinhala and its prestige. In order to disseminate his ideas, he also started a Sinhala journal in 1939 under the name *Subasa* (Good Language) and another journal in English, *The Helio* (1941).

Consequently, Cumaratunga's linguistic policy was best known for linguistic purism. As a language purist, later in his career Cumaratunga suggested a pure Sinhala style (*Hela*), which proved not to be acceptable to contemporary writers. During the first three decades of the twentieth century, Sanskrit and Pali played an important role in the intellectual life of *pirivena* or oriental scholars. Mostly the *pirivena* educated scholars tried to model Sinhala grammars on Sanskrit or Pali exemplars. In reaction to this scholarly tradition, Cumaratunga emphasized the unique features of the Sinhala language and distanced it from some other languages, mainly from Pali and Sanskrit. By denying the Indo-Aryan identity of Sinhala, Cumaratunga asserted an indigenous *Hela* identity for the language and people. He rejected the Sanskritized form of the Sinhala literary language (or the Sanskritization of Sinhala) and focused on the pure Sinhala or *Hela* language ideology. His desire was to show that the Sinhala language was an independent and superior language, not one hybridized by excessive borrowings from, or mixing with, other languages. This *Hela* movement at first gained the support of Sinhala language loyalists because of its ethno-nationalistic implications, but it later failed to gain mass support. Spolsky (2004) points out that purism becomes important during a time of 'language cultivation' and 'modernization'. Language cultivation involves norms of correctness, efficiency, purity, and aesthetics that are invoked in the development of a linguistic feature (Dua, 1996). As an individual language planner, Cumaratunga held the view that, before a language could attain official status and serve as a medium of communication, it should be 'idiomatic, grammatical and systematically correct'. Therefore, Cumaratunga pointed out the importance of *language cultivation*, referring to the treatment of problems related to matters of correctness, efficiency, style, and terminology (Coperahewa, 1999). With regard to the lexical expansion of Sinhala, Cumaratunga outlined some principles for the coining of new Sinhala terms, and he coined a large number of new terms for various communicative needs. Most of these terms were based on 'pure' (Hela) indigenous roots, and consequently failed to gain the acceptance of the Sinhala speech community and Sinhala writers. Discussing purism and language planning, Thomas (1991, p. 220) remarked: 'by preferring nativisation of the lexicon, purism may be seriously detrimental to the drive for modernisation'.

Wickramasinghe (1891–1976), a leading literary figure, journalist and critic during the twentieth century, expanded the horizons of the Sinhala literary idiom and crafted a vocabulary for modern Sinhala usage. His views on the development of the Sinhala language differed significantly from Cumaratunga's. In his numerous writings, Wickramasinghe stressed the fact that Sinhala is a 'living language'; he therefore used the colloquial idiom in his novels and short stories. As a journalist, he modernized contemporary Sinhala usage and created a corpus of material for modern Sinhala literary criticism. Moreover, during the first half of the twentieth century, the Sinhala print media also played an important role in the process of corpus planning. The media acted as an outlet for new terms, phrases and discourses pertaining to all spheres of national and daily life (Karam, 1974).The literary activities of the post-independence period also contributed to vocabulary expansion, simplification of registers and stylistic development. As Obeysekera (1974, p. XXXV) pointed out:

> The magazines, newspapers, controversies and debates helped to give to the Sinhalese language a new blend of classical and colloquial forms and created a vehicle of communication which could reach both the scholar and newly created mass reading public.

Thus, with the expansion of modern Sinhala literature in the mid-twentieth century, Sinhala language became a popular vehicle for the new reading public.

Diglossia and discourses of language standardization

As stated previously, the Sinhala language has been characterized as diglossic. Diglossia is a common feature in many South Asian societies where writing was considered a 'sacred' heritage, not to be polluted by ordinary people. Moreover, as M.W.S. De Silva (1976) points out, 'all South Asian diglossias have evolved within the availability of a reference grammar' (p. 95), and 'most diglossic societies suffer from colonial hang-overs' (M.W.S. De Silva, 1974, p. 82). Literary Sinhala is the prestige variety, enjoying a broad body of classical literature extending back over several centuries. Due to the great emphasis laid on the literary language as the 'correct' form, the spoken language was completely neglected by the Sinhalese grammarians of the last century. However, modern Sinhala linguists have recently made some attempts to analyse the structure of contemporary spoken Sinhala in the context of modern linguistics (Disanayaka, 1991).

One aspect of corpus planning involves the process of language standardization. According to Ferguson (1968), the concept of 'standardization' includes notions of increasing uniformity of the norm itself and explicit codification of the norm. When a language becomes the medium of wider communication within a linguistic community, it tends to produce deviations of usage. There is always a constant interaction between 'standard' and non-standard usage (Krishnamurti, 1998). On the other hand, standardization of the written form is a complex activity, especially in a diglossic environment. In the early twentieth century, the spread of vernacular literacy and the growing demand for printed books created a greater need for the 'standardization' of Sinhala usage. Discussing the controversy over written standard Sinhala, Dharmadasa (1977) stated:

> During the early decades of the twentieth century with expansion of modern education and the broadening of intellectual horizons concomitant with modernization in society, attention came to be focussed on the anomaly of retaining for literary purposes an idiom far removed from the language in everyday use. (p. 23)

As a result, standard Sinhala became closely associated with written Sinhala in general. Generally, standardization is involved when a language achieves national or official status, and it gives privilege, authority, and legitimacy to a particular variety. The new status accorded to Sinhala in 1956 broadened its usage as a medium in education, in government activity, and in the mass media; in other words, the shift to Sinhala from English inevitably increased the functional load on the Sinhala language. However, in the midst of language change, elaboration of functional varieties and modernization there is no evident decrease in Sinhala diglossia (Gair, 1983).

There was also a problem of evolving a style and developing a vocabulary suitable for the new genres and a new epoch. As a 'diglossic' language in which variety or style should be given prominence in the production of school textbooks and government publications, the 'popular' variety became a major issue that sparked controversies. While the purists were organizing themselves in defense of the literary grammar, there were a few scholars who wrote in favour of adopting the spoken grammar for literary purposes. With the spread of education and of literary activities, a movement for bringing literary language closer to the speech of the common people developed in the decades of 1950 and 1960s.[26] A small group of scholars launched that movement, but the idea was strongly opposed by the *Hela Havula* scholars on the ground that serious writings were not possible in the spoken language. With the growth of the mass media, the expansion of mass education and the impact of information technology, some writers and scholars felt strongly that it would be desirable to use spoken Sinhala as the standard medium of communication.

The new trend of using patterns of spoken Sinhala in writing is seen more often in creative work than in scientific and technical writing. Sinhala fiction encouraged the expansion of spoken Sinhala as a medium for literary expression. According to Disanayaka (1976), a modern grammarian, 'the gradual but steady influx of spoken Sinhala into writing, coupled with changes within literary Sinhala itself, has brought about a number of variants in literary usage' (p. 31). Some contemporary Sinhala writers, including Siri Gunasinghe, Ajit Tilakasena, argue that there is no need to maintain such a distinction between spoken and written language. They have published creative works – such as novels and short stories in a more colloquial variety of Sinhala. Most of the private radio and TV channels use a variety of spoken Sinhala in news reading, but state radio broadcasting still uses a highly literary variety in news bulletins. As a result, the difference between spoken and written Sinhala is diminishing, and this change is partly due to the natural ignorance of the users and partly due to the work of scholars who, from a language planning perspective, deliberately encourage changes in language. Moreover, both varieties of language are influencing each other and producing new forms. The school education system, however, promotes written Sinhala as the standard form of language. All textbooks are written in standard written Sinhala, and the public examination system also encourages proficiency in written standard Sinhala. There is also a large body of normative opinion concerning the superiority of the written norm. However, as the history of Sinhala *diglossia* indicates, 'the strength of the forms of purism [derive] from the nativistic undercurrents at work in society' (Dharmadasa, 1977, p. 25).

From the 1960s, modern linguistics also contributed to the various corpus- planning activities related to Sinhala. The first course on modern linguistics to be conducted in Sinhala at the University of Ceylon, Peradeniya was introduced by Dr M.W.S. De Silva, who was trained in this discipline in Britain. As a result of his pioneering work, the focus of linguistic study 'shifted from written literary Sinhala to spoken Sinhala', and the need for writing 'new grammars for modern Sinhala' was considered by Sinhala linguists as a matter of high priority (Disanayaka, 1999, p. 268). As pointed out by M.W.S. De Silva (1969, p. 235), there was rivalry between writers who were attempting to bridge the gap between spoken and written Sinhala and their opponents who adhered to the 'traditional compartmentalization of these two aspects of the language'. Commenting on the effects of the 1956 language act, Gair (1983, p. 43) pointed out that there had been 'an elaboration of functions, but no apparent decrease in diglossia, a striking example of the persistence of tradition in the midst of change and modernization'. Discussing language purism in Sinhala, Jernudd (1989, p. 11) remarked, '[t]he idea of the preservation and protection of the Sinhalese language had been a considerably appealing political and cultural slogan, in relation to Tamil as well as in relation to English'. However, there continues to be a widening debate in Sinhala newspapers about the correct 'standard' usage of written Sinhala and the use of the grammar of spoken Sinhala for literary purposes. This debate reflects the strong feelings and attitudes of purists about the preservation of Sinhala.

In 1960, a few scholars raised the necessity for a written Standard Sinhala for textbook writing, government documents and the media; consequently, a debate arose regarding the choice of style for written Sinhala. In 1965, the Department of Education launched a programme to prepare a uniform set of textbook to be used in schools. In 1967, a Standard Sinhala (*Sammata Sinhala*) committee was appointed by the Minister of Education, I.M.R.A. Iriyagolla; that committee was charged to produce a Standard Sinhala (*Sammata Sinhalaya*) report with the objective of concretizing a standard language to be taught in schools, used in government documents, and in all other written communications. The report of the Committee (published in 1968) was severely attacked, especially by the universities which considered the report to be an attempt to 'fix an ultra-puristic archaic usage' as the standard for written Sinhala (Dharmadasa, 1977, p. 28). The promulgation of the idea of Standard Sinhala became a battlefield for Sinhala scholars. Parties representing both sides of the debate held several public meetings, and the print media gave wide coverage to the issue. As a result, a revised edition of the report was published in 1970. Since then, a few more state-sponsored attempts have been made to standardize modern Sinhala usage, the most recent effort being the report of a committee appointed by the Minister of Education, W. J. M. Lokubandara, under the patronage of the National Institute of Education (NIE). That report (National Institute of Education, 1989) documented standard written Sinhala rules; one of the positive achievements of the report (*Sinhala Lēkhana*

Rītiya) was the standardization of the Sinhala alphabet, as consisting of 60 symbols (National Institute of Education, 1989). As Joseph (1987, p. 113) asserts, language planning boards, and academies attempt to 'organize and systematize individual grammarians' efforts'. Recently, a few scholars undertook some practical steps toward standardizing Sinhala orthography, by compiling spelling dictionaries and manuals (Coperahewa, 2000). In 2005, a Sinhala spelling handbook was published under the direction of the Minster of Cultural Affairs; the ministry also made an effort to regulate the use of language in private radio and TV broadcasting. At present, issues related to Sinhala spelling are of real concern to many grammarians reflecting the social, cultural, and political aspects of spelling in society (Sebba, 2007).

Modernization of Sinhala

Modernization is undertaken when a language needs to expand its resources in order to meet the demands of the modern world (also called *elaboration* by Haugen, 1983). Lexical innovation and stylistic discoursal expansions are essential characteristics of the language modernization process (Ferguson, 1968). The function of *lexical modernization* has been defined as 'the sum of activities aimed at assisting a language – fully developed and 'mature' – to overcome the difficulty that accompanies concept borrowing which is too fast for its natural development' (Nahir, 1979, p. 106). The modernization process in Sinhala began at the end of the nineteenth century, in response to the impact of European languages, and to the availability of printing and journalism. However, in the early twentieth century, to help the study of the national languages and also to facilitate their use in education and administration, technical terms became a necessary. In 1932, the Executive Committee for Education saw the importance of creating a committee of specialists to coin 'Sinhalese equivalents of new terms' that were coming into use daily (GOSL, 1931, p. 111). In the 1930s there were three Text Book Committees in the Department of Education for Sinhala, Tamil, and English. The main function of these committees was to recommend to the Director of Education, the books to use in schools from those produced and submitted for consideration by authors and publishers (Ariyadasa & Perera, 1969). The decision to make Sinhala and Tamil medium of instruction in schools and the rise of Sinhala as an official language in the mid-1950s laid the foundation for a more systematic language modernization process. There was a need for technical vocabulary in response to social and political change. In 1959, the *Report of the Ceylon University Commission* pointed out some of the practical problems of implementing the policy of Swabhasha in the university:

(1) the need for glossaries of scientific terms,
(2) the need for the translation of important books into Sinhala and Tamil,
(3) the need for the writing of original books in Sinhala and Tamil,
(4) the question of identifying competent authors,
(5) the need for supplementary reading in Swabhasha,
(6) the issue of university teachers' proficiency in Swabhasha (GOSL, 1959b).

In 1965, the Educational Publications Department was established in Colombo to translate and publish textbooks for use in higher education and also to prepare and publish readers and companion works in grammar and composition.

One of the initial problems Sinhala scholars had to overcome was the absence of suitable technical terminology for administrative and educational purposes. At the start of the process, the task of coining new technical terms in Sinhala fell upon 'Glossary Committees' set up under the Official Languages Department. A glossary committee consisted of a Chair, a Secretary and one or more language scholars and representatives of the field of study with which the committee would deal. During the period of transition from English to Sinhala (1956–1960), four kinds of glossaries were published by the Department:

(i) Glossaries of Administrative Terms, containing words needed to transact official business in government departments, corporations, banks, etc.;
(ii) Glossaries of Academic Terms, containing words needed to teach new, non-traditional subjects in school and university curricula;
(iii) Glossaries of Cluster Words, specially intended for translators dealing with more than one discipline, and
(iv) Composite Glossaries, representing words taken from all subjects, arranged in two separate alphabetical orders, one for Sinhala and another for English.

By 1955, the official terminology committee had indexed 43,000 Sinhala and 48,117 Tamil terms and phrases used in the public sector (Samarasinghe, 1996).

The linguistic policy dealing with word coinage had been a burning issue among Sinhala scholars in the 1950's and 1960's, and there had been considerable debate about technical terms. Jernudd (1977) pointed out that creators of new terms may face conflicting goals. With regard to Sinhala, there were three main schools of thought:

(i) The first school advocated the use of words of Sanskrit origin;
(ii) the second school maintained a 'puristic' approach; and
(iii) the third school supported a more English-oriented approach (Disanayaka, 1999).

Hettiaratchi (1952), Professor of Sinhala at the University of Ceylon, stressed: 'with regard to the important steps to be taken in making the national languages the medium of instruction in the higher schools and the Universities, a great deal can be learnt from the work being done in India in that direction' (p. 150). He further noted: 'of the thousands of terms coined by the Indian scholars, some are quite suited to the genius of our language as Sinhalese is a sister dialect of the modern Indo-Aryan languages' (Hettiaratchi, 1952, p. 154). In view of the urgency of the word coinage project, some glossary committees looked to India where similar arrangements had been made to teach new subjects in Hindi and other Indian languages. Commenting on this situation, Disanayaka (1999, p. 263) explained:

> Hindi glossaries of technical terms were based on models suggested by an Indian scholar named Raghuvira. The decision to take Raghuvira as the model resulted in the production of many technical terms with a Sanskrit bias. As a result, some of the terms came under severe attack and even ridicule. Since the sound patterns of Sanskrit are more complex than those of spoken Sinhala, some of these terms produced difficulties in pronunciation.

The extremely large newly created vocabulary of Sanskritic words was viewed by some scholars as 'an attempt to hybridize or Sanskritize Sinhala' (Disanayaka, 1976, p. 32). However, the Official Languages Department had allowed different committees to make their own policies in word coinage. Commenting on this issue, Hettiaratchi (1969, p. 739) stated 'before the committees met for discussions, certain policy decisions were reached with regard to the preparation of these equivalents so as to ensure simplicity, uniformity and consistency'. In the field of official language research, the Department made steady progress with regard to the preparation of glossaries during the 1950–1960s. However, in the earlier period (in the1950s), there had been no uniformity in style nor consistency in the use of technical terms in some government translations, but later on (after the

1960s) advisory boards were appointed for the purpose of scrutinising and standardizing the terms and phrases in the various glossaries.

In the 1970s, other institutions were also given the authority to produce glossaries in their individual fields of study; for example, the Department of Educational Publications of the Ministry of Education produced several glossaries in social sciences, humanities and arts. Textbook writers adopted many of these technical terms in their textbooks, and in addition, they independently coined many additional technical terms. The Sinhala vocabulary has expanded immensely in the areas of education and government administration in the last 50 years. As Disanayaka (1999) notes, three kinds of words were added to the vocabulary:

(1) administrative terms that were needed to transact official communication,
(2) academic terms that were needed to teach academic subjects, and
(3) words in everyday usage.

Apart from the previously cited authorities, Sinhala journalists have coined a number of terms for modern concepts that have come into daily usage. Lexical expansion is the consequence of expanding the functional roles of any language. Some of the new words in Sinhala contribute to what Fishman (1968) called the *efficiency* of Sinhala as a 'modern' means of communication.

In the 1950s and 1960s, the approval of a standard keyboard for Sinhala typewriters used in government departments has been a long felt need. In 1955, in response to that need, a special committee was appointed to report on the arrangement of the Sinhala typewriter keyboard. This committee, after examining the different keyboards available for Sinhala, devised a standard keyboard for the Sinhala typewriter.[27] The committee also recommended a trial period of 5 years to judge the suitability of the new keyboard (GOSL, 1959a). For designing a standard keyboard for the Sinhala typewriter, another committee was appointed under the chairmanship of the Commissioner of Official Languages, Dr Nandadeva Wijesekera – thus, the label, 'Wijesekera Keyboard' was adopted for the Sinhala keyboard approved by this Committee. The problem of devising a standard Sinhala typewriter keyboard led to a vigorous discussion on the issues related to the Sinhala alphabet and orthography. Consequently, Sinhala scholars focused their attention on the elimination of non-functional letters and the addition of new ones, on the removal of anomalies and irregularities, and on the modification of letters (Disanayaka, 1999). Spelling reform should be understood here as one aspect of graphization intended to facilitate the use of printing and typewriters. Romanization was also proposed for Sinhala, but with no success, for the weight of the Sinhala writing tradition has been too great. With regard to the Sinhala stenography, another committee was appointed under the Director of the Government Technical College to examine and evaluate all the systems of Sinhala shorthand. The two systems that were considered most 'practical and efficient' were the 'Lawrence system' designed by Lawrence Perera, an instructor in Sinhala shorthand at the Department of Official Languages and the 'Canter system' designed by Austin Canter, an instructor at the Government Technical College (Disanayaka, 1999). The formal corpus planning activities of the Official Languages Department ended in the 1970s following the completion of the work of the glossary committees.

Under the direction of the Ministry of Cultural Affairs, work on the Sinhala Encyclopaedia was also undertaken in 1956. Under the pioneering editorship of Prof. Hettiaratchi, the first volume of the Sinhala Encyclopaedia was out in 1963. After the demise of Prof. Hettiaratchi, there was a period of inactivity in this project. The most recent volume to be published was its eleventh volume in 2007. In year 1972, the work of

Sinhala dictionary was taken over by the Ministry of Cultural Affairs, and in the 1980s, the Ministry launched an accelerated programme to finish the work of the Sinhala dictionary, completed in 1992. This dictionary contains 26 volumes. In view of the voluminous nature of this dictionary, the Ministry of Cultural Affairs published a shorter and practical Sinhala dictionary for everyday use. This dictionary titled *Prayōgika Sinhala Śabdakōshaya* (Practical Sinhala Dictionary), consisting of two volumes, was published in 1982 under the editorship of Harischandra Wijetunga. On the other hand, the work of the Sinhala–English dictionary was considerably slower both due to the lack of competent editorial staff and the lack of priority. Most English–Sinhalese dictionaries have been written as aids to the Sinhala students learning English. The most popular English–Sinhala dictionary is *Malalasekera Ingrisi-Sinhala Śabdakōshaya* (Malalasekera English–Sinhala Dictionary) compiled by famous oriental scholar Prof. G.P. Malalasekera in 1948. Recently, the Official Languages Department has launched a project to compile a tri-lingual (Sinhala–Tamil–English) dictionary for practical everyday use. At present, however, there is no government or private 'language planning' body at the national level charged to carry on any activities related to the modernization and standardization of Sinhala.

Computers and language technology

With the introduction of microcomputers in the early 1980s, Sri Lanka too embarked on the use of computers with local language input and output. One of the major obstacles to use Sinhala in computers was the lack of system level support in many operating systems. Currently, both Microsoft and Linux operating systems provide Sinhala support. In recent years, modern computer technology has also made a considerable impact on Sinhala corpus planning with regard to orthography and typography. As a result, most of the current language engineering activities are focused on such issues as the standardization of the Sinhala character code for information technology, the development of Unicode-compatible fonts and other computer-based language tools such as spelling checkers. These activities are carried out with the assistance of the Information Communication Technology Agency of Sri Lanka, after the Council for Information Technology (CINTEC) was dissolved. With regard to local language computing, the CINTEC and Sri Lanka Standards have cooperated over the years to register with the International Standard Organization for the standard coding of Sinhala. The Unicode-based Sinhala standard was formulated by the CINTEC and thereafter by a Sri Lanka Standards Institute. In 1998, the Sinhala Unicode Chart was published in *The Unicode Standard, Version 3.0.* (Samaranayake, Nandasara, Disanayaka, Weerasinghe, &Wijayawardhana, 2003). Despite the inclusion of Sinhala in Unicode in 1998, no existing Sinhala font or application supports Unicode. According to computer scientists, the main reasons for this are:

  (i) a lack of awareness of Unicode,
  (ii) its incompatibility with legacy systems,
  (iii) the complexity of Unicode, and
  (iv) the lack of a single standard.

A number of Sinhala and Tamil fonts and applications are available in Sri Lanka, but they suffer from a number of problems:

  (1) Each Sinhala /Tamil package uses its own propriety standard.
  (2) Each package is specialized (e.g. for word processing) and does not integrate with other applications and standard databases.

(3) Most applications use character representations based on how the characters are displayed on the screen.

(4) Many of the available fonts are commercial, needing to be purchased at additional cost (Dias, 2004).

The University of Colombo has pioneered work in Sinhala Localization since the 1980s by developing fonts and keyboard drivers for DOS and Windows. In the 1990s, work on Sinhala Language Processing was carried out at the undergraduate project level with such tools as dictionaries and spell checkers which were being produced at a research level. With the award of a Canadian grant, the Language Technology Research Laboratory (LTRL) was set up in early 2004 to address the growing need of local language computing in Sri Lanka with the specific aims of producing: (1) a large Sinhala corpus and lexical resource, (2) a text-to-speech engine, (3) a tri-lingual electronic dictionary, and (4) an optical character recognition application. In addition to the development of natural language processing (NLP) tools, several research activities have been carried out at the LTRL on various issues related to Sinhala language in the context of computational linguistics, corpus linguistics and NLP. Some of the ongoing projects of the LTRL include:

- building monolingual lexical corpus,
- developing parsers, morphological analysers, and spell checkers for Sinhala language and annotation of Sinhala language corpora,
- creation of transfer lexicon and grammar, etc.

One of the major resources developed at the LTRL is the 10-million-word Sinhala corpus containing a wide variety of genres such as newspaper, creative writing and technical writing. LTRL also provides technical assistance for various governmental and private organizations in dealing with language processing and localization activities (Language Technology Research Laboraratory, 2006).

Part IV: language maintenance and prospects

This final section describes some important recent developments in language planning in Sri Lanka related to language rights and the process of globalization.

Language rights

Establishment of the OLC

Chapter III (Fundamental Rights) of the present Constitution guarantees the freedom to use one's own language and lays down the concept that no citizen shall suffer any disadvantage by reason of language. In the field of LPP in Sri Lanka, the issue of language rights is a new concern; however, there is a lack of public awareness of existing language law. According to a study conducted by D. Mendis (2002, pp. 182–183), 'many people are not aware of the existing policies, especially as they are set out in the country's Constitution'. On the other hand, when new policies are proposed, accurate and sufficient information is not conveyed to the public about these proposals and their implications. This study further says: 'native speakers of Sinhala and Tamil have distinctively different perceptions of the linguistic status quo in Sri Lanka' (D. Mendis, 2002, p. 182). A fundamental right under the Constitution guarantees that no citizen shall be discriminated against on the ground *inter alia* of race or language. Throughout Sri Lanka, any person (other than an official acting in his/her official capacity) shall be entitled:

(a) to receive communications from and to communicate and transact business in Sinhala, Tamil or English;
(b) to inspect, obtain copies of or extracts from any official register, record, publication or other document or transaction thereof as the case may be in Sinhala, Tamil or English.

In December, 1991, under the administration of President R. Premadasa, the UNP government took an important policy decision, in connection with linguistic human rights, i.e. to establish an *OLC*, under Act No. 18 of 1991, intended 'to recommend principles of policy, to take all such actions and measures relating to the use of the official languages, and to monitor and supervise compliance with the provisions contained in Chapter IV of the Constitution' (GOSL, 1991). The principles outlined here were based on a Canadian model, and the Act provided the legal framework for the Commission. On receiving a complaint, the Commission has the duty, under the OLC act, to inquire into that complaint. If it finds that the complaint is justified, it has the power to ask the relevant authority to redress the grievance. As a last resort, if the relevant authority fails to comply, the Commission can ask the Courts to issue a directive. Section 28(1) of the OLC Act No. 18 of 1991 also states:

> When a public officer wilfully fails or neglects to transact business or make such communication or issue copies or extracts in the relevant language, s/he shall be guilty of an offence and shall on conviction after summary trial before a Magistrate be liable to a fine not exceeding one thousand rupees or to imprisonment for a term not exceeding three months or to both such fine and imprisonment.

During President Premadasa's administration (1988–1992), the government encouraged a bilingual policy (Sinhala and Tamil) in official functions. Most public official functions were conducted in Sinhala and Tamil. President Premadasa, addressing UNP Heads of local bodies in 1991, stressed the value of using official languages:

> [...] remember to fall in line with the government language policy too. Sinhala and Tamil are the official languages and English is the link language. Use both Sinhala and Tamil in all communications. Don't think of not using Tamil, because there are only two or three families in your area. Use all three languages if possible...All citizens in this country belonging to all communities big and small are entitled to the same rights and same justice. (cited in Theva Rajan, 1995, p. 92)

In 1997, President Cumaratunga issued a letter entitled 'Implementation of the Official Language Policy' to all Ministries with copies to all Secretaries and Heads of Departments. The letter stated: 'in order to ensure that every citizen is afforded an opportunity to exercise his/her language rights without hindrance, all Government institutions are directed to comply with the following instructions within a period of two months':

- All regulations, legal provisions and information shall be available in all three languages;
- All printed forms must be available in all three languages;
- All letters received from the public should be answered in the language in which they are received (where there is a difficulty, at least a translation in English should be attached);

- All name boards of public institutions and other instructions or directives meant for the public must be displayed in all three languages;
- Action should be taken to fill immediately all the vacancies in the posts of Sinhala-Tamil translators and Tamil typists' Service. Institutions that do not have a cadre should make use of persons on a contractual basis.
- A senior officer must be identified in every institution and charged with the responsibility for implementing the law relating to language.

However, for various reasons, officials failed to comply fully with these instructions, which are of a minimal nature as far as the implementation of the language policy is concerned (Official Languages Commission, 2005, p. 8).

The parity between Sinhala and Tamil is prominently displayed on official signposts, but there is continuing distortion, as is evident from a recent report of the Official Languages Commission (2005). The tardiness in the implementation of statutes making Tamil an official language is so evident that the OLC has admitted 'there is an enormous gap between the constitutional provisions and their application'. According to official statistics, only 8.31% of the total numbers of public servants are Tamil-speaking. This group consists of three ethnic categories having Tamil as their first language: Sri Lankan Tamils, Muslims, and Tamils of recent Indian origin (plantation Tamils), collectively constituting 25% of the country's population.

Under the 'needs-based approach', there are three categories of language proficiency:

(a) Those requiring mainly conversational ability, such as police and health officials who have to attend to the basic needs of the people;
(b) Those requiring a degree of proficiency in the second official language that enables them to onverse and attend to correspondence; and
(c) Those who need to acquire knowledge of the second official language sufficient for them to read, analyse and draft reports when necessary (Official Languages Commission, 2005).

In 1998, the Ministry of Public Administration issued a new circular (No. 29/28) in accordance with the provisions of Article 18 of the Constitution, for the payment of incentive allowances to public officers proficient in more than one language. For the successful implementation of the language policy, it is necessary to motivate public servants effectively so that they will want to learn the second official language. Given that the presently available incentives are not adequate to inspire language learning, an attractive package should be introduced for those who acquire considerable proficiency in the second language.

In June 2005, the OLC submitted a *Memorandum of Recommendations* to President Cumaratunga for the effective implementation of the official language policy. In this set of recommendations, the Commission described the present state of the use of the Official Languages in the country and examined the problems that impede the implementation of the official language policy as embodied in the Constitution. The OLC observed that successive governments have failed to implement the policy fully as it is laid down in the constitution, since the constitution calls for a bilingual administration at all levels and throughout the country. The Commission also drew up a set of recommendations for the proper and speedy implementation of the policy, taking into account the present realities as well as the practicalities of the current situation. The proposals are described under the following topics:

(1) Implementation of the Official Languages Policy
(2) Language Training
(3) Departments of Official Languages
(4) Development of National/Official Languages
(5) Training of Translators and Interpreters
(6) Training in Link Language (English)
(7) Bilingual Secretarial Divisions
(8) New Categories of Cadre – for the Government Translators' Service and the Government Interpreters' Service[28]
(9) Allowances
(10) Implementation

As pointed out by the Constitutional Affairs and National Integration Minister, D.E.W. Gunasekera (Daily News, 2007b), 25% of the country's population are Tamil speaking (nearly 61% of them living outside the North and the East), but only 6% of the employees in the public service and 16% of those in the provincial public service are conversant in Tamil. Consequently, the language barrier is one of the main problems faced by the general public in obtaining the services of state institutions. Similar problems are faced by the Sinhalese in the North and the East where the activities in most government offices are conducted in Tamil. Accordingly, the government has started to address the issue of the language barrier. For instance, one of the OLC's proposals – making it compulsory for new recruits to gain proficiency in the second official language within a specific period – has gained approval (Sambandan, 2006). With a view to implement bilingualism in the public service, the government recently decided to make knowledge of Sinhala and Tamil compulsory for new recruits to public service at all levels as part of its efforts to implement the official language policy. Under the new plan, public servants would be offered 'attractive incentives' to learn the second official language, and their proficiency, tested through periodic examinations, would count toward promotions. As a further step in the implementation of the official language policy, the National Institute of Language Education and Training Bill was enacted in Parliament in June 2007. The Act provides for the establishment of a separate institute for the intensive training of government employees in the official languages (Daily News, 2007b). At present, the Official Languages Department promotes a 'tri-lingual policy' in order to maintain national integration and linguistic rights. However, it is clear that several complex issues related to LPP remain unresolved in Sri Lanka.

Globalization and language policy

It has become clear that globalization has made a profound impact on language policies in Asian countries and there are many questions related to language, culture and identity (Tsui & Tollefson, 2007). Sinhala, like many other languages, faces cultural, linguistic, and political demands to change with the times. Due to globalization and the impact of English as a global language, there are some current issues related to LPP in Sri Lanka. One significant response to globalization revolves around the issue of the re-introduction of English as a medium of instruction and which undertakes to understand the impact on both the public and private sectors. According to Raheem and Ratwatte (2004), the role and status of English have been determined through various means, giving rise to many complex factors, and the re-introduction of English continues to be crucial to the concerns of the nation. In the past decade, successive governments have decided to bring English back into the higher domains of society (such as administration, education, and commerce) in order to support globalization and development. Those who have adhered to the English medium of education have argued that a common international language serving as the medium of instruction will bring about harmony between the two major ethnic groups. However, as Punchi (2001, p. 377) points out, suggestions for the re-introduction of English medium at secondary level and the emergence of international schools in urban areas would 'lead to a fusion of two thin groups, namely the English educated Tamils and the English educated Sinhalese'. Moreover, the influx of English words in various spheres such as business, commerce, technology, mass media, and industry underlines the fact that language is a social phenomenon; for example, sign boards of commercial enterprises are written mostly in English or in a mix of Sinhala and English. The persistent use of English in these domains demonstrates the significant impact of English on the society.

Although the constitution guarantees the language rights of all citizens in several areas, in practice, however, there are problems concerning the maintenance and continuance of the status, equality, and right of use of the Sri Lankan languages (Samarasinghe, 1996; Theva Rajan, 1995). The practice of 'linguistic exclusion', a policy that excludes some language(s) from certain domains of society, is one of the current issues in language policy implementation in Sri Lanka. Furthermore, in a multilingual setting, lack of coordination between different areas in the *implementation* of language policy also induces people to choose their own policy (Annamalai, 2003, p. 128). English remains the language of power and high social status in Sri Lanka. As Fernando (1987, p. 49) correctly points out 'the gatekeeper positions associated with policy and decision making are still held by bilinguals who have a fluent command of English'. The phenomenon of globalization, together with the increasing hegemony of English, has motivated many policy makers to revisit their language planning policies, with a view to ensuring the pre-eminence of their own language. However, in the public sector, the lack of proficiency in English is a problem. As observed by the Official Languages Commission (2005, p. 2):

> Here it is pertinent to note that very few citizens could benefit from the provisions enabling communication in the English language or translations being available in English because there are very few people proficient in English. Most offices engaged in administration also have hardly any competent persons to attend to such matters in the English Language. Therefore emphasis has to be on the use of the two official languages in the administration of the country.

According to the government agenda for development, the present policy and planning decisions have targeted these objectives:

(1) improving competence in the official languages for government officers;
(2) improving knowledge of English;
(3) establishing bi-lingual administration at all levels throughout the country.

Regarding corpus planning of Sinhala, there are a few issues that will engage the attention of language planners in the years to come. These issues are:

- orthographic innovation,
- grammar revision or simplification and
- the use of spoken Sinhala grammar for literary purposes.

However, as Disanayaka (1976, p. 33) points out, 'these attempts at reform – i.e., orthographic innovation, grammar revision or simplification and the use of spoken Sinhala grammar for literary purposes – have been viewed with great alarm by traditional scholars, who hold that there are no substantial grounds for radical reform'. Fishman (1983) refers to the linguistic tension between traditional usage and modernization of language in corpus planning. In past years, the process of language development seems to have been impeded by the normative policies of academies and textbook bodies. Nevertheless, there is an urgent need for the development of suitable, updated terminology as well as for language genres for use in specialized fields. A special programme of language planning is also needed for areas such as government interpreting and translation and for the effective implementation of language policy.

Accordingly, an important part of corpus planning for Sinhala relates to the rapid changes taking place in the fields of science and technology as well as in new academic fields. There is also a need to enrich existing vocabularies continually and to compile new glossaries to serve usage in different fields. Commenting on the compilation of glossaries, the OLC also observed:

> The compilation of glossaries related to educational and academic domains may be entrusted to an appropriate institution. The government may also consider setting up a separate institution for the development of the National languages to meet the continually expanding vocabulary needs pertaining to the use of these languages (Official Languages Commission, 2005, p. 16).

Ferguson (1968) notes that the main aim of modernization of a language is to make it the equal of other developed languages as a medium of communication, so that it may join the world community of increasingly inter-translatable languages recognized as appropriate vehicles for modern forms of discourses. Indeed, some scientists and academics prefer publishing in English instead of in their own language because of the lack of scholarly journals in Sinhala, the deficiency of appropriate terms in Sinhala and the hegemony of English as a global language. Unfortunately, Sinhala and Tamil linguists are not actively associated with the current language problems of the country, and there is little official support for language planning activities. These issues have further implications for the language planning situation in Sri Lanka.

Conclusion

This monograph has discussed the historical, social, and political ecology of Sri Lanka's language planning situation from the colonial period to the post-colonial period, with special emphasis on the planning of Sinhala as an official language. Although language planning frequently attempts to solve conflicts over language, it can also create conflicts (Wiley, 1996). As the Sri Lankan situation demonstrates, post-independence language policy decisions not only have failed to solve language problems, but rather have created whole ranges of new social, ethnic, and political problems. In post-colonial Sri Lanka, as in other South Asian countries, language has been utilized as a weapon in the struggle for power. As noted earlier, under certain socio-political, economic and linguistic conditions, 'language can be mobilized for political ends and become a source of conflict' (Dua, 1996:6). Language controversy arose in close association with social, cultural, political, and ideological changes involved in the process of modernization. The rise of linguistic nationalism has led, on the one hand, to the revitalization of Sinhala as a medium of communication, education, and administration and, on the other, to political and ethnic conflicts between the Sinhalese and the Tamils. The case of Sri Lanka reveals the complex interaction between language policy and nationalist ideologies. According to Ager's (2001) motivational explanation of language policy, the Sri Lankan LPP issue was motivated by feelings of *identity* (Sinhala and Tamil), *ideology* (debate over standardization and diglossia), *insecurity* (majority versus minority), and *inequality* (relative political power).

LPP decisions in post-independent Sri Lanka have been largely underpinned by political objectives and by language ideological debates. As Ricento (2000, p. 7) points out, 'language policies are essentially political documents'. Disputes over language policies have led to ethnic tensions and violent conflicts. Language status planning began in Sri Lanka in 1944, before independence, when it was decided that Sinhala and Tamil should be the official languages of the country. However, the situation changed dramatically in 1954–1955 with the beginnings of a campaign in the country for the elevation of Sinhala to the status of the sole official language. Making Sinhala 'the sole official language' of the country (1956) was one of the key incidents involving Sinhalese in politics. This policy also served as a turning point for demonstrations and ethnic tensions. As a result, in less than a decade after the transfer of power, language conflict erupted in Sri Lanka, accompanied by the outbreak of riots in 1956 and 1958. The official language issue has been an important factor in the cultural dimensions of the ethnic conflict until the movement for a separate state for Tamils manifested itself in1976. The accommodation reached in language policy after the communal violence associated with the introduction of language policy reform in 1956 is noteworthy. According to some scholars, post-1977 linguistic accommodation was 'too little, too late' (De Votta, 2004). Amendments initiated between 1956 and 1978, through political necessity (in 1958) and a realistic adjustment to life in a multi-ethnic society (1978), all but conceded parity of status between Sinhala and Tamil languages. Unfortunately, there were some disparities between language policy as laid down in the constitution and language policy as actually practiced in the society.

As in many other newly independent nations, language status planning in Sri Lanka rested in the hands of politicians. LPP have evolved from what Kaplan and Baldauf (1997) refer to as a 'top-down' process, whereby different ethnic groups are manipulated by politicians – who seek to gain and retain power. In many situations, language-status planning is by its very nature a political activity. In Sri Lanka, the 'Sinhala-only' policy was politically more advantageous to some than was a 'parity of status' policy. As Dharmadasa (1996, p. 5) puts it, 'Sri Lanka's national LPP exercises have seen a series of twists and turns as politicians grappled with the consequences of their own policy changes'. Much of status planning has been bound up with the notion of 'one language, one nation', a notion that became the main argument during the period of nation building after independence. In this context, Bourdieu (1991, p. 45) has argued that the.

> official language is bound up with the state, both in its genesis and in its social uses. It is in the process of state formation that the conditions are created for the constitution of a unified linguistic market, dominated by the official language.

With regard to corpus planning in Sinhala, there were both government and individual language planning activities aimed at the *cultivation* of Sinhala as an official language. Language planning in general gained momentum in the second half of the twentieth century in response to new needs resulting from the changing status of Sinhala. A comprehensive language planning programme was carried out under the auspices of the government during the policy implementation transition period. The close integration of status policy and corpus policy is demonstrated in this activity. Corpus planning activities carried out by the Department of Official Languages during the period between 1955 and 1965 enabled Sinhala to cope with its extended role and new function as an 'official language'. In this period, the terminological modernization of Sinhala generated extensive discussion in the area of corpus planning. As an official language, Sinhala has been increasingly used in various domains and in the educational and administrative system. Like all languages, Sinhala as a modern language must serve the communicative needs of the modern epoch in the national context. In order to survive, Sinhala needs modern terminology for all specialized fields. As a result of lexical expansion, Sinhala has become an efficient medium for instruction and communication. However, due to the lack of government sponsored language planning in the past few years, no language planning agency or academy was set up to look into the language-related problems of the society. The Official Languages Department and the Cultural Affairs Department are the only government bodies actually charged to act in the area of language and cultural problems. Non-governmental organizations are also not active in the area of LPP. As a result, various language issues have arisen in Sinhala society related to:

  (i) Sinhala orthography,
  (ii) the acceptability of a standard,
  (iii) the development of specific registers, and
  (iv) modernization.

Due to Sinhala diglossia, the choice of styles has also led to language controversies. A number of corpus planning programmes have been dominated by puristic attitudes and prescriptive practices – activities paving the way for hyper-standardization involving correct, pure forms of Sinhala. As M.W.S. De Silva (1974, p. 82) argues, 'a declared policy to maintain and protect the "pure" language is often politically advantageous'. Connections between the discourse of purity, standard Sinhala and the broader political and ideological developments in Sinhalese society must also be explored further. Commenting on 'verbal hygiene', Cameron (1995, p. 4) pointed out: '[a]ll attitudes to language and linguistic change are fundamentally ideological, and the relationship between popular and expert ideologies, though it is complex and conflictual, is closer than one might think'.

Further empirical research is required to look at the linguistic, political, and social problems related to the planning of Sinhala as an effective medium of communication in an age of globalization, as well as the implications of past language planning programmes. Furthermore, there is an urgent need both for clearly stated goals and for a detailed long-term plan for effective *implementation* of the country's official language policy. As Rubin (1983, p. 330) observed, language planning is an ongoing process, or 'one continuous integrated event', which is, therefore, never completed. Hence, LPP in a multilingual country like Sri Lanka constitutes a sensitive and complex process – one needing constant serious consideration. Finally, as Fishman (1974, p. 26) points out: 'Like other types of planning [language planning] requires evaluation and feedback in order to proceed more successfully in the future than it has in the past'.

Acknowledgements

I began to work on this topic during my postgraduate studies as a Commonwealth scholar at Lancaster University, UK (2003–2004). I must, therefore, thank Dr Mark Sebba and Dr Uta Papen at the Department of Linguistics and Modern English Language for their comments on an earlier draft of this monograph. I gratefully acknowledge the comments made by the anonymous reviewers. Thanks are due to the editors of this series for their help in preparing this monograph. I must thank Ms. Kanchana Chandrasekera, Department of Geography, University of Colombo, for preparing maps for this monograph. I am also thankful to Mr Dulip Herath, LTRL, University of Colombo for providing information on computers and language technology research in Sri Lanka. The material for this monograph was collected at the following libraries and archives:

- the Sri Lanka National Archives,
- the National Library of Sri Lanka,
- University of Colombo,
- Lancaster University,
- University of Cambridge.

Notes

1. A *national language* is the language of a political, cultural, and social unit. An *official language*, in contrast, is simply a language that may be used for government business (Holmes, 1992, p. 105).
2. On 22 May 1972, Sri Lanka became a free, sovereign, and independent republic within the British Commonwealth.
3. Some scholars suggest using *Sinhala* for the language, and *Sinhalese* for the people who speak it, or using *Sinhala* as the adjective (Sinhala Culture) and *Sinhalese* as the noun (we are Sinhalese) (Disanayaka, 1998, p. 6). The origin of the name goes back to the myth of origin, as recorded in the *Dipavamsa* and *Mahavamsa*. According to this myth of origin, the Sinhalese are said to be descendants of an Indian prince, named Vijaya, the grandson of a Sinha, literary lion.
4. (1) Language purification, (2) language revival, (3) language reform, (4) language standardization, (5) language spread, (6) lexical modernization, (7) terminology unification, (8) stylistic simplification, (9) interlingual communication, (10) language maintenance, (11) auxilary-code standardization (Nahir, 1984).
5. There were, and still are, two main theories in vogue; they may be referred to as the North-Eastern and North-Western hypotheses (M.W.S. De Silva, 1979).
6. Tamil language has influenced the structure and vocabulary of Sinhala to such an extent that some scholars were erroneously led to believe that Sinhala belongs to the Dravidian family of languages (Gnanaprakasar, 1936; Gunawardhana, 1924). However, according to historical linguistic evidence, it is true that non-Aryan influences – not necessarily only Dravidian, but also pre-Dravidian as well – have been at work in the development of the Sinhala language (Geiger & Jayatilaka, 1935).
7. Literary Sinhala utilizes two different alphabets: *Miśra Sinhala* (mixed Sinhala) and *Śuddha Sinhala* (pure Sinhala). The 'pure' Sinhala alphabet has been used mainly for versification by classical writers.
8. The script of these cave and rock inscriptions is the same as that of the most ancient historical inscriptions of India, the most notable of which are the Asokan inscriptions (Paranavitana, 1967).
9. Wijesekera (1965), however, suggests that the Veddas are not the aboriginal people of Sri Lanka, but rather that they migrated to the island from South India in prehistoric times.
10. Dr U. Ansalado, Assistant Professor, Amsterdam Center for Language and Communication, has launched a project (2004–2007) for comprehensive documentation of the Sri Lanka Malay varieties under the title 'The documentation of Sri Lanka Malay: Linguistic and cultural creolization endangered' (see http://www.onderzoekinformatie.nl/en/oi/nod/onderzoek/OND1301812/).
11. Sinhala has a number of words that also exists in Pali, but not in Sanskrit (Geiger & Jayatilaka, 1935, p. xix.)
12. Census Reports dated prior to 1901 classified the population into seven groups, i.e.: (i) Europeans, (ii) Sinhalese, (iii) Tamils, (iv) Moors, (v) Malays, (vi) Veddas (vii) others. The Census of 1901 further divided the Sinhalese into low-country Sinhalese and Kandyan Sinhalese. The 1911 Census introduced more races and divided Tamils into Ceylon Tamils and Indian Tamils, and divided Moors into Ceylon Moors and Indian Moors (see Sarkar, 1957, p. 190).
13. The July 2001 census was not conducted in areas controlled by the LTTE.
14. The *pirivena* is a monastic college that provided education for monks. In modern times it has been transformed into a more substantial centre for academic pursuits.

15. *Kaduwa* literally means 'the sword'; it is Sinhala slang for English, common among Arts undergraduates.

16. A few years after the Colebrooke Commission, Lord Thomas Babington Macualay's famous minute (1835) on education and colonial language policy in India also pointed out the intent: '... to form a class Indians in blood and colour, but English in tastes, in opinions, in morals, and in intellect; a class who could serve as interpreters between the government and the masses, and who, by refining the vernaculars, would supply the means of widespread dissemination of western knowledge' (cited in Phillipson, 1992, p. 110).

17. The extent of English influence is confirmed by the founding of:

    • St Thomas' College in Colombo (1851) and of Trinity College in Kandy (1872) by the Anglicans;
    • Jaffna Central College (1870) and of Wesley College in Colombo (1874) by the Methodists;
    • St. John's College in Panadura (1891) by the Church Missionary Society and
    • St. Joseph College in Colombo (1891) by the Catholics.

18. The influence of missionary linguistic work on the process of modernization in Sinhala still needs to be studied in detail.

19. Language renovation may involve language purification, i.e. the removal of foreign (lexical) influences or the adherence to the classical forms and lexicons of language (Kaplan & Baldauf, 2003: p.214).

20. *Swa* = own, *bhāshā* = language (*Swabhāshā* = own language), Sinhala, or Tamil.

21. The SLFP constitution, drafted in 1951, adopted Sinhalese and Tamil as official languages.

22. The Federal Party was dedicated to 'the attainment of freedom for the Tamil –speaking people of Ceylon by the establishment of an autonomous Tamil state on the linguistic basis within the framework of a Federal Union of Ceylon' (Kearney, 1978, p. 529).

23. S.W.R.D. Bandaranaike had allowed a transitional period of 5 years, with January 1961 as the date when the Act would be implemented in full.

24. The Marxist parties originally supported linguistic parity.

25. It is useful to compare Cumaratunga's notion of purity with the notions of eighteenth century English grammarians and also with Maraimalai Adigal's *tanittamil* movement in Tamilnadu, from 1930 to the 1950s.

26. In 1947, Ven. Yakkaduwe Prajnarāma, an oriental scholar from the *Vidyālankāra Pirivena*, Colombo, made this suggestion in order to bridge the gap between spoken and written forms, and this idea was supported by Martin Wickremasinghe, one of the foremost novelists and literary critics of that time; it was also supported by a group of university teachers in the 1960s (Dharmadasa, 1977).

27. After comparing all the existing typewriter keyboards, D.A. Jayakody, (a member of the committee) and L. L. Perera, (an independent expert from the Official Languages Department) worked out a basic design for a standard keyboard for a Sinhala typewriter (GOSL, 1959a). [Keyboard design was not a problem unique to Sinhala (Zhao, 2005).].

28. According to a survey conducted in 2000, there were only 166 translators available throughout the country. Out of that group, only 44 persons were able to translate from Sinhala into Tamil while only 108 persons were able to translate from Sinhala into English and a mere 14 persons were Tamil–English translators (Daily News, 2007a).

References

Ager, D. (2001). *Motivation in language planning and language policy.* Clevedon, UK: Multilingual Matters.

Anderson, B. (1983). *Imagined communities: Reflections on the origin and spread of nationalism.* London: Verso.

Annamalai, E. (2003). Reflections on a language policy for multilingualism. *Language Policy, 2*(2), 113–132.

Ansaldo, U. (2005). *Typological admixture in Sri Lanka Malay: The case of Kirinda Java.* Retrieved April 10, 2007, from home.medewerker.uva.nl/u.ansaldo/ bestanden/SLM-KJcase-new.pdf

Ansaldo, U. (2008). Sri Lankan Malay revisited: Genesis and classification. In D. Harrison, D.S. Rood, & A. Dwyer (Eds.), *Lessons from documented endangered languages* (pp. 13–42). Amsterdam: John Benjamins.

Arasaratnam, S. (1964). *Ceylon.* Englewood Cliffs, NJ: Prentice-Hall.

Ariyadasa, K.D., & Perera, E.S.W. (1969). Text books. *Education in Ceylon – A centenary volume* Part 3 (pp. 1009–1022). Colombo, Sri Lanka: Government Press.

Bakker, P. (2006). The Sri Lanka *sprachbund*: The newcomers Portuguese and Malay. In Y. Matras, A. McMahon, & N. Vincent (Eds.), *Linguistic areas: Convergence in historical and typological perspective* (pp. 135–159). Houndmills, Basingstoke, UK: Palgrave Macmillan.

Baldauf, R.B., Jr. (1990). Language planning: Corpus planning. In R.B. Kaplan *et al.* (Eds.), Annual review of applied linguistics (Vol. 10, pp. 3–12). New York: Cambridge University Press.

Baldauf, R.B., Jr. (2006). Rearticulating the case for micro language planning in a language ecology context. *Current Issues in Language Planning, 7*(2 & 3), 147–170.

Bell, H.C.P. (1916). The 'ahigunthikayo' or Ceylon gypsies. *Ceylon Antiquary and Literary Register, II*(II), 108–114.

Blommaert, J. (Ed.). (1999). *Language ideological debates.* Berlin, Germany: Mouton de Gruyter.

Bourdieu, P. (1991). *Language and symbolic power.* Cambridge, UK: Polity Press.

Bourhis, R.Y. (1984). Introduction: Policies in multilingual settings. In R.Y. Bourhis (Ed.), *Conflict and language planning in Quebec* (pp. 1–28). Clevedon, UK: Multilingual Matters.

Brown, M.E., & Ganguly, S. (Eds.). (2003). *Fighting words: Language policy and ethnic relations in Asia.* Cambridge, MA: The MIT Press.

Cameron, D. (1995). *Verbal hygiene.* London: Routledge.

Canagarajah, A.S. (2005). Dilemmas in planning English – vernacular relations in post-colonial communities. *Journal of Sociolinguistics, 9*(3), 418–447.

Clyne, M. (2003). Language planning: Overview. In W. Frawley (Ed.), *Oxford international encyclopaedia of linguistics* (2nd ed., 4 Vols, Vol. II, pp. 409–412). New York: Oxford University Press.

Coates, W.A. (1961). The languages of Ceylon in 1946 and 1953. *University of Ceylon Review, 19*(1), 81–91.

Cooper, R.L. (1989). *Language planning and social change.* Cambridge University Press.

Coperahewa, S. (1999). Language planning and Cumaratunga. In P. Wijemanna (Ed.), *Uvasara: A collection of papers in honour of Prof. A. Kulasuriya* (pp. 483–489). Colombo, Sri Lanka: S. Godage.

Coperahewa, S. (2000). *Sinhala Akshra Vinyāsa Akārādiya* [*A dictionary of Sinhala spelling*]. Colombo, Sri Lanka: S. Godage.

Coperahewa, S. (2004). *Language policy and planning in Sri Lanka: The planning of Sinhala as an official language.* MA dissertation. Department of Linguistics and Modern English Language, University of Lancaster.

Coperahewa, S. (2007). Language contact and linguistic area: Sinhala–Tamil contact situation. *Journal of the Royal Asiatic Society of Sri Lanka, 53,* 133–152.

Coperahewa, S., & Arunachalam, S.D. (2002). *Sinhala Bhāshāve Demala Vacana Akārādiya* [*A dictionary of Tamil words in Sinhala*]. Colombo, Sri Lanka: S. Godage.

Crystal, D. (1997). *The Cambridge encyclopaedia of language.* Cambridge University Press.

Cumaratunga, M. (1938). *Vyākarana Vivaranaya* [*An elucidation of grammar*]. Colombo, Sri Lanka: M.D. Gunasena.

Daily News. (1946, March 22). Adoption of Sinhalese as official language, p. 3.

Daily News. (2007a, May 16). Ignoring each other's language cause of ethnic problem. Retrieved May 16, 2007, from http://www.dailynews.lk/2007/05/16/news22.asp

Daily News. (2007b, June 14). Bilingual proficiency must for new government recruits. Retrieved June 14, 2007, from http://www.dailynews.lk/2007/06/14/news20.asp

Daily News. (2008, April 23). Arming the people with a weapon of choice. Retrieved April 23, 2008, from http://www.dailynews.lk/2001/pix/PrintPage.asp?REF=/2008/04/23/fea01.asp

Daoust, D. (1997). Language planning and language reform. In F. Coulmas (Ed.), *The handbook of sociolinguistics* (pp. 436–452). Oxford, UK: Blackwell.

Das Gupta, J. (1969). Official language problems and policies in South Asia. In T.A. Sebeok (Ed.), *Current trends in linguistics* (Vol. 5, pp. 578–596). The Hague, The Netherlands: Mouton.

Das Gupta, J. (1970). *Language conflict and national development.* Berkeley: University of California Press.

De Alwis, J. (1852). *The Sidat Sangarava, a grammar of the Sinhalese language, translated into English, with introduction, notes, and appendices.* Colombo, Sri Lanka: Government Printer.

De Lanerolle, J. (1945). The future official languages of Ceylon. *University of Ceylon Review, 3*(2), 35–43.

Department of Census and Statistics, Sri Lanka (Ceylon) (1952). *Census of Ceylon, 1946.* Colombo, Sri Lanka: Government Printer.

Department of Census and Statistics, Sri Lanka (Ceylon) (1981). *Census of population and housing in Sri Lanka.* Colombo, Sri Lanka: Government Printer.

Department of Census and Statistics, Sri Lanka (2006). Population Characteristics. Retrieved May 20, 2008, from http://www.statistics.gov.lk

De Silva, M.W.S. (1964). *Dambānē vädibasa* [*The Vedda language of Dambāna*]. Gampaha, Sri Lanka: Sarasvati.

De Silva, M.W.S. (1967). Effects of purism on the evolution of the written language: Case history of the sinhalese situation. *Linguistics, 36,* 5–17.

De Silva, M.W.S. (1969). Sinhalese. In T.S. Sebeok (Ed.), *Current trends in linguistics* (pp. 234–248). The Hague, The Netherlands: Mouton.

De Silva, M.W.S. (1970). Some affinities between Sinhalese and Maldivian. *Journal of the Royal Asiatic Society of Ceylon Branch, 14,* 20–27.

De Silva, M.W.S. (1972). *Vedda language of Ceylon (texts and Lexicon).* Munich, Germany: R. Kitzinger.

De Silva, M.W.S. (1974). Some consequences of diglossia. *York Papers in Linguistics, 4,* 71–90.

De Silva, M.W.S. (1976). *Diglossia and literacy.* Mysore, Karnataka: Central Institute of Indian Languages.

De Silva, M.W.S. (1979). *Sinhalese and other island languages in South Asia.* Tübingen, Germany: Narr.

De Silva, K.M. (1981). *A history of Sri Lanka.* London: C. Hurst.

De Silva, K.M. (1986). *Managing ethnic tensions in multi-ethnic societies: Sri Lanka 1880–1985.* Lanham, MD: University Press of America.

De Silva, K.M. (1993a). Ethnicity, language and politics: The making of Sri Lanka's Official Language Act No. 33 of 1956. *Ethnic Studies Report, 11*(1), 1–28.

De Silva, K.M. (1993b). Language problems: The politics of language policy. In *Sri Lanka: Problems of governance* (pp. 275–304). Kandy, Sri Lanka: International Centre for Ethnic Studies.

De Silva, K.M. (1996). Coming full circle: The politics of language in Sri Lanka 1943–1996. *Ethnic Studies Report, 14*(1), 11–48.

De Silva Jayasuriya, S. (1999). Portuguese in Sri Lanka: Influence of substratum. *Journal of the Royal Asiatic Society (Third Series), 9*(2), 251–257.

De Silva Jayasuriya, S. (2001). *Indo-Portuguese of Ceylon: A contact language.* London: Athena.

De Silva Jayasuriya, S. (2003, July 31). Malay contacts with Sri Lanka. *IIAS Newsletter,* p. 29.

Deumert, A. (2000). Language planning and policy. In R. Mesthrie, J. Swann, A. Deumert, & W.L. Leap (Eds.), *Introducing sociolinguistics* (pp. 384–418). Edinburgh University Press.

De Votta, N. (2004). *Blowback: Linguistic nationalism, institutional decay and ethnic conflict in Sri Lanka.* Stanford University Press.

Dharmadasa, K.N.O. (1972). Language and Sinhalese nationalism: The career of Munidasa Cumaratunga. *Modern Ceylon Studies, 3*(2), 125–143.

Dharmadasa, K.N.O. (1974). The creolization of an aboriginal language: The case of Vedda in Sri Lanka (Ceylon). *Anthropological Linguistics, 16*(2), 79–106.

Dharmadasa, K.N.O. (1977). Nativism, diglossia and the Sinhalese identity in the language problem. *International Journal of Sociology of Language, 13,* 21–31.

Dharmadasa, K.N.O. (1981). Language conflict in Sri Lanka. *Sri Lanka Journal of Social Sciences*, *4*(2), 47–70.

Dharmadasa, K.N.O. (1988). Buddhist resurgence and Christian privilege in Sri Lanka, c. 1940–1965. In K. De SilvaM., P. Duke, E.S. Goldbers, & N. Katz (Eds.), *Ethnic conflict in Buddhist societies: Sri Lanka, Thailand and Burma* (pp. 110–125). London: Pinter.

Dharmadasa, K.N.O. (1989). The people of the lion: Ethnic identity, ideology and historical revisionism in contemporary Sri Lanka. *The Sri Lanka Journal of the Humanities*, *15*(1 & 2), 1–36.

Dharmadasa, K.N.O. (1992). *Language, religion and ethnic assertiveness: The growth of Sinhalese nationalism in Sri Lanka*. Ann Arbor: University of Michigan Press.

Dharmadasa, K.N.O. (Ed.). (1996). *National language policy in Sri Lanka*. Kandy, Sri Lanka: International Centre for Ethnic Studies.

Dharmadasa, K.N.O. (1998). Formative stages of Sinhala journalism. In G.H. Peiris (Ed.), *Studies on the Press in Sri Lanka and South Asia* (pp. 149–165). Kandy, Sri Lanka: International Centre for Ethnic Studies.

Dharmadasa, K.N.O. (2007). Sri lanka. In A. Simpson (Ed.), *Language and national identity in Asia* (pp. 116–138). Oxford University Press.

Dias, G. (2004). *Using it in local languages*. Retrieved April 4, 2006, from ICTA language website: www.fonts.lk

Disanayaka, J.B. (1976). *National languages of Sri Lanka I – Sinhala*. Colombo, Sri Lanka: Department of Cultural Affairs.

Disanayaka, J.B. (1977). *Sinhala Jana Vahara [Sinhala folk usage]*. Colombo, Sri Lanka: Lake House.

Disanayaka, J.B. (1990). *Studies in Sinhala Literacy: Traditional knowledge as reflected in folklore*. Colombo, Sri Lanka: National Association for Total Education.

Disanayaka, J.B. (1991). *The Structure of Spoken Sinhala- 1: Sounds and their Patterns*. Maharagama, Sri Lanka: National Institute of Education.

Disanayaka, J.B. (1994). *Sinhala: A unique Indo-Aryan language*. Colombo, Sri Lanka: M.H. Publications.

Disanayaka, J.B. (1998). *Understanding the Sinhalese*. Colombo, Sri Lanka: S. Godage.

Disanayaka, J.B. (1999). Sinhala: Changing trends in status and structure. In Y. Janaka Kumara (Ed.), *Milestones to independence* (pp. 259–270). Colombo, Sri Lanka: The Peoples Bank.

Disanayaka, J.B., & Coperahewa, S. (1998). Changing trends of the Sinhala media scene. In G.H. Peiris (Ed.), *Studies on the press in Sri Lanka and South Asia* (pp. 167–179). Kandy, Sri Lanka: International Centre for Ethnic Studies.

Dissanayake, W. (2005). *Enabling traditions: Four Sinhala cultural intellectuals*. Boralesgamuwa, Sri Lanka: Visidunu Prakasakayo.

Dua, H.R. (1996). The politics of language conflict: Implications for language planning and political theory. *Language Problems and Language Planning*, *20*(1), 1–17.

Ferguson, C.A. (1968). Language development. In J.A. Fishman, C.A. Ferguson, & J. Das Gupta (Eds.), *Language problems of developing nations* (pp. 27–35). New York: John Wiley & Sons.

Ferguson, C.A. (1977). Sociolinguistic settings of language planning. In J. Rubin, B.H. Jernudd, J. Das Gupta, J.A. Fishman, & C.A. Ferguson (Eds.), *Language planning processes* (pp. 9–29). The Hague, The Netherlands: Mouton.

Fernando, C. (1977). English and Sinhala bilingualism in Sri Lanka. *Language in Society*, *6*(2), 341–360.

Fernando, C. (1987). The nature of language inequality: The case of English and Sinhala from a functional point of view. *Nawasilu*, *9*, 47–59.

Fernando, C. (1996). The post-imperial status of English in Sri Lanka 1940–1990: From first to second language. In J.A. Fishman, A.W. Conrad, & A. Rubal-Lopez (Eds.), *Post-imperial English: Status change in former British and American colonies, 1940–1990* (pp. 485–512). Berlin, Germany: Mouton de Gruyter.

Fishman, J.A. (1968). Sociolinguistics and the language problems of developing countries. In J.A. Fishman, C.A. Ferguson, & J. Das Gupta (Eds.), *Language problems of developing nations* (pp. 3–16). New York: John Wiley & Sons.

Fishman, J.A. (1971). The impact of nationalism on language planning. In J. Rubin & B.H. Jernudd (Eds.), *Can language be planned? Sociolinguistic theory and practice for developing nations* (pp. 3–20). Honolulu: University of Hawaii Press.

Fishman, J.A. (1973). *Language and nationalism*. Rowley, MA: Newbury House.

Fishman, J.A. (Ed.). (1974). *Advances in language planning*. The Hague, The Netherlands: Mouton.

Fishman, J.A. (1980). Language maintenance. In *Harvard encyclopaedia of American ethnic groups* (pp. 929–638). Boston, MA: Harvard University Press.

Fishman, J.A. (1983). Modeling rationales in corpus planning: Modernity and tradition in images of the good corpus. In J. Cobarrubias & J.A. Fishman (Eds.), *Progress in language planning* (pp. 107–118). The Hague, The Netherlands: Mouton.

Fishman, J.A., Ferguson, C.A., & Das Gupta, J. (Eds.). (1968). *Language problems of developing nations*. New York: John Wiley & Sons.

Gair, J.W. (1968). Sinhala diglossia. *Anthropological Linguistics, 10*(8), 1–15.

Gair, J.W. (1982). Sinhala, an Indo-Aryan isolate. *South Asian Review, 6*(3), 51–64.

Gair, J.W. (1983). Sinhala and English: The effects of a language act. *Language Problems and Language Planning, 7*(1), 42–59.

Gair, J.W. (1985). Sinhala diglossia revisited or diglossia dies hard. In Bh. Krishnamurti, C. Masica, & A. Sinha (Eds.), *South Asian languages: Structure, convergence, and diglossia* (pp. 322–336). Delhi, India: Motilal Banarsidass.

Geiger, W. (1902). Etymological vocabulary of the Maldivian language. *Journal of the Royal Asiatic Society (Great Britain & Ireland), 30,* 909–938.

Geiger, W. (1935). Language of the Väddas. *Indian Historical Quarterly, 11*(3), 504–516.

Geiger, W. (1938). *A grammar of the Sinhalese language*. Colombo: The Royal Asiatic Society Ceylon Branch.

Geiger, W., & Jayatilaka, D.B. (1935). Sinhalese language and literature. In *A dictionary of the Sinhalese language* (Vol 1, Part I, pp. xvii–xxxviii). Colombo: The Royal Asiatic Society Ceylon Branch.

Rev. Gnanaprakasar, D. (1936). Dravidian element in Sinhalese. *Journal of the Royal Asiatic Society Ceylon Branch, 33,* 16–43.

Godakumbure, C.E. (1955). *Sinhalese literature*. Colombo, Sri Lanka: Colombo Apothecaries.

Goonetilleke, D.C.R.A. (1983). Language planning in Sri Lanka. *Navasilu, 5,* 13–18.

GOSL (Government of Sri Lanka (Ceylon)). (1926). *Debates of the Legislative Council of Ceylon*. Colombo, Sri Lanka: Government Press.

GOSL (Government of Sri Lanka (Ceylon)). (1929). *Report of the Commission to Inquire into and Report upon the Present System of Education in Ceylon* (Sessional Paper XXVII of 1929). Colombo, Sri Lanka: Government Press.

GOSL (Government of Sri Lanka (Ceylon)). (1931). *Debates of the State Council of Ceylon*. Colombo, Sri Lanka: Government Press.

GOSL (Government of Sri Lanka (Ceylon)). (1932). *Debates of the State Council of Ceylon*. Colombo, Sri Lanka: Government Press.

GOSL (Government of Sri Lanka (Ceylon)). (1943). *A report of the Special Committee of Education,* (Sessional Paper XXIV of 1943). Colombo, Sri Lanka: Government Press.

GOSL (Government of Sri Lanka (Ceylon)). (1944). *Debates of the State Council of Ceylon*. Colombo, Sri Lanka: Government Press.

GOSL (Government of Sri Lanka (Ceylon)). (1946). *Sinhalese and Tamil as official languages,* (Sessional Paper XXII of 1946). Colombo, Sri Lanka: Government Press.

GOSL (Government of Sri Lanka (Ceylon)). (1949). *Parliamentary Debates – House of Representatives*. Colombo, Sri Lanka: Government Press.

GOSL (Government of Sri Lanka (Ceylon)). (1951). *First interim report of the Official Languages Commission* (Sessional Paper XXI of 1951). Colombo, Sri Lanka: Government Press.

GOSL (Government of Sri Lanka (Ceylon)). (1953a). *Fourth interim report of the Official Languages Commission* (Sessional Paper of VIII 1953). Colombo, Sri Lanka: Government Press.

GOSL (Government of Sri Lanka (Ceylon)). (1953b). *Final report of the Official Languages Commission* (Sessional Paper XXII of 1953). Colombo, Sri Lanka: Government Press.

GOSL (Government of Sri Lanka (Ceylon)). (1954). *Interim report of the Commission on Higher Education in National Languages* (Sessional Report XXI of 1954). Colombo, Sri Lanka: Government Press.

GOSL (Government of Sri Lanka (Ceylon)). (1955). *Parliamentary Debates – House of Representatives*. Colombo, Sri Lanka: Government Press.

GOSL (Government of Sri Lanka (Ceylon)). (1956a). *Official Language Act No. 33 of 1956*. Colombo, Sri Lanka: Government Press.

GOSL (Government of Sri Lanka (Ceylon)). (1956b). *Parliamentary Debates – House of Representatives*. Colombo, Sri Lanka: Government Press.

GOSL (Government of Sri Lanka (Ceylon)). (1957). *Administration report of the Special Commissioner for Official Language Affairs for 1957*. Colombo, Sri Lanka: Government Press.

GOSL (Government of Sri Lanka (Ceylon)). (1958a). *Administration report of the Special Commissioner for Official Language Affairs for 1958*. Colombo, Sri Lanka: Government Press.

GOSL (Government of Sri Lanka (Ceylon)). (1958b). *Parliamentary Debates – House of Representatives*. Colombo, Sri Lanka: Government Press.

GOSL (Government of Sri Lanka (Ceylon)). (1959a). *Report of the Committee on the Arrangement of the Sinhala Typewriter Keyboard* (Sessional Report IX of 1959). Colombo, Sri Lanka: Government Press.

GOSL (Government of Sri Lanka (Ceylon)). (1959b). *Report of the Ceylon University Commission* (Sessional Paper XXIII of 1959). Colombo, Sri Lanka: Government Press.

GOSL (Government of Sri Lanka (Ceylon)). (1960). *Report of the Committee of Inquiry into the Teaching of English in Ceylon Schools* (Sessional Paper V of 1960). Colombo, Sri Lanka: Government Press.

GOSL (Government of Sri Lanka (Ceylon)). (1962). *Administration report of the Commissioner of Official Languages for 1962*. Colombo, Sri Lanka: Government Press.

GOSL (Government of Sri Lanka (Ceylon)). (1967). *Ceylon year book – 1967*. Colombo, Sri Lanka: Government Press.

GOSL (Government of Sri Lanka). (1972). *The Constitution of Republic of Sri Lanka*. Colombo, Sri Lanka: Government Press.

GOSL (Government of Sri Lanka). (1978). *The Constitution of Democratic Socialist Republic of Sri Lanka 1978*. Colombo, Sri Lanka: Government Press.

GOSL (Government of Sri Lanka). (1991). *Official Languages Commission Act No. 18 of 1991*. Colombo, Sri Lanka: Government Press.

GOSL (Government of Sri Lanka). (1997). *General education reforms*. Sri Lanka: The Presidential Task Force on Education.

Gunasekera, A.M. (1891). *A comprehensive grammar of the Sinhalese language*. Colombo, Sri Lanka: Government Press, [Reprint Sri Lanka Sahitya Mandalaya, Colombo, 1962.].

Gunasekera, R.G.O. (1996). The implementation of the official language policy, 1956–70. In K.N.O. Dharmadasa (Ed.), *National Language Policy in Sri Lanka* (pp. 17–78). Kandy, Sri Lanka: International Centre for Ethnic Studies.

Gunasekera, M. (2005). *The postcolonial identity of Sri Lankan English*. Colombo, Sri Lanka: Katha.

Gunatillake, G., Perera, M., Wanigaratne, R.A.M.C., Fernando, R.E., Lakshman, W.D., Chandrasiri, J.K.M.D., et al. (1992). The poverty discourse and the poor in Sri Lanka: Rural poverty in Sri Lanka: Priority issues and policy measures. *Asian Development Review, 10,* 164–198.

Gunawardana, R.A.L.H. (1979). The people of the lion: The Sinhala identity and ideology in history and historiography. *The Sri Lanka Journal of the Humanities, V*(1 & 2), 1–36.

Gunawardhana, W.F. (1924). *Siddhānta parīkshanaya or svabhāshā nītisāraya, being first principles of Sinhalese grammar 1*. Colombo, Sri Lanka: N.J. Cooray and Sons.

Haarmann, H. (1990). Language planning in the light of a general theory of language: A methodological framework. *International Journal of Sociology of Language, 86,* 103–126.

Haugen, E. (1966 [1972]). Dialect, language and nation. *The ecology of language: Essays by Einar Haugen*, [Selected and introduced by Anwar S. Dil] (pp. 237–254). Stanford University Press.

Haugen, E. (1983). The implementation of corpus planning: Theory and practice. In J. Cobarrubias & J.A. Fishman (Eds.), *Progress in language planning* (pp. 269–289). The Hague, The Netherlands: Mouton.

Hettiaratchi, D.E. (1952). Sinhalese today. *University of Ceylon Review, 10*(2), 140–155.

Hettiaratchi, D.E. (1969). Linguistics in Ceylon I. In T.A. Sebeok (Ed.), *Current trends in linguistics* (pp. 736–751). The Hague, The Netherlands: Mouton.

Holmes, J. (1992). *An introduction to sociolinguistics*. London: Longman.

Hussainmiya, B.A. (1987). *Lost cousins: The Malays of Sri Lanka*. Kuala Lumpur, Malaysia: Universiti Kebangsan.

International Centre for Ethnic Studies (ICES) (1989). *Official languages and the administrative report of the workshop*. Colombo, Sri Lanka: The Commissioner of Official Languages and the International Centre for Ethnic Studies.

Jayaweera, S. (1971). Language and colonial educational policy in Ceylon. *Modern Ceylon Studies*, *2*(2), 152–169.

Jernudd, B.H. (1977). Linguistic sources for terminological innovation. In J. Rubin, B.H. Jernudd, J. Das Gupta, J.A. Fishman, & C.A. Ferguson (Eds.), *Language planning processes* (pp. 215–236). The Hague, The Netherlands: Mouton.

Jernudd, B.H. (1989). The texture of language purism: An introduction. In B.H. Jernudd & M.J. Shapiro (Eds.), *The politics of language purism* (pp. 1–19). Berlin, Germany: Mouton de Gruyter.

Jernudd, B.H., & Das Gupta, J. (1971). Towards a theory of language planning. In J. Rubin & B.H. Jernudd (Eds.), *Can language be planned? Sociolinguistic theory and practice for developing nations* (pp. 195–215). Honolulu: University of Hawaii Press.

Joseph, J.E. (1987). *Eloquence and power: The rise of language standards and standard languages*. New York: Basil Blackwell.

Kailasapathy, K., & Sanmugadas, A. (1976). *National languages of Sri Lanka II – Tamil*. Colombo, Sri Lanka: Department of Cultural Affairs.

Kandiah, T. (1981). Disinherited Englishes: The case of Lankan English. *Navasilu, 4*, 92–113.

Kandiah, T. (1984). 'Kaduwa': Power and the English language weapon in Sri Lanka. In P. Colin-Thome & A. Halpe (Eds.), *Honouring E. F. C. Ludowyck* (pp. 117–154). Dehiwala, Sri Lanka: Tisara Prakasakayo.

Kaplan, R.B., & Baldauf, R.B., Jr. (1997). *Language planning from practice to theory*. Clevedon, UK: Multilingual Matters.

Kaplan, R.B., & Baldauf, R.B., Jr. (2003). *Language and language-in-education planning in the Pacific Basin*. Dordrecht, The Netherlands: Kluwer Academic.

Karam, F.X. (1974). Toward a definition of language planning. In J.A. Fishman (Ed.), *Advances in language planning* (pp. 103–124). The Hague, The Netherlands: Mouton.

Karunatilake, W.S. (1982). Nominal inflection in Sri Lanka Gypsy Telugu: An outline. *International Journal of Dravidian Linguistics, 11*(2), 377–382.

Kasyanathan, S.V., & Somasundarm, N.P. (1981). Bilingualism among Tamils in Sri Lanka. *Sri Lanka Journal of Social Sciences, 4*(1), 55–77.

Kearney, R.N. (1964). Sinhalese nationalism and social conflict in Ceylon. *Pacific Affairs, 37*(2), 125–136.

Kearney, R.N. (1967). *Communalism and language in the politics of Ceylon*. Durham, NC: Duke University Press.

Kearney, R.N. (1973). *The politics of Ceylon (Sri Lanka)*. Ithaca, NY: Cornell University Press.

Kearney, R.N. (1978). Language and the rise of Tamil separatism in Sri Lanka. *Asian Survey, 18*(5), 521–534.

Kekulawala, S.L. (1982). Kinship terminology in Sri Lankan malay: Contribution to the study of language universals. *Kalyäni – Journal of Humanities and Social Sciences of the University of Kelaniya, 1*(1 & 2), 207–225.

Kloss, H. (1969). *Research possibilities on group bilingualism: A report*. Quebec, Canada: International Centre for Research on Bilingualism.

Krishnamurti, Bh. (1998). *Language, education and society*. New Delhi, India: Sage.

Language Technology Research Laboratory (LTRL). (2006). Language Technology Research Laboratory. Retrieved May 7, 2006, from http://www.ucsc.cmb.ac.lk/research/ltrl/index.html

Loganathan, K. (1996). *Sri Lanka: Lost opportunities*. Colombo, Sri Lanka: Centre for Policy Research and Analysis (CEPRA), University of Colombo.

Malalgoda, K. (1976). *Buddhism in Sinhalese society 1750–1900*. Berkeley: University of California Press.

Manogaran, C. (1987). *Ethnic conflict and reconciliation in Sri Lanka*. Honolulu: University of Hawaii Press.

Masica, C.P. (1991). *The Indo-Aryan languages*. Cambridge University Press.

May, S. (2001). *Language and minority rights: Ethnicity, nationalism and the politics of language*. Harlow, UK: Pearson Education.

Mendis, G.C. (Ed.). (1956). *The Colebrooke–Cameron Papers: Documents on British colonial policy in Ceylon 1796:1833* (Vol. I). London: Oxford University Press.

Mendis, D. (2002). Language planning and ethnicity: Attitudes and perceptions from the education sector. *The Sri Lanka Journal of the Humanities, 27 & 28*(1 & 2), 161–184.

Mesthrie, R., Swann, J., Deumert, A., & Leap, W.L. (Eds.). (2000). *Introducing sociolinguistics*. Edinburgh University Press.

Meyler, M. (2007). *A dictionary of Sri Lankan English*. Colombo, Sri Lanka: Author Publication, Retrieved August 2, 2008, from http://www.mirisgala.net/index.html

Musa, M. (1981). *Language planning in Sri Lanka*. Dacca, Bangladesh: Bhuiyan Muhammed Imran.

Nahir, M. (1979). Lexical modernization in Hebrew and the extra-academy contribution [Special Issue: National Language Planning and Treatment]. *Word, 30*(1–2), 105–116.

Nahir, M. (1984). Language planning goals: A classification. *Language Problems and Language Planning, 8*(3), 294–327.

National Institute of Education (NIE), Sri Lanka (1989). *Sinhala Lēkhana Rītiya [Rules of written Sinhala]*. Maharagama, Colombo, Sri Lanka: Author.

Nuhuman, M.A. (2004). *Understanding Sri Lankan Muslim identity*. Colombo, Sri Lanka: International Centre for Ethnic Studies.

Obeysekera, R. (1974). *Sinhala writing and the new critics*. Colombo, Sri Lanka: M.D. Gunasena.

Official Languages Commission (OLC) (2005). *Memorandum of recommendations*. Rajagiriya, Sri Lanka: Author.

Pakeman, S.A. (1964). *Ceylon*. London: Ernest Benn.

Panditaratne, B.L., & Selvanayagam, S. (1973). The demography of Ceylon – an introductory survey. *University of Ceylon history of Ceylon (UCHC)* (Vol. 3, pp. 285–302). Peradeniaya, Sri Lanka: University of Ceylon Press.

Paolillo, J.C. (1997). Sinhala diglossia: Discrete or continuous variation? *Language and Society, 26*(1), 269–296.

Parakrama, A. (1995). *De-hegemonizing language standards: Learning from (post) colonial Englishes about 'English'*. London: Macmillan.

Paranavitana, S. (1967). *Sinhalayo* (4th ed., 1999). Boralesgamuwa, Colombo, Sri Lanka: Visidunu.

Passé, H.A. (1943). The English language in Ceylon. *University of Ceylon Review, 1*(2), 50–65.

Passé, H.A. (1949). The importance of English in Ceylon. *University of Ceylon Review, 7*(3), 162–170.

Paulston, C.B. (1994). *Linguistic minorities in multilingual settings*. Amsterdam: John Benjamins.

Peiris, G.H. (1996). *Development and change in Sri Lanka: Geographical perspectives*. Kandy, Sri Lanka: International Centre of Ethnic Studies.

Rev. Perera, S.G. (1922). Portuguese influence on Sinhalese speech. *The Ceylon Antiquary and Literary Register, 8*(Part I), 45–60.

Phadnis, U. (1976). *Religion and politics in Sri Lanka*. London: C. Hurst.

Phillipson, R. (1992). *Linguistic imperialism*. Oxford University Press.

Ponnambalam, S. (1983). *Sri Lanka: National conflict and the Tamil liberation struggle*. London: Zed Books.

Powell, R. (2002). Language planning and the British empire: Comparing Pakistan, Malaysia and Kenya. *Current Issues in Language Planning, 3*(3), 205–279.

Punchi, L. (2001). Resistance towards the language of globalization – the case of Sri Lanka. *International Review of Education, 47*(3–4), 361–378.

Raghavan, M.D. (1957). *Handsome beggars: The Rodiyas of Ceylon*. Colombo, Sri Lanka: Colombo Book Centre.

Raheem, R., & Ratwatte, H. (2004). Invisible strategies, visible results: Investigating language policy in Sri Lanka. In S. Mansoor, S. Meraj, & A. Tahir (Eds.), *Language policy, planning & practice: A South Asian perspective* (pp. 91–105). Karachi, Pakistan: Oxford University Press.

Rahman, T. (1996). *Language and politics in Pakistan*. Oxford University Press.

Ricento, T. (Ed.). (2000). Introduction. *Ideology, politics and language policies*. Amsterdam: John Benjamins.

Roberts, M.W. (1973). Elite formation and the elites, 1832–1931. In *University of Ceylon history of Ceylon* (Vol. 3, pp. 263–284). Peradeniya: University of Ceylon Press Board.

Rubin, J. (1971). Evaluation and language planning. In J. Rubin & B.H. Jernudd (Eds.), *Can language be planned? Sociolinguistic theory and practice for developing nations* (pp. 217–252). Honolulu: University of Hawaii Press.

Rubin, J. (1983). Evaluating status planning: What has the past decade accomplished? In J. Cobarrubias & J.A. Fishman (Eds.), *Progress in language planning* (pp. 329–343). The Hague, The Netherlands: Mouton.

Russell, J. (1981). Language, education and nationalism – the language debate of 1944. *Ceylon Journal of Historical and Social Studies, VIII*(2), 38–64.

Ryan, B. (1961). Status, achievement and education in Ceylon. *Journal of Asian Studies, 20*(4), 463–476.

Samarakkody, M., & Braine, G. (2005). Teaching English in Sri Lanka: From colonial roots to Lankan English. In G. Braine (Ed.), *Teaching English to the world: History, curriculum and practice* (pp. 147–157). Mahwah, NJ: Lawrence Erlbaum Associates.

Samaranayake, V.K., Nandasara, S.T., Disanayaka, J.B., Weerasinghe, A.R., & Wijayawardhana, H. (2003). *An introduction to UNICODE for Sinhala characters* (UCSC Technical Report 03/01). Colombo, Sri Lanka: University of Colombo School of Computing.

Samarasinghe, S.G. (1996). Language policy in public administration 1956–1994: An implementor's perspective. In K.N.O. Dharamadasa (Ed.), *National language policy in Sri Lanka* (pp. 79–112). Kandy, Sri Lanka: International Centre for Ethnic Studies.

Samaraweera, V. (1973). The Colebrooke–Cameron reforms. *University of Ceylon history of Ceylon* (Vol. 3, pp. 77–88). Peradeniya, Sri Lanka: University of Ceylon Press Board.

Samaraweera, V. (1977). The evolution of a plural society. In K. De SilvaM. (Ed.), *Sri Lanka: A survey* (pp. 86–107). London: C. Hurst & Company.

Sambandan, V.S. (2006, February 25–March 10). Language barrier. *Frontline, 23*(4). Retrieved April 8, 2008, from http://www.frontlineonnet.com/fl2304/stories/20060310001305500.htm

Sannasgala, P.B. (1976). *Sinhala Vocables of Dutch Origin*. Colombo, Sri Lanka: The Netherlands Alumni Association of Sri Lanka.

Sarathchandra, E.R. (1950). *The Sinhalese novel*. Colombo, Sri Lanka: M.D. Gunasena.

Sarathchandra, E.R. (1973). Language and literature in the nineteenth and twentieth centuries. In *University of Ceylon History of Ceylon* (Vol. 3, pp. 342–355). Peradeniya, Sri Lanka: University of Ceylon Press Board.

Sarkar, N.K. (1957). *The demography of Ceylon*. Colombo, Sri Lanka: Government Press.

Sebba, M. (2007). *Spelling and society*. Cambridge University Press.

Second National State Assembly. (1978). *Report from the Select Committee of the National State Assembly appointed to consider the revision of the Constitution* (Parliamentary Series No. 14). Colombo, Sri Lanka: Government Press.

Simpson, A. (Ed.). (2007). *Language and national identity in Asia*. Oxford University Press.

SLBC (Sri Lanka Broadcasting Corporation). (2004). About SLBC. Retrieved May 20, 2008, from http://www.slbc.lk/about.htm

Smith, I.R. (1979). Convergence in South Asia: A creole example. *Lingua, 48*(2–3), 193–222.

Somaratne, G.P.V. (1990). The history of the Sinhala Bible. *Indian Church History Review, 24*(2), 122–143.

Spolsky, B. (1998). *Sociolinguistics*. Oxford University Press.

Spolsky, B. (2004). *Language policy*. Cambridge University Press.

Sumathipala, K.H.M. (1968). *History of education in Ceylon, 1796–1965*. Dehiwala, Sri Lanka: Tisara Prakasakayo.

Suseendirarajah, S. (1970). Reflections of certain social differences in Jaffna Tamil. *Anthropological linguistics, XII*(7), 239–245.

Suseendirarajah, S. (1980). Religion and language in Jaffna society. *Anthropological Linguistics, 23*(8), 345–363.

Thambiah, S.J. (1986). *Sri Lanka: Ethnic fratricide and the dismantling of democracy*. Chicago University Press.

Thanajayarajasingham, S. (1975). Aspiration in Jaffna Tamil. *Linguistics: An International Review, 149*, 59–63.

Thanajayarajasingham, S. (1978). The Tamil diglossia situation in Sri Lanka. *The Ceylon Historical Journal, 25*(1–4), 275–284.

Theva Rajan, A. (1995). *Tamil as official language*. Colombo, Sri Lanka: International Centre for Ethnic Studies.

Thomas, G. (1991). *Linguistic purism*. London: Longman.

Times of Ceylon. (1955, December 8).

Tollefson, J.W. (1991). *Planning language, planning inequality*. London: Longman.

Tsui, A.B.M., & Tollefson, J. (2007). *Language policy, culture and identity in Asian contexts*. Mahwah, NJ: Lawrence Erlbaum Associates.

Turi, G. (1994). Typology of language legislation. In T. Skutnabb-Kangas & R. Phillipson (Eds.), *Linguistic human rights: Overcoming linguistic discrimination* (pp. 111–119). Berlin, Germany: Mouton de Gruyter.

UNESCO. (2000). *World Education Report 2000*. Paris: Author.

Uyangoda, J. (2001). *Questions of Sri Lanka's minority rights*. Colombo, Sri Lanka: International Centre for Ethnic Studies.

Vamadevan, M. (1996). Tamil in public administration. In K.N.O. Dharmadasa (Ed.), *National language policy in Sri Lanka* (pp. 113–142). Kandy, Sri Lanka: International Centre for Ethnic Studies.

Weerawardana, I.D.S. (1952). The general election in Ceylon [Special supplement]. *The Ceylon Historical Journal, 2*(1 & 2), 111–178.

Wickramasuriya, S. (1978). The beginnings of the Sinhala printing press. In L. Preamtilleke, K. Indrapala, & J.E. Van Lohuizen-De Leeun (Eds.), *Senarat Paranavitana commemoration volume* (pp. 283–300). Leiden, The Netherlands: E.J. Brill.

Wijesekera, N.D. (1965). *The people of Ceylon*. Colombo, Sri Lanka: M.D. Gunasena.

Wijesinha, R. (2003). Bringing back the bathwater: New initiatives in English policy in Sri Lanka. In C. Mair (Ed.), *The politics of English as a world language* (pp. 367–374). Amsterdam: Rodopi.

Wiley, T.G. (1996). Language planning and policy. In S.L. McKay & N.H. Hornberger (Eds.), *Sociolinguistics and language teaching* (pp. 103–147). Cambridge University Press.

Wilson, A.J. (1979). *Politics in Sri Lanka 1947–1979* (2nd ed.). London: Macmillan.

Wilson, A.J. (1988). *The break-up of Sri Lanka: The Sinhalese–Tamil conflict*. London: C. Hurst.

Woodward, C.A. (1969). *The growth of a party system in Ceylon*. Providence, RI: Brown University Press.

World Bank. (2006). *Sri Lanka at a glance*. Retrieved May 20, 2008, from http://devdata.worldbank.org/AAG/lka_aag.pdf

Wriggins, W.H. (1959). Ceylon's time of troubles – 1956–58. *Far Eastern Survey, 28*(3), 33–39.

Wriggins, W.H. (1960). *Ceylon: Dilemmas of a new nation*. Princeton University Press.

Wright, S. (2004). *Language policy and language planning: From nationalism to globalisation*. London: Palgrave Macmillan.

Zhao, S. (2005). Chinese character modernization in the digital era: A historical perspective. *Current Issues in Language Planning, 6*(3), 315–378.

Index

INDEX

Australian Journal of Linguistics

Official journal of the Australian Linguistic Society

Now listed in the SSCI

EDITORS:

Kate Burridge, *Monash University, Australia*
Keith Allan, *Monash University, Australia*

The ***Australian Journal of Linguistics***, the official journal of the Australian Linguistic Society, is concerned with all branches of linguistics, with preference given to articles of theoretical interest. The journal maintains an international focus, while at the same time encouraging articles on Australian languages, Australian English, and language in Australian society.

The Australian Linguistic Society is the national organization for linguists and linguistics in Australia. Its primary goal is to further interest in and support for linguistics research and teaching in Australia.

Australian Journal of Linguistics welcomes submissions of articles within the aims and scope of the journal. Authors should submit electronic copy of their article in MS Word RTF or preferably in (Adobe Acrobat) PDF as email attachments jointly to both editors, Keith Allan and Kate Burridge: keith.allan@arts.monash.edu.au and kate.burridge@arts.monash.edu.au

Routledge
Taylor & Francis Group

Critical Discourse Studies

EDITORS:
Norman Fairclough, *Lancaster University, UK*
Phil Graham, *Queensland University of Technology, Australia*
Jay Lemke, *University of Michigan, USA*
Ruth Wodak, *Lancaster University, UK*

Critical Discourse Studies is an interdisciplinary journal for the social sciences. Its primary aim is to publish critical research that advances our understanding of how discourse figures in social processes, social structures, and social change.

Critical Discourse Studies has been established in response to the proliferation of critical discourse studies across the social sciences and humanities. We will consider for publication papers that meet the needs of scholars in diverse disciplines and areas of study which develop critical perspectives on the relationship between discourse and social dynamics. Relevant areas and disciplines include: anthropology, communication, linguistics, sociology, politics, political economy, education, psychology, media studies, geography, urban studies, cultural studies, management studies, literary studies, history, technology studies, legal studies, philosophy, gender studies, migration studies, ethnic studies and others. We also welcome papers which connect critical academic research with practical concerns and agendas, including those of activist and grassroots political movements.

The scope of *Critical Discourse Studies* is not limited to linguistic studies, or articles that are primarily empirical or analytical. Critical examination of non-linguistic phenomena that take a significant discourse orientation, as well as theoretical and methodological papers that advance critical understandings of discursive phenomena, are welcomed.

Recognising the diversity, depth, and history of scholarship in the growth of critical discourse studies, no particular theoretical, disciplinary, or methodological "schools" or paradigms will be privileged over others in the selection of papers for publication. The primary criteria for publication are originality, scholarly rigor, coherence of argument, relevance and timeliness of research.

To sign up for tables of contents, new publications and citation alerting services visit **www.informaworld.com/alerting**

updates
Taylor & Francis Group

Register your email address at **www.tandf.co.uk/journals/eupdates.asp** to receive information on books, journals and other news within your areas of interest.

Powered by
informaworld

For further information, please contact Customer Services at either of the following:
T&F Informa UK Ltd, Sheepen Place, Colchester, Essex, CO3 3LP, UK
Tel: +44 (0) 20 7017 5544 Fax: 44 (0) 20 7017 5198
Email: subscriptions@tandf.co.uk Website: www.tandf.co.uk/journals

Taylor & Francis Inc, 325 Chestnut Street, Philadelphia, PA 19106, USA
Tel: +1 800 354 1420 (toll-free calls from within the US)
or +1 215 625 8900 (calls from overseas) Fax: +1 215 625 2940
Email: info@taylorandfrancis.com Website: www.taylorandfrancis.com
When ordering, please quote: XB90103A

View an online sample issue at:
www.tandf.co.uk/journals/cds

For Product Safety Concerns and Information please contact our EU representative GPSR@taylorandfrancis.com Taylor & Francis Verlag GmbH, Kaufingerstraße 24, 80331 München, Germany

Batch number: 08158847

Printed by Printforce, the Netherlands